How the Idea of Religious Toleration Came to the West

⚭

How the Idea of Religious Toleration Came to the West

PEREZ ZAGORIN

Princeton University Press Princeton and Oxford

Copyright © 2003 by Princeton University Press
Published by Princeton University Press, 41 William Street,
Princeton, New Jersey 08540
In the United Kingdom: Princeton University Press,
3 Market Place, Woodstock,
Oxfordshire OX20 1SY

All Rights Reserved

Library of Congress Cataloging-in-Publication Data

Zagorin, Perez.

How the idea of religious toleration came to the West / Peter Zagorin.

p.   cm.

Includes bibliographical references (p.) and index.

ISBN 0-691-09270-2 (alk. paper)

1. Religious tolerance—Christianity—History. I. Title.

BR1610 .Z34 2003

261.7′2′09—dc21   2002042565

British Library Cataloging-in-Publication Data is available.

This book has been composed in New Baskerville

Printed on acid-free paper. ∞

www.pupress.princeton.edu

Printed in the United States of America

1   3   5   7   9   10   8   6   4   2

THIS BOOK IS DEDICATED TO MY WIFE,

Honoré Sharrer,

WITH LOVE AND GRATITUDE FOR
OVER FIFTY YEARS OF MARRIED HAPPINESS
AND INTELLECTUAL COMPANIONSHIP.

God is always on the side of the persecuted. If a just man is
persecuted by a wicked one, God is with the persecuted just
man. If a wicked man is persecuted by a wicked man, God is with
the persecuted. And if a wicked man is persecuted by a
just man, God is on the side of the persecuted wicked man
against the persecutor.
—The Talmud

To kill a man is not to defend a doctrine, it is to kill a man.
When the Genevans killed Servetus, they did not defend a
doctrine, they killed a man.
—Sebastian Castellio, *Contra libellum Calvini*

After a careful investigation into the meaning of the term
heretic, I can discover no more than this, that we regard those
as heretics with whom we disagree.
—Sebastian Castellio, *De haereticis*

It is accordingly on this battlefield [of religion], almost solely,
that the rights of the individual against society have been
asserted on broad grounds of principle, and the claim of society
to exercise authority over dissentients openly controverted. The
great writers to whom the world owes what liberty it possesses,
have most asserted freedom of conscience as an indefeasible
right, and denied absolutely that a human being is accountable
to another for his religious belief.
—John Stuart Mill, *On Liberty*

CONTENTS

PREFACE

※

In August 1790 the Hebrew Congregation of Newport, Rhode Island, sent an address of praise and congratulations to President George Washington on the occasion of his visit to Newport. Speaking in the name of the "children of the stock of Abraham," it voiced gratitude for a government "erected by the Majesty of the People . . . which to bigotry gives no sanction, to persecution no assistance," but generously affords to everyone "liberty of conscience, and immunities of citizenship." Washington's cordial letter of reply, which thanked the congregation, also confirmed its sentiments, extolling the "Citizens of the United States" for "having given to mankind examples of an enlarged and liberal policy . . . worthy of imitation" in which all people "enjoyed the exercise of their inherent natural rights," including "liberty of conscience."

This noteworthy exchange between the Hebrew Congregation of Newport and the first president of the United States is even more memorable because Washington directed his remarks to Jewish citizens, members of a religious community that had been oppressed and persecuted by the Christian world for many centuries. His words may be taken as an eloquent testimony to the central importance religious toleration and the free exercise of religion have held among American values since the founding of the United States. The Bill of Rights, which became part of the United States Constitution in the following year, 1791, prohibits Congress from establishing any state religion, thereby forbidding

the introduction of any government-imposed barrier to religious
pluralism. Needless to say, Americans have not always lived up to
the ideal of religious freedom that the founders of the United
States professed. The past two centuries of American history contain numerous examples of episodes and entrenched institutional
policies reflecting animosity and systematic discrimination, bigotry, and exclusion directed against Catholics, Jews, and other religious minorities. In spite of this, however, it is also true that most
of the American people have never ceased to regard freedom of
religion as one of their basic and most precious rights. Today, following our recent entrance into the new millennium and the
deadly attack on the United States by Islamic terrorists on 11 September 2001, we cherish this right more than ever as an essential
attribute of a free society.

But how and where did the concept of religious tolerance and
freedom originate? In the United States, to the extent that Americans may think about this question at all, they are most likely to
look for the answer in the writings of the American founders like
Thomas Jefferson and James Madison, and in the United States
Constitution with its provisions for the toleration of religious differences and the protection of religious freedom. The founders'
thoughts on this subject were largely derivative, however, and a
product of the European Enlightenment of the eighteenth century and of what came before. The rationale of religious toleration
and the theological, moral, and philosophical justification of religious freedom had their real beginning in the sixteenth century;
they were forged in the bitter denominational conflicts, the continued struggle against persecution, and the fierce intellectual
controversies arising out of the religious divisions created in Europe by the Protestant Reformation.

The modern concepts of religious toleration and freedom are
thus Western in origin and the offspring of European civilization.
They are almost entirely due (the main exception is the Jewish
philosopher Spinoza) to the work of Christian thinkers, mostly
unorthodox Protestants, of the sixteenth and seventeenth centuries, all of whom were powerfully motivated by their religious be-

liefs to fight against the intolerance of both the Catholic and Protestant churches. It is very true that expressions and values of
tolerance, respect for other faiths, and religious coexistence can
be found in the teachings of other world religions such as Judaism,
Islam, Hinduism, and Buddhism, even though fanaticism and religious hatreds on the part of members of these religions, past and
present, have often belied such teachings. It is only in Western
society, nevertheless, and only since the sixteenth century because
of the conflicts and debates between contending Christian
churches, sects, and confessions, that there has appeared a mas-
sive body of writings by many different authors exploring the problem of religious toleration from many angles and presenting an
array of arguments in behalf of the principles of liberty of conscience, mutual tolerance, and religious coexistence and diversity.
This literature was produced at a time when, as in the previous
five centuries of Christian history, an accusation of heresy could
mean death for the person charged. At its heart, the controversy
over religious toleration and liberty of conscience in the sixteenth
and seventeenth centuries was a combat against the cruelty of persecution, a refutation of its rationale, and a plea to end the bloodshed and killing among Christians caused by confessional enmity.
This controversy played a vital role in the long-term development
of religious freedom as one of the distinctive features of contemporary Western civilization.

A few years ago, the British philosopher A. J. Ayer observed in
an essay entitled "Sources of Intolerance" that religious intolerance has probably done greater harm than all other forms of intolerance and was also exceptionally hard to explain. "I do consider
it extraordinary," he said,

> that persons who have somehow managed to convince them-
> selves that the course of nature is dependent on the volition
> of one or more supernatural beings should consequently be
> impelled not merely to despise and traduce but to torture
> and murder those who do not share their view. Not only that
> but those who affirm their faith in the existence of what is

nominally the same supernatural being have been as viciously divided among themselves. If anything, they have displayed even more enthusiasm in reviling, oppressing, torturing, and murdering those who held a different opinion concerning the properties of this being or the details of the ritual which was appropriate for its worship.

I have undertaken this book with the question Ayer broached never far from my mind. Its aim is to present readers with a broad historical account of the ideas of tolerance and religious freedom in their appearance and formative period in the early modern era between the sixteenth and the first decades of the eighteenth century. Within these years I have concentrated on a considerable number of writers and thinkers whose work concerned with toleration seems to me of particular importance, and which I have tried to set in its historical context. Although I have had to be very selective, I have done my best to include an adequate representation of the authors and works that made a major contribution to the discussion and defense of toleration. The book begins with a chapter on the historical problem of explaining the emergence of religious toleration in the West and which also examines the meaning of the concept of tolerance and its relation to religious freedom. The second chapter, on the Christian theory of persecution, deals with the evolution of the concept of heresy and the rationale that enabled Christians of high intellectual and moral standing, like the church father Saint Augustine, to persecute and approve the persecution of other Christians for religious error. The next five chapters survey the controversy over religion toleration in Europe from the time of humanists like Erasmus and Sir Thomas More and the great persecuting Protestant reformers Luther and Calvin, in the sixteenth century, until that of the two foremost champions of toleration at the end of the seventeenth century, John Locke and Pierre Bayle. In these five chapters I have discussed a number of the most significant writings on toleration, in several different countries where the controversy raged, by thinkers such as Sebastian Franck, Sebastian Castellio, Dirck Coornhert and the Dutch

Arminians, Roger Williams, the poet Milton, and others. The fourth chapter, on the work and career of Calvin's courageous opponent the Frenchman Castellio—a seminal thinker and fighter in the history of the idea of toleration—is, I believe, the fullest modern account of Castellio in English since the publication in 1935 of an English translation and edition of his book *De haereticis*, by the distinguished American historian of religious liberty Roland Bainton. The concluding chapter contains a concise overview of the progress of the idea of toleration in Europe and America from the eighteenth-century Enlightenment, Voltaire, Jefferson, and Madison up to the present, which includes a discussion of the view of religious freedom in the United Nations Universal Declaration of Human Rights of 1948 and the Second Vatican Council of the Catholic Church's Declaration on Religious Liberty of 1965. Although I touch in the following pages on the subjects of both anti-Semitism and attitudes toward Jews and of irenic conceptions of tolerance between different faiths, I have done so only occasionally, since my focus in this work is on the problem that was of the greatest import in the West, that of toleration between Christians.

While engaged in the research for this project, I have been able to draw on a large number of historical studies dealing with the idea and practice of toleration, and on recent discussions of toleration by moral and political philosophers. Most of the former are quite specialized rather than broad, while the writings on the subject by philosophers are sometimes not well grounded historically. I have striven in the present book to convey a wide general understanding of the history of the idea of toleration by centering on the succession of writers who figure the largest in this history. So far as I am aware, no work of this kind exists at present in the English language. Within the historical literature from which I have profited, I owe a special debt to the American historian W. K. Jordan's *The Development of Religious Toleration in England*, and the French historian Joseph Lecler's *Toleration and the Reformation*, two outstanding large-scale and indispensable works of synthesis and scholarship. I should also draw the reader's attention to

Henry Kamen's *The Rise of Toleration* as a short, well-informed treatment of the subject.

   At the conclusion of this preface, I must express my thanks to
the friends and colleagues with whom I have frequently discussed
the subject of religious toleration; to the Shannon Center for Advanced Study at the University of Virginia, which has encouraged
my work by making me a Fellow; and to the library staff of the
Alderman Library of the University of Virginia for their unfailing
assistance and cooperation.

How the Idea of Religious Toleration Came to the West

CHAPTER 1

Religious Toleration:
The Historical Problem

క∘3

Of all the great world religions past and present, Christianity has been by far the most intolerant. This statement may come as a shock, but it is nevertheless true. In spite of the fact that Jesus Christ, the Jewish founder of the Christian religion, is shown in the New Testament as a prophet and savior who preached mutual love and nonviolence to his followers, the Christian church was for a great part of its history an extremely intolerant institution. From its inception it was intolerant of other, non-Christian religions, first Greco-Roman polytheism, then Judaism, from which it had to separate itself, and later on Islam. Early in its history, from the time of the apostles, it also became increasingly intolerant of heresy and heretics, those persons who, although worshipers of Christ, dissented from orthodox doctrine by maintaining and disseminating beliefs—about the nature of Christ, the Trinity, the priesthood, the church, and other matters—that ecclesiastical authority condemned as false, and incurring the penalty of damnation. During the fourth century C.E., following the grant by the first Christian emperor Constantine and his colleague Licinius of legal toleration to Christianity, and their imperial successors' decision to make it the sole legal religion of the Roman Empire, the Christian

or Catholic Church, as we may now call it, approved both the
Roman government's suppression of paganism as idolatry and its
use of punitive laws and coercion against Christian heretics who
denied Catholic teaching and formed schismatic churches. This
initiated a development that led during the Middle Ages to the
forcible conversion of pagan Germans and Slavs, Jews, and Muslims
at the hands of Christian rulers, and to the long Christian enmity
toward the religion of Islam, which gave rise to the crusading movement of holy war in medieval Europe. It likewise led, because of
the prevailing hatred of Jews as enemies of Christ, to frequent
charges of ritual murder against Jews and to the instigation by Catholic religious preachers of repeated massacres of Jews in Europe.
And it led also to the medieval church's legitimation of religious
persecution, the creation of the papal Inquisition and its machinery of heresy hunting and prosecution, the Albigensian Crusade
in the thirteenth century against the Catharist heresy in southern
France, and the killing of innumerable fellow Christians whom the
church denounced as heretics.[1]

The sixteenth century, which witnessed the Reformation and
the beginning and spread of Protestantism, was probably the most
intolerant period in Christian history, marked not only by violent
conflict between contending Christian denominations but by an
upsurge of anti-Judaism and anti-Semitism in western Europe.
When Martin Luther, John Calvin, and other outstanding religious reformers undertook their successful revolt against the Catholic Church and established their own Protestant churches, the
latter showed themselves to be no less intolerant of heretics and
dissenting Christians than was the Catholic Church. In the attempt by Catholic and Protestant governments in Europe to stop
the spread of heresy, and in the civil and external wars of religion
waged between Catholicism and Protestantism in the sixteenth
and seventeenth centuries, countless thousands of people on both
sides perished or were forced to go into exile as the victims of
religious persecution. It was the long and terrible history of the
inhumanity of Christianity in its dealing with differences of religious belief, a history not yet ended even in his own time, that

caused the famous eighteenth-century French thinker Voltaire to declare that "of all religions the Christian is undoubtedly that which should instill the greatest toleration, although so far Christians have been the most intolerant of men."[2]

It is at this point that we confront the problem mentioned in this chapter's title. If Christian Europe and the Western world were so intolerant in religion for so many hundreds of years, and indeed in some places down to the later nineteenth century and even beyond,[3] how did it happen that their leaders and members came eventually to change their opinion and to endorse the principle of religious toleration? Anyone today who looks at the values and practices associated with Western liberal democracies in Europe and America can hardly fail to observe that most of their citizens prize none of them more highly than they do religious toleration and freedom of religion. To be sure, they regard political freedom as equally precious and indispensable; but they also commonly recognize that in our own time this freedom with its related political rights is so closely tied to the existence of religious toleration and liberty that the two have become essentially inseparable.[4]

Between the sixteenth and twentieth centuries, therefore, a huge and enormously significant shift of attitudes and values regarding differences in religion gradually occurred in Western societies. Instead of the age-old assumption that it is right and justifiable to maintain religious unity by force and to kill heretics and dissenters if necessary, the opposite assumption came to prevail that it is wrong and unjustifiable to use force and to kill in the cause of religion, and, moreover, that religious toleration and freedom are morally and politically desirable and should be given effect in laws and institutions. This is the very momentous, far-reaching change in Western civilization that needs to be explained, and with whose origins and earlier development this book is concerned.

It will help us grasp the magnitude of this change if we keep in mind that it is in some ways even more novel than the emergence in the West of liberal and democratic societies during the past several hundred years in the aftermath and principally as the result of the English, American, and French revolutions of the seven-

teenth and eighteenth centuries. I stress this point because some
of the conceptions and practices underlying liberal and democratic polities were of very old origin, having been a part of the
Western tradition since classical antiquity and familiar in both
Greek and Roman political thought and experience. Ancient Athens in one of the greatest periods of its history was, despite the
existence of slavery, a democracy of free (male) citizens, and there
were other Greek city-states, although we know much less about
them, that were also democracies. Similarly, republican Rome, the
feudal regime in medieval Europe, and numerous cities of medieval and Renaissance Italy, the Netherlands, and Germany, were
all well acquainted with certain ideas, institutions, and principles
of civic and political liberty, ruler limitation, and self-government.
In comparison with these, the fundamental principles and values
that sustain religious toleration and freedom of religion are innovations and late arrivals in world history and did not become a
part of the Western tradition until recent times. Imperial Rome,
it is true, was tolerant in practice in permitting the existence of
many diverse religious cults, provided their votaries also complied
with the worship of the divine emperor as part of the state religion.
Unlike Christianity and Judaism, Roman religion had no sacred
scriptures and did not depend on any creed, dogmas, or ethical
principles. It consisted very largely of participation in cult acts connected with the worship of various deities and spirits that protected the Roman state and were associated with public, family,
and domestic life. At nearly all stages of their history the Romans
were willing to accept foreign cults and practices; this de facto
religious pluralism is entirely attributable to the polytheistic character of Roman religion and had nothing to do with principles
or values sanctioning religious toleration, a concept unknown to
Roman society or law and never debated by Roman philosophers
or political writers.[5]

Rome's religious pluralism, however, although officially tolerant of Judaism, did not extend to Christianity. Christians were intermittently persecuted and put to death by the Roman government from the first century C.E. to the beginning of the fourth

century, a history culminating in the great persecution under Emperor Diocletian between 303 and 305. The main reason for this treatment was the refusal of Christians to worship any god but their own or take part in the imperial cult by offering sacrifices to the gods on the emperor's behalf. Christians proclaimed that the pagan gods did not exist or were malevolent demons, an attitude deeply offensive to Romans, who believed that it endangered the relationship between gods and men and alienated the goodwill of the gods. On the other hand, the Roman regime tolerated Judaism despite its exclusive monotheism. The Jews were widely regarded as devotees of an ancient and venerable faith; unlike Christians, they did not attack Roman paganism as a religion of demons, and while they would not participate in the imperial cult, their priests could offer prayers for the emperor in the Temple at Jerusalem.[6]

Thus far in my discussion, I have been speaking of religious toleration and religious freedom as though they are closely related or synonymous. Before going further, however, I feel it essential to offer a few clarifications concerning the use of these two concepts.

The English word "tolerance," which is virtually identical in other Western languages (French *tolérance,* German *Toleranz,* Italian *tolleranza,* etc.), stems from the Latin verb *tolerare,* which is defined as "to bear or endure" and carries the further meaning "to nourish, sustain, or preserve." Some philosophers and historians, taking the first of these meanings as their point of departure, regard toleration and religious freedom as quite distinct things and emphasize the differences between the two. They understand toleration to signify no more than forbearance and the permission given by the adherents of a dominant religion for other religions to exist, even though the latter are looked upon with disapproval as inferior, mistaken, or harmful. In contrast, these thinkers see religious liberty as the recognition of equal freedom for all religions and denominations without any kind of discrimination among them. In the case of toleration, it is also pointed out that those in authority who have the power to tolerate a religion have likewise the power to refuse or withdraw toleration, whereas in the case of religious liberty, no one is rightfully possessed of the power not to tolerate or to cancel this liberty. A typical formulation of this view of the subject is the statement by D. D. Raphael that "toleration is the practice of deliberately allowing or permitting a thing of which one disapproves. One can meaningfully speak of tolerating, i.e. of allowing or permitting, only if one is in a position to disallow."[7]

I do not deny that this distinction is a valid one, or that it can be very useful at times in its application to certain historical circumstances. It is also feasible, nevertheless, to think of religious toleration in its broadest terms as equivalent to the condition of religious freedom, and this, I believe, is not only how it is widely understood today, but also how some of the best-known historians of toleration, such as W. K. Jordan and Joseph Lecler, have often regarded it in tracing its evolution.[8] The British historian Henry Kamen states in his *Rise of Toleration* that in its widest sense toleration means "the concession of liberty to those who dissent in religion" and "can be seen as part of the process in history which has led to a gradual development of the principle of human freedom."[9] Johannes Kuhn, a German scholar of the subject, speaks of the historical sense of toleration as encompassing both forbearance toward another and treating another with respect.[10] In the latter formulation, we can perceive the germ of an approximation to the condition of religious freedom. The Swiss historian Hans R. Guggisberg, one of the foremost recent students of the history of toleration, noted that among the latter's synonyms in European tongues were such terms as *souffrance*, "indulgence," *caritas* (love or charity), and *mansuetudo* (gentleness or mildness), and also pointed out its close relationship to phrases like "religious freedom," "liberty of conscience and belief," and "freedom of worship."[11] In the 1560s in France, we find the words *liberté de conscience* beginning to be used to oppose the forcing of consciences as a form of oppression.[12] As we shall see later, moreover, the most noted early fighters for toleration, such as Sebastian Castellio, Roger Williams, and John Locke, also tended to conceive of religious toleration as related to religious freedom. Unless I indicate otherwise, therefore, I shall treat the concept of religious toleration as also implying religious freedom in some measure. In this sense, the belief in and the practice of toleration, as they have evolved and become established in the United States and other countries of the Western world, depend on a very simple and basic principle. This principle is that society and the state should, as a matter of right, extend complete freedom of religious belief and expression to all their members and citizens and should refrain from imposing any religious tests, doctrines, or form of worship or religious association upon them. I take this to be the proper understanding of religious toleration, in its fullest meaning, as it would be conceived today. The struggle to achieve such toleration has the further significance, moreover, that its effects extend beyond the domain of religion and are closely connected with the broader goals of freedom from censorship and intellectual freedom. For the centuries in which intolerance reigned also witnessed the attempt by religious authorities and governments to censor and control the expression of philosophical, political, and other ideas in speech and writing in the interests of a dominant religious orthodoxy. Hence the advance of toleration, by helping to weaken such efforts, played a major role over time in widening the scope of freedom of thought and expression in areas other than religion.

Toleration entails at a minimum the willingness to recognize and accept a degree of religious coexistence and pluralism. In Europe it has pertained historically to the acceptance of coexistence both with members of non-Christian minorities, like Jews and Muslims, and with people who were defined as heretics or belonged to other Christian churches. Those in the former category, not having been baptized into the Christian faith, were regarded by the Catholic Church or Christian governments not as religious traitors or schismatics, but as infidels and external religious enemies, and were therefore often officially tolerated under

various disabilities and despite intermittent outbursts of persecution. Such was the case, for example, of the Muslim and Jewish
communities that lived in Spain amid Christian populations and
under Christian rulers in the fourteenth and fifteenth centuries,
and also of the Jewish communities that could be found in various
parts of Europe since Roman times. As regards the Hispanic Jews,
their relatively peaceful *convivencia* with Spanish Christians until
the late fourteenth century is well known. Thereafter, however,
the intensification of anti-Judaism and anti-Semitism fueled by a
variety of motives led to increasing persecution, massacres and
forced conversions, and finally to the expulsion of the Jews from
Spain in 1492.[13] In the course of the sixteenth century the Muslim
Moriscos in Spain were subjected to growing persecution and
forced conversion, which drove them to revolt, and in 1609 were
also expelled from Spain.[14]

Beyond non-Christians the problem of coexistence and pluralism was one that concerned the relationship of the Catholic
Church to Christian heretics during the Middle Ages and, after
the coming of the Reformation, the relationships among Catholics, the new Protestant churches—chiefly Lutheran, Calvinist,
and Anglican—and the new religious communities and sects, such
as Anabaptists, Spiritualists, and Antitrinitarians, who dissented
from both Catholicism and the major Protestant denominations.
To the medieval church and papacy, coexistence with heretics was
unthinkable, and its possibility was never considered. Thus it was
only with the appearance and steady expansion of Protestantism
in the sixteenth century that ecclesiastical authorities, secular rulers, and European intellectuals were forced for the first time to
confront the issue of reconciling themselves to some degree of
toleration and coexistence.

To the question of why the willingness to tolerate and accept
coexistence between rival religious confessions emerged in Christian Europe, several answers have been given. Perhaps the two
most common reasons cited for this development are the growth
of religious indifference and unbelief, and political expediency.[15]
With regard to the first, it is impossible to deny that these two

factors, indifference and unbelief, made an important contribution over the long run to the creation of a climate of opinion averse to religious fanaticism and zealotry and therefore conducive to a willingness to tolerate. This is obvious when we consider the widening presence between the years 1600 and 1700 of a number of interrelated trends, such as skepticism, libertinism, latitudinarianism, rationalism, the movement of scientific ideas, biblical criticism, deism, and natural religion, all precursors of the Enlightenment in Europe, which had the effect of modifying and liberalizing religious beliefs, weakening clerical authority, and undermining theological orthodoxy.[16]

It should be borne in mind, however, that the impact of these various trends was largely limited to intellectual elites and the educated. Moreover, indifference, incredulity, and the dominance of a secular mentality do not necessarily make for toleration; in some people, on the contrary, they may give rise to a lack of concern about toleration and whether it exists or not. There were quite a few skeptical thinkers in early modern Europe who supported persecution in the interests of political stability and were convinced that maintaining religious faith and conformity among the masses of common people was an essential safeguard of social and political order and subordination.[17] In any case, though, the intellectual changes mentioned above, since they occurred only gradually, cannot possibly account for the theories and defenses of toleration that appeared in the second half of the sixteenth century. The latter were the work of profoundly Christian if also unorthodox thinkers, not of minds inclined to religious indifference or unbelief; and the same is also true of nearly all the major theorists of toleration in the seventeenth century. We must therefore dismiss these factors as an explanation of the emergence of a willingness to accept religious coexistence.

The second reason cited for the appearance of the latter is political expediency, of which a good account has been given by Herbert Butterfield, an eminent English historian of early modern Europe, who emphasized the overwhelming importance of the political factor. Butterfield maintained that the emergence of toleration was entirely due to the mutual exhaustion resulting from the religious conflicts of the Reformation era. As then understood, he argued, toleration was not an ideal or positive end but simply the lesser evil and last resort "for those who often still hated one another but found it impossible to go on fighting any more." Moreover, it was hardly even an idea but something that appeared when no other choice or hope of further struggle remained. It did not stem from any belief in freedom of religion and assuredly not from the belief that religion doesn't matter. Rather, he considered, it "came in the end through *exhaustion*, spiritual as well as material," which made room for reason-of-state and hence the possibility of political solutions and compromises. He also noted that wherever religious toleration was established in the sixteenth century, it was always subject to serious limitations and regarded as no more than a temporary measure.[18]

There is undoubtedly a fair amount of truth in Butterfield's explanation. Although he doesn't expressly say so, he seems to have had in mind chiefly the effects of the religious divisions of the sixteenth century in the Holy Roman Empire, which included all of the German principalities, and in France. In the former, years of conflict and religious war between Catholic and Lutheran princes brought about their agreement in 1555 to the Peace of Augsburg, which provided for the coexistence in the empire of both Catholic and Lutheran states and princes, together with the right of each territorial ruler to determine the religion of his subjects. It also envisaged the parity of Catholics and Protestants in the imperial cities. Calvinists were excluded from this compromise, and the alternative of emigration to another territory was accorded to persons unwilling to conform to the religion of the ruler and state under which they lived.[19]

In France, the religious settlement known as the Edict of Nantes was promulgated in 1598 by the Catholic monarch Henry IV in order to put an end to the bloody and anarchic civil war between French Catholics and Calvinist Protestants, or Huguenots, of the Reformed Church, which had continued for more than thirty years.[20] A religious compromise that sprang from the urgent need

to restore peace, order, and the political authority of the French
monarchy, the edict reflected the realization by the Catholics that
they could not extirpate Protestantism in France, and by the Protestants that they had no hope of making France into a Protestant
country. It granted legal toleration to the Protestant minority, who
were allowed to have their own churches and freedom of worship
in a number of designated places, and were also given certain political and military privileges as securities for their religious liberties.[21]

These two attempts at religious coexistence between antagonis-
tic Christian denominations, though quite limited, are certainly
landmarks in the early history of toleration, and they fit Butterfield's argument, since they were very largely due to political
expediency, which accepted them as lesser evils in preference to
unending religious war. But what we cannot overlook is that both
of these settlements were unstable, and neither lasted for very
long. To recall some well-known facts, during the later sixteenth
century and the first years of the seventeenth, frequent violations
and local conflicts, as well as the exclusion in its provisions of toleration for Calvinism, undermined the Peace of Augsburg. Confessional enmity in Germany increased and was aggravated by the
growing successes of the Catholic Counter Reformation in its battle to reverse the spread of Protestantism. In 1618, as the result
of a Protestant rebellion in Bohemia, one of the states of the Holy
Roman Empire, a new religious struggle began, the Thirty Years
War, which by stages engulfed most of Germany and also drew in
other powers to become a major European war.[22] As several recent
historians of toleration in early modern Germany have pointed
out, pragmatism was a fragile support for the meager degree of
religious pluralism among the German states and cities, and sixteenth-century Germans lacked the intellectual means to concep-
tualize the amicable coexistence of religious communities divided
by fundamental doctrinal differences.[23]

In France, as elsewhere, neither Catholics nor Protestants believed in religious toleration, which they had reluctantly accepted
as a political necessity. Most Catholics and their spiritual guides
remained unreconciled to the existence of Protestantism in their

midst and considered the concessions granted to the Protestant minority as merely temporary. In the earlier seventeenth century, the Protestants themselves launched several revolts, as a result of which they lost the political and military privileges given them by the Edict of Nantes. During the second half of the century, Louis XIV's government, after subjecting the Protestants to increasing persecution to compel them to become Catholics, finally revoked the edict in 1685 and decreed the abolition of Protestantism in France. This action forced many thousands of Protestants to leave their homes and seek refuge in other countries willing to receive them.[24]

Thus the legal regime of coexistence between Catholics and Protestants in sixteenth-century Germany and seventeenth-century France, each the product of political expediency, failed to survive or to create an enduring foundation for toleration. We could cite other historical instances of such failures of what might be called pragmatic coexistence. Among them would be the breakdown of the previously mentioned Christian-Jewish *convivencia* in medieval Spain, and, in our own time, the calamitous collapse of peace and tolerance between Serbian Christians and Bosnian Muslims in the 1990s in the former Yugoslavia as a consequence of abiding religious and ethnic division and animosities.

These cases suffice to show that, contrary to Butterfield's view, while political expediency may have been a reinforcing factor, it alone, unaccompanied by a genuine belief in and commitment to toleration as something inherently good and valuable, was not enough to bring about a permanent peaceful coexistence between hostile religious confessions in Reformation Europe. What this distinguished scholar's discussion strangely ignored is the very great contribution made to the achievement of toleration and denominational coexistence by the formation of religious, philosophical, moral, and humanitarian arguments that can support and justify them. For in a certain sense ideas rule the world, and the attitudes and actions of human beings are greatly affected by reasons and justifications. In the absence of convincing reasons showing why toleration is right and desirable, the institutional accommodation and the change in individual and social values needed to establish it could hardly occur.

Moreover, Butterfield was mistaken in claiming that toleration had scarcely become even an idea in the sixteenth century, when expediency and the exhaustion from religious strife supervened to try to free Germany and France from that strife. For by the latter part of the sixteenth century, a conception and theory of religious toleration had definitely come into being. Generally speaking, moreover, and in spite of the previously mentioned examples of pragmatic toleration in antiquity and the Middle Ages, the appearance and development of the idea of toleration largely preceded its realization. This development required a long and arduous intellectual effort down through the seventeenth century and was the work of a number of thinkers. Without an underlying theoretical rationale that was both philosophical and religious—one that reflected a complex mixture of scriptural, theological, ecclesiological, epistemological, ethical, political, and pragmatic arguments—and without the gradual acceptance by political and intellectual elites and others of principles and values enabling them to subordinate and set aside religious differences and strive for concord through mutual understanding, religious toleration and the freedom it implied could not have been attained as one of the predominant and most cherished attributes of modern and contemporary Western societies. That proposition is the main thesis of this book, and it explains why I have chosen to discuss the notable writers and the religious and intellectual controversies concerning toleration that are the subject of the following chapters.

CHAPTER 2

The Christian Theory
of Religious Persecution

I n 1887 the famous English historian and liberal Catholic Lord Acton had an exchange of correspondence with Dr. Mandell Creighton concerning the latter's *History of the Papacy during the Period of the Reformation,* in which he commented as follows about the popes of the thirteenth and fourteenth centuries and their responsibility for the medieval Inquisition:

> These men instituted a system of Persecution, with a special tribunal, special functionaries, special laws. They carefully elaborated, and developed, and applied it. They protected it with every sanction, spiritual and temporal. They inflicted, as far as they could, the penalties of death and damnation on everybody who resisted it. They constructed quite a new system of procedure, with unheard of cruelties, for its maintenance. They devoted to it a whole code of legislation, pursued for several generations.[1]

Profoundly opposed to persecution for religion, Acton criticized Creighton's history for treating the misdeeds of the popes with too much leniency, and he maintained that those who fashioned the persecutory machinery of the Inquisition were guilty of

The Martyrdome and burnyng of Maifter W.Tyndall,in Flaun-
ders,by Filford Caftle.

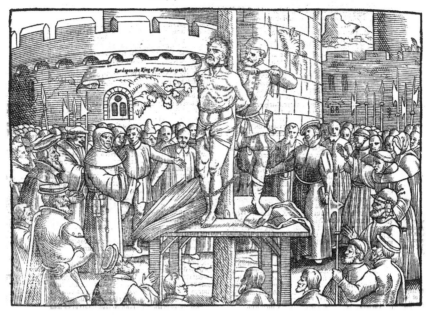

Posthumous woodcut depiction of the execution of the Protestant William
Tyndale, a great translator of the New Testament into English. Tyndale was
strangled and burned at the stake in Brussels in 1536 for the crime of heresy.
Reproduced from John Foxe, *The Ecclesiasticall History*, or *Book of Martyrs*,
1576 edition. Courtesy of The Albert and Shirley Small Special Collections
Library, University of Virginia Library.

a crime. His attitude on this subject grew out of his conviction that
one of the supreme duties of the historian was to brand wrongdo-
ing with eternal infamy by pronouncing a severe moral indictment
on the corruption of power and criminal acts of popes, kings,
statesmen, and other persons who had occupied high positions in
the past.[2] Creighton, who did not share Acton's opinion of the
place of moral judgment in history, stated in reply that

> wrongdoing for an idea, an institution, the maintenance of
> an accepted view of the basis of society, does not cease to be
> wrongdoing: but it is not quite the same as personal wrong.

It is more difficult to prove, and it does not equally shock the moral sense of others or disturb the moral sense of the doer. The acts of men in power are determined by the effective force behind them of which they are the exponents.[3]

This striking exchange between the two historians invites us to inquire why Christians and their spiritual and theological mentors were so intolerant of other Christians in the past that they were even willing to punish or kill them for their beliefs. Was it, as Acton thought, because the persecutors and those who justified persecution were wicked and immoral? According to some philosophers, toleration is a moral virtue;[4] and if this is the case, it would follow that intolerance is a vice. But virtue and vice are qualities solely of individuals, while the intolerance and persecution that characterize centuries of Christian history were, as Creighton implied, not simply a fault of individuals, but a social and collective phenomenon sanctioned by society and for a long time hardly questioned by anyone. Religious intolerance and persecution, therefore, were seen not as evils but as necessary and salutary for the preservation of religious truth and orthodoxy and all that was believed to depend on them. What chiefly rendered persecution commendable was a set of doctrines and an underlying rationale that explained and justified it. There was, in short, a Christian theory of persecution that long antedated any concept or philosophy of religious toleration and freedom, and without which the Catholic Church, the later Protestant state churches, Christian governments, and religious persons could not have undertaken or approved of the repression of Christian heretics and dissenters. Because this theory was embraced by men of high moral character, it is possible to describe the religious persecution of earlier centuries as persecution with a good conscience. W. H. Lecky, author of the nineteenth-century classic *History of Rationalism in Europe* (1865) had this fact in mind when he observed that the peculiar evil of persecution was that it took its seat in the realms of duty and conscience and was defended by sentiments of the deepest piety.[5] A similar comment was made by Henry C. Lea, the greatest historian of the medieval and Spanish inquisitions, who pointed out that men of the kindliest tempers, the profoundest intelligence, the noblest aspirations, the purest zeal for righteousness, professing a religion founded on love and charity, were ruthless when heresy was concerned and were ready to trample it out at the cost of any suffering.

Among these men, as he noted, were such persons as Saints Dominic, Francis of Assisi, and Bonaventura, Pope Innocent III, and Saint Louis, king of France. With all of them it was not desire of gain or lust of blood or pride of opinion or wanton exercise of power, but "sense of duty" that made them unsparing of the heretic; and in this, said Lea, they "represented what was universal public opinion from the thirteenth to the seventeenth century."[6]

THE CONCEPT OF HERESY

The concept of heresy formed an essential part of the theory of persecution, and its introduction in the early Christian church was the fateful first step that initiated the history of religious intolerance and persecution of Christians by other Christians. Heresy was the persistent denial of any authoritatively defined doctrine of the church, and as W. K. Jordan explained, the persecution of heresy depended fundamentally

> on the conviction that there is an ascertained body of religious truth which must be believed . . . in order to attain salvation. The Church was regarded as the sole custodian of this body of truth, and hence rebellion against the Church was, in part, a rebellion against Truth. Thus, according to universal opinion, all who were external to the Church were doomed to eternal damnation.[7]

How did this idea of heresy become part of the earliest Christianity? It is not easy to obtain an answer to this question. Standard works of scholarship on church history and the development of Christian doctrine tell us a great deal about the different heresies in the church of the first four centuries but often seem to ignore the problem of why the idea of heresy as false and prohibited religious belief ever took root in the first place, especially since no precedent for this idea existed in either contemporary Judaism or Greco-Roman religion.[8] The seventeenth-century English philosopher Thomas Hobbes was one of the first thinkers to attempt to deal with this problem, and in several of his writings he gave a short historical sketch of the evolution of heresy and the source of the idea. An accusation of heresy against heterodox thinkers still remained a live possibility in his time, and his main reason for tracing its history was less to write a disinterested account than to produce a brief defending himself from the charge of heresy that his critics made against him, and to reinforce the argument of his political philosophy that the civil sovereign must be the sole judge of heresy.[9]

Etymologically, the word "heresy" originated in the Greek term *hairesis*, signifying "choice," and it could also refer to opinions and the philosophical sects or schools that professed them.[10] Transliterated into classical Latin, the word appeared as *haeresis*, retaining its meaning of a philosophical or religious sect or its tenets.[11] Understood in this sense, it had no negative connotations in either language. The Greek term *hairesis* was also used in the New Testament, but here it had ceased to be a neutral description and already began to take on a pejorative meaning. In Paul's letter to the Christians of Corinth, he told them that "when ye come together in church, I hear that there be divisions [*schismata*] among you," and then went on to say that "there must be also heresies [*haireseis*] among you, that they which are approved may be made manifest among you" (1 Cor. 11:18–19).[12] In this letter it is significant that Paul associated heresy with *schismata*, the Greek parent of the English word "schism," which is defined in both languages as a separation, division, and disharmony. In his letter to the Galatians, he listed heresies (*haireseis*) as one of the "works of the flesh," along with idolatry, witchcraft, hatred, sedition, and other sins (Gal. 5:20). The Latin Vulgate translation of the Bible, made by Saint Jerome in the fourth century, renders *haireseis* in the latter passage as *sectae*, or sects, with the implication of something divisive. In the second letter of Peter, the apostle definitely connected heresy with false and wicked belief in his declaration that "there shall be false teachers among you, who privily shall bring in damnable heresies, even denying the Lord" (2 Pet. 2:1). Finally, in Paul's letter to Titus, after first exhorting him to tell his fellow Christians to avoid foolish questions and contentions, he then stated that they should reject "a man that is an heretick [*hairetikon anthropon*] after the first and second admonition," because "he that is such is subverted and sinneth, being condemned of himself" (Titus 3:10–11).

These examples indicate that the New Testament authors tended to conceive of heresy not in the older sense of philosophical schools or their opinions, but mainly as the fomenting of divisions and sects among Christians through the propagation of false and evil opinions. This impression is further confirmed by such passages as Paul's warning in his letter to the Romans to avoid those who "cause divisions and offences contrary to the doctrine which ye have learned" (Rom. 16:17); and his beseeching the Corinthians in the name of Christ "that ye all speak the same thing, and that there be no divisions [*schismata*] among you" (1 Cor. 1:10).[13] The evidence of the New Testament, therefore, makes it clear that Christians of the first and second centuries were already being taught to think that heresy signified erroneous and evil beliefs contrary to the apostles' and the church's teachings and was related to schism or the creation of divisions in the Christian communities.

Although the concept of heresy thus emerges in the New Testament, the latter never enjoins any coercion or silencing of those who introduce heresies and cause divisions. The utmost severity that the New Testament recommends to the Christian churches in dealing with heresy is first to admonish the persons responsible and then, if this was unsuccessful, to reject and avoid them, which presumably meant their expulsion or excommunication from the religious community. Such treatment would be in keeping with the pacific message of Christ as the founder of Christianity. In any case, until the fourth century, the Christian churches were purely voluntary societies subject to persecution by the Roman state and powerless to use coercion against erring members even had they believed in doing so.

There were, of course, numerous theological differences and quarrels that arose in the church with the spread of the new religion, and the developing importance of the concept and identification of heresy and its distinction from orthodoxy can be seen in the treatises written against heretics and heresy by a succession of early Christian authors.[14] The first writer outside the New Testament to designate error in doctrine as "heresy" was the venerated Saint Ignatius of Antioch, martyred at the beginning of the second century, who used the word in reprobation of Docetism, a form of Gnostic heresy.[15] Orthodoxy, which represents the principle of religious authority, was in general equated with the teachings and tradition of the apostles. The gradual formation of the canon of the New Testament during the second and third centuries, along with the evolution in the church of a Rule of Faith of apostolic origin summarizing the divinely ordained events leading to redemption through Christ, contributed to the establishment of orthodoxy.[16] Speaking of this period, Gibbon declares that

> the Christians formed a numerous and disciplined society; and the jurisdiction of their laws and magistrates was strictly exercised over the minds of the faithful. The loose wanderings of the imagination were gradually confined by creeds and confessions; the freedom of private judgment submitted to the public wisdom of synods . . . and the episcopal successors of the apostles inflicted the censures of the church on those who deviated from the orthodox belief.[17]

One of the first widely circulated antiheretical works was Bishop Irenaeus of Lyon's *Against All Heresies*, dating from around 180 and directed especially against Gnosticism, a major heresy in the early church. As an exponent of the apostolic and Catholic tradition, Irenaeus described heretics as bringers of alien doctrines to the altar of God and as rebels against the truth and church whom God would punish for their separation from the church's unity.[18] Another polemic against heresy came from Tertullian, a rhetorician, lawyer, and leading Christian theologian of the later second and early third centuries. His *Barring of Heretics* (ca. 200) contained an exposition of Catholic principles and included a Rule of Faith that he called it heresy to question. Heretics, in his opinion, could not be Christians.[19] Although he insisted on the truth of Christianity, Tertullian was nevertheless opposed to compulsion in religion and stated in other works that "to do away with freedom of religion [*libertas religionis*]" was wrong. While Christians, he said, worship the one God and pagans worship demons, both "human and natural law" ordain that "each person may worship whatever he wishes."[20] Other authors who carried on the theological warfare against heresy were Hippolytus of Rome (d. ca. 235), a Christian martyr whose *Refutation of All Heresies* condemned heretics as atheists dependent on pagan philosophies;[21] the historian Eusebius of Caesarea, whose *Ecclesiastical History* (ca. 311), an account of the church from its supernatural beginnings to the reign of the emperor Constantine, dealt with heresies and heretics among its many subjects;[22] and Epiphanius of Salamis (d. 403), whose book entitled *Medicine Chest* was the most extensive chronicle of the numerous heresies that had afflicted the church since the beginning of Christianity.[23]

THE CHRISTIAN ROMAN EMPIRE

The fourth and fifth centuries saw the Roman Empire gripped by increasing troubles caused by economic and military deterioration, the decline of the urban middle classes, civil wars, pressure on the frontiers, and invasion of the Roman provinces by migratory Germanic tribes. Government regimentation of society steadily grew as various occupations were made hereditary and prices and wages regulated in an effort to cope with economic problems and extract taxes. Toward the end of the third century the emperor Diocletian (284–305), recognizing that the Roman Empire was too big for one person to rule, carried out a sweeping administrative reorganization that divided the empire into an eastern and

a western part governed under a system of coemperors and in
which the city of Rome was no longer the imperial capital. Roman
government thereafter became more and more a type of despo-
tism with theocratic trappings under the control of emperors who
maintained themselves in power with the support of their armies.
It was in this period, in which Roman civilization was declining
and the empire in the West was destined to disappear and give
way to successor Germanic barbarian kingdoms, that the Christian
church rose to ascendancy.

The fourth century marked the great and decisive transforma-
tion in the position of the church and likewise in the history of
heresy. It began with the emperor Constantine's conversion to
Christianity in 311 and the legalization of the Christian religion in
313, thus ending its persecution by the Roman state. In the course
of the century Christianity was adopted as the exclusive religion of
the empire and became itself a persecutor in the prohibition of
paganism and heresy. From the reign of Constantine, the Christian
emperors played a dominant role in ecclesiastical affairs and show-
ered the church with wealth and privileges, placing behind it the
power of the imperial government. In 325, Constantine convened
the Council of Nicaea comprising about three hundred bishops,
the first general council of the Christian church, to deal with the
Arian controversy concerning the divinity of Christ and the Trinity.
Its initiator, Arius, a theologian of Alexandria who had many followers, denied the true divinity of Christ and affirmed that Christ as
Son of God was not coeternal but created by God the Father. The
council condemned and anathematized Arianism as heresy and
sanctioned a declaration of orthodoxy in the Nicene Creed, according to which Christ was true God, begotten—not made—and
of one substance with the Father and the Holy Spirit, which is worshiped together with the Father and the Son. Thereafter Constantine issued an edict banning various heresies and confiscating
the churches of "these enemies of the truth"; and he likewise took
various measures against paganism, demolishing some famous
pagan temples and despoiling them of their treasures and estates.[24]
Although Arianism persisted for a number of years and enjoyed

the patronage of several subsequent emperors, the Nicene Council was a landmark in prescribing a definition of the orthodox Catholic faith in opposition to Arianism and other heresies.

Several of Constantine's heirs permitted the toleration of heretics, but in 385 Maximus, coemperor in the western part of the empire, condemned and executed Priscillian, a Spanish bishop, and four of his adherents for various heretical doctrines and practices. This violent act to stamp out Priscillianism, which some Catholics of the time deplored, was the first execution for heresy in the history of the church.[25]

In the eastern empire Theodosius I (379–395) was a pious, fanatical Christian and a relentless champion of Catholic orthodoxy. In a momentous edict issued with his coemperors in 380, he recommended all his subjects to "profess the faith . . . communicated by the Apostle Peter to the Romans" and to "believe only in one deity consisting of the sacred Trinity of Father, Son, and Holy Spirit, to be worshipped in equal majesty." Those who follow this Rule of Faith, he commanded, "should embrace the name of Catholic Christians," while all others were to be considered heretics "condemned . . . to suffer divine punishment" and the emperor's vengeance and chastisement. In 381 he summoned the Council of Constantinople, the second general council of the church, which reaffirmed the Nicene doctrine as the faith of the church. Theodosius was an implacable enemy of heresy, against which he issued no fewer than eighteen edicts. He proscribed various heresies by name, ordered the confiscation of churches and private houses where heretics met for worship, and deprived them of the right to make wills or receive inheritances. In the case of certain heretical sects he commanded that their members be hunted down and executed. In his attempt to enforce uniformity of belief he also instituted legislation against paganism, including a comprehensive enactment in 395 forbidding anyone of whatever rank or dignity to sacrifice to or worship "senseless images" constructed "by human hands," on pain of heavy fines and other penalties. He was likewise the first emperor to impose penalties on Christians who profaned their baptism by reverting to paganism.[26]

The reign of Theodosius I marked a major step in the creation of a new religious order in the late and fast declining Roman civilization. This order was founded on the spread of Christianity and the union between the Roman imperial government and the Catholic Church, which was now the sole legally recognized religious society of the Roman Empire and in which the primacy of the bishop of Rome, the pope, as head of the church was gradually coming to be acknowledged. All subjects were expected to be worshipers in this church; and in addition to the spiritual and political authority its bishops wielded, it had the power of the state at its disposal to enforce its faith against heretics. The practical toleration and religious pluralism that had formerly been the Roman custom no longer existed. The change that took place is epitomized in an appeal made in 384 by Quintus Aurelius Symmachus—a Roman senator, orator, and prefect of Rome, and a defender of paganism—to the emperors Theodosius I and Valentinian II to restore the altar of the goddess Victory to the Senate House (it had been removed by imperial decree after standing there for over 350 years, since the reign of the emperor Augustus at the beginning of the first century). Speaking in the name of the proscribed ancient religion of Rome, Symmachus declared that

> each nation has its own gods and peculiar rites. The Great Mystery cannot be approached by one avenue alone.... Leave us the symbol on which our oaths of allegiance have been sworn for so many generations. Leave us the system which has given prosperity to the State.[27]

His plea was of no avail, however, for the cross of Christ had conquered the Roman Empire, and the altar of Victory remained banished and abandoned.

SAINT AUGUSTINE AND THE COERCION OF HERETICS

By the early fifth century religious intolerance and the concept of heresy had become firmly established within the Catholic Church, various doctrines had been condemned as heresies that Christians must not believe, and the legal repression of heretics by the civil authorities was a familiar phenomenon. Heresy was understood to be religious error maintained in willful and persistent opposition to religious truth as authoritatively defined and declared by the church. From the orthodox viewpoint, heresy was a moral defect no less than a religious error, since the heretic adhered to a false belief pertinaciously, despite warnings and remonstrances, and caused divisions by factiously seeking to win over others to his doctrine. Although heresy and schism were not identical, they tended to be associated, and the distinction between them was easily elided. Among heresies, some were more speculative and intellectual in their doctrinal deviations, others more directly critical of the institutional church and clergy. The orthodox considered them all as dangers to the church and its salvific mission. Christian writers of the fourth and fifth centuries estimated the number of heretical sects by the score, including Gnostics, Arians, Manichaeans, Donatists, Montanists, Marcionites, Monophysites, Nestorians, Pelagians, and others. All were inspired by the teachings of theologians, ecclesiastics, and prophets, and some acquired a mass following. They were all subject to punitive legislation, and in 407 an edict of the emperor Arcadius declared heresy a public crime "because any offence which is committed against divine religion involves an injury to all." The punishment of heretics still included death only exceptionally, although in 510 the emperor Anastasius inflicted the death penalty on Manichaeans, as did also the emperor Justinian in the sixth century. The suppression of paganism likewise continued, and in 529 Justinian ordered all pagans to come to church with their families, receive instruction, and undergo baptism.[28]

Whether the divinely founded Catholic Church, which proclaimed the message of salvation through Christ, was justified in using coercion in behalf of religion was a question that deeply concerned Saint Augustine (354–430), who after Saint Paul was the greatest of Christian thinkers and one of the foremost religious minds of any age. Born in Roman Africa of a pagan father and a Christian mother, educated in Latin letters and philosophy and a professor of rhetoric first in Africa and then in Italy, Augustine in his search for wisdom and truth had been during his youth an adherent of the Manichaean heresy for a number of years. Experiencing a conversion, in 387 he was baptized into the Catholic Church and dedicated himself thereafter to a religious life. Returning to Africa, he became a priest in 391 at the insistence of the people of Hippo, a port on the Mediterranean coast, and was appointed bishop of the city four years later. He spent the rest of his life there involved in the affairs of the church and as a prolific and eloquent author, preacher, biblical exegete, and theologian whose work exercised a vast influence on the Christian thought of the subsequent centuries.

Augustine carried on a long theological combat with three formidable heresies, Manichaeanism, Pelagianism, and Donatism. Among his writings against the last of these and its followers, the Donatists, he left an invaluable record of his reflections on the justification of coercion against heretics to enforce religious truth. At the time he became bishop of Hippo, Donatism, which took its name from one of its first leaders, Donatus, bishop of Carthage, had already existed in North Africa for more than eighty years and had undergone considerable persecution. Originating in the early fourth century in an ecclesiastical controversy over a bishop who had compromised with paganism during the persecution by the emperor Diocletian and was therefore considered a betrayer of the faith, the Donatists formed a schismatic and rival church with its own clergy. Rigorists who believed in a church composed exclusively of the holy, they maintained that an unworthy priest could not perform a valid sacrament. By insisting on the rebaptism of converts, the Donatist church declared its rejection of the sacramental character of Catholic baptism. To some extent Donatism represented an expression of social protest against the profane world as a domain ruled by Satan. Its more extreme adherents, a fanatical fringe of zealots and ascetics known as Circumcellions, sought a martyr's death by any means, including suicide; they gathered as bands of marauding peasants who attacked estates and

committed other acts of violence. As a self-described church of
martyrs, the Donatists condemned the alliance between Catholicism and the Roman authorities as a renunciation of Christ in
favor of Caesar, and their bishop Donatus was reported to have
said, "What has the Emperor to do with the Church?" In the
course of its history Donatism became a considerable movement,
although it remained largely confined to North Africa.[29]

In his numerous writings against this heresy, one of Augustine's
constant aims was to persuade its followers by means of reason
and argument to abandon their errors and return to the Catholic
Church. He did his best to refute its doctrines in a number of
treatises and at first opposed any use of coercion against these
heretics.[30] A lost work of 397 repudiated coercion,[31] and in an
undated letter to a Donatist churchman he wrote: "I do not intend
that anyone should be forced into the Catholic communion
against his will. On the contrary, it is my aim that the truth may
be revealed to all who are in error and that . . . with the help of
God, it may be made manifest so as to induce all to follow and
embrace it of their own accord."[32] To several Donatists he wrote
in around 398 that those who maintain a false and perverted opinion but without "obstinate ill will"—and especially those "who have
not originated their error by bold presumption" but received it
from their parents or others, and who seek truth with a readiness
to be corrected when they have found it—are not to be included
among heretics. The heretic himself, however, "swollen with hateful pride and with the self-assertion of evil contradiction, is to be
avoided like a mad man."[33]

Nevertheless, Augustine eventually reversed his position and
decided to endorse coercion. Looking back at this development
some years later, he said that at first he had believed that no one
should be forced into the unity of Christ, and that the church
should rely only on speaking, reasoning, and persuasion "for fear
of making pretended Catholics out of those whom we knew as
open heretics." But then proven facts caused him to give up this
opinion when he saw Donatists in his own city "converted to Catholic unity by the fear of imperial laws" and those in other cities

recalled by the same means. Reclaimed Donatists, he contended, were now grateful that "fear of the laws promulgated by temporal rulers who serve the Lord in fear has been so beneficial" to them.[34]

We first learn of Augustine's change of mind in the treatise he wrote (ca. 400) as a reply to a letter by the Donatist bishop Parmenian, a leading spokesman of the movement.[35] In this work he justified the intervention of the imperial government against the Donatists by invoking Saint Paul's theology of the state, as the apostle outlined it in the thirteenth chapter of his letter to the Romans (Rom. 13:1–7). There Paul instructed Christians to be obedient to the higher powers as the minister ordained by God and armed with the sword for the repression of evildoers. In the light of this apostolic teaching, Augustine insisted that the emperors and political authorities had the God-given right and duty to crush the sacrilege and schism of the Donatists, since they were as obligated to repress a false and evil religion as to prevent the crime of pagan idolatry. He further pointed out that the Donatists were guilty of many cruelties and had themselves appealed to the emperors in the past against the dissidents in their own church. Denying that those of them condemned to death were martyrs, he described them instead as killers of souls and, because of their violence, often killers of bodies.[36]

One of the arguments he put forward in defense of force in this work was his interpretation of Jesus' parable of the tares in the Gospel of Matthew (Matt. 13:24–30). This famous text was destined to be cited often during subsequent centuries in discussions of toleration and persecution, and to occupy a prominent place in the tolerationist controversies of the era of the Protestant Reformation. The parable first likens the kingdom of heaven to a good seed and then relates how a man sowed good seed in the ground, whereupon his enemy came in the night and planted tares, or weeds, there as well. When the wheat appeared, so did the tares. The man's servants asked their master if they should pull up the tares, but he forbade them lest they also uproot the wheat. He ordered that both should be left to grow until the harvest, and then the reapers would remove and burn the tares and gather the wheat into the barn. The parable's point would seem to be that good people and sinners alike should be allowed to await the Last Judgment to receive their due, when God would reward the good with the kingdom of heaven and punish the bad with the flames of hell. Augustine, however, drew from it a very different lesson: if the bad seed is known, it should be uprooted. According to his explanation, the only reason the master left the tares to grow until the harvest was the fear that uprooting them sooner would harm the grain. When this fear does not exist because it is evident which is the good seed, and when someone's crime is notorious and so execrable that it is indefensible, then it is right to use severe discipline against it, for the more perversity is corrected, the more carefully charity is safeguarded.[37] With the help of this interpretation, which reversed the parable's meaning, Augustine was able not only to justify the Roman government's repression of the Donatists but to provide a wider reason for religious persecution by the civil authorities.[38]

Augustine elaborated his position in favor of coercion in religion in a number of letters. In a lengthy epistle to the Donatist Vincent, he argued for the utility of coercion in inducing fear that can bring those who are subject to it to the right way of thinking. Maintaining that people could be changed for the better through the influence of fear, he concluded that "when the saving doctrine is added to useful fear," then "the light of truth" can drive out "the darkness of error."[39] To reinforce his view, he quoted the parable of the feast in the Gospel of Luke (Luke 14:21–23), another of the texts that was to figure prominently in future tolerationist controversy. In this parable, a man prepared a great feast to which he invited many guests who failed to appear. After summoning from the city the poor, blind, and lame to come and eat, he found that room still remained, so he ordered his servants to "go out into the highways and hedges, and compel them to come in [*compelle intrare* in the Latin Vulgate], that my house may be filled." "Do you think," Augustine asked in a comment on this passage, "that no one should be forced to do right, when you read that the master of the house said to his servants, 'Whomever you find, compel them to come in.' " He referred also to the example of the conversion of the apostle Paul, who "was forced by the great violence of Christ's compulsion to acknowledge and hold the truth" (Acts 9:3–18).[40] The main point, he claimed, was not whether anyone was being forced to do something, but whether the purpose of doing so was right or wrong. While no one could be made good against his will, the fear of punishment could persuade a person to repudiate a false doctrine and embrace the truth he had previously denied, as had happened to many Donatists who had thankfully become Catholics and now detested their diabolical separation.[41]

In dealing with heresy, Augustine thus laid great stress on what might be called the pedagogy of fear to effect a change of heart. He did not see coercion and free will as opposites in religious choice but claimed that fear plays a part in spontaneous acts of the will and may serve a good end.[42] In one of his most important statements on the subject, contained in a letter of 417 to Boniface, the Roman governor of Africa, he propounded a distinction between two kinds of persecution. "[T]here is an unjust persecution," he said, "which the wicked inflict on the Church of Christ, and . . . a just persecution which the Church of Christ inflicts on the wicked." The church persecutes from love, the Donatists from hatred; the church in order to correct error, the Donatists to hurl men into error. While the church strives to save the Donatists from perdition, the latter in their fury kill Catholics to feed their passion for cruelty.[43] Augustine was convinced that the coercion of heretics was therefore a great mercy because it rescued them from lying demons so that they could be healed in the Catholic fold. He rejected the objection of those who said that the apostles had never called upon the kings of the earth to enforce religion, since in the apostles' times there had been no Christian emperor to whom they could appeal. It was necessary and right, however, for kings to forbid and restrain with religious severity actions contrary to God's commandments, and to serve God by sanctioning laws that commanded goodness and prohibited its opposite.[44]

While admitting that it was better to lead people to the worship of God by teaching than to force them through fear of suffering, Augustine nevertheless averred that the latter way could not be neglected. Experience proved, he claimed, that for many heretics it had been a blessing to be driven by fear of bodily pain to undergo instruction in the truth and then follow up with actions what they had learned in words.[45] Schismatics, he noted, protested that men have freedom to believe or not to believe, and that Christ never used force on anyone. To this objection he countered with his previous argument that Christ had first compelled Paul to cease his persecution of the Christian church by striking him blind at his conversion and only then taught him. "It is a wonderful thing," he said, "how he [Paul] who came to the gospel under the compulsion of bodily suffering labored more in the gospel than all the others who were called by words alone." Once again he drew on the injunction *compelle intrare* in the Gospel of Luke to affirm that the Catholic Church was in accord with God when it compelled heretics and schismatics to come in.[46] In other letters he denied that the "evil will" should be left to its freedom, and cited not only this same parable and the example of Christ's compulsion of Paul, but also God's restraint of the Israelites from doing evil and compelling them to enter the land of promise (Exod. 15:22–27), as proof of the church's justice in using coercion.[47]

Although after his change of mind Augustine consistently approved the policy of subjecting heretics to coercion, he never desired that they should be killed. In writing to Donatists, he often stated that he and his brethren loved them and acted for their good, and that if they hated the Catholic Church, it was because "we do not allow you to go astray and be lost."[48] Donatists had been subject to previous imperial legislation against heresy, but between 405 and 410 the emperor Honorius decreed a number of heavy penalties against them that put them outside the protection of the law for their seditious actions; he ordered their heresy to be put down in "blood and proscription."[49] Augustine frequently interceded with the Roman authorities to spare their lives. In 408 he wrote to the proconsul of Africa urging Christian clemency and

praying that though heretics be made to feel the effect of the laws
against them, they should not be put to death, despite deserving
the extreme punishment, in the hope that they might be converted. To another high official he pleaded in behalf of some Donatists tried for murder and other violent acts that they should be
deprived of their freedom but not executed that they might have
the chance to repent.[50]

Although repression weakened Donatism, it failed to eliminate
this deeply rooted heresy, which survived until the later seventh
century when the Islamic conquest of North Africa destroyed
every form of Christianity in this region.[51] In the course of his
career, Augustine, who was not only an outstanding thinker but a
man of keen and sensitive conscience, wrestled strenuously with
the problem of heresy and the achievement of Catholic unity by
the use of coercion. It is regrettable that one of his major legacies
to the Catholic Church was the formulation of a theory of persecution founded entirely on Christian grounds and supported with
numerous examples from the Old and New Testaments. As a great
rhetorician he knew how to find arguments and present them per-
suasively; but a leading twentieth-century Catholic theologian,
Yves Congar, who edited some of his anti-Donatist treatises, has
expressed the opinion that the texts he relied on, such as the parable of the feast and the conversion of Paul, did not serve well for
his purpose. As Congar also pointed out, however, his belief in
justice and the right of truth conditioned his ideas about the use of
force; its exercise in behalf of these values was completely different
from its use in behalf of a lie or injustice.[52] He defended religious
persecution provided its ends were good, and was confident that
the coercion of heretics served such an end. In his view, persecuted heretics like the Donatists could not claim to be Christian
martyrs, because they did not suffer in a righteous cause. Not only
did they separate from the Catholic Church, but they were guilty
of repeated seditions and violence that necessitated the intervention of the civil authorities. While he never supposed that heretics
could be converted by force, he regarded their fear of pain and
suffering as conducive to their repentance and acceptance of the

truth. It is rather appalling that Augustine was willing to rely on the pedagogy of fear as a way to convert heretics and failed to see the terrible dangers in this position. "Pride," he once wrote, "is the mother of all heretics," and fear could break down this pride and thus act as an auxiliary in the process of conversion. Whether the heretic was really sincere in professing a change of mind under the threat of bodily pain was a question that could best be left to God. Augustine certainly did not recommend the death penalty for heretics but strove tirelessly to save their souls from eternal perdition. He supported their repression by the Roman imperial government in the hope of restoring them to the Catholic Church, and because, as he said in a letter to some Donatists, "nothing can cause more complete death to the soul than freedom to disseminate error."[53]

Peter Brown, a historian with a deep understanding of Augustine's mind, has warned that an academic consistency should not be imposed upon him, and that coercion was not a doctrine for him but an attitude derived from a long and painful attempt to embrace and resolve tensions. While this may be true, it is also the case that Augustine contributed very significantly to the justification of such a doctrine. The great church father and theologian had thought hard about the use of coercion, but as Brown also noted, if one removes the foundation of honesty from his attitude, "his phrases become fallacious, horrible and insidious."[54]

HERESY IN THE MIDDLE AGES

By the time Augustine died in the year 430, the provinces of the western Roman empire were being overrun and occupied by Teutonic tribes who were founding kingdoms and becoming Christianized. While in the East the shrunken empire survived and gave birth to a new Greek-speaking Christian Byzantine civilization ruled by an emperor and centered on its capital, Constantinople, in the Latin West the Roman world and centralized government came to an end in the fifth century. During the next five hundred years Europe was subject to a succession of pagan Germanic, Slavic, Asiatic, and Scandinavian invaders and was hemmed in and separated from Byzantium by the creation of an Islamic empire stretching from Arabia, Persia, and the lands of the eastern Mediterranean to Egypt, North Africa, and Spain. The European society and economy became predominantly rural and agrarian as commerce declined and towns, contracting or vanishing, no longer functioned as centers of trade. Public authority ceased to exist and was only slowly re-created in the following centuries. Classical culture disappeared, and civilization gave way to primitive conditions. What remained in the West of the literary and intellectual heritage from antiquity was preserved by the Catholic Church in the Benedictine monasteries that had been founded in various parts of Europe as asylums of the religious life and refuges from the world. From the era of imperial Rome and its greatness the Catholic Church, led by the popes, who were bishops of Rome and successors to Saint Peter the Apostle, remained as the chief living link with the Roman past.

During these centuries of upheaval, movement of peoples, violence, insecurity, and disorder that marked the earlier Middle Ages, a new Christian society and civilization gradually emerged in the West with new social and political institutions and new feudalized kingdoms united in allegiance to the Catholic Church. Before the eleventh century the latter, still engaged in the work of conversion, was not much concerned with the problem of heresy. The older heresies had been vanquished or had become largely extinct, and the church was as yet little troubled by new ones. With the great economic, political, religious, cultural, and intellectual revival of the later eleventh and twelfth centuries, however, a variety of heresies appeared that led to the further development of instruments of persecution in law and institutions.

The new heresies were broadly of two types. Some were doctrinal deviations stigmatized as heretical that affected only a relatively small number of learned clerics and were the product of the theological and philosophical speculations and debates in the schools and universities that came into existence during this period. Other heresies, however, had a far wider impact, generating popular movements of radical religious protest against the doctrines and the wealth, power, and worldly practices of the church and higher clergy, which they condemned as a departure from the gospel of Christ and its moral message. These popular heresies, which were of different kinds and inspired by preachers, prophets, and in some cases by the teachings of radical or visionary theologians, were the most threatening to the church between the twelfth and fifteenth centuries and often represented a direct challenge to its institutional dominance in medieval society. They were propagated primarily among laypeople, although they also attracted disaffected monks and clergy whose religious and spiritual aspirations the church failed to satisfy. Such heresies created sects of believers outside of and uncontrolled by the church. One of the most widespread in the twelfth and thirteenth centuries was the Cathars, or the pure. Their dualistic conception of the world as a battleground between two forces—a spiritual and all-good God versus an evil power that ruled the material universe may have been a revival of the ancient Manichaean heresy, and they had their own religious organization, ministers, rituals, and doctrines diametrically opposed to the church's. Popular heretical movements began to appear in the later eleventh century and more noticeably in the twelfth in different parts of Europe, in Italy, France, the Low Countries, and Germany, and they multiplied rapidly after 1150. Among the features common to a number of them were an impulsion to asceticism, anticlericalism, and an aspiration to a Christian life based on poverty, renunciation, repentance, and the example of the apostles.[55]

To the Catholic Church and all its faithful members it was an essential and unchallengeable truth that there could be no salvation outside the church; and the response of ecclesiastical authority to heresy was that heretics were violators of Christian unity who brought damnation on themselves by separating from the church and rebelling against its teachings. As Malcolm Lambert has observed, all the heresies that appeared between the twelfth and fifteenth centuries were failures, unable either to impose their views on the church or to gain toleration for their opinions and practices. The papacy's condemnation of dissident religious bodies as heretical led either to their extirpation, as in the case of the terrible persecution of the Cathars—against whom Pope Innocent III proclaimed the Albigensian Crusade in 1209—or their survival as persecuted underground sects like the Waldensians in France and Italy and the Lollards in England, the latter of whom owed some of their heretical beliefs to the radical teachings of the Oxford theologian John Wyclif (d. 1384). Wyclif's ideas also spread to Bohemia, where they helped influence the heretical national reform movement led by the popular Czech preacher John Hus. In 1415, following his condemnation by the Council of Constance, Hus was burned for his heresy, and the church launched a series of crusading wars in Bohemia and central Europe against the Hussite revolt that his teachings inspired.[56] Thus throughout the Middle Ages, in spite of significant manifestations of opposition, the Catholic Church preserved its institutional and doctrinal supremacy in Europe as the one religious body of Western Christendom, maintaining its dominance both by teaching and evangelistic preaching and by force. Not until the Protestant Reformation of the sixteenth century was its supremacy overthrown by heresies that successfully resisted all efforts at repression. Persecuted heretics like the Waldensians, Cathars, and Lollards hated and rejected the Catholic Church as anti-Christ. To their way of thinking the wicked and ungodly had always oppressed the good, and they recalled Christ's words to his disciples, "If the world hates you, know that it has hated me before it hated you" (John 15:18) and "I send you out as sheep in the midst of wolves" (Matt. 10:16).[57] There is no reason to think that heretics were more tolerant than their persecutors; had the followers of popular heresies possessed the power, they would surely have abolished the Catholic Church and hierarchy and imposed a religious order of their own.

The Catholic faith of the Middle Ages was composed of doctrines based on the Gospels and other parts of the Bible as discussed and defined by the church fathers of the early centuries of Christianity, by the popes, and by ecclesiastical councils and synods. Some philosophical and doctrinal disagreements, to be sure, always existed in the universities among clerical intellectuals and Scholastic theologians, which might be the subject of vigorous debate and testified to the intellectual vitality of medieval civilization. Such disagreements, though, did not commonly cross the line into heresy and dealt with unsettled questions on which opinions could legitimately differ. To determine whether a doctrine was heretical was not necessarily easy, in any case. In the twelfth century, however, the definition and criminality of heresy as elements of the Christian theory of persecution were made part of the law of the church as a result of their inclusion in Gratian's *Decretum* (ca. 1140). This authoritative legal compilation, which was later augmented by the decrees of a number of medieval popes and commented on by jurists for centuries, became the first part of the great code or body of canon law, the *Corpus iuris canonici*, and exerted an immeasurable influence upon medieval and early modern Catholic civilization.[58] One of the first defiant acts of Martin Luther when he began his career as a religious rebel against Catholicism was to burn the canon law.

The materials Gratian used for his great collection included patristic texts, decrees of church councils, and papal pronouncements. In its treatment of heresy, which is found in the second part of the *Decretum*, we meet with citations from various Catholic writers and especially Saint Augustine, who is treated as the principal authority on this subject. Saint Jerome is first cited in a passage showing the distinction between heresy and schism; he explains that heresy is the Greek word for choice and refers to a bad choice of doctrine contrary to the meaning of Scripture given by the Holy Spirit. A definition of the heretic then follows, taken from the statements of Augustine: the heretic is someone who invents or follows false and new opinions. A person who defends a false and perverse opinion not by his own boldness and presumption but seduced into error by the influence of parents or others, and who seeks the truth and is willing to be corrected, should not be considered a heretic; heretics are those who introduce into the church of Christ depraved and diseased beliefs, and who contumaciously resist correction, persistently defending their pestiferous, deadly dogmas.[59] The essential mark of the heretic is therefore the perversion of Christian truth by the obstinate maintenance of an opinion that the church has condemned as false and indefensible. From Augustine's writings a number of passages are also cited justifying the use of coercion in the cause of justice and against heretics, the church's enlistment of the assistance of kings against its enemies, and its persecution of evildoers.[60] A further citation from an early pope declares that heretics and schismatics are subject to the coercion of the secular powers.[61]

The *Decretum* does not speak of killing heretics, and before the eleventh century, heresy, although penalized with various censures and excommunication, was not punishable by death. Thereafter we hear of heretics being killed by mobs, while the first execution for heresy by the secular authority is said to have occurred at Orléans in 1022 at the order of King Robert the Pious of France. In 1034 heretics were burned in Italy in the diocese of Milan, and in Germany in 1051 the Holy Roman Emperor Henry III executed some members of the Manichaean sect lest their heresy infect many other people.[62] At this period, nevertheless, the death sentence for heretics remained rare, and the control of heresy was left to bishops and local secular officials. By the latter half of the twelfth century, however, the rapid growth of heresy caused the papacy to initiate further measures against it. The third Lateran Council of 1179 anathematized all heretics, together with all who defended or received them, and prohibited anyone from sheltering or transacting business with them. Referring to the Cathars and other heretics in southern France, it offered spiritual rewards to those who would take up arms against such pests and enemies of the Christian people and authorized the confiscation of their possessions and their reduction to slavery. In 1184 Pope Lucius III and the Holy Roman Emperor Frederick Barbarossa jointly proscribed a number of heresies, and the pope issued a noted decretal, *Ad abolendam*, to pursue them. This declaration, which was incorporated with other papal decretals in the canon law,[63] spoke of heretics as all those who presumed to think or to teach concerning the sacraments of the church "otherwise than as the Holy Roman Church teaches and observes." Among its provisions was an order to all archbishops and bishops to conduct investigations into heresy in their dioceses once or twice annually by calling credible local persons to testify under oath whether there were heretics or people holding secret conventicles in their neighborhoods. Convicted heretics, unless they abjured their errors, were to be handed over to the secular authority for punishment, and civil officials were required to take an oath to pursue heresy when asked by the bishops.[64]

The church's efforts to crush heresy were further intensified during the pontificate of Innocent III (1198–1216), who encouraged the French nobility to join in the crusade against the Cathars in Languedoc and also made strenuous efforts to convert heretics through preaching and persuasion. His decretal of 1199, *Vergentis*, likened heresy to lèse-majesté, a form of treason in Roman law, and subjected heretics to various penalties.[65] The Fourth Lateran Council of 1215, which was summoned by Innocent III, took various actions in behalf of orthodoxy and against heresy. It solemnly declared that "there is one Universal Church of the Faithful, outside of which there is absolutely no salvation." All the faithful were required to go to confession and receive the Eucharist at least once a year on pain of being cut off from the church in life and deprived of Christian burial in death. The council reiterated the church's excommunication and anathema of "every heresy," under whatever name, "that raises itself against the holy, orthodox, and Catholic faith." It ordered condemned heretics to be delivered to their secular rulers for punishment and specified that all secular authorities of whatever office were to be admonished and if necessary compelled, as they wished to be numbered among the faithful, to swear that they would strive to exterminate in the territories under their jurisdiction all heretics pointed out by the church. Those persons who gave credence to the teachings of heretics, or who received, defended, or patronized them, were to be excommunicated, and if they failed to make satisfaction within a year, they were to be stigmatized as infamous, expelled from any office they held, and deprived of the right to give testimony in a court of law, make a will, or receive an inheritance. Bishops were reminded to go around their dioceses at least once every year to uncover the secret assemblies of heretics.[66]

In the works of thirteenth-century commentators on the canon law, the descriptions and definitions of the heretic and heresy became more detailed than in Gratian's *Decretum*. One canonist described the heretic as any person who perverts the sacraments of the church, or who separates himself from the unity of the church, or is excommmunicated, or who errs in the exposition of Holy Scripture, or who invents or follows a new sect, or who understands the articles of faith differently from the Roman church, or who thinks ill of the sacraments of the church. Other canonists listed six ways to identify a heretic, which included the following signs: someone who begets or follows a false opinion in matters of faith, or who understands Holy Scripture differently from the Holy Spirit by whom it was written, or is separated from the sacraments of the church and the community of the faithful, or is a perverter of the sacraments, or is dubious in faith, since we are required to believe firmly, or who attempts to remove the Roman church as the head of all the churches.[67] The definition of heresy given by the thirteenth-century English theologian Robert Grosseteste, one of the leading thinkers of the period, was more succinct: "Heresy is an opinion chosen by human faculties, contrary to Holy Scripture, openly taught and pertinaciously defended."[68]

The Catholic religion, its institutions, and its values were so closely intermingled with the political regimes, social order, and culture of medieval Europe that the danger which popular heresy presented to the church was seen with good reason by churchmen and governments alike as equally a danger to society. It is therefore not surprising that by the first half of the thirteenth century the death penalty was being established as the common remedy for heresy, with the concurrence of the church. Secular rulers such as Louis IX of France (Saint Louis) and the Holy Roman Emperor Frederick II, king of Germany and also sovereign of parts of Italy and the Kingdom of Sicily, introduced capital punishment for heresy into their law codes. In an edict of 1224 Frederick imposed the death penalty for heresy in Lombardy. The constitutions he promulgated for Sicily in 1231 ordered that heretics be publicly burned, and this provision was subsequently extended throughout his empire. The popes who succeeded Innocent III required these laws to be enforced by the magistrates in the territories in Italy subject to papal rule. In France the burning of heretics became universal during the thirteenth century and was made part of Louis IX's legislation in 1270. England acted later: it was not until 1401 that the English Parliament instituted death by fire for the crime of heresy as a reaction to the heretical Lollard movement.[69]

Heresy, although treated as a crime by secular law, was first of all a spiritual offense that could be ascertained and judged only by the church. The culminating step in the church's creation of machinery for the eradication of heresy was the inauguration of the Inquisition. Papal legislation of the late twelfth and early thirteenth centuries had placed the detection of heretics in the hands of the bishops by ordering them to undertake circuits of their dioceses once or twice annually to ferret out heresy. In 1233 Gregory IX issued two bulls that made the persecution of heresy a special responsibility of members of the Dominican order, who were empowered to go as judges into different places to investigate heresy and to proceed without appeal against heretics and their receivers, defenders, and helpers. The pope may not have intended by these measures to found a new and permanent ecclesiastical institution, but they evolved into such during the rest of his pontificate and under his immediate successors. As a result the Inquisition superseded the bishops in importance as the chief instrument of the church and papacy in the discovery and suppression of heresy, and inquisitors were appointed for this purpose in various regions.

Administered by the Dominicans under a jurisdiction delegated by papal authority, the Inquisition inherited a body of ecclesiastical legislation against heresy to which the popes of the thirteenth

century after Gregory IX made further additions to aid and direct
its work. It also developed a procedure peculiar to itself. It was
both an investigative organ and an ecclesiastical tribunal, conducting inquiries (inquisitions) into the existence of heresy in a particular place, initiating prosecutions and summoning suspected heretics, examining accused persons and witnesses under oath,
holding trials, and pronouncing judgment and sentence. All of its
proceedings were secret, their attendance limited to inquisitors
and officials, but verdicts and sentences were publicly announced.
Heresy could be an elusive crime, and inquisitorial procedure
compelled suspected heretics to testify against themselves. The
chief aim of the inquisitors was to extract a confession from the
accused. Their methods of achieving this end ranged from inten-
sive questioning to the application of torture if necessary. Convicted heretics were asked to abjure their false and damnable beliefs, and if they did so, various penances plus other penalties, such
as imprisonment, might be imposed upon them. If they refused,
the punishment was death. Because the church always maintained
the principle that it did not shed blood, it handed over convicted
heretics to officials of the secular power for execution. Heretics
who abjured and again relapsed into heresy forfeited any claim to
mercy and were condemned to die.[70]

The creation of the Inquisition during the thirteenth century
completed the system of intolerance and persecution of religious
dissent that marked the history of medieval Christianity. It was also
the predecessor and model of the inquisitions subsequently established in Catholic Spain and Italy in the late fifteenth and the
sixteenth centuries. The surviving handbooks for the guidance of
inquisitors, which were written by inquisitors themselves, indicate
that they were learned, conscientious, dedicated men, well informed about the different heresies, who believed they were performing a holy and necessary task. These handbooks also show
the difficulties they encountered during questioning in trying to
entrap suspected heretics, who often pleaded ignorance and resorted to evasion, equivocation, and dissimulation, even feigning
madness, to escape conviction.[71]

In the later Middle Ages the belief seems to have been universal that heresy was a defilement and an infection that must be removed, and that it was right to punish and kill impenitent heretics. Among those who gave authoritative expression to this view was Saint Thomas Aquinas (1225–1274), a Dominican and one of the foremost medieval philosophers and theologians. Examining the question of whether heretics should be tolerated, he concluded that their sin is such that

> they deserve not only to be separated from the Church by excommunication, but also to be shut off from the world by death. For it is a much more serious matter to corrupt faith, through which comes the soul's life, than to forge money, through which temporal life is supported. Hence if forgers of money or other malefactors are straightway justly put to death by secular princes, with much more justice can heretics, immediately upon conviction, be not only excommunicated but also put to death.

This great thinker obviously looked upon heresy as a threat to society as well as a personal sin. Taking note of the parable of the tares in the Gospel of Matthew, he gave it the same harsh interpretation as had Saint Augustine: when the tares are recognized and there is no chance of a mistake, then Christ's command against uprooting them no longer applies. He also discussed the further question of whether "those who return from heresy ought to be taken back by the Church." His answer was that those who returned for the first time should be received to penance and their lives preserved if they seemed to be genuinely converted; but if they relapsed after being taken back and then again returned, they should be admitted to penance but nevertheless sentenced to die.[72]

The discourse of heresy by Catholic theologians and jurists depicted the heretic as an alien Other who had no place in the community of the faithful. Jews and Muslims were likewise regarded as alien Others and enemies of Christ, but the heretic differed from them in being a Christian who had betrayed his baptism and separated himself from the church. He was an excommunicate, condemned to damnation and given over to execution by the secular arm, since the church did not shed blood. He was guilty of divine lèse-majesté, or treason against God. He was a putrid limb that had to be cut off to preserve the health of the body. He was a fox who destroyed the vines of the Lord and a wolf who preyed on Christian souls. Orthodox writers of the twelfth and thirteen centuries, as R. I. Moore has pointed out, ransacked the language of disease for metaphors to describe heresy. Heresy was called a plague, a cancer, an infection, a contagion, a lethal poison, and was compared especially to leprosy. Moore suggests that the analogy between heresy and disease was not simply a convenient figure of speech or random collection of images but a comprehensive model for depicting heresy and how it worked.[73]

Such descriptions were attributes of the Christian theory of persecution, which rested on a number of widely accepted premises that persisted through the Middle Ages into the era of the Protestant Reformation in the sixteenth and seventeenth centuries: that salvation was the chief goal of mankind; that there was no salvation outside the church divinely founded by Jesus Christ; that heresy was a contagious evil that killed souls and had to be stamped out as a peril to human salvation. Heresy was defined in relation to orthodoxy, and a belief became heretical when it was condemned by the church. The practice of persecution was undergirded by a normative conception of religious and ecclesiastical unity that left no room for heterodoxy or dissent from articles of faith. Both the Catholic Church and the later Protestant state churches of the sixteenth century took for granted the traditional principle that unity of faith as expressed in belief and sacraments was a necessity for the spiritual welfare of the Christian people. The heretic violated this unity by pertinaciously adhering to a false faith despite all persuasion and was therefore rightly punishable even with death. Religious unity was considered equally indispensable to the preservation of the political unity and internal peace of kingdoms and states, and to the maintenance of social stability and order. The theory of religious persecution was concerned essentially with belief as a condition of mind. The aim of persecution was not primarily to achieve external conformity, but to affect conscience and induce or compel a change of mind. The convicted heretic, if he were not to face punishment and death, had to admit his error, perform penances, and recant his belief.

The assumptions supporting the Christian theory of persecution constituted what appeared to be a body of unquestionable truths accepted for ages. For anyone to attack and criticize these assumptions was a formidable undertaking that demanded exceptional moral and intellectual independence and courage.

CHAPTER 3

The Advent of Protestantism
and the Toleration Problem

꿏

It is easy to idealize or exaggerate the unity of medieval civilization because it shared a single religion under papal headship
and was still comparatively free of the divisive nationalism of
later centuries. As we have seen, however, the medieval Catholic
Church was never a spiritual monopoly in which all religious faith
and worship were concentrated. Beginning during the eleventh
century, it was continually forced to deal with heretical movements
opposed to its central tenets and to its institutional wealth and
power. In addition, since the year 1054 it had been formally separated by a schism from the Greek Orthodox Church of the Byzantine Empire, which differed with certain of its doctrines and did
not recognize the supremacy of the pope. We should not forget,
either, that Jewish and Muslim communities were also elements
within Christian society with a long history in various regions of
Europe as alien but intermittently tolerated minorities. In spite of
these qualifications, though, we are not mistaken when we think
of the Catholic Church until the sixteenth century as identical
with Western Christendom and the one institution in which nearly
all the Christian peoples of western and central Europe placed the
hope of their salvation.

It is because the Protestant Reformation of the sixteenth century gave rise to lasting Christian division that it looms so large in Western history. The Reformation, which started in Germany in the 1520s with Martin Luther as its inspirer and leader, was neither planned nor foreseen; no one in the years immediately preceding its beginning had any premonition of the great religious upheaval that was about to occur. But by overthrowing the Catholic Church in parts of Europe, by creating new churches and forms of religious life, Protestantism shattered forever the unity of Western Christianity and led to civil conflict and religious war, as well as to profound changes in society, politics, and culture. One of its greatest immediate consequences was a diversity of churches and sects on such a scale that it made the problems of religious disunion and toleration inescapable and gave them a centrality they had never previously had in European experience.[1]

During the century and a half before the Reformation, the most significant intellectual movement in European culture was the growth of humanism, which in one of its principal manifestations, known as Christian or biblical humanism, envisaged a renewal of Christian life. A distinctive development identified with the period we call the Renaissance, humanism first originated in Italy in the fourteenth century as an educational and cultural program aiming at a revival and deeper knowledge of the languages, literature, and civilization of classical antiquity. The subjects it pursued, from which its name derived, were the humanities, or *studia humanitatis*, including grammar and rhetoric, or the arts of language, philology, history, moral philosophy, and poetry. The humanists, those who cultivated these studies, were an intellectual elite made up of teachers, scholars, churchmen, civic officials, secretaries to kings and prelates, diplomats, and men of letters who were devoted to the works of Greek and Roman writers, in which they found a model for literary imitation and the inspiration for a fresh ideal of culture and of living. Popes, princes, kings, great noblemen and ecclesiastics increasingly acted as patrons of these studies, which were often referred to as "the new learning" and *bonae litterae*, a phrase best translated as "humane letters." They were distinct from the logic, metaphysics, and Scholastic theology taught in the universities. Many humanists tended to be critical of Scholastic theology in particular because of what they considered its hair-splitting intellectualism and preoccupation with recondite speculative questions that seemed to have nothing to do with the teachings of Christ or the life of Christians in the world. During the fifteenth and earlier sixteenth centuries the humanist educational-cultural program spread from Italy to Spain and northern Europe, where it not only acquired many followers but expanded its scholarly interests to encompass the study of the early Christian church fathers and the historical-philological investigation of the Bible itself.[2]

Several fifteenth-century thinkers antedating the Protestant Reformation who belonged to the world of humanism held a conciliatory and irenic conception of Christianity and religion that has sometimes led historians to align them with the idea of toleration. One of them was the German ecclesiastic and philosopher Cardinal Nicholas of Cusa (1401–1464), who in one of his works, *The Peace of Faith* (*De pace fidei*), imagined a colloquy among representatives of the world's religions, who appeal to God to overcome their differences. In the course of their discussion, although Christianity remains foremost, the religions associated with various nations are united in the recognition of a universal truth based on their common belief in the one supreme God toward whom all of them aspire in their different rites and observances.[3] Other philosophers—like the Italians Marsilio Ficino (1433–1499), the translator of Plato into Latin and a devotee of Hermeticism and magic, and Giovanni Pico della Mirandola (1463–1494), one of whose main interests was the secret mystical wisdom of the Jewish Cabala—fashioned a body of ideas that took a positive view of pagan philosophies and non-Christian religions as anticipating and sharing various spiritual beliefs with Christianity.[4] In the sixteenth century also there were a few well-known scholars like the French humanist, jurist, and philosopher Jean Bodin (1529–1596), who in one of his unpublished works expounded the idea of concord among different religions and Christian denominations.[5] While such thinkers may be seen as exemplifying a certain type of tolerance in their irenic outlook, they can hardly be said to have contributed anything to the formation of a doctrine or theory of religious toleration. Concerned among other things with the relationship and perhaps harmony between Christian and non-Christian religions and philosophies, they did not deal with the subjects of heresy or religious dissent. A doctrine of toleration could take shape in European thought only if it directly addressed the problem of the internal divisions separating Christians themselves and questioned the traditional attitude toward heresy.

CHRISTIAN HUMANISM AND TOLERATION: ERASMUS AND MORE

In the countries of northern Europe, the dissemination of the humanist cultural-educational program through schools and teaching, the publication of classical texts and translations, and works of scholarship was greatly assisted by the rapid diffusion of printing following its invention in the mid–fifteenth century. In contrast to Italy, in Germany and the Holy Roman Empire, France, the Netherlands, and England, the humanistic pursuit of the knowledge of classical antiquity and literature often took on a more distinctive religious character, which has given it the name of Christian, or sometimes biblical, humanism. Christian humanists pursued the study of the humanities not only for their independent educational value but as a possible catalyst for religious and moral reform in both society and the individual. The main hallmark of Christian humanism was therefore its attempt to achieve a union of Christian and classical erudition and education and its close association with the hopes and goal of a renovation of Christianity and the church through the spread and effect of the new learning. These hopes were shared by humanists of various countries at the end of the fifteenth century and in the first two or three decades of the sixteenth. They rested particularly on the application of humanistic scholarship to the works of early Christian writers and to the Bible, especially the New Testament, with the ultimate goal of making the latter and its image of Christ an essential part of the personal lives of Christian people.

Desiderius Erasmus of Rotterdam (ca 1466–1536) was the greatest Christian humanist in Europe of the generation that spanned the beginning of the Reformation, a man admired and acclaimed by his contemporaries as the foremost scholar, writer, teacher, and disseminator of classical culture of his era. Beyond all other intellectuals he exemplified through his many writings, vast correspondence, and enormous contribution to scholarship the aim and hope of revitalizing religion and personal piety through humanistic studies and education. Among his good friends was the Englishman Sir Thomas More (1478–1535), whom he met on a first visit to England in 1499–1500, and who for number of years shared some of his most cherished values. Both men usually figure in histories of religious toleration, and their place in this history must be accurately ascertained.

The two had quite different careers. Erasmus, the illegitimate son of a priest, was placed as an adolescent in an Augustinian monastery in the Netherlands. Disliking the monastic life, he left his cloister in his early twenties to become a cosmopolitan intellectual dependent on patronage and dedicated to study, scholarship, and the earning of his livelihood by his writings. He traveled widely, residing for periods of time in Paris, London, Cambridge, Venice, Louvain, Basel, and other places. Although he was ordained a priest, there is no evidence that he ever celebrated Mass after leaving the monastery. More, in contrast, was a married man and father, a practicing lawyer, and an important legal official of the city of London who in 1517 entered the service of King Henry VIII. Devoutly Catholic with a longing toward the ascetic life of a monk, a brilliant writer and outstandingly able practical statesman, he had strong humanistic values that united him in warm friendship with Erasmus, whose work he supported. As one of Henry VIII's ministers, he had a very successful political career, which culminated in 1529 with his appointment to the great position of lord chancellor, yet he died a victim of the king's anger, executed for

IMAGO · ERASMI·ROTERODA
MI · AB · ALBERTO · DVRERO·AD
VIVAM· EFFIGIEM · DELINIATA·

ΤΗΝ·ΚΡΕΙΤΤΩ·ΤΑ·ΣΥΓΓΡΑΜ
ΜΑΤΑ·ΔΙΞΕΙ

·M D X X V I·

Engraved portrait of the famous humanist scholar Erasmus of Rotterdam, made in 1526 by Albrecht Dürer. The Greek inscription states that Erasmus's writings show his image better. In these first years of the Protestant Reformation, Erasmus argued in vain against the Catholic Church's use of force in the treatment of heresy. Courtesy of the University of Virginia Art Museum.

treason in 1535 because of his loyalty to the Catholic Church. The life of each of these distinguished men may be said to have been divided, if not indeed split, by the effects of the Reformation, which began when they were mature thinkers who had already accomplished most of the work for which they remain renowned. Their attitude to and understanding of toleration is accordingly best examined in relation to two successive and distinct periods,

the first preceding the emergence of Luther and the Protestant
revolt, the second following it.[6]

Between 1500 and 1520 Erasmus, an astonishingly prolific author who wrote only in Latin, produced a wealth of publications,
frequently reprinted in numerous editions, which gave expression
to his Christian humanism. Some of these were editions and translations from Greek into Latin of classical authors and the church
fathers. Others dealt with methods of study and teaching. Many
threw open to readers treasures of Greek and Latin literature and
wisdom joined with helpful comments; they provided instruction
in points of grammar and style by such means as collections of
classical adages, amusing imaginary colloquies or conversations
on religious and other topics, and directions for writing letters in
correct form for various occasions. Among them also were a book
on the education of a virtuous Christian prince, tracts opposed to
war, which Erasmus hated, and a manual of personal piety and
faith, *Handbook of a Militant Christian* (*Enchiridion militis Christiani*).
This last composition, one of his most popular, stressed, as did
many of his other writings and letters, the importance of the moral
and spiritual side of Christian living, with Christ as its model, in
preference to external religious observances like fasting, pilgrimages, devotion to saints, and works of penance. Although Erasmus
decried popular religious superstitions, he did not condemn these
ritualistic practices as such, since they were an intrinsic part of
the Catholic religion. He devalued and often objected to them,
however, because he felt that for too many people, both laity and
clergy, they had become a mechanical substitute for a vital personal and ethical relationship to Christ. Another of his works,
which he dedicated to Sir Thomas More, was *The Praise of Folly*
(*Moriae encomium*), a wise and witty satire on the foibles and fool-
ishness of human beings in all walks of life, which included many
caustic comments ridiculing the folly and failings of clergy, monks,
and theologians. Erasmus's writings offered a moral guide that
disparaged doctrinal disputes and the exterior side of religion and
gave priority to the precepts of Christian living. They combined
instruction and learning with humor and serious critical observa-

tions on contemporary manners and religious practices in a way that made them tremendously popular throughout Europe with readers whom his books reached by means of the printing press. The term he generally used as a synonym for his Christian humanism was *philosophia Christi*, "the philosophy of Christ," or Christian philosophy. It placed the human figure of the Christ of the Gospels at the heart of religion as an emblem of love, kindness, tenderness, humility, and simplicity, urging that Christians of every station in life take and follow him as their example.[7]

Erasmus's most significant achievement as a Christian humanist was his work on the New Testament. In 1516 he published a new edition of the entire Greek text of the New Testament based in part on the study and collation of some new manuscripts.[8] This was the earliest appearance of the Greek New Testament in print, and he dedicated his edition to Pope Leo X. In this dedication he stated that "our chiefest hope for the restoration and rebuilding of the Christian religion" was for Christians the world over "to absorb the principles laid down by their Founder from the writings of the evangelists and apostles," in which the heavenly word from the heart of God the Father "still lives and breathes for us and acts and speaks with more immediate efficacy . . . than in any other way."[9] To accompany the Greek text he produced a parallel Latin translation of the New Testament that departed in some respects from the Latin Vulgate, the official translation of the Bible by Saint Jerome, which the Catholic Church had used for centuries in its religious services and theological teaching and interpretation. He also supplied his Greek text with many annotations, which contained some views at odds with prevailing theological opinion. His humanist beliefs had convinced him that expert knowledge of the ancient languages and philological-historical scholarship were as necessary to the understanding and interpretation of Scripture as was theological learning, and that the second was insufficient without the first. In the brief *Paraclesis*, or Exhortation, preceding the Greek text and Latin translation of the New Testament, he offered a further statement of his Christian philosophy. There he lamented how much effort men gave to the study of abstruse questions in the writings of Plato, Aristotle, and other philosophers, while neglecting or remaining ignorant of the philosophy of Christ, which was understandable to everyone of whatever age, sex, or condition. He favored the translation of the Bible into all the vernacular tongues, voicing the wish that ordinary people everywhere—women and men, Turks and Arabs, laborers at the plow, weavers at the loom, and travelers on their journey— might know and recite the Gospels and the letters of Paul in their own languages.[10]

His edition and Latin translation of the Greek New Testament enjoyed great success. It went through a number of revised editions and was widely used by scholars, including the reformer Martin Luther. But it also came under attack from conservative theologians who strongly disapproved of Erasmus's tampering with the New Testament's Greek text and his changes from the Vulgate version in his Latin translation. These critics accused his work of questionable orthodoxy, and they were likewise angered by his satires and negative comments on Scholastic theology and contemporary religious practices in his various writings.

In the decade between 1510 and 1520 Erasmus reached the height of his fame and influence. Courted and honored by popes, kings, prelates, noblemen, and rich businessmen, his books known in every country, he found it possible to hope that the progress of the new learning might lead to a gradual reform of the church and religion. During this period religious toleration was not a problem that engaged his mind, and none of his writings had a direct bearing on the subject. The most one can say is that certain major themes in his work implied a tolerant attitude toward religious differences among Catholics. This attitude, however, did not extend to Jews. He accepted without any reservation Christianity's traditional anti-Semitism and expressed a virulent hostility to Judaism and the Jewish people. In 1512 a long controversy arose in Germany when some Dominican theologians of Cologne University launched an attack upon John Reuchlin, an eminent Christian humanist and pioneer Hebrew scholar, because of his interest in the Jewish Cabala and his opposition to the destruction of Hebrew books. Despite the fact that Reuchlin had written a Hebrew grammar and was a student of Jewish knowledge, he was not a friend of the Jews and believed that God had justly punished them for their collective guilt in rejecting Christ. Even though Erasmus disapproved of the lack of moderation shown by some of Reuchlin's humanist supporters, who attacked the theologians as enemies of enlightened learning, he sided with Reuchlin against his adversaries. He took no interest himself, though, in Hebrew literature other than the Old Testament, considering the Talmud and the lore of the Cabala unprofitable for Christians.[11] Like the mass of Catholics, he regarded the Jews as enemies of Christ; in a letter defending Reuchlin to Jacob van Hoogstraten, the Dominican inquisitor in the archdiocese of Cologne, he stated that "if it is Christian to detest the Jews, on this count we are all good Christians and to spare."[12]

Toward disagreements among Christians, his writings of this period implicitly suggest a tolerant spirit. The reasons for this can be easily understood. His philosophy of Christ made him oppose violence and fanaticism of any kind. As a humanist scholar and student of classical rhetoric, he believed strongly in dialogue and persuasion rather than compulsion. Although he was a loyal Catholic, his critical view of Scholastic theology included an aversion to dogmatism and the multiplying of articles of faith. He always felt a deep distaste for the overintellectualization of religion and the concern of theologians with recondite subjects that seemed to him irrelevant to the core of Christianity. A large dose of skepticism entered into his negative attitude to Scholastic theology, since he was convinced that most of the questions theologians delighted to debate were unanswerable and touched on problems not essential to the conduct of a Christian life. In a letter of 1519 to a Bohemian nobleman, which was subsequently printed, he characteristically complained of the "readiness . . . to define everything" in religion and advised instead that faith should consist only of things clearly laid down in the Scriptures as necessary to salvation. For this purpose, he thought, "a few truths are enough, and the multitude are more easily persuaded of their truth if they are few. As things are, we make six hundred articles out of one, some of them of such a kind that one can be ignorant of them, or unconvinced, without peril to one's religion."[13] This point of view, which appeared frequently in his writings, reflected his constant conviction that the Christian faith consisted of a small number of easy truths clearly stated in the New Testament and focused on Christ's teaching and redemptive mission.[14] He insisted that it was in keeping with the gospel's message to distinguish between essential and nonessential doctrines, and that Christians needed to believe only the former, which were few and plain, in order to be saved. All these aspects of Erasmus's thought contributed to his comparatively tolerant attitude toward intellectual differences in religion in the years prior to the Reformation. They fail to tell us, however, what his response would be to the unanticipated shock of the disruption of Catholic unity that resulted from the heresy of Martin Luther and the movement he inspired.[15]

During this same period Erasmus's friend Sir Thomas More did actually deal directly with the question of religious toleration in one of his writings. This was in his famous fictional creation, *Utopia*, written in Latin during an interval of leisure and published in 1516 at a time when his association with Erasmus was at its closest. Its purpose was to present his conception of a good society, or, as its title says, "The Best State of a Commonwealth," and it remains the most original as well as one of the greatest expressions of Christian humanism in the years before the Reformation.[16] Its story, as told by the narrator More, consists of his meeting and dialogue in Antwerp with an imaginary voyager, the wise and learned Raphael Hythloday, who has traveled to the remote, unknown island of Utopia, or Land of Nowhere, and reports what he saw there. The first part of the work is a discussion that consists mainly of an unsparing indictment of the many injustices of England's social order: its idle nobility, the oppression of the poor by the rich, the cruelty and partiality of the criminal law, which protects the interests of property and hangs poor men for petty offenses, and the greed of noblemen and landlords, who expropriate the lands of peasant cultivators and use them to reap profit by grazing sheep on them. The second part offers a description of the commonwealth of Utopia, whose institutions and values, based on social justice and economic equality, differed fundamentally from those of Christian Europe. More's picture of Utopian society is complex, but its most prominent characteristics are common ownership and the nonexistence of private property, and religious toleration and the absence of an official church or religion.

Utopus, the king who founded Utopia, ordained for the sake of peace that all should be free to follow their own religious faith and to try to convert others, provided they relied solely on persuasion and refrained from abuse. Those who resorted to violence in religion or contended too forcibly in argument were punished with exile or enslavement. In Utopia there were accordingly a number of religions and forms of worship, although the Utopians generally agreed that there was one supreme being who had created and now governed the world. Utopus had the idea that perhaps God desired a variety of religions and therefore inspired people to hold different views. He was sure in any case that it was wrong to try to force belief, and that if there were one true religion, its truth would eventually become evident through its own power. Although he thus left religion to be decided as each person thought best, he did decree a single limit on the freedom of belief. In order to maintain the dignity of human nature, Utopians were required to believe that the world was ruled by divine providence, not chance, and that the soul was immortal and would be rewarded or punished in an afterlife for its virtues and vices. The citizens of Utopia considered these propositions to be founded on reason and their denial therefore a kind of madness. Persons who rejected them were not harmed or compelled by threats to hide or lie about their opinion; they were deemed, though, to have a low mind and were not entrusted with any office. The Utopians had never heard the name of Christ until the arrival of Hythloday and his companions, who informed them about Christ's teachings and miracles. Some then became Christians, but when one of these converts aggressively preached against other religions and their followers, he was exiled not for his belief but for inciting disorder. The Utopians, Hythloday said, "count this principle among their most ancient institutions, that no one should suffer for his religion."[17]

In the Land of Nowhere as More visualized it, the concept of heresy did not exist. The citizens of Utopia, a society in which the common good prevailed, were free to hold any religious belief and to worship as they pleased. Utopian tolerance and religious liberty stood in complete contrast with the religious persecution that marked the history of Christian Europe. It is uncertain whether More in the halcyon time in which he wrote *Utopia* was merely indulging in depicting an imaginary alternative or seriously wanted his readers to embrace toleration as a genuine and desirable possibility. One may wonder whether he would have been willing to approve of religious pluralism in a Europe that had already been Christian and Catholic for over a thousand years. In any event, within a few years of the publication of his picture of a just and tolerant society, he was to become a persecutor and scourge of heretics himself.[18]

The years after 1520 marked a watershed in the lives of Erasmus, More, and many other European humanists and religious intellectuals. They were compelled to take a stand as they saw the reformer Martin Luther (1483–1546), an Augustinian monk, priest, and professor of theology at the newly founded University of Wittenberg in Saxony, emerge from obscurity to become the leader of a revolt against Catholicism. Luther's public career began in the autumn of 1517 with the publication and widespread circulation of his Ninety-five Theses against the sale of indulgences. Indulgences at this period were a device for raising money regularly approved by the pope and ecclesiastics; Catholics bought them from the church to obtain for their souls or those of departed relatives a remission of the time they would have to spend after death in the flames of purgatory doing penance for their sins. Luther found many reasons to condemn the sale of indulgences as a mercenary practice, spiritual deformity, and flagrant abuse. The printing presses spread his theses so quickly that in a short time their author's name was known throughout Germany. Soon he was being accused of heresy, although humanists and many others who desired the reform of the church welcomed his arguments. The pope, Leo X, ordered an investigation of his actions, but Luther stood his ground, resisting all efforts and threats to persuade him to renounce his opinions. At a public disputation in Leipzig in 1519 where he faced a well-known Catholic theologian, he defended the Bohemian heretic John Hus and denied the primacy of the pope and the infallibility of general councils of the church.

Within four years his ideas had developed to the point where they conflicted radically with Catholicism. In a group of celebrated works written in 1520, he condemned the Catholic Mass and sacramental system, the distinction between priests and laity, the notion that celibacy and the monastic state were spiritually superior to marriage and life in the world, and other Catholic teachings and practices. Every true Christian believer was a priest, he held, the clergy were in no way more holy than the laity, and the only religious authority binding on Christians was the word of God in the Bible. Attacking the papacy, ecclesiastical corruption, and the church's and clergy's claim of independence of the secular power, he appealed directly to the German princes and nobility to carry out a thorough reformation of the church on their own initiative. His fundamental theological doctrine of justification by faith alone taught that the profound and pervasive sinfulness of human beings deprived them of free will to do anything by their own power that could satisfy God's law or attain salvation; all their attempts to please God by their acts or the good works and ritual performances authorized by the church meant nothing. Only by acknowledging their worthlessness and helplessness, only through trusting exclusively in the righteousness of Christ as their redeemer, could they be justified and saved. One of the major consequences of the principle of justification by faith alone, which Luther had come to believe especially through his study of Saint Paul's letters, was the elimination of the mediating, sin-absolving

role of the Catholic Church and priesthood between God and the
believer in the process of salvation; for according to this principle,
human salvation depended completely on God's grace as manifested in an immediate, direct relationship between the faith of
the individual Christian and his savior Christ. The Lutheran conception of justification by faith alone, together with the belief in
Scripture as the sole source of Christian truth, became the two
central doctrines of sixteenth-century Protestantism.

In 1520 the pope excommunicated Luther and condemned a
large number of his tenets as heretical. In reply, Luther burned a
copy of the papal bull of excommunication and the canon law.
Summoned in 1521 before the diet (the representative assembly)
of the Holy Roman Empire, where he was ordered in the presence
of the emperor Charles V to recant his opinions, he refused in the
name of conscience. For this defiance he was declared an outlaw
and placed under the ban of the empire. He was now a notorious
heretic who in ordinary circumstances would have been a doomed
man and destined for the flames. He was protected, however, by
his prince, the elector Frederick III of Saxony, who gave him refuge in one of his castles for nearly a year. There Luther wrote a
number of pamphlets against the Catholic Church and, starting
with the New Testament, began his enormously successful German
translation of the Bible.[19]

In the following years the movement led by Luther gathered
growing numbers of supporters from all classes in Germany.
Among them were many clergy who began to preach against Catholic teaching and institute the new doctrines in their own congregations and communities. New sects appeared with principles
more radical than Luther's. Assisted by evangelical preachers, the
Lutheran message also spread among the agrarian population and
urban classes. In 1524–1525 a great peasant rebellion accompanied by revolts in a number of cities swept southern and western
Germany, Austria, and parts of Switzerland, caused in some measure by the high hopes and expectations of social emancipation
aroused by the Lutheran religious reformation. Luther published
a violent denunciation of the insurrectionary peasants for daring

to rise against their lords, whom he exhorted to put them down, and their rebellion was crushed with great bloodshed and loss of life by the armies of the German princes and nobility.

The unfolding of these events confirmed Erasmus's worst fears about the disorders that might result from Luther's fierce attack on the church. His initial attitude to Luther, when the latter first became known to him, was one of friendliness but also of misgiving. Although the two men never met in person, they exchanged some letters, and Erasmus repeatedly discussed the actions of Luther and his followers in his correspondence with others.[20] It is fair to say that he never felt any strong personal sympathy for Luther and certainly failed to recognize the greatness of his personality or his profundity as a religious thinker. He saw him mainly as a passionate, impulsive reformer and soon as an extremist who went too far, with disastrous consequences. Since he agreed on the necessity of the reform and purification of religion and the church from the papacy downward, he defended Luther, while continually urging him to moderate his bitter language and refrain from publishing anything derogatory to the pope's authority or Catholic dogma. At the same time, he consistently refused to associate himself with Luther or to endorse his cause, even pretending to be little acquainted with his writings. While he detested Luther's opponents and critics, whom he regarded as defenders of an unreformed church and enemies of humane letters, he worried that Luther's intemperate statements and uncompromising course would lead to violence. He also had considerable reservations about certain of Luther's religious conceptions. He did not share Luther's deep pessimism about human nature and disagreed with his denial of freedom of the will, which rendered all the moral actions of Christians useless in gaining salvation. Zealous partisans who opposed Luther likewise suspected Erasmus's orthodoxy and were convinced that the great humanist scholar was the inspirer of some of Luther's ideas or had even collaborated in certain of his writings. Many thought, as a saying of the time put it, that Erasmus laid the egg that Luther hatched. Although he was often urged to write against Luther, he resisted the pressures to do so for a number of years. For his part, Luther at first expressed great admiration and respect for Erasmus but, finding him a weak and doubtful ally, soon turned against him. Erasmus, however, was thoroughly opposed to rebellion against the church. Striving to preserve a mediating position between Luther's supporters and adversaries, he found himself distrusted and denounced by both sides. In 1524 he finally broke openly with Luther over the question of freedom of the will. In a book entitled *Free Will* (*De libero arbitrio*), whose argument was based on the Scriptures, Christian writers, and reason, he defended the position that human nature was not utterly corrupt, and that God had endowed mankind with some measure of free will to cooperate in the attainment of salvation. This was a critique and rejection of Luther's deeply rooted conviction that man's will was totally enslaved to sin and could do nothing to gain salvation, which depended wholly on divine grace. Underlying Erasmus's irreconcilable difference with Luther on this vital point was his veneration of Catholic tradition, the *consensus ecclesiae*, or common consent and belief of the church, to which he said he could never be untrue.[21] In spite of his rupture with Luther, however, he never joined the German reformer's enemies, nor did he ever publicly attack him as a heretic.

Not even Luther's dissent and condemnation by the church caused Erasmus to produce any formal work dealing with toleration and religious persecution. Hence his thoughts on this subject in relation to the church's treatment of Luther must be extracted from scattered letters and writings. Perhaps the main point he reiterated was his opposition to the use of force against heresy. Writing in October 1519 to Cardinal Albert of Brandenburg, in a letter that was was full of complaints against his own critics but also defended Luther, he deplored the way Luther's enemies were bent on his destruction and their use of the words "heresy" and "heretics" against him. In the old days, he pointed out, the extreme penalty for heresy was excommunication, and a heretic was someone who dissented from the Gospels or the articles of faith; at the present day, however, any disagreement with a theologian or university sophister was enough to bring accusations of heresy, and the punishment of heresy was far different.[22] Explaining his stand on Luther to another churchman, the Roman cardinal Campeggi, he declared that whatever Luther was, it was wrong to kill him. He cited the example of Saint Augustine, who, in dealing with the perniciously heretical Donatists,wished them not to perish but to live so that they might repent. While in the past excommunication had been the worst penalty inflicted on the heretic who persisted in his error, in his own day, Erasmus said, "no proscription is more brutal than an accusation of heresy." He blamed the attack on Luther on those who had an incurable hatred of the ancient tongues and humane studies, and maintained that the sole result of their denunciations and clamor was to make Luther's books famous. If Luther erred, he contended, he should be refuted by arguments from Holy Scripture and recalled from his errors rather than destroyed.[23]

In the autumn of 1522 the Netherlands Inquisition tried and convicted three Augustinian monks for Lutheran heresy; two of them were later burned in Brussels, while the third died in prison. The two executed monks were the first Protestant martyrs. Erasmus followed the case from Basel, where he then lived; although he regretted their death, he commented that they had died "not for the articles of faith but for Luther's paradoxes; for which I should not be willing to die myself, because I do not understand them."[24] All the same, he criticized the physical repression of heresy, certain that violence was counterproductive, that it would only beget more violence and make new converts for Luther's cause.[25] Thus he told the duke of Saxony that while it might arguably be right to send someone to the stake who opposed an article of faith or any other doctrine accepted by the general consent of the church, it was wrong to punish every error with death unless the offense involved sedition or some other crime for which the civil law imposed the death penalty. He denied, moreover, that the common remedies against heresy, "recantations, imprisonment, and the stake," were effective. Far from crushing heresy, they "make the evil worse," he insisted, claiming that only after the two monks were burned in Brussels did the city begin to support Luther. This was one of Erasmus's constant refrains, that the usual methods against heretics, forcible suppression and extorting recantations through terror of the stake, achieved nothing except to spread the evil of heresy more widely and "provoke anger in a sect which is far from insignificant in the number of its members."[26]

Because he hated persecution, Erasmus believed that heresy should be combated only with spiritual weapons so long as it consisted simply of error and did not give rise to crimes against civil peace and the secular authority. He sometimes cited the parable of the tares in the Gospel of Matthew (13:24–30) in support of this position. In his *Paraphrase of Saint Matthew* (*Paraphrasis in Matthaeum*), a popular exposition of the Gospel text published in 1522, he interpreted the parable to mean that the servants who wanted to gather up the tares before the harvest "are those who think that . . . heretics should be destroyed by the sword and put to death; whereas the Master did not wish them destroyed, but rather tolerated," so that they might repent and the tares become wheat.[27] In 1524 he advised Cardinal Campeggi that he should act with complete impartiality in dealing with Lutheran dissent so as to cure rather than suppress it, and to let it be seen that he had no wish "to weed out the tares in such a fashion" as to "pull up the wheat by the roots at the same time."[28] Erasmus was opposed to the imposition of religious opinions by coercion or their fettering by definitions laid down by theologians. To Archbishop Jean de Carondelet, a councillor of the emperor Charles V, he observed that "the sum and substance of our religion is peace and concord," but that this could not be the case "unless we define as few matters as possible and leave each individual's judgment free on many questions." He lamented that "we force men by intimidation to believe what they do not believe . . . and to understand what they do not understand. Compulsion is incompatible with sincerity, and nothing is pleasing to Christ unless it is voluntary."[29]

In 1527 some Franciscan and Dominican theologians at a conference in Spain censured certain passages in Erasmus's writings as heretical, including some of his statements on heresy.[30] In his reply to these charges, he maintained that he had a right to give his opinion on questions unsettled by the church and denied that he had ever questioned any articles of faith. These articles, he pointed out, were based not on the pronouncements of Scholastic theologians but on clear scriptural evidence, the Catholic creeds, and the decisions of general councils. Refusing to retreat from his position on heresy, he reaffirmed his interpretation of the parable of the tares and protested against burning people for slight and apparent errors as defined by the theologians. Although Christian princes, he said, had the duty of wielding the sword for the repression of evildoers and the protection of the community, they should be admonished not to inflict capital punishment except as a last resort and only in the most necessary cases; and that theologians should likewise be admonished to discern the difference between simple error and godless belief, and between an individual who simply errs and one who wickedly propagates false doctrine. Pleading for mildness in the treatment of heresy, he asked whether it was not better for the church for heretics to be reclaimed rather than killed.[31]

One of the religious groups whose errors Erasmus was unwilling to tolerate, however, was the Anabaptists, the most persecuted Christians of the sixteenth century, who made their appearance in the 1520s. The hallmark of this sect was adult, or believer's, baptism and hence rebaptism, in itself a crime since the legislation of the Christian Roman emperors of the fourth century. In addition, many of the early Anabaptists favored community of property and were opposed to war and the use of arms, the taking of oaths, and civil magistracy, all of which they considered un-Christian. These convictions caused them to be widely regarded as rebels against secular authority and fomenters of disorder. Likening them to anarchists, Erasmus held that they were "by no means to be tolerated; for the Apostles command us to obey the magistrates, and these men object to obeying Christian princes."[32]

On the whole, the advent of the Reformation was a sad and disillusioning period for Erasmus. He felt, as he told a friend in 1527, that he was living through a long tragedy, and the religious conflicts created by the progress of the Lutheran movement made him foresee a cruel and bloody century ahead. He cared neither for the theologians and vested interests in the church who opposed reforms, nor for the Lutherans who were responsible for such drastic changes in religion as the abolition of the Catholic Mass.[33] He lamented to the archbishop of Cologne that humane letters had been flourishing in every region until the wickedness of seditious people who were trying to create a new world had all at once destroyed the harmony of the entire church and almost torn the state apart with dissident opinions and contentious dogmas. As a result, he said, all the fruit and reward for his long years spent in labor as a scholar had vanished.[34]

Despite his lenient view of heresy and fear of religious war, Erasmus never conceived of religious pluralism as a permanent solution for the conflicts of his time. Seeing the expansion of the Lutheran movement, he occasionally proposed toleration as a temporary expedient until unity in the church could be restored.[35] Touching on the subject in a letter in 1526 to a minister of Archduke Ferdinand, brother of the emperor Charles V, he suggested that it would perhaps be better in those cities where the Lutheran evil had increased to allow both religious parties a place and leave everyone to follow his conscience until time brought an opportunity for agreement. But in the meanwhile, he added, any attempts at sedition should be severely punished and some of the abuses in the church corrected that had caused the evil.[36] In 1530 he wrote in a similar vein to Cardinal Campeggi, the papal legate in Germany, saying that it might be better if the two parties remained balanced until God found a remedy for the present misery.[37] In a subsequent letter to Campeggi, he stated that while he knew and abhorred the brutality of the leaders and supporters of the sects (by which he meant the followers of Luther), the world's demand for peace was more important than what these evildoers deserved. Hence he broached the thought that until time itself provided a remedy for incurable evils, the sects might be tolerated on certain conditions. Although admitting that this would be a grave evil, he called it a lesser evil than a religious war.[38]

The unity in religion that Erasmus longed to see restored was hardly possible, however, since Protestantism represented much more than merely a religious opinion that might perhaps be tolerated. It was also a revolutionary agent against the status quo. Reformation Protestantism felt a deep revulsion against what it called Catholic superstition. When a city or principality became Protestant through the action of its civic governing body or ruler, what usually followed was the compulsory suppression of the Catholic Mass, the doctrine of purgatory, and the cult of devotion to the Virgin Mary and the saints; the destruction of altars, religious images, and ornaments used in Catholic rites; the taking over of Catholic churches for Protestant worship; the abolition of monasticism and expropriation of monasteries; the confiscation of ecclesiastical property by the state, and other far-reaching changes. In its rejection of Catholicism, Protestantism sought to bring about a great alteration in the religious beliefs and practices of Christians, with all manner of political and social repercussions. It was understandable that Catholic sovereigns, churchmen, and communities should perceive it as a direct threat to public stability, a potential cause of civil war, and a grave danger to society and Europe's inherited civilization.

Until the end of his life Erasmus continued to believe that the breach in the church was not irreparable. He expressed this view in 1533 in his *On Repairing the Unity of the Church* (*Liber de sarcienda ecclesiae concordia*), which proposed various means of restoring unity, including concessions by the contending parties and the introduction of reforms in the church, but which also described heresy and schism, the separation from the community of the faithful, as a far worse evil than an immoral life.[39] In his response to the Lutheran revolt and the appearance of new religious bodies, he never went beyond the idea of a Catholic Church broad enough to permit room for differences of opinion in nonessentials, while of course reducing as much as possible the number of beliefs he deemed essential. As one of his biographers has commented, he was a pioneer not of toleration but of the ideal of religious concord within Catholicism based on doctrinal compromise and concurrence on a small number of fundamental articles of faith.[40] The tradition of religious reconciliation that he founded remained an active force in the later sixteenth century through the efforts of a few thinkers in Germany and France, such as the irenic Catholic theologian Georg Cassander and the Catholic humanist jurist François Baudouin, while his moderate temper and opposition to dogmatism were an important influence upon religious groups in the Netherlands and England in the seventeenth century.[41] But although he stood out among his contemporaries for his relatively tolerant perspective at a time of increasing confessional strife and hardening division, he cannot be said to have developed any theory of toleration, much less to have envisaged religious tolerance as a necessary principle of Christian society. Like nearly everyone else in the first half of the sixteenth century, he failed to reach the understanding that the only way to solve the problem created by the emergence of Protestantism was the acceptance of religious pluralism and respect for individual religious conscience.

Sir Thomas More responded to the appearance of Protestantism in a very different fashion from that of his friend Erasmus. Even though desirous of religious reform and an advocate of the new learning, he was never as critical as Erasmus of the state of the church, the monastic life, and popular devotional practices. The enlightened picture he drew in 1516 of religious tolerance among the Utopians does not justify the conclusion that he thought the same principle should apply in his own country or Europe. During the 1520s he was increasingly disturbed by the presence of Lutheran heresy in England; these teachings were being disseminated in forbidden books and beginning to gain converts in the universities and among some humanist scholars, clergy, and merchants.[42] As early as 1521 he had assisted Henry VIII in the book in defense of the Catholic sacraments that the king wrote against Luther. Knowing of the German peasant revolt, More was concerned as a royal minister not only about the danger to souls from the new Protestant doctrines but about their effect in promoting political disorder and sedition. In 1528 the bishop of London urged him to write some works in English to help ordinary unlearned people understand the cunning malice of heretics as subverters of the church. More complied willingly with this suggestion, the result of which was a series of polemical books in the next six years upholding the Catholic faith against Luther and his English disciples such as William Tyndale, whose English translation of the New Testament, illegally published in 1526, made a major contribution to the growth of Protestantism. Beside his writings in defense of the church, More was also engaged during this period in the interrogation and prosecution of heretics. In 1532, however, he resigned his great office of lord chancellor, to which he had been appointed three years earlier, because he was unwilling to support Henry VIII's attempt to divorce Catherine of Aragon in order to remarry. When the pope, despite repeated threats and pressure, proved unwilling to grant him a divorce, the king cut England's ties of allegiance to the papacy and in repudiation of Catholic tradition had himself recognized by act of Parliament as the supreme head of the English church and clergy. More, a faithful Catholic to the end, was imprisoned and then executed as a traitor in 1535 for refusing to violate his conscience by swearing an oath that would have signified his consent to England's disavowal of the papacy.[43] His death as Henry VIII's victim was the inception of his posthumous career as a Catholic martyr and eventually a saint.

We need look only at the earliest of his writings of this period, *A Dialogue concerning Heresies* of 1529, to understand his view of heresy and initial reaction to the new doctrines coming out of Germany.[44] The dialogue presents a conversation between two speakers, More and a young man somewhat attracted to the heretical ideas of Luther and Tyndale. The older, wiser More reasons with him in a friendly fashion, with characteristic touches of humor, and in the end, of course, persuades his young interlocutor to his own point of view as he affirms the church's teaching against the errors of the heretics on such subjects as the veneration of images, prayers to the saints, pilgrimages, miracles, and the use of the Bible in English.[45] It was evident to him that the new heresies were intellectually puny when matched against the consensus of the faithful, the knowledge of Catholicism's learned doctors, and the teachings of the saints. He described heresy as false belief, faction, and a "secte and a syde way" of those who, though baptized, had fallen from God and the common faith of the whole church. Although heretics, he said, had no care for truth and made a practice of lying to conceal their heresy, he wished, nevertheless, that they should be treated with as little rigor and as much mercy as possible "where symplenes appeared and not hyghe harte or malyce." After recalling how Saint Augustine was compelled to support force against the Donatists because of their violence and sedition, he recounted the outrages committed in later times by heretics in Europe, which caused rulers to repress and punish them by fire in all parts of Christendom both to preserve the peace and to protect the spiritual welfare of subjects.[46]

More devoted an entire chapter of the *Dialogue* to showing that it was lawful, necessary, and beneficial to burn heretics, and that the imposition of this punishment was due not to the clergy but to the prudent provision of the secular authorities. Although there had been a time in the history of the church when heretics were not physically punished but only excommunicated, the violence they incited had made it necessary to repress them by force. No fault was more offensive to God than heresy, he maintained, and Lutherans ought to be destroyed as ravenous wolves who prey on Christ's flock.[47] In his depiction of the heretics' psychology he placed pride uppermost; it was their presumptuous pride in their own knowledge, he declared, and their hidden partiality toward themselves that made heretics obdurate in the face of demands that they relinquish their heresy.[48]

In More's subsequent writings in defense of the church, the tone of his comments on heresy became more urgent, intense, and pessimistic. Alistair Foxe has seen in these vehement polemics against Protestantism signs of a deterioration of personality

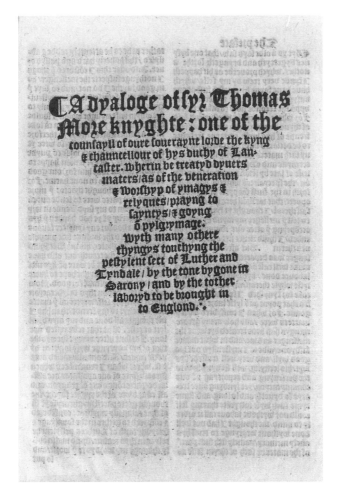

¶A dyaloge of syr Thomas More knyghte: one of the counsayll of oure souerayne lorde the kyng & chauncellour of hys duchy of Lancaster. Wherin be treatyd dyuers maters/as of the veneration & worshyp of ymagys & relyques/prayng to saynteys/& goyng o pylgrymage: wyth many other thyngys touchyng the pestylent sect of Luther and Tyndale / by the tone bygone in Saxony / and by the tother laboryd to be brought in to Englond.

Title page of Sir Thomas More's *Dialogue concerning Heresies,* 1529. This was More's first polemical work in English against Protestant heresy and included a justification of the forcible suppression and killing of heretics. Six years later More himself became a religious martyr, put to death by Henry VIII for his loyalty to Catholicism. Courtesy of the Folger Shakespeare Library.

and loss of psychological balance on More's part, while W. K. Jordan has taken them as evidence of the tragic effect the Reformation had upon him.[49] He denounced the heretic as a "false traytour to God" whose crime was treated by all laws both spiritual and temporal as "the wurst crime that canne be," and far worse than treason. The heretic, he believed, was properly deprived during trial of knowledge of his accusers, and he warned against any communication with heretics except to condemn their heresy, for fear that folk who were weak in the faith might contract their infection.[50]

More's view of heresy contained nothing original and merely reiterated the traditional position of the church. Indeed, on the Catholic side there was probably no longer anything new that could be said on this subject. But his comments were important as those of a celebrated Catholic intellectual and responsible statesman faced with the reality of Protestant heresy in the first years of the English Reformation. His justification of the killing and burning of heretics constituted his personal version of the Christian theory of persecution. For the humane author of *Utopia*, as for all other Catholics, there could be no salvation outside the church. Toward heresy More was relentlessly punitive. He would rather have reclaimed than killed heretics, but he never doubted that they should be silenced and deserved death for the souls they destroyed in undermining the faith of the church.

PROTESTANTS AND TOLERATION

Martin Luther was the great pathbreaking leader of the first generation of Protestant reformers. In the generation following, the preeminent leader was the Frenchman John Calvin (1509–1564), a great systematic theologian and religious organizer who after Luther was the foremost influence in the development of Protestantism in France, Geneva and other Swiss cities, Scotland, the Netherlands, and parts of Germany and central Europe, as well as a major intellectual influence upon the Anglican Church and English Puritanism in the later sixteenth century. What was the attitude of these two founders of Protestantism to religious toleration? Let us look at Luther first.

In the papal bull of 1520 excommunicating Luther, one of the forty-one heresies and "pestiferous errors" of which he was accused was the opinion that "the burning of heretics is against the will of the Holy Spirit."[51] This statement, however, should not mislead us into supposing that he ever held any theory or even possessed a genuine conception of toleration. He did give some thought to the question of heresy and the enforcement of belief, and until about 1525—during his first years as a reformer and rebel against the church, when he and his followers stood condemned as heretics and threatened with persecution—he advocated mildness toward heresy. In the following years, he witnessed the German peasant war, the appearance of radical preachers, and the growth of sects, and Protestantism in Germany gained the adherence of various princes and civic regimes and began the creation of a new religious order with its own ecclesiastical institutions; all these events caused his view of dissent to become much harsher.[52] At no time, though, is there any indication that the idea of tolerating freedom of religious belief and association ever entered his mind. For Luther, as for his medieval Catholic predecessors, religious unity presupposed that Christian society and the church must be coterminous. It is therefore not surprising that in the German lands that became Protestant under Lutheran influence, and where the prince replaced the pope and ecclesiastical hierarchy in the control and supervision of the church, all Christians were required to belong to the latter as the only religious body recognized by the state.[53] This principle was enshrined in the Peace of Augsburg of 1555, which provided for the coexistence in the Holy Roman Empire of both Catholic and Lutheran states (Calvinism was excluded) and mandated that individual subjects must adhere to the religion of their ruler or else emigrate.[54]

In the earlier period of Luther's career, several of his publications of 1520, when he was under attack by Catholic authorities for his doctrinal deviations, contain typical expressions of his attitude to heresy at the time. His *Address to the Christian Nobility of the German Nation* condemned the church's burning of John Hus and claimed that "we should vanquish heretics with books, not with

burning, for so the ancient fathers did. If it were a science to vanquish the heretics with fire, the hangmen would be the most
learned doctors on earth." In the same work, he also maintained
that certain differences of opinion concerning the Real Presence
of the body and blood of Christ under the forms of bread and
wine in the sacrament of the Eucharist should be tolerated until
the two sides came to agreement.[55] He reiterated this view in *The
Babylonian Captivity of the Church*, where he declared that everyone
should feel free to believe either of two opinions about the Real
Presence of Christ in the sacrament of the altar without fear of
being called a heretic. This did not prevent him, however, from
describing as heretical the belief in indulgences, freedom of the
will, and good works, which he opposed.[56]

One of his principal statements on the attempt to compel belief
appeared in his treatise of 1523, *Of Secular Authority and How Far
It Should Be Obeyed*. Reflecting a consistent feature of Luther's
thinking, this work sharply distinguished between the secular and
spiritual domains, and while strongly affirming the right and necessity of secular rulers to use force and the sword to maintain
civil order and punish wrongdoers, it denied them any power to
prescribe laws for the soul to compel it to believe. God, said Luther, wished faith to be based solely on his word; all were responsible for their own faith, nobody could believe or go to hell or
heaven for another, and "since . . . belief or unbelief is a matter
of . . . conscience," secular rulers should refrain from coercing
belief, over which they had no authority. He went on to observe
that while people could be forced to obey in word and deed, they
could not be made to do so in their hearts, because thought and
faith were free. Hence it was better to let them err than to constrain them to lie. He called heresy a "spiritual matter which no
iron can strike, no fire burn, no water drown." If it exists, he declared, "let it be overcome, as is proper, with God's word," not by
the brandished sword.[57]

These sentiments might be taken as indicating a somewhat tolerant acceptance of difference. They must be understood, however, in relation to the fact that when he wrote them, his own reli-

gious doctrines stood accused as heresies. In invoking conscience and denying the right of rulers to impose belief, he was essentially pleading in opposition to the enforcement of Catholic orthodoxy against himself and those who thought as he did. The view that belief cannot be compelled was a truism, well known from the words of Saint Augustine that Luther quoted: "no one can or ought to be constrained to believe."[58] This principle, though, had not prevented Augustine from recommending coercion as an aid to persuasion,[59] nor did it deter sixteenth-century Christian governments and the major Protestant denominations created by the Reformation from enforcing external conformity and church membership. Luther understood Augustine's statement particularly as referring to Catholic compulsion, and he certainly never intended to advocate freedom for any and every religious opinion however unorthodox or extreme.

One of Luther's fundamental theological concepts was Christian liberty, which he discussed in *The Freedom of a Christian Man* (1520) and other works. Derived from the teachings of Saint Paul, especially his letter to the Galatians, it designated a freedom that was purely spiritual and inward, having nothing to do with a latitude of religious belief or with emancipation from political or economic forms of injustice, bondage, or oppression, such as serfdom or the tyranny of rulers or lords. What it essentially meant to Luther was acceptance of the doctrine of justification and redemption through faith in Christ alone, and thereby the deliverance of the individual Christian's conscience from the burden of sin through failures to comply with God's law and from the ceremonies and meritorious works imposed by the Catholic Church as a means of salvation. He described the freedom of the Christian as a "spiritual liberty" far more "excellent than all other liberty which is external." He condemned those who misconceived it as "an occasion for the flesh and think that now all things are allowed them."[60] In the sense that Luther gave it, therefore, Christian liberty never implied religious toleration or the right of Christians to join together in churches based on their personal convictions. This conception of Christian liberty also prevailed in the Lutheran Evangelical churches, and as

Steven Ozment has pointed out, wherever Lutheranism was established, it created "a new bondage to a dogmatic creed"; the freedom of the Christian meant no more than "the right to dissent from Rome and to agree with Wittenberg."[61]

Luther was not generally tolerant. He hated Judaism and the Jewish people and was the author of a number of anti-Semitic tracts.[62] He was, needless to say, highly intolerant of Catholicism. Although at first he advocated preaching and persuasion rather than the use of force to eliminate Catholic worship, he soon came to maintain, as he told the elector of Saxony in 1525, that it was the duty of rulers and public authority to suppress the Catholic Mass as an outward abomination and blasphemous crime.[63] His advice to the German princes who embraced Protestantism was that they compel their subjects to submit to religious instruction and allow them to hear only authorized preachers. Such compulsion, he held, did not infringe the freedom of faith, because no one was forced to believe but all were required to listen to the word of God. He gave no weight to the argument of Catholics who appealed to their right of conscience to celebrate Mass, since their conscience was not guided by Scripture and was thus merely "a conscience in appearance."[64] Although he held that the word of God in Scripture was the sole Rule of Faith, he implicitly arrogated to himself the right to be the Scripture's infallible interpreter.

Toward Protestants he showed himself very intolerant of the Swiss theologian Zwingli, the spiritual leader of the Reformation in Zurich, and of those called "Sacramentarians," to whose doctrine denying Christ's physical presence in the Eucharist, or sacrament of the altar, he was violently opposed. At the colloquy of Marburg in 1529, where he and Zwingli, accompanied by other theologians, acrimoniously debated the nature of the Eucharist, they failed to agree. Luther was unwilling to make any doctrinal concession on this subject and condemned Zwingli's position as blasphemy.[65] He was also fiercely intolerant of the new sects of Spiritualists, Anabaptists, Antinomians, and others to which the Reformation gave birth and which insisted on separation from the Protestant state churches. While the cruel persecution of the Anabaptists at the hands of Protestant authorities occasionally troubled him, he considered them guilty of blasphemy and sedition and therefore deserving of death.[66] In a letter of 1541 he made the comment that he "could not conceive of any reason by which toleration could be justified before God," and this statement may be regarded as a definitive expression of his attitude on the subject.[67]

Calvin, as a Protestant leader, was as intolerant as Luther, if not more so, since he always maintained that heretics should be punished and killed if necessary. He had none of Luther's human warmth, spontaneity, or peasant humor. A man of severe and inflexible character, he succeeded in dominating everyone around him by virtue of his intellectual power and theological learning, his literary skill and polemical ability, and his single-minded will as a Protestant disciplinarian, educator, and organizer. Trained in theology and law at Paris, Orléans, and Bourges in preparation for a career in the Catholic Church, Calvin was at first attracted to Christian humanism. Following his conversion to Protestantism in his early twenties, however, he left France in 1534 to escape religious persecution. While staying in Basel in 1536, he published his *Institutes of the Christian Religion* (*Institutio religionis Christiani*), a treatise that went through a number of revisions in succeeding editions before reaching its final version. This renowned and influential work became the fundamental statement of the theological principles of Calvinist Protestantism and the Reformed churches it created in France, the Netherlands, and elsewhere. One of its essential teachings was the doctrine of predestination, according to which God in his inscrutable sovereign will has from the beginning of creation ordained some human beings for eternal salvation and others for eternal damnation. Later in the same year Calvin arrived in Geneva, which had only recently accepted the Reformation and cast off the bishop of Geneva's authority. Persuaded by the Protestant minister Guillaume Farel to remain, he became a minister and preacher who threw his very exceptional abilities into the struggle to entrench Protestantism in the city. Calvin believed that the church must be an autonomous institution embracing the entire community but not subject in its inter-

nal affairs to the secular authority, an institution that appointed
its own ministers and other officers and exercised through its own
organs an independent pastoral discipline in morals and religious
belief over all its members high and low. Conflicts with the civic
government forced him to leave Geneva in 1538, but three years
later it recalled him. Upon his return, he introduced his *Ecclesiastical Ordinances,* which established the constitution of the Protestant
Reformed Church of Geneva on Calvinist lines as a body with a
large degree of self-government and disciplinary powers but still
nevertheless subordinate in certain matters to the Geneva magistrates. Between 1541 and his death in 1564, despite the considerable resistance he met from some of the civic elite, Calvin, although formally only a minister and private citizen, gradually
achieved an unchallengeable personal ascendancy in Geneva.
Under his guidance the city became a theocracy based on the
dominant position of the church, which supervised morals and
did not permit dissent. As a result of his influence, Geneva gained
the reputation in Protestant Europe of a model Christian commonwealth, and Protestant refugees flocked there from France
and other countries. Although he had many critics and enemies,
Calvin's stature gave him an almost pontifical authority in his city.[68]

Calvin's intolerance manifested itself in numerous ways. Bitterly
opposed to Catholicism as a false, idolatrous religion, he would
not have permitted its existence in a Protestant state. He was
against attempts at the mediation of differences between Catholics
and Protestants and attacked those who favored a conciliatory policy of doctrinal compromise. He had no tolerance for the Protestants in Catholic Italy and France who continued for fear of their
lives to attend Catholic services; he denounced them as hypocrites
and traitors to Christ. He was extremely hostile to Protestant sectarians such as Spiritualists and Anabaptists, whom he excoriated
as libertines and fanatics.[69]

A whole chapter of Calvin's *Institutes* dealt with the subject of
Christian liberty but said nothing concerning toleration or the
freedom to differ in religion. Like Luther, he understood the freedom of the Christian as a purely spiritual gift that, enjoining ad-

herence to the doctrine of justification by faith in Christ alone, liberated the Christian conscience from the yoke of the law and Catholic observances. Naturally, he warned against misapplying the gospel teaching of Christian liberty to the political order, lest believers imagine that their emancipation of conscience freed them from subjection to "outward government" and "human laws."[70] In another chapter, on ecclesiastical discipline, Calvin explained the Reformed Church's biblically based authority to exercise jurisdiction over sinners in order to preserve the good from the corruption of the wicked by admonishing, censuring, and excommunicating offenders.[71] Such offenders, needless to say, would have included not only violators of good morals but those guilty of adhering to a false doctrine. In a chapter on civil government, he made clear that the foremost duty of Christian rulers and magistrates as God's deputies on earth was the care of religion and the church, a duty that involved the protection of the outward worship of God and defense of sound doctrine, as well as the suppression of idolatry, sacrilege, and blasphemy against God's truth.[72] The relationship of church and state that Calvin outlined in his *Institutes* provided ample justification for the repression of heterodoxy and religious dissent by ecclesiastical and political authority. Although the *Institutes* attacked heresies like Antitrinitarianism and Anabaptism as the work of Satan, it said nothing about the treatment of heresy as such. In refuting, however, the Catholic claim that Protestants were heretics, Calvin defined heresy and schism in the usual way. Heretics were those who, by creating dissension, broke the communion of the church and corrupted the faith with false dogmas; schismatics were those who broke the bond of fellowship in religion.[73]

Calvin's most notorious act of intolerance was the prominent role he played in the trial and execution of the Spaniard Michael Servetus, condemned for heresy as an Antitrinitarian and Anabaptist and burned at Geneva in October 1553. I shall return to this very significant event and its sequel in the following chapter. Here, however, we must note Calvin's defense of Servetus's execution; for while Geneva's action in killing Servetus received some sup-

port in other Swiss Protestant cities, there were also reservations
and criticisms from several quarters, which Calvin hastened to answer. He published his reply, *Defense of the Orthodox Faith*, in Latin
in February 1554 and in a French version immediately thereafter.[74] Most of this work consisted of fulminations against Servetus's
monstrous heresies and of documents pertaining to his case, but it
also contained a short section justifying the Christian magistrate's
obligation to repress heretics with the sword, which remains the
principal statement of his theory of religious persecution.[75]

Calvin maintained that none but simple, ignorant people and
malicious hypocrites and libertines who hated the Christian religion would deny the justice of punishing heretics with the sword.
He dismissed the argument that the Protestants' punishment of
heretics would likewise justify the Catholics' persecution of Protestants, answering that Catholics were wrong because they persecuted the truth, whereas Protestants defended the true religion
ordained by God. To the further objections that faith could not
be compelled and that Christ and the apostles never used force
to spread their teachings, he pointed out that God desired men's
aid in sustaining religion, and that Christ's coming did not abolish
the duty of judges and political authorities to punish evildoers.
Since magistrates could punish thieves and murderers, it was absurd to suppose that they had no right to punish heresy and suppress sacrilege as offenses against God's honor.

Throughout his discussion, Calvin's main theme was the duty of
Christians to uphold God's honor. Although acknowledging that
princes were unable to penetrate the hearts of men with their
edicts and touch them so that they submitted themselves to God
and the truth, he insisted that "their vocation nevertheless required them not to allow God's name to be reviled and wicked
and venomous tongues to tear God's word to pieces." Since Christ
himself had used force to expel the money changers who were
polluting the temple, Calvin asked "why good magistrates
shouldn't draw the sword given them by heaven to repress the
apostates who openly mock God and profane and violate his sanc-
tuary." Those who would pardon heretics on the grounds of hu-

manity, he declared, were more than cruel, because to spare the
wolves, they let the poor sheep become prey. Was it reasonable,
he demanded, "that heretics should murder and poison souls with
their false doctrines, and the sword ordained by God be prevented
from touching their bodies, and the whole body of Christ be lacer-
ated so that the stench of one rotten member should be un-
touched." He reminded the "merciful persons who take such great
pleasure in leaving heresies unpunished" how little "their fanta-
sies" accorded with God's commandment. For God had decreed
(here he referred to Deuteronomy 13) that all those who tried to
lead the people away from the right road in religion by worshiping
false gods should be put to death, with no one spared, neither
brother, child, wife, or neighbor. God had destroyed whole cities
and peoples as a sign of his detestation of their infection; and
when the maintenance of God's honor and glory was in question,
he stated, all considerations of humanity must be forgotten.

Several times Calvin cited Saint Augustine's dealing with the
Donatist heretics and quoted his comment that what made a martyr was not his punishment but the cause for which he died. Touching upon the parable of the tares, he found nothing in it to prohibit the punishment of heretics along with other malefactors. He
was not uniformly severe, however, but recognized three grades of
error, each deserving different treatment. Light errors could be
overlooked and pardoned, while others needed moderate castiga-
tion to correct and deter those whose contumacy and wickedness
attempted to rend the unity of faith. But in the case of the worst
errors such as those he attributed to Servetus, which blasphemed
God and destroyed the foundations of religion by their impious
and pestiferous dogmas, the extreme penalty of death was necessary to prevent the poison from spreading.[76]

For Calvin, accordingly, there could be no question that an
incorrigible heretic—a person whose false doctrines insulted
God and directly threatened the Christian religion—was guilty of
a crime that both God and man deemed worthy of death, and
that was rightly punishable with the sword of the civil magistrate.
The tone of his discussion was by turns reasonable, angry, con-

temptuous, and magisterial. Although he begged some questions (for instance, neither Servetus nor Catholics would have conceded that Calvin was defending the true religion), he seemed to make his case with a crushing logic that obliterated objections. He was apparently unable to conceive that any sincere, well-informed Christian could truly believe that religious persecution and the killing of heretics were wrong and contrary to the teaching of Christ.

What I have said about Luther and Calvin was also true of the lesser sixteenth-century leaders of the Protestant Reformation. Melanchthon (d. 1560), Zwingli (d. 1531), Oecolampadius (d. 1531), Bucer (d. 1551), Brenz (d. 1570), Bullinger (d. 1575), and other prominent ministers and theologians were all intolerant in varying degrees. None of the Protestant churches—neither the Lutheran Evangelical, the Zwinglian, the Calvinist Reformed, nor the Anglican—were tolerant or acknowledged any freedom to dissent. The right that the younger Luther had assumed to challenge the spiritual deformities of Catholicism in the name of conscience and Scripture found no home in any of the major Protestant denominations, which in principle remained persecuting institutions. As some form of Protestantism came to be adopted by princes and governments in Germany, England, Scandinavia, Switzerland, and elsewhere, the result was the rise of confessional states based on a single official church and worship to which subjects were required to conform without regard for individual conscience or personal belief. Although some of these regimes and churches were more stringent than others in enforcing conformity, all of them, as well as the Catholic Church and governments, reflected the common opinion of statesmen, churchmen, and intellectuals in an era of religious division and strife that such conformity was necessary not only for religion's sake but for the preservation of political unity and peace. It should be noted and underlined, moreover, that the intolerance generally characteristic of both Catholicism and Protestantism in the sixteenth and seventeenth centuries had its horrible counterpart in the widespread fear and persecution of witchcraft that likewise marked this period of history in various countries of Europe with a heavy toll of victims.[77] Both the heretic or religious dissenter and the witch who made a pact with Satan were considered as a menace to Christian society and justly punishable for the harm they committed.

Among the few exceptions to the general intolerance of sixteenth-century Protestantism were some of the sectarian and Spiritualist dissenters from Protestant orthodoxy. These belonged to the fringe groups of early Protestantism who constituted what has been commonly described as the Radical Reformation.[78] The Anabaptists, who were the most numerous victims of Catholic and Protestant persecution alike, were not a single body but composed of numerous sects of Christians that grew up in Switzerland, Germany, and the Netherlands during the 1520s and thereafter.[79] Hostile to the union of religion and the state, they were completely voluntary societies adhering to the gospel ethic and practicing rebaptism as the sign of entry into membership. Although the Anabaptists were mostly pacifists, some of them took part in the great German peasant rebellion of 1525. Moreover, one notorious episode of violence in particular marked their early history. In 1534–1535 a movement of six or seven thousand Dutch and German Anabaptists, gripped by messianic hopes, took over the city of Münster and, led by charismatic prophets, forcibly established their rule as the kingdom of the New Jerusalem founded on Old Testament laws, polygamy, and community of goods. Besieged and soon crushed by German princes, this Anabaptist revolt with its enormities gave the sect a long-lasting but undeserved reputation as violent fanatics and enemies of morality and social order.[80] In the aftermath of the Münster tragedy, however, Anabaptism as a whole was fundamentally peaceable, even quietist, and tolerant in that it rejected all compulsion in religion. In 1524, Balthasar Hubmaier, executed for heresy four years later as one of the early Anabaptist martyrs, wrote a short tract against the burning of heretics. Naming the devil the first heretic, he described heretics as those who set themselves against the truth of Scripture as understood by the Holy Spirit. Such people, he held, should be dealt with mildly and only by persuasion. If they refused to accept the true meaning of the gospel, they should be excluded from one's company as unclean persons. To prove that heretics should not be killed, he invoked the parable of the tares. His conclusion contended that those who were not blind would see that the advice to burn heretics proceeded from the devil.[81]

The exclusion and shunning of those who went astray in doctrine or conduct was a key Anabaptist principle, which came to be expressed in the concept of the ban. A tract on the ban written in 1550 by Menno Simons, Anabaptist founder of the Mennonites, explained its meaning and purpose. Authorized by Scripture, it was a mandatory separation of the erring member from the religious community. The ban was the ultimate sanction, and the person so treated suffered no other harm. Simons described it as a work of divine love, not an instrument of cruelty, and he pointed out that the true Christian, who commiserates with everybody, would not deny necessary services, love, and mercy even to a banned person.[82] While the Anabaptists of this period did not develop any general ideas about toleration, their repudiation of the killing of heretics and of violence in religion reflected a strain of tolerance that stood in striking contrast with the principles and practice of the mainline Protestant churches.

Spiritualism in its essential features represented a distinctive type of religion that based the Christian faith and source of religious authority on the Holy Spirit dwelling in the believer instead of on the literal biblical word. Spiritualists, whose numbers were small, considered the Spirit that inspired the Bible and the prophets superior to the biblical letter and record itself, and they placed the spiritual Christ whom they sought to follow above the historical Christ depicted in the Gospels. They accordingly disavowed all visible churches, dogmatic formulas and creeds, and external ceremonies as needless and false. They tended toward a somewhat mystical relationship to Christ and the Holy Spirit and hence in the main to an extreme form of religious individualism.[83] Among sixteenth-century Spiritualists, the foremost exemplars of a tolerant attitude toward difference in religion were Sebastian Franck

(1499–1542) and Caspar Schwenkfeld (1490–1561), both of whom passed through Lutheranism to a sort of Christian universalism. Of the two, it will suffice to discuss only the first in order to note the bearing of Spiritualism on toleration.

Franck, a university graduate and ordained priest who became a Lutheran preacher in 1526, left the ministry two years later in disagreement with some of Luther's teachings. He questioned both the doctrine of justification by faith and the Lutheran denial of free will. An original and visionary thinker, he supported himself thereafter as a printer and author of historical and other works, living in a number of different cities and finally in Basel, where he died. Although he was exposed to occasional persecution during his career, it was never enough to prevent him from publishing his writings.[84] His was an intensely inward and ethical Christianity, with pacifism as one of its basic principles, which alienated him from all the existing churches of the time. He held a deeply pessimistic view of history as a ceaseless conflict of the Spirit against the flesh and the letter, and between God and the world. The good were always made to suffer, the Crucifixion always recurred, and the true church was a dispersed, invisible community of those in whom the Spirit worked, who were always a small persecuted minority. This tragic picture was relieved, however, by Franck's firm belief that at the end of time Christ's coming would restore mankind.[85] In a remarkable letter of 1531 (later published) to an unorthodox Protestant friend, he declared that for over fourteen hundred years, since the death of the apostles, Antichrist had reigned and no true visible church or sacraments had existed. The church fathers were "doctors of unwisdom" whose doctrines and human inventions had corrupted the church. The Lutherans were as bad as the Catholics, because both mixed the Old Testament with the New to try to prove the legitimacy of war, oaths, the power of magistrates, priesthood, and tithes, falsely ascribing this conclusion also to Christ. According to Franck, everything taught by the papists and by Luther and Zwingli would have to be unlearned and abandoned. "I maintain against all ecclesiastical authorities," he stated, "that all outward things and ceremonies

. . . customary in the church of the apostles have been done away
with and are not to be reinstituted." The true church would remain scattered among the heathen until the end of the world,
when the advent of Christ would at last destroy Antichrist and his
church and gather together the remnants of fugitive Israel from
the different parts of the earth.[86]

Franck had no theory of religious toleration or of religious freedom as a Christian's right. His Spiritualist approach toward a religious universalism, however, made him an exceptionally tolerant
thinker and an enemy of persecution. In the preface to a historical
account of heretics in his *Chronicle of World History* (1531), he almost dissolved the conception of heresy by explaining that those
whom the Catholic Church denounced as heretics—Luther, Zwingli, Hus, Wyclif, the Anabaptists, and others—were all true Christians. He had no doubt, he wrote, that among the church's list of
heretics were many godly people who had more of the Spirit in
one finger than did Antichrist in all the existing churches. The
world had never recognized truth; what it took as truth were invariably lies and darkness. The present world, which was no better
than the past, has always persecuted the truth as heresy.[87] For
Franck, therefore, it was the heretic rather than his persecutors
who was most likely to possess the truth. Elsewhere he declared
that God loved both pagans and Jews, and that there was hardly
a pagan, philosopher, or heretic who did not have a glimpse of
something good.[88] He often said that he wished to regard everyone
as his brother, whether papist, Lutheran, Zwinglian, Anabaptist,
or Turk, even though they differed in religion, and "to love . . .
especially those who, among all sects, beliefs, and peoples, belong
to Christ."[89] Franck's Spiritualism was thus both moral and religious in its inspiration and led him to embrace a humane and
tolerant perspective that transcended all distinctions of belief
among Christians, as well as between Christians and other religions. His defense of heretics, together with his skepticism about
heresy, was a rare phenomenon in his time and is one of the most
significant elements that marked the gulf between the Spiritualists' type of Christianity and that of orthodox Protestantism.

CONCLUSION: THE REIGN OF PERSECUTION

The emergence of Protestantism confronted the Catholic Church with its greatest threat since the persecutions centuries before in Roman times. The new Protestant denominations aimed at much more than merely being allowed to exist. They wished to convert Christians wherever they could and, with the help of the state, to impose their own belief and exclusive ecclesiastical order on society. While the religious divide went on widening in Europe, there were Christian humanists and political men who continued to believe, as Erasmus did, in the possibility of overcoming confessional disunion through conciliation and doctrinal compromise. Among the measures to promote this end in Germany were several religious conferences, most notably the meeting at Regensburg in 1541 between leading Catholic and Protestant theologians. In France a similar meeting was sponsored by the French government at the colloquy of Poissy in 1561, where Calvinist and Catholic divines fruitlessly debated their differences. These attempts at religious mediation by means of conferences all ended in failure.[90] Some Catholic humanists and ecclesiastics in the 1530s and 1540s also placed their hope of repairing the religious split in the convening of a general council of the church that would order reforms and resolve doctrinal disagreements with Protestants. After several postponements, the Council of Trent, which was summoned by Pope Paul III, assembled for its first session in 1545 and continued to meet with several intermissions until 1563. While the council and the reforms it initiated played a major role in the Catholic revival of the later sixteenth century, no representatives of Protestant churches or princes took part in its deliberations, and its doctrinal decrees, far from seeking compromise and reconciliation, drew the line sharply and irremediably between Catholic dogma and Protestant teaching.[91]

In the meantime, the Catholic Church also extended its machinery of repression against heresy. In 1542 Pope Paul III created in succession to the medieval Inquisition the Roman Inquisition, or Congregation of the Holy Office, which had branches in a number of Italian cities and whose main task was to detect and punish Protestant heresy along with any other kind of heterodox opinion. The Roman Index of Prohibited Books was inaugurated by Pope Paul IV in 1559 for the censorship of Protestant and other publications of questionable orthodoxy. This Index was subsequently expanded, and in 1571 Pope Pius V created a separate Congregation of the Index to supervise the investigation of suspect books.[92] In Spain the Inquisition, or Holy Office, had been founded in 1478 for the purpose of detecting secret Judaism on the part of Jewish converts to Christianity, but from the 1530s it also undertook the suppression of the Spanish disciples of Erasmus and of Protestant heresy.[93]

The Catholic Church's judicial prosecution of heresy in the sixteenth century took thousands of lives. Tabulations of the executions inflicted for heresy are bound to have a wide margin of error; however, according to one recent estimate by a very competent scholar, there were approximately three thousand legally sanctioned deaths for heresy in Europe in the period 1520–1565.[94] In England the short reign of Henry VIII's Catholic daughter, Queen Mary I (1553–1558), witnessed the burning of nearly three hundred Protestant heretics condemned under the heresy laws by the ecclesiastical courts.[95] In the Netherlands and France, the governments of the earlier sixteenth century did their best to eradicate heresy by prosecutions carried on by both ecclesiastical and secular tribunals.[96] In both countries, however, Protestantism, mainly in its Calvinist form, continued to grow in spite of repression, and in each of them a long rebellion and religious civil war began in the 1560s, caused in part by Catholic persecution.[97] Catholic persecution was responsible for a far greater number of executions for religion than was persecution by Protestants. The only sixteenth-century Catholic martyrs were those put to death in England under Henry VIII in the 1530s and 1540s and during the reign of Queen Elizabeth I (1558–1603), who reestablished Protestantism as the state religion.

Of course, the intolerance between Catholics and Protestants was mutual. Protestant authorities and theologians treated Catholicism not as a heresy but as a corrupt and idolatrous faith that should be suppressed. Hence Protestant governments generally prohibited Catholicism and persecuted Catholics and their priests who tried to preserve their religion through private or clandestine worship. Protestant zealots attacked Catholic churches in violent outbreaks of iconoclasm, defacing and destroying altars, tombs, and the sacred images and symbols of worship. Protestant and Catholic armies of fighting men slaughtered each other during the religious civil war in France and the Netherlands rebellion, and both sides were guilty of religious massacres. The most famous of these massacres, that on Saint Batholomew's Day, which began in Paris on 24 August 1572 and spread to a number of other French cities, was a killing spree in which Catholic mobs murdered thousands of Protestants.[98]

To be sure, there were also a few moves toward religous coexistence. The Peace of Augsburg of 1555, of which I have spoken previously, was the sequel to a religious war in Germany in the 1540s between the Catholic emperor Charles V and the Lutheran princes. This settlement, however, which excluded Calvinism and was inherently unstable, did not provide for the existence of two religions in the same state. It only authorized the coexistence in the Holy Roman Empire of Catholic and Lutheran states and princes, requiring that individual subjects conform to the religion of their prince or else emigrate.

In France on the eve of the religious civil war that began in 1562, the government of the boy king Charles IX and his mother the queen regent Catherine de Medici sought to pacify the country by replacing the previous policy of repression with a measure of toleration for the French Protestants, or Huguenots, as they were also known. This new policy of coexistence was advocated by the highest royal official, the newly appointed chancellor of France, Michel de L'Hopital, an able, humanistically educated statesman who was something of an Erasmian. He distinguished between Protestants who used religion as a pretext for sedition and those who were peaceable believers and should be treated leniently. In a speech to the French Estates General in December 1560, he deplored the religious division in the kingdom, which was endangering its political unity, and argued that it could not be cured by force, and that violence was alien to the Christian religion. The following year he told the Parlement of Paris that while there were some among the Reformers who were atheists and criminals, others were moved by zeal and commitment, convinced that their religion was the salvation of their souls and willing for its sake to risk their lives and possessions. In a subsequent address to the French bishops, he declared that force could not overcome religious differences nor constrain conscience, which could be persuaded only by reason. The Protestants, he pointed out, believed that "the word of God strictly obliges them to assemble to hear the preaching of the gospel and participate in the sacraments, and they hold this as an article of faith." He did not think it was possible to prevent their religious assemblies and therefore called for the toleration of Protestant worship in France. Again in January 1562, speaking to a political assembly summoned to advise the king, he said that to try to crush Protestantism by force could lead to the ruin of the state. He therefore favored the legal recognition of Protestantism and maintained that people could be citizens (*citoyens*) without sharing the same religion. Thus, to deal with the unprecedented political crisis brought on by the conflict between Catholics and Protestants, he was willing to depart from the wisdom enshrined in the venerable French maxim envisaging France as a country of "one faith, one law, one king" (*une foi, une loi, un roi*).[99]

It was at this time, in 1561–1562, that the terms "tolerance" and "liberty" first began to be used in France to designate the policy of permitting Protestant worship.[100] In January 1562, Charles IX issued his well-known edict conceding the Protestants freedom to hold religious services until a general council of the church was able to restore unity. Conceived as a temporary measure, it contained many restrictions. Protestants were allowed to meet for worship only in daylight and outside the walls of the kingdom's cities. They were likewise prohibited from holding synods and consistories, except with the permission of royal officials and in their presence, and from performing various other acts.[101] Despite all its limitations, however, the January edict marked the first legal recognition of Protestantism and the Reformed Church in France. It was also the first indication of the possibility that citizenship and the political allegiance of subjects to their king and country might be consistent with a diversity of religions in the state.

The promulgation of what has been termed licensed coexistence between Protestants, or Huguenots, and Catholics was a prudential concession and political expedient rather than an act of principle.[102] In this it was no different from the Peace of Augsburg in Germany. Nearly all Catholics opposed the January edict. Among them was Etienne de La Boétie, the dear friend of the great French writer Montaigne, who warned of the dangerous and divisive consequences of permitting two religions, which could lead to two opposed states in the same country. The most he would have allowed the Protestants was the right to worship in private, and he pointed out their own intolerance of Catholics. His policy for religious peace was one of conciliation and concord through reforms in the church that would eventually persuade the Protestants to reunite with Catholicism. Montaigne himself once agreed with this policy but eventually came reluctantly to believe in the necessity of toleration as the only alternative to civil strife.[103]

The January edict did not avert the civil war in France between Catholics and Protestants, which began soon afterward in the summer of 1562 over a number of intertwined religious and political differences. This war, or series of wars, of organized religious parties, led on both sides by members of the highest French nobility, deeply weakened the monarchy and plunged France into anarchy for more than thirty years. Throughout this period the large majority of Catholics remained opposed to any concession of toleration. As for the Protestants, or Huguenots, they failed to abide by the limitations prescribed in the January edict, and nearly all of them were against toleration in principle.[104] Calvin, their chief

spiritual guide, condemned it unconditionally, and, as we shall
note later, so did his colleague and successor the minister Theodore Beza, one of the foremost figures in the French Reformed
Church. In the territories that the Protestants held and governed
during the civil war, they did not permit Catholic worship. In
1598, at the war's conclusion, Henry IV, in order to pacify his
wasted kingdom, issued the Edict of Nantes, which assured toleration under certain restrictions to the Protestants, now a much reduced minority. This arrangement, too, was a product of political
expediency and a result of the mutual exhaustion caused by the
civil war.[105] Thus, at the beginning of the seventeenth century, belief in the principle of toleration and freedom of conscience was
still very far from being widely accepted either in France or anywhere else in Europe.

CHAPTER 4

The First Champion of
Religious Toleration:
Sebastian Castellio

ᔥᔤ

On Friday, 27 October 1553, Michael Servetus, forty-two years of age, was taken as a prisoner from the town hall of Geneva to the hill of Champmel just outside the city gate. There, soon after midday, he was burned alive for the crime of heresy. His captors had earlier rejected his terrified plea that they kill him by the sword instead of fire. On his *via dolorosa* to the place of execution, the pastors accompanying him pressed him to repent of his beliefs, but he refused. Tied to his body when he was chained to the stake was one of the heretical books he had written, which was also consumed in the flames.[1]

The unfortunate Servetus, a creative thinker, theologian, and physician, was notorious for his controversial personality and extremely unorthodox writings. The dangerous thoughts contained in his books were an amalgam of recondite ideas, including Antitrinitarianism, which made him one of the founders of modern Unitarianism, a somewhat Neoplatonic emanationist conception of Christ as the divine but noneternal Son of God begotten by the Holy Spirit, a strain of pantheism, and believer's baptism as a way of union with Christ and with God. He was also a biblical scholar, geographer, student of astrology, and medical doctor, credited with the discovery of the pulmonary circulation of the blood. The heterodox opinions advanced in his works on religion such as *The Errors of the Trinity* (*De Trinitatis erroribus*), *Dialogues on The Trinity* (*Dialogorum de Trinitate duo libri*), and *The Restoration of Christianity* (*Christianismi restitutio*) horrified and scandalized Protestants and Catholics alike. He was a critic of both Lutheranism and Calvinism.[2] Because of his reputation for heresy he was a hunted man, forced for his own safety to conceal his identity under a false name. For twelve years prior to his arrest in Geneva he lived under the alias of Michel de Villeneuve in the French city of Vienne, where he practiced medicine. Unhappily, in March 1553 the Inquisition in Vienne accused him of heresy in connection with his book *The Restoration of Christianity*, which he had arranged to have secretly printed.[3] Placed under investigation, he was in due course condemned to death but succeeded during his trial in escaping from the Inquisition's grip at the end of April. For a few months thereafter he wandered about in search of a refuge. Then on 13 August 1553, a Sunday morning, he entered Geneva on his way to Italy and was recognized and imprisoned later the same day. The Geneva authorities had no legal jurisdiction over him, since he was merely a passer-through who had committed no offense in the city. Nonetheless, they proceeded to try him for heresy, Calvin being his main accuser. Calvin, who had previously corresponded with Servetus and was well informed about him and his writings, detested him for his argumentative character and various heresies concerning the divinity of Christ, the Trinity, and other Christian doctrines. A few years previously he had told his friend the minister Farel that should Servetus ever come to Geneva, "if my authority is of any avail, I will not suffer him to get out alive."[4] In all probability he also played a major part in March 1553 in supplying the evidence to the Inquisition in Vienne that helped betray Servetus to his Catholic persecutors.[5]

Servetus's condemnation was based on a law in the code of the Roman emperor Justinian prescribing the death penalty for the denial of the doctrine of the Trinity and rejection of infant bap-

Sixteenth-century portrait of the Protestant reformer John Calvin. A fierce enemy not only of the Catholic Church but of dissenters from orthodox Protestantism, Calvin did not hesitate to defend the execution of heretics. He bore the main responsibility for the notorious burning of the Antitrinitarian heretic Michael Servetus in Geneva in 1553. The painting in the Boymans Museum, Rotterdam, is reproduced from a copy in E. Doumergue, *Iconographie calvinienne*, 1909.

tism. In sentencing him, the officials who conducted his trial spoke with horror of the stinking poison of his heretical writings and of his execrable blasphemies against the Holy Trinity, the Son of God, and the baptism of infants, which were an affront to the majesty and honor of God and caused the murder, perdition, and ruin of many poor souls. Declaring that it was necessary to purge the church of God of such infection and to cut off the rotten member, they ordered Servetus to be attached to the stake and burned to ashes, so that he would finish his days as an example to others who might think of committing the same crime.[6]

In the course of the sixteenth century thousands of people were executed as heretics, among them such well-known victims as the English churchman Thomas Cranmer, archbishop of Canterbury, burned at Oxford in 1556, the French humanist scholar Etienne Dolet, hanged and burned in Paris in 1546, and the Italian philosopher Giordano Bruno, burned in Rome in 1600. Pious Protestant and Catholic authors of various nations compiled martyrologies and memorials recording the names and steadfastness of the men and women who had accepted death rather than renounce their faith.[7] Amid so many martyrs and victims of intolerance in the century of the Reformation, why should the tragic fate of Servetus stand out so prominently? The answer is threefold. First, since Calvin was his main adversary and the man most responsible for his death, Servetus's trial and sentence proclaimed to Christian Europe the readiness of a founder and one of the foremost leaders of Protestantism to inflict the death penalty on heretical opinions. Second, Servetus's heresies were abstruse religious conceptions without any seditious or political implications. His condemnation, as Lord Acton noted, was "the most perfect and characteristic example of the abstract intolerance of the reformers. [He] was guilty of no political crime. . . . His doctrine was speculative, without power of attraction for the masses . . . and without consequences subversive of morality, or affecting in any direct way the existence of society."[8] In other words, Servetus was judicially murdered by a Protestant government simply because of the fear and hatred aroused by his errant theological convictions and for no other reason. Third and most important, Servetus's trial and execution provoked the first major controversy in Western history over the question of religious toleration and the killing of heretics. Calvin's and Geneva's actions met with criticism in Basel and other Swiss Protestant cities among a number of persons who, while not sharing Servetus's beliefs, were against putting heretics to death.[9]

One of the critics was the French Protestant scholar Sebastian Castellio, a resident of Basel. If this book has any kind of a hero, it is Castellio, who, in a series of writings distinguished by both their reasoning power and their moral courage and mental independence, became the first great advocate and defender of tolerance and pluralistic freedom for differing religious beliefs.

SEBASTIAN CASTELLIO AND SERVETUS'S EXECUTION

Following Servetus's execution, the earliest protest against his punishment was an anonymous, well-informed tract dating from late December 1553, *Historia de morte Serveti* (*The History of Servetus's Death*), which appeared in Basel and circulated in manuscript copies. Its first part, a summary of events from the time of Servetus's arrest by the Inquisition in Vienne to his pitiless burning in Geneva, brought out Calvin's involvement and responsibility for his death. Its second part explained why so many pious people regarded Servetus's persecution and execution as "a scandal of scandals." Among the reasons given were that in Geneva a man was killed, with Calvin's complicity, because of his religion; that in killing him Protestants had conspired with papists and the Inquisition; that in a practice learned from the pope Geneva had burned Servetus's books; and that after his death preachers publicly preached that he was condemned to eternal damnation. The author of this tract was most likely Sebastian Castellio.[10] Moreover, it was quite surely because of criticisms like these that Calvin felt the need to write the work discussed in the previous chapter, his *Defense of the Orthodox Faith*, printed in February 1554, which justified the killing of heretics such as Servetus.

But who was Castellio?[11]

Born in 1515, he was the child of a poor peasant family named Chasteillon (Chatillon, Chateillon) belonging to a village in a region of the Duchy of Savoy conquered by France in the 1530s. He must have shown unusual intellectual ability, because in 1535 he went to Lyon to spend five years in poverty as a student at the

municipal Collège de la Trinité. Lyon at that period was an international commercial crossroads and a center of culture and the
book trade where a number of well-known humanist scholars and
men of letters lived and worked. There he was exposed to humanism and acquired a humanistic education in the languages and
literature of Greece and Rome. Under its influence he Hellenized
his name to "Castalio," after the Castalian fountain on Mount Par-
nassus that was the spring of the Muses. While in Lyon he came
in contact with the Protestant Reformation and probably read Calvin's *Institutes of the Christian Religion*, first published in 1536. In
January 1540 he could have seen the first execution in Lyon of
Protestant heretics who were burned at the stake. Later the same
year he left Lyon and moved to Strasbourg, a city that had accepted the Reformation. This change was quite certainly connected with his conversion to Protestantism. On arriving in Strasbourg, he met Calvin, whom he had perhaps come to see and who
had gone there to live after his banishment from Geneva in 1538.
For a few days he lodged in Calvin's house, and he formed a
friendly relationship with the reformer and some of his associates.
After a year in Strasbourg during which he supported himself by
teaching, he went to Geneva in June 1541 to become head of the
Collège de Rive, an employment for which Calvin's friend, the
minister Farel, had recommended him. Calvin himself was recalled to Geneva in September 1541 by the city government and
immediately proceeded to introduce there the new church order
outlined in his *Ecclesiastical Ordinances*.[12]

During the four years he spent in Geneva, Castellio worked very
hard as head teacher at the Collège de Rive, a school whose purpose was to offer children a Protestant and humanistic education.
He also did some preaching in nearby villages, began a French
translation of the New Testament, and published a pedagogical
work in 1543 that went through enlarged later editions and remained popular for many years, *Dialogi sacri* (*Sacred Dialogues*), a
collection of biblical children's stories that combined the teaching
of Latin with Christian instruction.[13] Although Calvin, his mentor,
was well disposed toward him at first, frictions soon developed

between them. Castellio wanted to become a minister, but Calvin
and the Geneva Company of Pastors decided that he was unsuit-
able for this position and should remain at his school. There were
also theological disagreements. One centered on a disputed point
in the Apostles' Creed, another on divergent understandings of
the biblical Song of Solomon, which Calvin interpreted in accord
with Christian tradition as a spiritual allegory of Christ's love for
his church, while Castellio maintained that it was a shameless, las-
civious love poem by the Hebrew king. At a meeting of Calvin and
other ministers in May 1544, Castellio bitterly attacked some of
the latter for their moral faults, including cowardice in refusing
to serve during a recent outbreak of the plague, and compared
them most unfavorably with the apostle Paul. This incident resulted in a breach with Calvin and led to Castellio's censure for
misconduct by the Geneva magistrates. Soon afterward he resigned his teaching post, and in the spring of 1545 he moved to
the city of Basel. Calvin's attitude toward him had by now become
quite hostile. He reported to Farel that Castellio "vomits his
venom," and described him as saying that it is "because of my [Cal-
vin's] tyranny that he has been debarred from the ministry so that
I can reign alone."[14] On Castellio's departure, Calvin, who must
have been much relieved to see him go, wrote a letter of reference
for him which, though mentioning the doctrinal deviations that
had prevented his admission to the ministry, nevertheless attested
his ability as a teacher and stated that he had left his position
voluntarily.[15]

It is obvious that Castellio's critical attitude and readiness to differ made his conflict with Calvin inevitable. Calvin considered that
a man with such traits would be detrimental to the unity of the new
Reformed Church he was straining every nerve to build in Geneva.
Although he recognized some of Castellio's merits, he judged that
his independence of mind in theology and other matters made
him unreliable as a minister and church leader. On Castellio's side,
it is more than likely that by the time he left Geneva, he had come
to dislike and resent Calvin's domination and perhaps also to

doubt, if not altogether reject, the Calvinist doctrine of predestination and denial of free will, which he was later to attack.

Besides its importance as an economic center, Basel, with a population of about ten thousand, was a city of letters and art containing an interesting mixture of inhabitants. Following its embrace of the Reformation in 1529, it attracted numerous religious
refugees, including some distinguished Italians. Erasmus, who had
been a prominent resident there for some years until the establishment of Protestantism drove him away, nevertheless returned in
1534 to die there two years later. Basel had a university and was
famed for its printers, such as Froben and Amerbach, who hired
humanist scholars as editors and correctors of the books they published. When he arrived in Basel, Castellio secured employment as
a corrector with Johannes Oporinus, owner of one of the foremost
printing and publishing houses.[16] During his first years in the city,
as he made various friends in the civic elite and among the religious
exiles, he produced a large number of works published by Oporinus. They included editions of Greek and Latin texts, Latin translations of Greek authors and of the Psalms, poems in Latin on biblical subjects, and a new edition of his *Sacred Dialogues.* The most
significant of these publications were his translations of the Bible
into both Latin and French. The first, a version in fine classical
Latin, with the Old Testament translated directly from the Hebrew
original, appeared in 1551. The second, a French translation published in 1555, was based on the common speech and designed for
the ordinary uneducated reader.[17] Although Castellio looked upon
the task of biblical translation through the eyes of a scholar and
philologist, his approach to the Bible as a sacred book was both
spiritual and moral. In preliminary remarks to the readers of both
translations he said that the Bible revealed itself only to those who
possessed the Holy Spirit, were humble, and renounced the judgments of the flesh; those, on the other hand, who preferred their
own will, followed worldly wisdom, and failed to turn away from
their sins, would never understand it.[18]

Castellio dedicated his translations to two kings, the Latin version to Edward VI of England, the French to Henry II of France.

The dedicatory preface to the former is noteworthy as the earliest expression of his belief in toleration. It was an indictment of religious persecution by Christians and a call for charity, patience, and mildness in dealing with religious divisions. Castellio attached far higher importance to morality and a Christian life of brotherhood and love than to doctrine or dogma. He painted a dark picture of the Christians of his time as guilty of a general ignorance of religion and lacking in true piety and love of neighbor. In their quarrels over religion, they pursued and killed one another in the name of Christ and suppressed those of a different view. Lamenting the misunderstanding of the parable of the tares, he cautioned against condemning others for their beliefs and urged that the tares be left to the harvest and God's final judgment lest the good seed be uprooted. One of the conceptions passingly mentioned in this dedication was that the Bible contained obscurities and riddles that had been debated for over a thousand years without agreement, whereas what was necessary was charity, which allayed all controversies. In an allusion to the victims of persecution, he declared that since Christians permitted proud, envious, avaricious, drunken, and shameless people to live among them, they should also let those live who confessed the same Christ and showed such courage that they preferred to die rather than say what they did not believe. To the young King Edward, whose virtues he praised, he declared that he spoke not as a prophet sent by God but as a common man who detested quarrels and hatred and desired to see religion manifested in charity and piety of heart, rather than in contentions and external practices.[19] These sentiments foreshadowed in germ some of the ideas he was presently to develop much more broadly in his writings on toleration.

Castellio's numerous publications brought him a distinguished reputation as a humanist scholar. In 1553 the University of Basel, in which he had previously matriculated, appointed him as its professor of Greek and awarded him a master of arts degree. He had married in Geneva, but his wife died in 1549 and he remarried in the same year. With children from both wives to support, his circumstances were never easy, but his academic position and pub-

lications relieved the considerable poverty of his earlier period in
Basel. After 1553, although he remained a noted and productive
scholar, our interest in his career necessarily shifts to his series of
writings concerned with toleration on which his chief significance
depends.[20]

CASTELLIO'S *CONCERNING HERETICS*

Castellio's first printed response to the execution of Servetus was
his *De haereticis an sint persequendi, & omnino quomodo sit cum eis
agendum* (*Concerning Heretics and Whether They Should Be Persecuted,
and How They Should Be Treated*), which appeared in March 1554.
It was not an answer to Calvin's *Defense of the Orthodox Faith*, which
had only just been published in Geneva the previous month, but
what its subtitle described as "a collection of opinions of learned
men both ancient and modern . . . most necessary and useful to
all in a turbulent time, especially to princes and magistrates to
show them their duty in a matter so controversial and dangerous."
On its title page was a motto taken from Galatians (4:29): "He that
was born after the flesh persecuted him that was born after the
Spirit." This momentous book, a small volume of only 175 pages,
was anonymous and bore a false printer's name and imprint declaring its place of publication as Magdeburg; in reality, it was published secretly in Basel by Oporinus.[21] Despite its anonymity, Calvin and his colleague and disciple Theodore Beza, a leading
minister in the Reformed Church, quickly recognized Castellio's
hand in it. Although he may perhaps have had the assistance of
several collaborators among his friends in Basel, the book's conception was probably his, and he was not only its editor but its
main author.[22]

Concerning Heretics consisted of two main parts.[23] The first was a
preface by Martin Bellius, a pseudonym for Castellio, dedicating
the work to a German prince, Christophe, duke of Württemburg.
The second and much longer part was an anthology of carefully
selected texts opposed to religious persecution. Twenty authors

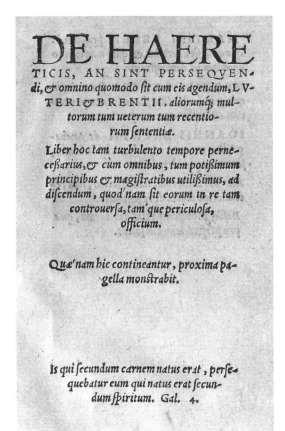

DE HAERE

TICIS, AN SINT PERSEQVEN-
di, & omnino quomodo fit cum eis agendum, LV-
TERI & BRENTII, aliorumq́; mul-
torum tum ueterum tum recentio-
rum sententiæ.

Liber hoc tam turbulento tempore perne-
ceßarius, & cùm omnibus, tum potißimum
principibus & magistratibus utilißimus, ad
discendum, quod'nam fit eorum in re tam
controuersa, tam'que periculosa,
officium.

Quæ'nam hic contineantur, proxima pa-
gella monstrabit.

Is qui secundum carnem natus erat, perse-
quebatur eum qui natus erat secundum spiritum. Gal. 4.

Title page of Sebastian Castellio's anonymously published *De haereticis, an sint persequendi* (*Concerning Heretics and Whether They Should Be Persecuted*), 1553, one of the first great protests in the sixteenth century against the persecution of heresy and a landmark in the struggle for religious toleration. Courtesy of the Folger Shakespeare Library.

were represented in this anthology, four of whom, Saint Augustine, Saint Jerome, Lactantius, and Saint John Chrysostom, were fathers of the early church. The other sixteen, with the exception of Erasmus, were all moderns and Protestants.[24] Among them were Luther, Sebastian Franck (under the thinly disguised name of Augustinus Eleutherius), Calvin, some Protestant ministers and scholars, and Castellio himself under his own name. The

last two names in this company, though, George Kleinberg and
Basil Montfort, were fictitious and probably served as additional
pseudonyms for Castellio. Since Saint Augustine, Luther, Calvin,
and most of the other Protestants in the collection either were or
became persecutors, it was quite an irony to include them in a
work against persecution and in defense of toleration. As Bellius's
preface explained, however, while some of the authors had later
held a different view, he had chosen to use their first opinion,
which accorded "with the meekness and mercy of Christ" and was
written at a time when they were poor and afflicted. By this he
implied that after religious leaders such as Luther and Calvin became prominent and powerful, they ceased to be defenders of
Christ but "defended Mars and converted true religion into force
and violence."[25] Some of the longest extracts in the collection were
taken from writings by Erasmus, Luther, and Sebastian Franck,
which we have noticed in the previous chapter, and by John Brenz,
a German Lutheran minister who at one time opposed the persecution of the Anabaptists. The selection from Calvin was among
the shortest, merely two passages, one of them from the first
(1536) edition of his *Institutes* on the use of exhortation and persuasion in dealing with the excommunicated.[26] Castellio's contribution in his own name consisted of a selection from the dedication to Edward VI in his Latin Bible.[27]

Concerning Heretics was undoubtedly intended as a protest
against the burning of Servetus, yet his name was never mentioned
in it. Why did Castellio choose to leave out all explicit reference
to Servetus and to mount his attack against religious persecution
in a work that was anonymous? The most likely reason for his not
discussing Servetus's condemnation was that he wished to keep
clear of all personal accusations and controversies in presenting
his case. To exclude issues of personality may also have been one
of the reasons that he withheld his name as author. In addition,
he may have done so because of the need for caution in the Basel
civic environment. He was merely a resident, not a free citizen of
Basel, a Protestant community in which legal toleration did not
exist. The city government authorized censorship of publications

partly to prevent the expression of religious opinions that might provoke religious disturbances or adversely affect its relations with other Swiss cities.[28] All these considerations would explain Castellio's decision against identifying himself publicly as the author or editor of the book.

The overwhelming significance of *Concerning Heretics* lies in its broad critical confrontation with the concept of heresy and its array of arguments undermining the Christian theory of persecution. Its most important part as a statement in behalf of toleration was not its anthology of well-known authors but the pseudonymous Bellius's prefatory dedication to Duke Christophe of Württemburg and the selections at the end attributed to George Kleinberg and Basil Montfort, all of which were the work of Castellio.

The dedication opens with a parable asking the duke to suppose that he has told his subjects he will come to them at an uncertain time, and has commanded them to meet him wearing white robes when he appears. Instead of preparing their white robes, though, they fall to quarreling and fighting about where he is and whether he will arrive on a horse or in a chariot and unattended or with an entourage. Some of them oppress and kill others, claiming that they act in the duke's name and by his command. The duke would, of course, be displeased by such conduct and punish it severely. The point is evident, and the dedication proceeds to make explicit the analogy with Christ, who told his followers that he would return at an uncertain hour, and that they should meanwhile live peaceably together and love each other. Few Christians, however, obey Christ's command by living in a just, religious manner while awaiting his coming. "We dispute," Bellius says, not about how to draw nearer to Christ by correcting our lives, but about Christ's state and office, how he is at the Father's right hand and one with the Father, and also about the Trinity, predestination and free will, the angels and the state of souls after death: all things that don't "need to be known for salvation by faith" or "make a man better."[29] Such perverse curiosity makes men conceited with a false opinion of their knowledge and contemptuous of others. Their pride leads

to cruelty and persecution so that few people can endure anyone
who differs, and nearly all sects condemn each other, desiring to
reign alone. From these vices have arisen "banishments, chains,
imprisonments, stakes, and gallows and this miserable rage to visit
daily penalties upon those who differ from the mighty about matters hitherto unknown, for so many centuries disputed, and not
yet cleared up." If someone tries, moreover, to prepare the white
robe by living innocently and justly, others who differ from him
call him a heretic, accuse him of horrible crimes, and bring about
his death, justifying this treatment as in accord with Christ's will,
although "Satan could not devise anything more repugnant to the
nature and will of Christ."[30]

Bellius next extends his parable to speak of those Christians
who strive to live by Christ's commandments but are convinced in
conscience that they will offend Christ unless they take communion in two kinds and baptize only those who are able to give a
reason for their faith. To put such people to death would certainly
be contrary to Christ's will and the example of his life. In all disputed articles of religion, Bellius says, on which Christians differ
and may err, no one should condemn others, and all should strive
to correct their own lives. What he most deplores is "the license
of judgement which reigns everywhere today and fills all with
blood . . . so wrongfully shed . . . of those called heretics." The
name of heretic has become so infamous and horrible that "when
it is pronounced men shut their ears to the victim's defense, and
furiously persecute not merely the man himself but also all . . .
who dare to open their mouths on his behalf, by which rage it has
come to pass that many have been destroyed before their cause
was really understood."[31]

Immediately following the preceding sentence comes this statement: "Now I say this not because I favor heretics. I hate heretics."[32]
The modern reader may be surprised and perhaps dismayed by this
remark, which seems to contradict the entire tenor of the previous
argument and its exhortation to Christian charity and love. It
should probably be read, however, as a rhetorical concession
Castellio felt obliged to make to his adversaries, and should not be

taken very seriously when we observe how he modifies and reduces the meaning of heresy in the course of this work.[33]

Bellius next goes on to explain that the purpose of his book and its collection of authors is to reduce persecution. For after the pagan persecution of Christians had ceased, Christians persecuted other Christians. He is convinced, moreover, that those who are saints have always been persecuted. Persecution has always oppressed genuine religion, and if there were no truly religious people in the present age, there would likewise be no persecution. Whenever the godly appear, there also appear persecutors.[34] Bellius thus conceives that suffering persecution is one of the signs of a true Christian. In perhaps the most significant part of his preface, he proceeds to consider the definition of a heretic, a subject, he says, "of prime importance" not dealt with by the authors in his anthology, and necessary because "not . . . all those are heretics who are so called." At present, he observes, "no one is put to death for avarice, hypocrisy, scurrility, or flattery, of which it is often easy to judge, but for heresy, of which it is not so simple to judge, so many are executed." Having carefully investigated the meaning of the term "heretic," he explains that

> I can discover no more than this, that we regard those as heretics with whom we disagree. This is evident from the fact that today there is scarcely one of our innumerable sects that does not look upon the rest as heretics, so that if you are orthodox in one city or region, you are held for a heretic in the next.[35]

To this deflationary definition of the heretic he adds a brief account of the word itself as used in the New Testament. From it he concludes that the heretic "is an obstinate man who does not obey after due admonition." There are two kinds of obstinate persons, however, those who are obstinate in their conduct and various vices, and those obstinate in spiritual matters and doctrine to whom the term "heretic" properly applies, since in Greek "heresy" means a sect or opinion. In this sense, the adherents of particular sects and opinions are called heretics. Conduct, though, is much easier to judge than doctrine. Everyone, whether Jew, Turk, or Christian, knows that robbers and traitors are evil and should be put to death; they agree without controversy because God has engraved this knowledge in their hearts. In religion, knowledge and the truth are not so evident. Jews, Turks, and Christians all disagree on many things, and Christians disagree with other Christians and condemn one another as heretics. Hence controversies over "obscure questions" like baptism, free will, communion, and invocation of saints lead Christian denominations to persecute each other. These dissensions, Bellius maintains, "arise solely from ignorance of the truth," for if the matters in dispute were as obvious as the proposition that there is one God, all Christians would readily agree.[36]

The one remedy Bellius proposes for these great contentions among Christians is avoidance of condemnation, mutual charity, and efforts to teach others by examples of true religion and justice. Those who think themselves wiser than others should also be better and more merciful. The more a man knows the truth, the less he will be inclined to condemn, as Christ and the apostles showed. By condemning others, the persons who do so prove that they do not know. If all acted charitably and with forbearance, they would live in unity and peace despite their disagreements. Unhappily, Bellius laments, because Christians at present strive with hate and persecutions, "we go from bad to worse." Who would wish to be a Christian, he asks,

> when he saw that those who confessed the name of Christ were destroyed by Christians themselves with fire, water, and the sword without mercy. . . ? Who would not think Christ a Moloch . . . if he wished that men should be immolated to him and burned alive?

He continues with what is clearly an allusion to Servetus and his behavior at the stake:

> Who would wish to serve Christ on condition that difference of opinion on a controversial point with those in authority would be punished by burning alive at the command of

Christ ... even though from the midst of the flames he should call with a loud voice upon Christ, and should cry out that he believed in him?[37]

With this statement the dedication arrives at its conclusion. It is an indignant peroration denying that Christ, so mild, merciful, and patient of injury, could command or approve of the cruel and terrible things, the killing and torture, done in his name, and denouncing the "blasphemies and shameful audacities of men" who dare to attribute to Christ what they do at the command and instigation of Satan.[38]

The French translation of *Concerning Heretics* includes an additional and much shorter dedication to Count William of Hesse, the son-in-law of Duke Christophe of Württemburg. A further plea against persecution, its main thesis is that princes should beware of killing and burning anyone for faith or religion, "which above all else should be free," because they are matters of belief beyond the reach of the sword. Bellius bases this view on the argument that the civil magistrate has no jurisdiction over spiritual offenses like heresy and infidelity, which are subject only to the word of God. Spiritual offenders should therefore be excommunicated from the church and nothing more. If they create disturbances, they are punishable by the civil magistrate, but only by banishment as the extreme penalty, not death.[39] We also meet in this dedication with the distinction between "dubious" or "ambiguous doctrines" that "transcend human understanding"—of which Bellius gives several examples, like the Trinity—and the "fundamental points of true religion," such as that Jesus is the savior. It is sufficient, he holds, for Christians to accept the latter, while being left to their own opinions regarding the former.[40]

We come finally to the pair of statements printed under the names of George Kleinberg and Basil Montfort, which bring us almost to the end of the work. Kleinberg's contribution, entitled "How Persecution Hurts the World," is an exhortation to rulers and magistrates against persecution. It bemoans the bloodshed committed, especially in Germany, by those who profess to have the true religion, and notes that from the cruelty first used against the Anabaptists a long series of atrocities began. People had been killed in thousands merely for differing in their understanding of obscure passages of Scripture and for no offense worse than ignorance and error. Rather than debate the truth, persecutors kill their opponents and burn the latter's books. Urging rulers not to listen to those who advise them to shed blood for religion, Kleinberg reminds them of Christ's command in the parable of the tares to leave the tares, even if they are heretics, until the harvest. The office of princes is to wield the sword to protect the good against evildoers, but not to defend a theological doctrine, which is beyond the reach of force. "If a good physician can defend his opinions without the aid of the magistrate, why cannot the theologian do the like? Christ could, the apostles could; surely their disciples can. Defend bodies with the bodily sword. The sword cannot touch the soul."[41] Kleinberg further maintains that it is the victims of persecution who are the truly godly people because they are sufferers for Christ. None "were ever killed for Christ," he says, "except with the title of heretic." He warns that persecution breeds seditions and civil wars that can destroy states; hence princes who desire peace and tranquillity should not persecute. "The dwelling of Christ," he concludes, "must be built by love. The persecutors wish to build it by hate and blood."[42]

Basil Montfort's statement is headed "Refutation of the Reasons Commonly Alleged in Favor of Persecution." Its main argument is directed against appeals to various precedents in the Mosaic books and other parts of the Old Testament to justify religious persecution, such as the command in Deuteronomy 13 to put false prophets to death. Diversity of opinions, Montfort observes, makes it difficult to decide who is a false prophet, and people are attacked for minor matters in religion even though they retain the fundamentals. If all errors and misinterpretations of Scripture were to be called heresy, it would be necessary to kill many people, and all the sects would have to kill one another because of their disagreements. Persecutors seek blood and therefore imitate the harsh features of the Mosaic law rather than the mild ones, contrary to the mercy of Christ.

In rejecting any scriptural justification of killing for religion, Montfort stresses that neither Christ nor the apostles ever used carnal or worldly weapons. The "sword of the Old Testament," he explains, is merely a figure or symbol of "the sword of the Spirit of God" on which the New Testament relies.[43] Besides insisting that nothing in the New Testament sanctions violence in religion, he points out that civil magistrates and ministers of religion have separate functions and should not meddle in each other's work. Heretics are punishable only by the word of God, while the sword of the magistrate is to be employed against criminals and to defend the good against injury. The magistrate lacks the power to make men good or to propagate religion by force. The apostles, although powerless, poor, and persecuted, accomplished far more for religion than others have been able to do with violence and the help of princes. When coercion prevails, religion becomes servile and men are compelled to approve whatever the persecutors assert. "Nothing is too monstrous to teach the people," Montfort declares, "when to doubt is prohibited, since if you doubt or do not believe, you are put to death." It is because religion is not "left free," he suggests, that error and spiritual tyranny are able to establish their dominion. He completes his statement with a series of biblical images to indicate that in a world divided between the forces of good and evil and the spirit and the flesh, the persecuted stand with Christ and the persecutors with Antichrist.[44] This point is followed by the conclusion of the work, a short impassioned declaration based on biblical passages showing that the persecutors belong with the Scribes, Pharisees, Herod, and Pilate as the cruel, ungodly children of the flesh, and the persecuted with the poor, humble, and meek as the godly children of the spirit. The very last words of the book are a quotation from Paul's first letter to the Corinthians (1 Cor. 4:5), an admonition to judge nothing before the advent of the Lord, who will bring the things of darkness to light and make manifest the counsels of all hearts.[45]

While Castellio undoubtedly had in mind a variety of readers, he evidently intended *Concerning Heretics* especially for princes and magistrates in the hope of persuading them to cease the persecution of heresy. Since the work was very largely a Christian indictment of the persecuting spirit, it is easy to understand why in his own contributions he quoted only the Bible, upon whose authority he relied exclusively. Biblical images and language suffuse his language and thought. Among the predecessors who helped shape his tolerationist perspective, the most important were Erasmus and Sebastian Franck. Erasmus criticized the killing of heretics; he also distinguished between the beliefs essential to the Christian faith and others not necessary to salvation that were wont to be the subject of endless theological disputes. Franck's spiritual religion, ethical consciousness, and depiction of heretics and the persecuted as the true Christians constituted an even stronger influence.[46] Not surprisingly, quotations from Erasmus and Franck provided Castellio with two of the longest selections in his anthology of authors opposed to persecution. But although he was indebted to both writers, neither of them made toleration the absolute center and focal point of his thought. Castellio's vision extended beyond theirs to make his own work, starting with *Concerning Heretics*, the first justification of a tolerant Christian society.

Two major themes dominated Castellio's attack upon religious persecution in *Concerning Heretics*. The first was skepticism regarding the concept of heresy itself. Castellio's discussion not only disarmed but went a long way toward deconstructing this concept. His investigation of its meaning led him to the conclusion that heresy was no more than disagreement between Christians on controverted points of religion. A heretic, accordingly, is not a person we can say for certain is guilty of error, but simply someone with whom others disagree. On this view, heresy is relativized so that it becomes merely a matter of differing opinions. Hence every sect looks upon other sects as heretical. One may wonder whether, in light of this analysis, Castellio really continued to believe in the existence of heresy as an objective fact. It is true that he also speaks of the heretic as an obstinate person in respect to doctrine. But about this there is an unstated implication that the heretic is seen as obstinate by those who disagree with him and vainly try to make him change his mind; in his own eyes, of course, he is neither obstinate nor in error but loyal to his faith. So understood, heresy in any case loses all its terrors, and it is difficult to see how it could ever be a danger to souls.

The second theme was the advocacy of toleration and acceptance of religious differences. Although Castellio did not use the word "toleration" either in this work or elsewhere, his ethical position and all of his reasoning pointed in the direction of a tolerant Christian society. Included in his understanding of toleration was also the perception of intellectual freedom, that is, the freedom to doubt, to question, and to hear differing opinions. He condemns the silencing of argument by calling people heretics and the destruction of the books of heretics, which makes it impossible to know their beliefs and what they can say in their own defense. Against persecution and in behalf of religious toleration he deploys a number of ideas. One is the claim that many things in the Bible and Christian doctrine are obscure and impossible to understand with any certainty, so they inevitably generate controversy. He distinguishes them from the obvious moral truths on which no one disagrees, and from the religious truths all Christians accept as essential to their salvation, such as the role of Christ as savior and redeemer. Castellio, however, is in no way a skeptic in religion, as he is convinced that the fundamental religious and moral teachings of the Christian faith are easily known and understandable to all believers. The distinction between the essential and the obscure, uncertain, and debatable parts of the Christian religion implies a charitable acknowledgment of the legitimacy and inevitability of dissent and differences. Connected with this thought are his statements in favor of mercy, mildness, gentleness, and persuasion, and his severe strictures against judging others. Basically, in accord with his interpretation of the parable of the tares, he holds that the unresolvable points in religious controversies should be left to the judgment of Christ and God alone, who will perhaps reveal the truth at the end of time. Implicit in his attitude to differences is also the recognition of a right of conscience. Although he does not spell this out, it is intimated in his treatment of heresy and heretics. He adumbrates a political condition for toleration in arguing that force is powerless to change belief or touch conscience, and that rulers and magistrates have no authority to judge or punish purely spiritual offenses such as heresy. Such offenses, he believes, can be judged only by the word of God and are punishable at most by excommunication. Finally, it cannot be stressed enough that his desire for toleration was actuated and sustained by deeply felt ethical and humanitarian motives based on the figure and life of Christ. He considered religious persecution to be morally wrong and contrary to Christ's teachings and will. He hated it also because it was cruel and inhumane, and the history of the Christian church had convinced him that the persecutors are invariably the ungodly children of the flesh while the persecuted are among the godly children of the spirit.

THE TOLERATION CONTROVERSY: CASTELLIO VS. CALVIN

Concerning Heretics was only the opening shot in the clash of ideas over heresy and toleration precipitated by the burning of Servetus. Castellio had many enemies in Geneva, foremost of whom was Calvin. He was divided from them not only by his opposition to their treatment of Servetus and heresy but also on the great issue of predestination. Both he and some of his friends in Basel rejected this Calvinist doctrine, which they considered contrary to God's goodness, mercy, wisdom, and desire that all men should be saved. Castellio criticized Calvin's opinion on predestination in some of his tolerationist and theological writings and also in a note in the second (1554) edition of his Latin Bible translation.[47] Needless to say, Calvin's reaction to *Concerning Heretics* was completely negative. He described the work as full of intolerable slanders against God, and he told Heinrich Bullinger, the chief Protestant minister in Zurich, that he hoped its evil influence would be prevented from spreading. To his mind those who produced the book were part of a New Academy (a reference to a Greek school of philosophical skeptics of the second century B.C.E.) who were trying to destroy religion by their unholy liberty of doubting. Calvin's friend and disciple, Theodore Beza, then professor of Greek in Lausanne, reacted similarly. Denouncing the impieties vomited forth in Bellius's preface, he declared that they left nothing intact of the Christian religion. He informed Bullinger of his intention to write a reply to the work in order to refute its blasphemies.[48]

Castellio on his side was determined to carry on the battle against Calvin's intolerance, and in 1554 he wrote an answer to the latter's *Defense of the Orthodox Faith* soon after its appearance. This reply, which was anonymous and bore the title *Contra libellum Calvini* (*Against Calvin's Book*), was never published in the author's lifetime. Castellio probably left it in manuscript because he believed the Basel censorship would have prevented its publication. It was first printed in 1612 in Holland, though without the author's name.[49] Circulated in manuscript, a copy reached Geneva as early as June 1554, whereupon Calvin attributed the work to Castellio.[50] While it is a further defense of toleration, it reflects a very different spirit from that of its predecessor. It is a direct, unsparing attack on Calvin's ideas and good faith, composed in a tone that is sometimes angry, bitter, and accusing. It consists of a very short preface followed by a lengthy dialogue between two characters, Vaticanus, the author's spokesman, and Calvinus— Calvin—whose statements are quoted almost entirely from his *Defense of the Orthodox Faith*. Vaticanus's remarks in the dialogue provide a running critical commentary on each of these excerpts by Calvin. In the preface Castellio explains that he does not defend Servetus's doctrines but shows "the falsity of Calvin's." Hence he will not dispute about the Trinity, baptism, or other difficult questions. He adds that "I have no books by Servetus; Calvin hastened to burn them. Therefore I am not acquainted with the opinions he defends." He himself, however, will not burn Calvin's books but will reproduce the latter's own words and answer them to demonstrate his errors "so that everyone can see them and learn how this author thirsts for blood."[51] The discussion that followed covered a variety of subjects, including some that were previously dealt with in *Concerning Heretics*, although in a far less polemical manner. The work as a whole offered a stinging critique of both Calvin personally and the entire structure of his argument in support of persecution and the execution of Servetus.

One of the dialogue's main points is the evil of Calvin's intolerance of difference. He and his disciples believe that everyone guilty of grave errors in religion is a heretic and should die. They would therefore burn all Christians except Calvinists. Speaking through Vaticanus, Castellio points to Calvin's domination in Geneva and the danger of offending him, which is even greater than the danger of offending the king of France in his palace. "If Christ himself came to Geneva," he says, "he would be crucified. For Geneva is not a place of Christian liberty. It is ruled by a new pope, but one who burns men alive, while the pope at Rome at least strangles them first." Calvin tries to render odious all who differ from him by branding them with such hellish names as atheists, libertines, and Anabaptists. In this way he can gain the victory without his adversaries' ever being heard. He does not follow the scriptural rule of dealing with erring persons mildly and by private admonition. Instead, his admonitions to Servetus consisted first of insults, then imprisonment, and then the stake. Castellio likens him to the wicked Haman in the biblical book of Esther; for just as the latter would have killed the whole Jewish people, so Calvin makes heretics of all who don't think as he does, and would have them killed for differing from him.[52]

Castellio also condemns Calvin's use of force to silence those who disagree with him instead of granting them the right, which he assumes only for himself, "of discussing freely, equal to equal." "If you are right," Castellio declares, "why do you not prove it? Why do you maintain your view by force?" Whereas Servetus had combated Calvin only with his writings, Calvin employed "the sword and the fire" against Servetus. How can he condemn the persecution and massacres committed by the Catholic Church when his own hands are stained with Servetus's blood? Castellio calls upon Calvin to renounce violence and persecution and acknowledge the freedom to speak and write that he has prohibited, and then he will see "what free truth can do."[53]

The obscurity of Scripture is another prominent feature of Castellio's argument. He first notes Calvin's anger that anyone could say the Scriptures are obscure. If they aren't obscure, he replies, why does Calvin write so many commentaries to make them clear? The Geneva reformer writes about them daily, differing from those who have written on the same topics before, and says that he has written his *Institutes of the Christian Religion* as an instrument necessary for the understanding of Scripture. Every day he harangues the people, writes and disputes, always to clarify the Scriptures, which he nevertheless affirms are perfectly clear.[54] It is one of Castellio's basic contentions, however, that parts of the Bible are obscure. In the New Testament, for instance, Christ spoke in parables to those outside the circle of his disciples, while to the latter only did he explain his meaning openly. The Apocalypse is a pure enigma, a closed book that only the Lamb and those who truly fear God can understand. But he also strongly denies that nothing is certain in religion. On the contrary, "everything necessary to our salvation, our obedience, our duty . . . is certain." Thus it is certain that the whole of Scripture is true, and that Jesus is the Christ, the Son of God, and did everything written of him in the New Testament. It is likewise certain that Christians have committed such manifest errors that one can touch them. And equally certain are the precepts of piety, such as the injunctions to love God and one's neighbor, to love one's enemies, to be patient, and other moral duties. But Christians neglect these duties that are known to them, thrusting themselves instead into the work of God as if they were his counselors. Hence "we have many disputes about eternal election, predestination, and the Trinity," from which "are born interminable arguments. And we spill the blood of the unhappy and weak people who do not share our opinions."[55]

The nature of heresy and the wickedness of killing heretics are pervasive themes in Castellio's discussion. The question of who is a heretic and the punishment of heresy, he contends, must be left to God at the Last Judgment in accord with Christ's command in the parable of the tares. In contrast with Calvin's concern that piety and the true church would suffer if heretics were free to utter their beliefs, Castellio repeatedly emphasizes the priority of obedience to Christ's moral precepts of love for others as the principal test of faith. These precepts are certain and all Christians know them, even though they remain ignorant of obscure matters like the Trinity, predestination, and other mysteries that God has kept hidden.[56] He charges that Calvin never defines what a heretic is, and continually confuses heresy with blasphemy and apostasy so that he can kill all those he views as religious malefactors. An apostate, however, is someone who renounces his religion, while a heretic worships the same God as other Christians but adheres to a sect or a false opinion. On Calvin's view, he himself was guilty of apostasy for leaving the Catholic Church and should have been burned for abandoning his faith in the pope. Castellio frequently insists, however, that there is no law of God ordering the killing of heretics, and that heretics are not blasphemers, for "to be mistaken is not to blaspheme."[57] As always he diminishes the significance of heresy, which he equates with obstinacy in maintaining an erroneous opinion, and he protests that Calvin persistently confounds error with impiety. "If a believer understands the words of Christ otherwise than I do, I do not consider him an impious person who wants to overthrow religion." Truly impious people such as blasphemers and contemners of the Scriptures are not heretics. If they deny God, blaspheme, and hate holiness and piety, they are punishable by the magistrate, although not for their religion but for irreligion. In passing, Castellio remarks that he does not defend blasphemers who openly turn away from God and deserve to die. This is the sole instance in which he seems to approve of punishment for an opinion, perhaps because he shares the general conviction of his time that irreligion inevitably leads to immorality and crime. As to heresy, however, he identifies it exclusively with erroneous opinion, and he points out that every religious sect considers other sects as heretics. One of his main contentions is that no one should be killed for their errors, and everyone should await the revelation of the truth.[58]

A fundamental part of Castellio's critique is his denial of Calvin's claim that the magistrate has the duty to support religion with the sword. To Calvin's statement that kings and magistrates are obliged to defend the true doctrine, he makes the following classic answer: "To kill a man is not to defend a doctrine, it is to kill a man. When the Genevans killed Servetus, they did not defend a doctrine, they killed a man." The defense of doctrine, he holds, "is not the business of the magistrate (what does the sword have to do with doctrine?)," but that of the learned. The magistrate's business is rather to protect the people under his jurisdiction against injustice.[59] Castellio strives consistently to demarcate the realm of the spiritual from the secular and to limit the civil government's power over religion. He maintains that the magistrate has no jurisdiction in spiritual matters nor any obligation to enforce the Mosaic law, since this law has been superseded by Christ's spiritual law of love and charity. Magistracy exists to prevent men from doing evil, and when the magistrate punishes crimes such as homicide or adultery, he upholds not the law of Moses but the law of nature and equity. Whereas the magistrate punishes actions, God punishes the thought; the magistrate is concerned with the body, God with the soul, and "not to distinguish" these two domains "is to confuse everything." After quoting Calvin's statement that a just government cannot neglect piety and religion if it is to preserve a legitimate order among men, Castellio comments that "a legitimate order" is one in which "the pastor occupies himself with souls and the magistrate with bodies."[60]

Finally, threaded through Castellio's dialogue is a clear recognition of the epistemological problem of subjective conscientious conviction as an argument against persecution. Calvin, Castellio observes, had Servetus put to death for speaking the truth, since he said what he thought was true even if he was mistaken. All people believe in the truth of their religion; none ever say their religion is false. While Calvin claims certainty for his religion, so likewise do many sects, who persecute each other because they think the religion of the others is false. Calvin, however, has made himself the sole judge over all of them. But who appointed him to this office of judge so that

> he has the sole right of condemning others to die? What judgment allows him to say that he alone knows? He invokes the word of God? So do the others. If the thing is so certain, for whom is it certain? For Calvin. But then the others think it is certain for them. . . . Why are there people ready to die for their belief in a second baptism and other matters of this kind, when they avow and revere the Holy Scriptures?

These considerations bring Castellio once again to the tolerant conclusion that many things in religion are unclear and controversial, with the evident implication that differences and alleged errors must be charitably permitted.[61]

An account such as the one above can hardly do justice to the cumulative polemical force of Castellio's reasoning in *Against Calvin's Book*. He was a formidable controversialist who advanced a variety of arguments—religious, theological, moral, and philosophical—to pick apart and refute the claims and assumptions on which Calvin based his justification of persecution. He may sometimes exaggerate and is prone to the use of reductio ad absurdum, but he never misrepresents or distorts Calvin's meaning.[62] In arguing his case, he quotes nothing except the Bible and repeatedly invokes the precepts of love and charity in the New Testament. What emerges from his dialogue is the rationale for a tolerant community and a pluralism in which peaceable religious bodies can freely coexist. He makes no attempt, of course, to work out the problems connected with the relationship between civil government and religion, which in an age of state churches, and one as religious as the sixteenth century, were exceptionally complex. His denial of the magistrate's right to punish religious opinions and spiritual offenses went very much against the grain of his time. He is convinced, however, that persecution does great harm to religion, and understands clearly that toleration and religious liberty are impossible without limitations on the magistrate's authority over religion. His denunciation of the destruction of Servetus's writings is evidence of his dedication to the principle of free discussion of religious differences. He opposes the suppression of unorthodox opinions; heretics should be permitted to defend their views, and he seems to think that the truth is most likely to emerge if Christians are able to debate their differences freely and openly. He regards the moral fruits of religious belief as much more important than doctrine. Christianity for him consists primarily in living according to the precepts of Christ. Its fundamental spiritual and moral truths, moreover, are certain and known, especially that Christ is the savior, and these suffice for unity and peace. He also recognizes the significance of conscientious conviction where the truth is uncertain as a major reason for toleration. The heretic is neither impious, an apostate, nor a blasphemer. He is someone who adheres obstinately to an erroneous opinion, yet to him his opinion is not an error but true. And considering that many religious questions are obscure and the subject of interminable disputes, how can one determine which opinions are erroneous on subjects like the Trinity, baptism, and predestination and free will? Since all Christian denominations believe their religion is the true one, and only God and Christ can finally judge among them, they should all be permitted to believe as they would.

Castellio's championship of toleration as the author of *Concerning Heretics* and *Against Calvin's Book* makes it understandable why both Calvin and Beza detested him for many years as a thorn in their side. In comparison with the small number of persons, however, mostly historians and scholars, who have ever heard of Castellio, millions of Christians know the name of Calvin. Calvin's work as the founder of one of the great branches of Protestantism was a monumental achievement that had enduring consequences in Western culture. It is impossible, though, to estimate his place in history without taking into full account the import of his defense of persecution and his personal responsibility for Servetus's death. Despite the intolerant spirit of the age, the approval and practice of religious persecution by the Protestant Calvin—the leader of a religious body whose members were themselves perse-

cuted in Italy, France, Spain, the Netherlands, Germany, and elsewhere in Europe—were very diffferent from the persecutions undertaken by the Catholic Church and governments. As for
Castellio's criticisms of Calvin, we must remember that he knew
the reformer well. He had worked with him, talked and argued
with him, and observed him closely in both Strasbourg and Geneva. His words in *Against Calvin's Book* must be given full weight as
an exposure of Calvin's self-righteous dogmatism and rigid, dominating character, his contempt and hatred of religious dissent,
and his readiness to set aside all pleas of humanity and mercy in
the interest of preserving religious orthodoxy.

THE TOLERATION CONTROVERSY:
CASTELLIO VS. BEZA

Born in France into a noble family, educated in Bourges and Orléans, where he studied law in preparation for a career in the Catholic Church, Theodore Beza (1519–1605) achieved an early reputation as a humanist poet and scholar. After his conversion to
Protestantism in 1548 and the life change it entailed, he settled
in the Swiss Protestant city of Lausanne, where he taught Greek.
In 1559 he was called to Geneva as head of the newly founded
Geneva Academy. A disciple and confidant of Calvin, he succeeded the latter after his death in 1564 as the leader of the Geneva church. He was well known as a religious poet, biblical translator, theologian, and political theorist who attained great prestige
as a prominent spokesman of European Calvinism and as an influential figure in the French Reformed Church before and during the religious civil war that began in France in 1562.[63]

Beza regarded Castellio's *Concerning Heretics* as a blasphemous
and sacrilegious work and lost no time in issuing a refutation. His
rejoinder, published in Geneva in September 1554 and printed
in 1560 in a French translation, was called *De haereticis a civili magistratu puniendis libellus, adversus Martini Bellii farraginem, & No-
vorum Academicorum sectam* (*Concerning the Punishment of Heretics by*

the Civil Magistrate, a Book against the Farrago of Martin Bellius and the Sect of New Academics). The reference in its title to the New Academics shows that, like Calvin, he was determined to associate Martin Bellius, the pseudonymous compiler and author of *Concerning Heretics,* with the school of skeptical philosophers of classical antiquity who might be thought inimical to a religion based on dogma. Beza's was a strong but conventional mind whose book offered no new reasons for its intolerant position. It was an eloquent reaffirmation of the Christian theory of persecution, buttressed with examples from the Bible and Christian history, which attacked each of Castellio's arguments in order to prove that the magistrate had the duty and right to punish and execute heretics.

Beza gave heresy a very wide meaning, explaining that it had come to signify more than the original Greek word. It referred to those who erred but let themselves be taught and others who, despite admonition, obstinately resisted the truth and disrupted the peace and unity of the church with their false teaching. The kinds of heretics were almost limitless; among them he included infidels, the ignorant, apostates, those who departed from the truth, disturbers of the church, and others. The magistrate does not, of course, decide himself what is heresy, but executes the judgments of the church. Beza based the magistrate's duty of punishing heresy on the main purpose of civil society, which was that men should live in peace and serve and honor God as their supreme obligation. Without the power to suppress those whose heresies undermined religion, the magistrate could neither protect the church nor ensure the true service of God. The only distinction Beza made between heresy and the civil crimes punishable by the magistrate was that heresy was far more heinous. Indeed, there could not be a worse crime; far worse than parricide, it was an extreme danger to society and an enormity for which no penalty could be adequate. Hence the denial of the magistrate's authority to protect religion and punish heresy amounted to contempt for the word of God and threatened the utter ruin of the church. Beza did not think the parable of the tares forbade the punishment of those whose guilt was beyond doubt, or that heretics deserved the love or patience preached by the apostle Paul. It was a cruel and diabolical kind of charity, he held, to expose the sheep of Christ as prey to the wolf, and to allow the contagion of heresy to spread for the sake of sparing the life of a single man. Ridiculing the notion that willingness to die for an opinion was proof of its truth, he refused to countenance the view that the beliefs of an erring and misguided conscience could have any immunity from the magistrate's authority. He was outraged by Bellius's claim that dogmas like the Trinity, long held by the church, should still be considered controversial, uncertain, and undecidable by Scripture. "You number the Trinity," he told the New Academics, "among the matters that need not be known, and if known make man no better. What can we call you but new devils who would drive God from the throne?" It seemed to him that nothing could exceed the wickedness of this skeptical position, whose spokesmen were emissaries of Satan and whose doubts about the necessity of believing fundamental doctrines of the church left nothing of religion intact. Beza saw no reason himself to question these doctrines. The only way to Christ, he averred, is through faith, and faith included all the dogmas Bellius and the New Academics considered uncertain and unnecessary.[64]

Upon reading Beza's book, Castellio felt bound to respond to its arguments and criticisms. This reply, which was completed in March 1555, was his third major treatise in the cause of religious toleration. It gave the author's name as Basil Montfort, one of the pseudonyms he had used in *Concerning Heretics*, and was entitled *De haereticis a civili magistratu non puniendis, pro Martini Bellii farragine, adversus libellum Theodori Bezae, libellus* (*Concerning the Nonpunishment of Heretics by the Civil Magistrate, a Book in Support of the Farrago of Martin Bellius against the Book of Theodore Beza*). I shall refer to it as *Against the Punishment of Heretics*. After he finished it, a French translation, probably his own, appeared. Although it would have been read in manuscript copies, the work remained unprinted during the author's lifetime and long afterward. Following the discovery of the original manuscripts in the 1930s, it was first published in both the Latin and French versions in 1971.[65] Anticipation of censorship—on the assumption that the Basel authorities would disapprove the appearance of a polemic against the Geneva estab-lishment—was probably the reason Castellio left it unpublished.[66]

Against the Punishment of Heretics is a brave, outspoken, and painstaking interrogation of Beza's views. It addresses him di-rectly, attacking not only each of his theses but his personal failings as a Christian. Castellio explained to the reader that he was forced to answer the many calumnies and misrepresentations of Beza, a formidable and eloquent opponent, because otherwise the latter might seem to have won the day. Although his work has no system-atic order and repeats many of the arguments in his preceding writings, it is valuable as a fuller reply to the charge of religious skepticism and adds to his thoughts on heresy and to his earlier account of the magistrate's relationship to religion. Over the whole work hung the long shadow of Servetus's recent execution, which it frequently mentioned as a signal example of the cruelty and injustice of religious persecution against which Castellio had protested from the beginning. In writing it, he indicates that he felt himself outnumbered by powerful enemies, the "Calvinians," as he calls them, "the Scribes and Pharisees of our time," who chose Beza as their spokesman and did all they could to silence their opponents. More than once he explains why the authors who condemned Servetus's trial and execution were obliged to use pseudonyms to conceal their identity. It was because Calvin and Beza wanted to kill heretics and treated as heretics all who dis-agreed with them. "You reprehend us," he says, "for not revealing our names so that being known, we can be reduced to the same ashes as Servetus. Have we not most just cause to dissemble our names since you conduct your dispute with the sword?"[67] In the course of the work he often calls Beza an unscrupulous rhetorician who speaks more like a Ciceronian than a Christian, a man to whom eloquence is dearer than truth, and who has mastered the Ciceronian art of speaking as easily against truth as for it.[68]

While Beza depicted his opponents as "the New Academics" in order to discredit them, Castellio defended these ancient skeptics as "the best sect among philosophers." It was their resistance to

pretended knowledge and the dogmatic presumption of certainty
that he valued. Their first founder, he pointed out, was Socrates,
praised for his wisdom in saying, "I know that I know nothing."
He compares Socrates' "prudent ignorance" with the "light and
rash knowledge" of the philosophers whom Beza follows, the Aris-
totelians, who failed miserably in all that they affirmed. Aristotle,
thinking he knew everything, taught that the world was uncreated
and other falsities, and such were "the fruits of the science of those
who want to affirm everything." The Jews, being likewise puffed
up by their science, killed the prophets of God, the apostles, and
the Son of God himself, something they could not have done had
they doubted about things that were uncertain. In the present age,
those who think everything is certain and clear when they encounter others who disagree with them are the ones who often put
good and innocent people to death for heresy. Beza was greatly
mistaken, Castellio avers, in supposing that to doubt of uncertain
things is a new doctrine. Not only did many good and wise men
subscribe to it, but it was commanded by Christ, who said, "Judge
not that you be not judged," and by Saint Paul, who in speaking
of uncertain things forbade judging before time. Beza shows his
malice by attacking Bellius and his supporters as New Academics
if they doubt and denouncing them as heretics if they affirm.[69]

Castellio reiterated his conviction that a Christian has no need
of knowledge of recondite doctrines like the Trinity and predestination in order to attain salvation. The way Christians know and
come to Christ is by amending their lives, not by disputing about
Christ's office and whether the Holy Spirit proceeded from the
Father and the Son. Contrary to Beza's claim, knowledge of such
matters does not make anyone better. Moreover, when people
carry on disputes over these obscure and difficult questions that
have troubled the church for centuries, they become worse if they
lack charity. If Beza thinks the Scriptures are not obscure but clear
and manifest, what reason has he for writing so many commentaries to explain their meaning? In his opposition to the Calvinist
doctrine of predestination, Castellio charged that Beza himself
distorted the plain sense of Scripture even in passages where the

meaning was manifest. Saint Paul, for example, affirmed clearly
that God desires all men to be saved (1 Tim. 2:4), and Saint Peter
wrote that God wishes no sinner to perish, and that all should be
received to repentance (2 Pet. 3:9). Beza nevertheless miscon-
strues these statements, saying to the contrary that God created a
certain number of people whom he decided to damn and who
can never be saved. As his answer to the imputation of religious
skepticism, Castellio denies that he disbelieves in truth, and carefully circumscribes the scope of doubt. Of course, the truth exists,
he declares, but Beza does not know it because he is too full of
hatred to understand the Scriptures. To the challenge of how he
could prove the existence of an eternal, all-powerful God, he re-
sponds that God's existence is not in doubt or dispute, nor is the
veracity of the Scriptures. The points in doubt are the ones debated on account of the obscurity of Scripture. As always he rele-
gates doctrine to a secondary place in the Christian scheme compared with the importance of modeling one's life on the example
of the savior Christ. "[D]octrine," he asserted, "is useless without
morals." Beza, who is so quick to condemn others because of obscure questions, pays no heed to the commandments to love one's
neighbor, to do good to enemies, and not to return evil with evil.
These latter are so clear that they were never in doubt, and all
sects accept them. But instead of concentrating on such things,
on which salvation depends, Beza troubles the world with matters
in dispute and contention.[70]

He summed up his position on the problem of Christian knowledge, certainty, and doubt in the following passage:

> I say that the Scriptures are partly clear and partly unclear.
> The commandments are clear: not to kill, or steal, or bear
> false witness . . . to follow Christ by faith, to bear the cross . . .
> these and the rest are all plainly stated. It is necessary to begin
> with faith and exercise the love and fear of God in order to
> achieve greater knowledge. . . . Christians do not disagree on
> these basic things which are clear, even though they may de-
> bate some other things that are obscure.

He explained further that it was no injury to God to say that his witnesses and oracles are obscure, because it was God's glory to speak so that only his own children would understand him. This was why Christ spoke obscurely in parables and similitudes to the people who were not his followers, while to his followers he spoke otherwise. He attains an almost mystical note in concluding that only those who, unlike Beza, possess Christ's spirit of charity can understand the divine secrets contained in the Scripture and judge of controversial matters.[71]

On the political question of the relationship between civil government and religion, Castellio once more attacked Calvin's and Beza's view that the magistrate had the care of religion and the right of punishing heresy. They favored this arrangement, he contended, because they wanted magistracy on their side in order to overcome their adversaries in Geneva and elsewhere. He warned, however, that if kings and magistrates exercised the care of religion, there would be no "freedom of religion [*libre religion*]."[72] He does concede that the magistrate is authorized to repress offenses like the manifest blasphemy of denial that God exists, because these are contrary to the law of nature known to all nations. But crimes of this kind, which are recognized by the common sense of all nations, do not need to be identified by theologians. The magistrate has no authority, however, to punish heretics, a claim Castellio bases on the fundamental distinction between the spiritual and the secular. The Christian's war is a spiritual one waged only with spiritual weapons. The sword of the magistrate is given him by God in the law of nature and the law of Moses to suppress evildoers and punish civil crimes like theft. For such crimes he may execute an offender, whether Jew, Turk, or Christian. But there is also another sword, the sword of Christ, which is made not of iron but of Christ's living word in the gospel. Christ rules his kingdom not as the world is ruled but through the power of righteousness, which conquers sin by the word. When Christ's kingdom comes, there will be neither swords nor magistrates, only eternal righteousness. Meanwhile the magistrate is necessary as the ordinance of God who may not be resisted, but whose jurisdiction is restricted to civil crimes. Only the sword of Christ, therefore, is competent to deal with heresy.[73]

Castellio denied that he favored heretics and repeated Bellius's earlier statement that "we hate heretics," adding that if they are really heretics, they should be excommunicated. But he indicted the terrible persecution of the Anabaptists and the defamation of many good people as heretics. He reinforced his opposition to the punishment of heretics by insisting against Beza that heresy is a vice, not a crime. The magistrate is concerned only with crimes, whereas vices, which hurt the soul, pertain exclusively to God, since the civil or corporal sword cannot affect the soul. While the magistrate's task is to protect bodies from injury, the spiritual sword has cognizance of the injuries done to the soul. He also noted that if the magistrate were free to use compulsion in religion, then the Lutherans could compel the Calvinists with the aid of the magistrate, and the Calvinists could compel the Lutherans in like manner. Although Beza maintains that what he enforces is the true religion, the other denominations make the same claim, and there is no way of providing a judge or a sign by which everyone can tell who is right.[74] It is significant in this connection that Castellio found nothing persuasive in Saint Augustine's argument in favor of religious coercion that "those are made willing who are constrained despite themselves." He rejects this view because constraint in religion is contrary to Scripture and forces people to pretend to believe. We must, he said, "obey God rather than Saint Augustine."[75]

In his interpretation of the parable of the tares, he again narrowed and relativized the meaning of heresy. He explains that Christ will pardon all the sins of those who repent except the sin against the Holy Spirit. The latter, the only sin that incurs damnation, consists of obstinately opposing the truth or refusing to acknowledge it even though one knows it in one's heart. The tares, or weeds, in the parable are sinners of this kind who will be condemned at the harvest, or Last Judgment. Heretics, on the other hand, are not guilty of this sin, because they speak the truth as they know it. While they may err, they cannot be condemned if they do, for people never willingly suffer for a belief they think false. Heretics accept death because they refuse to speak against their conscience. This is the reason Calvin and Beza, completely lacking in charity, want to punish them, despite the fact that their error, if any, is due to ignorance. Although Beza claims that a bad conscience is always united with heresy, he does not know the secret of hearts yet presumes to sit in judgment. Those who differ from Beza consider him among the tares, of course, and would kill him and his brethren if they followed his principles. By their readiness to kill heretics, Calvinists thus put themselves in the place of God and anticipate the final judgment.[76]

Castellio's understanding of the authority of the magistrate is dictated less by political interests than by an abiding concern for the principle of religious liberty, to which his belief in toleration is closely related. Accordingly, he defends Bellius against Beza's censure for "wanting Christians to have the liberty of saying what they think," commenting that without this liberty "the errors of the century" would never have been exposed. Because he wishes to leave "religion in liberty," he deplores the "alliance" between churches and the civil magistrate and princes, which is responsible for all the blood spilled for religion. Calvin and Beza are like their brothers, the Scribes and Pharisees who delivered Christ to Pilate; their aim is to use the magistrate to punish those they deem heretics in order to maintain and extend their tyranny.[77] He conceives the Christian magistrate's authority as concerned exclusively with the civil order common to all nations and not peculiar to Christians. As Christ enjoined men to render to Caesar what is Caesar's and to God what is God's, so Christians owe obedience to the magistrate only in civil matters; in religious and divine things, their obedience is due solely to God.[78] This latter was a conventional Protestant tenet but was not commonly understood to mean that the magistrate had no responsibility for the care of the church and religion. Castellio used it deviantly, however, to posit the separation of civil from religious and ecclesiastical jurisidiction, and to argue that the sole punishment for heretics (by which he meant those who remain obstinate after admonition by the church) should be excommunication without any further penalty. Just as guilds and corporations, he noted, may punish their own members for some fault without the intervention of the magistrate or any danger of ensuing anarchy, so should the church alone deal with those it considers heretics.[79]

Arriving at what he calls "the conclusion of the whole dispute," Castellio gave voice to a passionate exhortation against the unjust practice of religious persecution. He condemns the leaders of the Swiss churches who approved the execution of Servetus, the hatred and dissensions dividing Calvinists, Lutherans, and other Christians, and the killing of many God-fearing people in Italy, France, Germany, Spain, and England under the name of heretics. He warns the persecutors who flatter themselves with their domination that God would make them repent if they persevered in their blind error. The work ends with an epilogue listing all the logical fallacies Beza has committed, followed by some comments on the recent internal conflicts in Geneva. The final sentence is the fitting biblical quotation "Arise, O Lord, plead thine own cause" (Ps. 74:22).[80]

Against the Punishment of Heretics is a thoroughgoing critique, on very largely Christian grounds, of the entire theory of religious persecution. While Castellio retains a residual conception of heresy, he diminishes its significance to such an extent that it can no longer be considered a peril to Christian society. Beyond the essential principles of the Christian faith and moral conduct that are clear and unmistakable, he looks upon doctrinal disagreements as conflicting versions of truth inevitable among Christians because of the obscurity and uncertainty of parts of Scripture. Like Sebastian Franck, he holds that no one but Christ at the Last Judgment can decide who is a heretic. His understanding of heresy thus deprives it of any absolute content or meaning, since there is no orthodoxy against which it can be measured, and because Christian denominations will differ in their definitions of doctrinal error. What he emphasizes most is the necessity of charity and tolerance toward religious difference as a moral imperative of the Christian faith itself. There can be no question that he considers the persecution and killing of heretics to be profoundly anti-Christian. One of his uppermost concerns, accordingly, is freedom of religion—that is, freedom to believe and to express one's belief without fear or danger. It is for the sake of toleration coupled with this freedom that he strives to mark the boundary between the civil order and religion; he maintains that princes and magistrates have no authority over spiritual offenses, which belong to the realm of faith or belief, and hence no right to punish heresy.

Some may imagine that Castellio's aspiration toward a religiously tolerant political order makes him a thinker who was far ahead of his time. This, however, seems to me to be a mistaken view. While it is true that he fought against his time in contesting the intellectual and religious rationale for the persecution of dissent, he was nevertheless in essential respects a man of his time. He was very definitely a Christian humanist in the Erasmian mold but one who went much further than Erasmus. A devout though highly unorthodox Protestant of the age of the Reformation with strong leanings toward Spiritualism, Castellio was a thinker who found in the intellectual traditions and religious faith of his own era the resources to promulgate and defend the principle of toleration against such redoubtable opponents as Calvin and Beza.

CASTELLIO'S LAST COMBATS AND
FINAL TOLERATIONIST WRITINGS

Castellio's life was never free of strife and controversy. Although during his remaining years, which were filled with intense intellectual activity and scholarly work, he wrote on many subjects, he was frequently compelled to defend himself against his relentless adversaries in Geneva and some opponents in Basel as well. Beza and Calvin, who did their best to make his position in Basel untenable, attacked him abusively for his work as a biblical scholar and his theological convictions. In 1557, he wrote a defense of his biblical translations in response to Beza, but the Basel censor refused to allow its publication until 1562 and even then permitted it to appear only with important passages deleted.[81] Because he could discover no justification in the New Testament for the doctrine of predestination, some of the theologians in Basel charged him with denying the divine inspiration of Saint Paul's writings. In November 1557 their dispute with him was brought before the city council. To this official body he expressed his opinion that the Holy Spirit had inspired Paul's letters, and that he was unable to conceive that God had predestined some souls to damnation. He was cleared owing to the main part of his statement, which avowed that he would await Christ's will, would condemn no one who disagreed with him, and wished to live in peace with all Christians and not to disturb the church.[82] In 1558 he replied to attacks in separate tracts by Calvin and Beza in which they upheld the doctrine of predestination against the "calumnies" of its critics. His answer, circulated in manuscript and not printed until 1578, contained an appendix appealing to the Geneva theologians to renounce their intolerance and allow others to differ with them without being called impious. On his own behalf he pleaded "by the blood of Christ" that they cease persecuting him. "Grant me the freedom," he asked, "to believe and profess my faith . . . just as you would like me to leave you in freedom, which I do." He urged them also not to judge those who disagreed with them, who included many pious people. On the main points of religion, he added, "I do not differ from you. I want to serve in my way the same religion that you do. . . . We all err . . . so let us therefore get on in a friendly manner."[83]

Castellio's resistance to Calvinist orthodoxy was an important part of his thought. His main theological work was his *Dialogi IIII* (*Four Dialogues*), written in the later 1550s and posthumously published, which dealt with predestination, election, free will, and faith.[84] These dialogues were designed to contest Calvin's theology. They feature two fictional speakers, one representing Castellio's point of view, the other Calvin's. Castellio refused to accept the Calvinist denial of human free will and its deterministic conception of predestination founded upon God's absolute sovereignty and arbitrary decree at the time of the creation to elect some human beings to salvation and others to damnation. Convinced by his own examination of the biblical texts, he strenuously defended free will and human responsibility as indispensable conditions of salvation. Because God was a God of reason and love, Castellio could not credit him with an arbitrary will or think of him as the author of sin in his creatures for which they were to be eternally punished. God desired that all should be saved, and since he commanded nothing that was impossible, every human being through faith and with the aid of the Holy Spirit could strive to obey his commands. Salvation was therefore possible for all Christians.[85] Castellio's critical rejection of the Calvinist doctrine of predestination as contrary to reason and Scripture contained a strong strain of rationalism and reflected his allegiance to the Christian humanist tradition—the tradition that Erasmus had exemplified when he argued against Luther in favor of free will.[86] It stood likewise in close complementarity to his indictment of religious persecution and of Calvin's intolerance. Castellio's conviction that differing opinions should be allowed to express themselves freely, along with his emphasis on conformity to Christ's moral precepts as the true test and fruit of faith, made it impossible for him to believe in the God of Calvin, who meted out damnation to some of his creatures irrespective of how they lived or whether they sought to follow the example of Christ.

Castellio's last literary contributions to the tolerationist controversy were his *Conseil a la France désolée* (*Advice to a Desolate France*) and *De arte dubitandi et confidendi ignorandi et sciendi* (*The Art of Doubting, Believing, Being Ignorant, and Knowing*). The first, a short work published anonymously in 1562, was a tract for the times in the most immediate sense. An appeal for sanity against violence, it appeared soon after France had plunged into religious civil war, and called for tolerant coexistence to stop the French Catholics and Protestant Calvinists, or Huguenots, from slaughtering each other.[87] When copies of the book reached Geneva, they were suppressed.[88] Although earlier voices, like that of the chancellor Michel de L'Hopital, had been raised in France to arrest the drift toward a war of religion, they were all the expressions of Catholics who were politically motivated to advocate a restricted tolerance for Protestant worship to save the kingdom from a destructive civil war. While these writers also stressed that conscience was not subject to compulsion, their primary concern was for the unity and welfare of the state.[89] Castellio was the first author at this juncture to plead for confessional tolerance in France principally on the religious and moral ground of respect for conscience and not only for pragmatic reasons.[90]

His analysis of the conflict identified its essential cause as "the forcing of consciences," for which he blamed Catholics and Protestants equally. Beside arguing that religious persecution was contrary to Christ's teaching and never approved in Scripture, he emphasized that the evil advice given to princes and judges to punish heretics must result in endless war. To readers on both sides of the religious divide he declared that the only way to combat heretics was with the words of truth, which were always more powerful than lies. The sole remedy for the nation's miseries, he maintained, was "to settle the differences," "allow the two religions to remain free," and permit "two churches . . . in France." Summing up his advice at the conclusion of his tract, he urged France to "cease the forcing of consciences . . . stop persecution . . . and rather allow those who believe in Christ and . . . accept the Old and the New Testament, to serve God in your country, not in accordance with the beliefs of others, but in accordance with their own."[91]

Always among the points at issue in the controversies between Castellio and his opponents was his way of reading the Bible. One of the most momentous innovations of the Protestant Reformation was to make the word of God in the Scriptures the sole rule in questions of faith. It thereby rejected the Catholic belief that the tradition and doctrinal authority of the divinely founded church and papacy were coequal with Scripture as a source of religious truth. The Protestant principle of *sola scriptura*, the exclusive supremacy of Scripture, seemed in theory to open the door to an uncontrolled, unlimited freedom of interpretation by individual believers and sects. In fact, the mainline Protestant churches, Lutheran, Calvinist, and Anglican, averted this consequence to a con-

siderable extent by adopting formal confessions of faith and articles of religion that defined orthodoxy for them; in effect, they
made their own interpretations authoritative. Castellio's attitude
to Scripture, however, presumed an independence of all ecclesiastical authority. Standing for personal freedom of interpretation,
he held that the reverent and inquiring believer who lived a Christian life was qualified, with the help of the Holy Spirit, to conduct
his own search into the meaning of sacred text without the need
of authority. Nothing angered Calvin and Beza more than his
claim that parts of the Bible were obscure and their meaning uncertain. While they were determined to inculcate orthodoxy as the
truth to which Christians must conform, he tried to show the place
of doubt in religion and the study of the Bible.

His final work, *The Art of Doubting*, tackled the subject of doubt,
as well as those of belief, ignorance, and knowledge. This remarkable composition was probably begun in 1563, the year of his
death, and was left unfinished. After surviving in manuscript for
more than four centuries, it was at last published in full in 1981.[92]
Divided into two books of short chapters preceded by a preface,
it was an attempt to present the result of his prolonged reflection
on the widespread existence of religious dissensions and the problem of how anyone could claim to possess the truth in religion.
Although mainly a theological treatise and filled with biblical citations, it is also the most philosophical of his writings and a defense
of both toleration and reason in religion. The word "art" in the
title is important. As the preface states, the book's principal aim
is to show how to determine what things are appropriate to doubt
and to believe, and which ones need not be known, as contrasted
with those that must. It also explains that the art of doubting is
essential because men often sin owing to the fact that they believe
where they should doubt, doubt where they should believe, are
ignorant of what they should know, and think they know what is
unknown and can remain so without affecting their salvation.[93]

The opening chapters of the first book are mainly concerned
with establishing the divine authority and truth of Scripture. We
may pass over them and come at once to the discussion of

doubting. It begins with the claim that Christians need to know what to doubt and what to believe as beyond doubt. Those who would doubt nothing and assert everything boldly, Castellio says, also damn without doubt those who differ from them, and do not doubt the validity of calling someone an Academic who thinks that nothing can be certain or assured. To this last charge he answers, "I in truth hold more for certain than they would like. . . . For . . . I am certain that in affirming all things boldly and damning those who disagree with their opinion, they are very rash." The reason for doubting is that it is dangerous to consider uncertain things as certain; and that some things are uncertain is proved by the innumerable books and continual contentions about these things. Since men do not dispute about what is certain and assured, the conclusion is evident that uncertain things should be doubted. The evils, moreover, that come from not doubting what should be doubted are as great as those that come from not believing what should be believed. Had the Israelites doubted, they would not have killed so many prophets and Christ himself; and if Christians and the Christian churches of the present day doubted, they would not put the most holy men to death and commit so many wicked murders for which they will soon have to repent.[94]

Castellio next explains how to distinguish the doubtful from the certain and what need not be known from what ought to be known. Doubtful things are conjectures that may have some probability but cannot be known through the senses or intellect, or are not transmitted by authors worthy of belief. Those things are certain that are clearly and perspicuously transmitted by credible authors and do not contradict the senses or intellect. In this latter category was Saint Paul's statement (1 Cor. 6:9–10) that neither fornicators, idolaters, nor the covetous will inherit the kingdom of heaven. What should be known are the things necessary for the knowledge of God and man's duty. Of other things it is permissible to be ignorant. Thus while Christians may be ignorant of many things, they cannot fail to know the precepts of charity on which all of Christ's teaching depends, because these are naturally known to all human beings. Even the impious know them, because

they are written into the hearts of everyone and belong to the
common notions of the mind. Therefore what men need to know,
which is the way to salvation, they can know easily. The publicans
and sinners who were taught by Christ were saved, even though
they were ignorant and had never heard of the disputed questions
that lacerate the present-day churches.[95]

Castellio then goes on to demonstrate that many things have
been left obscure in Scripture, with the result that the theological
controversies which divide Christians have no conclusion. He argues that the senses and the intellect provide the proper instrument of judgment in dealing with these controversies. Faith has
no duty to believe what is contrary to the senses and the nature of
things, for then nothing would be so absurd, impossible, or false
that it could not be believed. While allowing that there are things
"above the senses" which the latter cannot perceive, he maintains
that all opinions contrary to the senses are to be rejected as false.
Christ never differed from other men in his judgment of colors
or tastes and never said or did anything contrary to the senses or
intellect; had he spoken to people as if they lacked senses and
intellect, no one would have believed him. Pursuing this theme,
Castellio is critical of those (he has Calvin in mind) who want
people to believe with closed eyes what is contrary to the senses
or to reason. The importance he assigns to reason in judging theological and other claims carries him on to a striking panegyric of
reason as "the daughter of God," who existed

> before all writings and ceremonies and even before the cre-
> ation of the world, and . . . will be always after writings and
> ceremonies have passed away and . . . the world is renewed
> and changed. God can no more abolish her than he can abol-
> ish himself. Reason . . . is like the eternal speech of God, far
> older and more certain than writings and ceremonies, . . . by
> which he taught his people before there were any writings or
> ceremonies.

Reason is thus "the discoverer and interpreter of truth." If something in either profane or sacred writings is obscure or changed

by time, reason either clarifies it or puts it in doubt until the truth manifests itself or it is conclusively judged to be uncertain.[96]

In support of this position, Castellio takes great pains to deny the objection that Adam's sin corrupted the senses and intellect of mankind. He calls this opinion, held by Calvin and before him by Saint Augustine,[97] an old error unsupported by any sacred author and contradicted by reason and experience. But while insisting that man's senses and reason have not been vitiated by the Fall and remain sound and whole, he points out that certain impediments affect their exercise. Of these, the main one lies in the will, which can cause men to avoid using their judgment to discern the truth. Reason is therefore "corrupted by disease when the intellect is affected in such a way that it is blind and unable to see or know the truth." Castellio is very interested in analyzing the nature of this disease and its effects. It is produced, he explains, by the "carnal affections," a sin he attributes to his opponents, which prevents them from judging correctly. The "carnal affections," by creating "disturbances of the mind," make one unable to weigh an opposing opinion fairly or even to follow it. They result in mental obstinacy; the "obstinate man sticks to his opinion and can hear or see nothing contrary to it, and if God and all his saints and angels speak against it, he prefers to condemn [them] rather than change his opinion." Their source is self-love, which leads to a desire for victory rather than truth and an inability to see another person's argument. In all contentions and wars, he states, "we always see blindness and obstinacy arising from love of self," and unless men learn to hate themselves, they will remain incurable. They must learn to see their own uncleanness as they see that of others. He tells his readers that if they "do this with a mind desirous of truth and ready to follow it whether it agrees with [their] opinion or not," they will "find some light of truth . . . and give thanks to God as the father of light."[98]

The above discussion, which teaches when to doubt and examines the prejudiced, dogmatic mind-set that renders discussion futile and bars the search for truth, occupies the first book of *The Art of Doubting*. In the second book Castellio applies his method

to some controversial theological questions—the Trinity, the nature of faith, justification, and the Eucharist, which he examines
by the criterion of whether they can or cannot be decided by the
senses and reason in relation to the reason and authority of Scripture. As always he proceeds by distinguishing the necessary from
the inessential in belief. On the Trinity, for example, he observes
that although it has been thought a belief necessary for salvation,
it was unknown to the publicans and sinners whom Christ taught,
and is not mentioned in Scripture. Putting the Trinitarian doctrine to the test of reason, he finds it wanting. One person cannot
be three persons, nor can three persons be one; if a man is a citizen, a tailor, and a father, he is not three persons; it is absurd to
say that when the Father begot the Son, he begot himself, or that
when he sent the Son and Holy Spirit, he sent himself; God and
nature, the speech of every nation, grammar, dialectic, and arith-
metic all teach that three are three and one is one, and if there
are three, there cannot be one, and if one, there cannot be three.
Accordingly, to believe in the doctrine of the Trinity, one would
have to "bid farewell to reason, the greatest gift of God" to man;
but "it is impossible to believe without reason, and those without
reason can believe nothing." For himself he states that his own
faith is in God, in his Son Jesus Christ, and in the Holy Spirit; this is
the simple faith given by the apostles that is sufficient for salvation
"without [our] needing to know or believe inexplicable things introduced after the time of apostolic simplicity."[99] In his disbelief
in and critique of the doctrine of the Trinity, Castellio was one of
the foremost precursors of the Antitrinitarian Socinian movement
that emerged in the late sixteenth century as the ancestor of modern Unitarianism.[100]

There is no need to discuss his comments on the other theological issues except to note that on nearly all of them his rational
critique, backed by arguments from Scripture, places him in direct
opposition to Calvin and Protestant orthodoxy.[101] Near the end of
the unfinished work, he emphasizes that no blindness is so great
that it cannot befall those who follow a blind guide and have scru-
ples against doubting. For in the past, Christian teachers, through

either ignorance or iniquity, wanted their own interpretations to be received as oracles and saw to it that succeeding generations feared to doubt or question them. The same practice continues in the present, as Christian doctors, like those of earlier times, forcibly impose their opinions and interpretations, even though false, and forge new articles of faith to ensnare the consciences of people. From this comes their persecution of those who disagree with them, who are treated as heretics.[102]

In 1558, in one of his replies to his adversaries, Calvin denounced Castellio in the following words: "You wish to subject the mysteries of God to a judgment according to human perception, and you make reason, which by its blindness extinguishes all of God's glory, not only the leader and teacher, but dare to prefer it to Scripture."[103] Except for the very last charge, which was certainly untrue, Calvin perceived clearly enough where Castellio stood. As *The Art of Doubting* makes evident, he was a rationalist to a considerable extent, with a strong faith in the power of reason in religion. Refusing on rational grounds to believe that Adam's sin had corrupted humanity's intellect and senses, he was convinced that all Christians had the capacity to know and follow Christ. As Elizabeth Feist Hirsch has observed, his "optimism about reason and the senses as sources of knowledge was matched by his high estimate of the moral consequences resulting from a will to believe in Christ."[104] The important place he gave to reason was qualified, however, by the still higher significance he attributed to the Holy Spirit as both a source of faith and an indispensable guide to the understanding of Scripture. The sixteenth century saw the questioning of all knowledge in the treatise *The Uncertainty and Vanity of All the Sciences and Arts* (1533), by the celebrated German physician, humanist, and occult philosopher Henry Cornelius Agrippa, and it likewise witnessed the revival of the skeptical philosophy of ancient Pyrrhonism in the *Essais* (1588) by the great French writer Montaigne and the work of other thinkers.[105] Castellio was never a true skeptic, however, and the doubt he recommended was far from a total skepticism about knowledge. He very definitely limited the need of doubt to what was obscure and uncertain, confi-

dent that the knowledge necessary for salvation was both certain
and accessible to all. He was not always a rigorous thinker in *The
Art of Doubting*. Like other Christian philosophers and theologians
of the age, he begged numerous questions, assuming, for example, that everyone knows that God exists, that Christianity is the
best religion, and that the same moral ideas are innate in all
human beings and nations because God has implanted them in
mankind as part of the law of nature. What emerges from his work,
nevertheless, is a great prescription for religious tolerance inextri-
cably tied to freedom of thought and opinion. It shows the value
of fair and open discussion of religious differences and stigmatizes
as a great moral fault the intellectual rigidity that is unable and
unwilling to hear opposing views. It justifies independence of religious authority and explains that toleration not only is mandated
by the doubtfulness and uncertainty of many religious doctrines
but is the only alternative to the injustice of persecution. It defends the principles of tolerance and religious liberty as both morally imperative for Christians and a great benefit to religion itself.

C astellio died in Basel in December 1563 while new proceedings were pending against him for religious unorthodoxy. These sprang from accusations addressed to the city
government by a local physician whose attack on him echoed
many of the charges previously made by Beza. Because of such
pressures, at the time of his death he was apparently considering
emigration to Poland, which offered a haven in the later sixteenth
century to the victims of religious persecution.[106] When he died,
he was not yet fifty years of age. Although the effect of his work
following his death is not always traceable, its importance was considerable. One of the first writers to show signs of his influence
was Jacopo Acontius (ca. 1500–ca. 1566), an Italian refugee
scholar whom he knew in Basel, whose book *Satan's Stratagems*
(*Strategmatum Satanae*), published in 1565, was a treatise in favor
of toleration.[107] Another was Mino Celsi, an Italian exile in Basel
whose treatise against Beza and the killing of heretics, published

in 1577, included extracts from Castellio's works.[108] As they were more widely circulated, Castellio's writings, including those posthumously printed, played a part in the struggles over religious toleration in the later sixteenth century and throughout the seventeenth. In the Netherlands during the rebellion against Spanish rule, Dirck Volckertszoon Coornhert, Dutch patriot and one of the staunchest contemporary fighters for toleration, was a disciple of Castellio and helped disseminate his work.[109] Protestant dissidents, opponents of Calvinist intolerance, latitudinarians, and Antitrinitarians, or Socinians, were especially receptive to his ideas, which became quite well known in the Dutch Republic and in England. His biographer, Hans Guggisberg, has even spoken of a "Castellio Renaissance" in the Netherlands in the later sixteenth and seventeenth centuries and has also shown that in England during the latter period some of the principal advocates of toleration were acquainted with his thought.[110]

The Protestant Reformation created unprecedented religious division in Western Christianity both between and within the countries of Europe. It aroused powerful forces of spiritual renewal and gave birth to new Protestant churches and sects, fierce theological hatreds and controversies, and rebellions, wars, and bloodshed stemming from confessional conflict. Allied to the state, the Protestant churches, although a product of the revolt against Catholicism, continued the Catholic Church's practice of persecuting heresy and suppressing dissent. On the chaotic scene of confessional strife, persecution, and religious civil war in parts of Europe that Castellio witnessed in his lifetime, his writings in behalf of toleration and freedom of religion stand out as a beacon pointing the way to peace. The issue of toleration generated a vast amount of debate in the sixteenth century, but he remains the most significant thinker of the age in developing for the first time a broad theory to justify religious tolerance and freedom. His writings struck a powerful blow against the concept of heresy, and his incisive comment in *Concerning Heretics*, that "after a careful investigation into the meaning of the term heretic, I can discover no more than this, that we regard those as heretics with whom we disagree," may be seen in retrospect to mark an epoch in the cause of toleration. It is noticeable that, unlike such irenic contemporary thinkers as Erasmus or Cassander, he never pleaded for doctrinal compromise or reunion between Catholics and Protestants by means of agreement on a limited set of fundamental beliefs. It is likely that he considered the Catholic Church far too authoritarian to ever want to reunite with it. He accepted denominational and theological differences among Christians as inevitable, striving to inculcate a spirit of charity, forbearance, and mutual understanding between them. His hatred of persecution was motivated by very real humanitarian and moral principles that prohibited force and violence in religion as contrary to the spirit of Christ. It was for this reason that he spoke out in behalf of such victims of persecution as the Anabaptists. While he did not attempt to solve the practical problems of establishing a tolerant regime, he devoted great effort to explaining the religious, philosophical, and moral rationale that made such a regime desirable and necessary. His achievement should be far more widely known and recognized, for his significance depends less on the extent of his influence than on the character of his thought and his intellectual and moral firmness as a great pioneer in the struggle for toleration.

CHAPTER 5

The Toleration Controversy
in the Netherlands

⚡

The problem of toleration that troubled so many of the states of western and central Europe in the later sixteenth and the seventeenth centuries, and which also affected the English colonies in North America, may be said, despite all its facets and complications, to have involved two fundamental issues. One was the question of religious toleration between Catholics and Protestants. The other was the question of toleration within Protestantism itself of dissenters and sects. After Protestant state churches replaced Catholicism in a number of countries, the second of these questions at times equaled or even exceeded the first in its importance for Protestant regimes and thinkers. In general, as we have seen, neither Catholic nor Protestant governments of the sixteenth century believed in toleration for those of their subjects who belonged to the opposite faith. Each regarded the other religion as an evil and, in their treatment of its adherents, took persecution and exclusion for granted as the norm. For Catholics, Protestantism in any form was both a heresy that condemned souls to eternal perdition and a danger to political stability. In Spain, Portugal, and the states and cities of Italy, where it never spread widely, it was virtually eliminated by persecution and repression during the six-

teenth century. If elsewhere in Europe Catholic governments sometimes consented to the compromise of coexistence with Protestantism, it was to avoid the still greater evil of civil conflict, not because
they accepted the principle of tolerance. During the French wars
of religion the term *politique* began to be used as a name for this
point of view. It described those Catholics, in time a numerous
party, who were in favor of subordinating religion to the political
interests of the state and hence willing to concede coexistence with
Protestants when necessary to preserve or restore civil unity and
peace.[1] Since hardly anyone considered religious pluralism other
than an evil, this pragmatic policy was generally regarded as a temporary expedient, not a lasting solution to religious division. It was
largely for *politique* reasons, as has been pointed out earlier, that
the Catholic princes of Germany agreed to the Peace of Augsburg
of 1555, which recognized the coexistence in the Holy Roman Empire of Catholic and Lutheran states and princes, and that in
France the Catholic monarch Henry IV issued the Edict of Nantes
in 1598, which granted freedom of worship under various restrictions to the Calvinist Protestant minority.[2]

There was one major exception in the later sixteenth century
to Catholicism's general intolerance. This was in the Catholic
kingdom of Poland, where the growth of Lutheranism and Calvinism among the Polish nobility led several of the kings of Poland
to support a moderate policy of coexistence between Catholics
and Protestants. This policy also encouraged Protestant religious
refugees to seek a home in Poland. Among those who found shel-
ter there were Antitrinitarians, also known as Socinians, whose
principal leader from whom they took their name, Fausto Sozzini
or Socinus (d. 1604), arrived in 1579. For about three decades
Poland became the European center of Antitrinitarianism and its
churches, until the renewal of Catholic persecution in the earlier
seventeenth century forced the suppression and expulsion of this
radical Protestant sect.[3]

Among Protestants the great majority were taught to fear and
hate Catholicism as a corrupt, idolatrous faith.[4] Many thought the
pope was Antichrist and doubted the loyalty of Catholic subjects

in Protestant countries because of their allegiance to the papacy. For both religious and political reasons Protestant regimes refused to tolerate Catholicism among their people. In some German cities members of the two religions coexisted under the terms of the Peace of Augsburg, but only as a concession to expediency. Whichever of the two were in the minority were always subject to disabilities imposed by the majority religion. Nowhere in Europe did Protestant governments embrace toleration as a principle of public life. Protestant political authorities usually maintained that they allowed Catholics their freedom of conscience. By this they meant that they punished actions, not belief, and refrained from conducting inquisitions into the thoughts and religious opinions of individuals. This claim was largely true. It did not prevent them, however, from prohibiting Catholic worship or from persecuting Catholics through a variety of punitive measures aimed at the suppression of their religion.

Among Protestant countries in the later sixteenth and the seventeenth centuries, the Netherlands and England became the sites of the greatest, most intense debates over the question of religious toleration and freedom. In each of the two toleration was strongly advocated, defended, and opposed, and the focus, generally, was less on Catholicism than on the relationship between the Protestant state and church and dissenting Protestant religious groups. In the course of the seventeenth century the Dutch Republic acquired the reputation of being the most tolerant, pluralistic society in Europe. It is necessary to ascertain what this toleration consisted of and the contribution that the toleration controversy made to its achievement. In England from the 1640s onward, the struggle for toleration became one of the biggest, most divisive problems in religion and politics, generating intellectual and political conflicts that were not resolved until the end of the century. Developments in both countries were a crucial stage in the reception and practice of the principle of toleration in European civilization. In this chapter we shall focus on the issue of toleration in the Netherlands, and in the next on the English toleration controversy.

THE NETHERLANDS REBELLION AND
THE DUTCH REPUBLIC

The Dutch toleration controversy was an outgrowth of the revolt
of the Netherlands against Spanish rule, a conflict that began in
1566–1567 and lasted for many years.[5] The revolt resulted in the
breakup of the seventeen provinces of the Netherlands that
were part of the Spanish monarchy, leading from the later 1580s
to the emergence in Holland, Zeeland, and the five other northern provinces of a new independent Protestant state, the Dutch
Republic. Resistance to the government of Philip II of Spain
(1555–1598), an absentee prince who ruled through an appointed governor-general and local officials, was due to both religious and political grievances. Like his father, the emperor
Charles V, from whom he inherited the sovereignty of the Netherlands, Philip II did everything in his power to enforce Catholic
uniformity by crushing the spread of Protestantism. Both mon-
archs established the Inquisition in the provinces and issued fearful edicts ordering the death penalty for heresy. Despite persecution, Lutheranism and Anabaptism increased among the
population, followed from the 1540s onward by Calvinism, which
grew steadily and formed underground congregations. At the time
of the revolt the Netherlands, or Low Countries, were, together
with Italy, the most economically advanced region in Europe.
They were comparatively highly urbanized and a major center of
the cloth industry, international banking and finance, and commercial enterprise, particularly in their southern provinces of
Flanders and Brabant. The latter's city of Antwerp, to which merchants came from all parts, contained one of the greatest concen-
trations of wealth in Europe. In the 1560s Philip II's religious persecution and financial exactions provoked such widespread
opposition that it plunged the country into a political crisis. Artisans, urban classes and elites, and members of the nobility both
Catholic and Protestant joined in demonstrations and protests
against the policies of the Netherlands government of the king of

Spain, which they condemned as a violation of their long-established provincial liberties and privileges.

With the outbreak of the revolt, William of Nassau, prince of Orange, who belonged to the country's highest nobility, emerged as its leader. Tolerant himself, he became a Lutheran and eventually a Calvinist but was essentially a *politique* who tried hard to overcome provincial particularism and religious divisions so as to unite Catholics and Protestants in a common resistance against the Spanish regime. Despite his methods of terror, Philip II failed to suppress the revolt. For some years the struggle against Spain was carried on in only a few of the provinces. Then in 1572 the Dutch rebels conquered and occupied Holland and Zeeland as a permanent base, which thereafter became the center of the revolt. Four years later, by their agreement to the Pacification of Ghent, all the provinces joined in a common effort to compel the departure of Spanish troops from their country. Their unity was precarious, however, because of the religious differences between them. Striving to keep them together, William of Orange in 1578 issued an appeal for a general religious peace based on the free exercise of their religion by both Protestants and Catholics. One of its purposes was to persuade reluctant Catholics to accept Protestant coexistence; for as the document declared,

> the . . . Reformed religion is much followed and loved in this country not only because of the war, but also because we are necessarily hosts to merchants . . . of neighboring realms who adhere to this religion. . . . [I]f we do not grant it freedom of exercise by an amicable agreement and peace in the matter of religion . . . then in the absence of such an agreement, our common enemy, who is in our land, will find it all the easier to harm us, while, if we are held together in close union by a peaceful accord, we shall be able to defend ourselves against all troubles and dangers.[6]

The policy of religious pacification failed, nevertheless, owing largely to the intolerance of the Calvinists, which alienated Catholics from the common cause. From its beginning Calvinist congre-

gations played a major part in the Netherlands rebellion as its
most resolute and militant element who supported it courageously
through its hardest trials. After the Dutch rebels occupied Holland and Zeeland in 1572, the Calvinists suppressed Catholic worship in both provinces, killing and expelling the Catholic clergy,
and took over the churches. While demanding freedom for themselves, they denied it to Catholics wherever they gained control.
In the years after 1579, in a development aided by the progress
of Spanish reconquest, the heavily Catholic southern provinces of
the Netherlands abandoned the revolt and returned to Spanish
rule. The northern provinces allied themselves in the Union of
Utrecht and in 1581 declared their independence of Philip II's
rule. This was the prelude to the gradual formation of a separate
federal republican state in the northern Netherlands, which
fought on to preserve its independence and was not fully recognized by Spain until 1648.

   In the Dutch Republic that thus came into being, Catholics constituted a much larger part of the population than Protestants.
The Calvinist Reformed Church, however, became the legally recognized public or state church in every one of the provinces. The
Catholic Church was banned, its property confiscated, and its worship prohibited. Although not physically persecuted or compelled
to attend the public church, Catholics had no freedom to practice
their religion and could do so only in secret conventicles. With
the passing of time, nevertheless, they were permitted to meet for
worship privately without interference and thus gained an increasing practical toleration. The Dutch Reformed Church, an intolerant Calvinist institution, worked to convert the population to its
teachings and way of life, but its members remained a minority.
Many people resisted its discipline, and many belonged to other
churches or to none at all. Lutherans, diverse sects of Anabaptists,
Spiritualists, and other Protestant religious bodies maintained a
separate existence outside the public church in a condition of de
facto toleration, and Jews also were gradually received in the republic and allowed to practice their religion.[7]

In the highly decentralized constitution of the federal Dutch Republic, each separate province was theoretically a sovereign entity governed by its own representative body called the States. The chief central organ of government was the States General, an institution composed of representatives of all the provinces. There was also the quasi-monarchical office of stadholder, which was invested with the military leadership and possessed great authority in the republic. This was a position always occupied by one of the members of the house of Orange-Nassau, offspring of the great Dutch leader William of Orange (d. 1584). Since Holland was the wealthiest province, exceeding the others in the magnitude of its mercantile and financial enterprise, manufactures, and shipping, it became the preponderant power in the republic and in the determination of its policy.

The governing class of Holland and the Dutch Republic as a whole were the regents, the life members and officials of the States General and the provincial States, plus the magistracy of the towns, who collectively administered the country's affairs. An elite that tended over time to become a hereditary patriciate, the regents were for the most part not zealous Calvinists; some of them prized the tradition of Erasmian humanism, and while they cannot be said to have favored religious diversity, they were mainly moderates who were opposed to persecution. Calvinist in doctrine and organization, the Dutch Reformed Church had marked theocratic tendencies and laid claim to a large degree of autonomy and power. To its ministers and preachers, the great goal of the Netherlands revolt had been to establish religion in purity against the tyranny of Catholicism and Spain. Through its synods, consistories, and the discipline it exercised over its members, the Reformed Church aspired to a major role in Dutch society in the enforcement of theological orthodoxy, regulation of morals, and influence upon politics. This was a potent cause of tensions and acute conflicts with the regents, not least in Holland, who were never willing to give the church the independence or power it desired. More tolerant than the Calvinist ministers, they tended toward the position known as Erastianism, a view that owed its name to the ideas expressed by the German anti-Calvinist physician and theologian Thomas Erastus (d. 1583), who held that the church, its ministers, and its ecclesiastical jurisdiction and discipline must be entirely subject to the civil magistrate.[8] In the Protestant countries of Europe during the Reformation era, many members of the governing classes were instinctively Erastians to some extent even if they had not read Erastus, because they were convinced that the prince or state must possess full authority over the church and clergy in order to maintain political unity and protect their subjects against excessive clerical power. While the Dutch regents supported the Reformed Church as the sole religious institution sanctioned by the state, they also denied it full autonomy, insisting on its subordination to the country's political rulers. The governing bodies on which they sat managed the church's property and appointed and paid the salaries of ministers. They strove to moderate doctrinal disputes that could trouble civil order and exercised ultimate control over the church's affairs. This relationship and regent primacy, while they gave rise to frequent conflicts, contributed during the seventeenth century, despite the absence of official toleration, to the growth of a broadly tolerant society in the republic.[9]

DIRCK VOLCKERTSZOON COORNHERT

Most of the discussion of religious coexistence during the earlier years of the Netherlands revolt tended to regard it mainly from a *politique* standpoint as necessary to maintain the cooperation of Catholics and Protestants in a common cause. Not that other more religious motives were entirely absent, of course. A tract of 1579 written in support of William of Orange's religious peace by one of his advisers reminded its readers that "all of us," Catholics and Protestants alike, "are men, Christians, people . . . who believe in one God, profess one Jesus Christ, desire one reformation in this state. As men, let us love; as Christians, let us instruct and support

Engraved portrait of Dirck Volckertszoon Coornhert by Hendrik Goltzius. Coornhert, an artist and popular Dutch writer, was one of the foremost advocates of religious toleration and pluralism in the nascent Dutch Republic in the later years of the sixteenth century. Courtesy of the New York Public Library.

each other." Much more emphasized than this plea for Christian love, however, was the author's warning that it would be better for the two religions "to live in peace . . . rather than ruin ourselves by internal discord. . . . [W]e can choose between two things: we can . . . either . . . live in peace . . . or we can all die together."[10] It was in view of this necessity that one of the articles of the Union of Utrecht of 1579, which brought the northern provinces together as the first step in the formation of an independent Dutch state, provided that "each individual" should "enjoy freedom of religion," and that "no one [should be] persecuted or questioned about his religion."[11] This requirement was never honored, though, since in the 1580s Catholic worship was outlawed in all the provinces.

The foremost thinker to argue in favor of toleration and confessional pluralism during the Netherlands revolution was Dirck Volckertszoon Coornhert (1522–1590), artist and engraver, poet, dramatist, humanist, moral philosopher, theologian, and Dutch patriot and activist. Although his name is even less familiar at the present day than Castellio's, he stands out in the later sixteenth century as the principal champion of religious freedom in the Netherlands. He was born in Amsterdam, the son of a prosperous cloth merchant, and practically nothing is known of his early years or education. Following his marriage at the age of eighteen, for which his father disinherited him, he lived for considerable periods of time in Haarlem working as an etcher and engraver. He became a well-known, highly regarded artist in this profession. In the 1560s he also served as the city's secretary and secretary to the burgomaster. When he was thirty-five, he learned Latin in order to read the church fathers, Cicero, Seneca, and other Roman writers. Closely associated with William of Orange and other leaders of the revolt, in 1567 he was tried and imprisoned by the Council of Troubles, a tribunal introduced by the Spanish governor, the duke of Alva, to punish rebellion and heresy. Six months later he escaped, however, and fled to Germany. After his return to Haarlem in 1572, Calvinist persecution forced him to leave the city several times, but he resided there between 1577 and 1586 employed as a notary. Compelled to leave yet again, he moved to Delft and then to Gouda, where he died in 1590.[12]

Coornhert wrote prolifically in Dutch, which made his compositions accessible to ordinary readers who lacked a classical education.[13] Besides Dutch translations of Homer, Cicero, Seneca, Boethius, and other authors, he published works on theology, religion, and moral questions. Among his best-known books was a manual on the art of living, *Zedekunst Dat Is Wellevenskunste* (1585)

(*Ethics or the Art of Living Well*), based on Christian principles, which identified the good life with the practice of virtue.[14] A life-long though most unorthodox Catholic, he never formally quit the church and defended the right of Catholics to religious freedom along with that of other groups. He engaged in numerous disputations with ministers of the Reformed Church, which he criticized for its intolerance and attempt to impose religious uniformity. His personal religion was a tolerant type of Spiritualism derived from the writings of Sebastian Franck and from his contacts with the Family of Love, an underground Spiritualist sect that had some distinguished secret disciples among Netherlands intellectuals and humanists. Although interested in the Familists' ideas, he never joined the sect and disliked the authoritarianism and some of the teachings of its founder and leader, Henrik Niclaes. His attraction to Spiritualism led him to regard dogma and external ceremonies as irrelevant compared to love of God and the inwardly working spirit of Christ in the believer. Like Castellio, he was very strongly opposed to the doctrines of predestination and original sin. He did not agree with Franck's pessimistic view that mankind contained few real Christians at any time. Instead, he tended toward a perfectionism that had faith in the ability of human beings to obey God and Christ and become united with them through a life of love and service. In 1562 Calvin published an attack on Coornhert for his belief in spiritual liberty, associating him with people the Geneva reformer denounced under the name of libertines.[15]

The main sources of Coornhert's commitment to toleration lay in his Erasmian Christian humanism and his allegiance to Spiritualism and perfectionism. Another considerable factor was the influence of Castellio, with whose tolerationist works, *Concerning Heretics* and *Advice to a Desolate France*, he became acquainted in the 1570s. He translated several of Castellio's theological writings and said of him that there was "more truth, more fear of God, and more edification in a single page of his . . . than in all the books of Calvin and Beza."[16] He shared Castellio's hatred of persecution and once declared, addressing some Dutch ministers, that the killing of heretics "was the prime, indeed . . . the only cause which first impelled me to take up the pen against Calvin and Beza and after that against you when I saw clear signs that you were planning to force conscience and to use physical punishment."[17]

The principal target of Coornhert's battle for toleration was the Dutch Reformed Church, of whose dogmatism and intolerance he was a fearless, irrepressible critic. In his earliest tract dealing with toleration (1579), which described a conversation between himself and the burgomaster of Haarlem, he attacked the persecuting mentality of the Reformed ministers and their desire to punish heretics. Insisting that such punishment had no warrant in Scripture or Christ's teaching, he maintained that those who persecute do not honor and obey God, as they claimed, but offend and despise God. The ministers had threatened him with prosecution by the civil authority, but he contended that the latter had no jurisdiction over heresy or power to use the sword in matters affecting the soul. He even went so far as to suggest that heretics might actually be in the right. Admonishing the Holland magistrates, he urged them not to repeat the mistakes of the Spanish regime by resorting to compulsion in violation of the law of Christ. It is clear from this work that Coornhert was a consistent advocate of religious pluralism. The burgomaster in the conversation refuses to agree that freedom of conscience means the right to practice any religion. "Is not everyone," he asks, "now allowed to believe what he likes without being punished?" Coornhert's answer to this claim was that belief is always free, since no one could be prevented from believing, but that without freedom to practice one's faith, whatever it might be, constraint of conscience remained.[18]

Coornhert supported the religious freedom of Catholics and Protestant dissenters alike. In 1581 he drew up a petition in behalf of the Catholics of Haarlem for freedom of worship in which the town's Catholic citizens, recalling earlier promises to permit freedom of religion, described themselves as faithful patriots and condemned the intolerance of the Reformed Church. Among their principles they stated that religion and faith were a gift of God, that no religion should ever be imposed by force, and that civil peace and unity required religious freedom. This petition had no effect in deterring the States of Holland from issuing a general decree prohibiting Catholic worship.[19] The following year Coornhert drafted a remonstrance from the magistrates of the city of Leiden to the States of Holland to protest the Reformed Church's intolerant treatment of Caspar Coolhaes, one of its ministers and a professor of theology at the University of Leiden. The somewhat heterodox Coolhaes, who was affected by Spiritualism and opposed the rigidity and intolerance of Calvinism, said that the preacher's office was "to preach Christ, not Calvin." Despite the support he received from the civic authorities, the church's national synod excommunicated him in 1582 and dismissed him from his professorship. The remonstrance Coornhert wrote for the Leiden magistrates upheld freedom of conscience and declared that compulsion could never achieve unity. It also affirmed the civil power's right to intervene in church affairs to protect freedom of religion. For the state's well-being, he declared, it was better that all should be free to hold their own opinions while remaining united for the common good, rather than strive to achieve an arbitrary religious uniformity by injuries and accusations of heresy.[20]

Coornhert's most important tolerationist works were his *Synod of Freedom of Conscience* (*Synodus van Der Conscientien Vryheyt*) (1582) and *Trial of the Killing of Heretics and the Forcing of Conscience* (*Proces van 't Ketter-Dooden onder Dwangh der Conscientien*) (1590). The *Synod* is an interesting dialogue that strikingly reflects the contemporary religious conflicts in the Netherlands and demonstrates how far the author was willing to go in upholding the right of the individual conscience in religion. It depicts an imaginary synod of a number of Catholic and Protestant spokesmen who meet in nineteen sessions to debate various religious questions. Among its characters are several noted Catholic theologians, Calvin and Beza as the most eminent Protestant representatives; Jezonias, the moderator who sums up each discussion; and Gamaliel, based on the wise Pharisee in the New Testament, who expresses Coornhert's views.[21] There are also references to an absent Daniel, the synod's president, who will ultimately decide everything and apparently stands for Christ. The Bible is frequently cited, and Coornhert tries throughout the discussions to give a fair presentation of the opinions of those who speak for the different churches, sometimes quoting from their own writings. The *Synod's* original 1582 edition bore the author's name but no publisher or place of publication. The title page stated that the synod took place in "Freetown" and showed how the "Ancients," the old Catholic Church, and the "Young," the new Reformed Church, had both sought and obtained the "domination of the people's conscience."[22]

The first nine sessions of the work cover theological topics like whether the church can err, the credibility of the church fathers, and the authority to judge doctrine. In the remaining ten sessions, the synod comes directly to grips with various issues relating to religious liberty. In each of them Protestant and Catholic speakers wrangle and disagree, while Coornhert in the person of Gamaliel offers a position that differs from both in its affirmation of confessional pluralism. Remarking that every church claims to be the true church and to possess the truth, he concludes from this that the only solution to their conflicts lies in freedom for all. The opinions he expresses are certainly bold and exceptional in his particular place and time. While seeming to retain the idea of heresy, he simultaneously undermines it by maintaining that neither civil nor ecclesiastical authorities have any competence to decide what heresy is or who is a heretic. He denies that the magistrate has jurisdiction over heresy, and reminds Calvin and Beza that they were not against two confessions in the same state when it was a question of toleration for the Reformed Church under Catholic rule. Claiming that the main aim of the Netherlands revolt was freedom of conscience, for which the people had to pay a high price, he holds that all constraint of conscience is contrary to God's law, and that the civil magistrate should permit freedom of worship to all denominations for the sake of unity and peace. He is, of course, completely opposed to killing anyone for religion, convinced that it is wholly without justification in Scripture.

In his eyes both Catholics and Reformed, prelates and ministers, are alike unjust persecutors who wrongly presume to instruct the civil magistrate as to what persons are worthy of death as heretics.

Perhaps Coornhert's most original theme is his repeated insistence on the value and necessity of open discussion and criticism based especially on Scripture in order to establish the truth in religion. All churches can and do err, and without criticism their errors cannot be exposed. Observing that the persecution of Protestantism was ineffective in preventing the dissemination of heterodox doctrines in France and the Netherlands, he contends that for the magistrate to prohibit the teaching of anything contrary to the doctrines of the official church is not only useless but an "open tyranny" that serves to perpetuate errors in the church. Proceeding further along this line, in the fifteenth session he takes up the question of the prohibition of printing and books. Although agreeing that political authorities are right to prohibit books that incite sedition, he is generally against the suppression of books or writings—a censorship that he considers harmful to the diffusion of truth. Ideas should be freely expressed, he maintains, and if mistaken should be refuted by Scripture. Finally, he criticizes the recourse of theologians to civil authority to impose their doctrines. Disapproving any form of compulsion in religion, he held that the magistrate had no place in the determination of religious truth, which could be decided only through free discussion and with reference to Scripture.[23]

A forceful critique of the intolerance of both the Catholic and mainline Protestant churches, Coornhert's *Synod* can be read only as a plea for universal toleration, at least for every Christian denomination. Both his religious principles and his moral sense caused him to repudiate persecution, which he points out cannot succeed in suppressing heresy and usually contributes to its spread. With regard to freedom of conscience, he leaves no doubt that it does not exist unless Christians can practice their religion freely. As he presents the differences between Catholics and Protestants and their exclusive claims to truth, confessional coexistence and pluralism seem the only way out of endless religious strife. He writes throughout as a Dutch patriot with a keen concern for his country's unity and welfare. While Castellio's influence is discernible in many of his comments, he gives even greater prominence than the French thinker to the importance of free and open discussion in matters of religion.[24] His belief in the ability of human beings to become more perfect in their relationship with God probably helps to account for his confidence that truth would vanquish error in free discussion.

Coornhert's final discussion of toleration, *The Trial of Killing Heretics*, published in 1590, the year of his death, does not add anything new to the ideas in his previous writings. Its context, however, as a controversy between himself and the celebrated Dutch humanist scholar Justus Lipsius gives it a distinctive importance among his works. Lipsius (1547–1606) made his great reputation through his achievements in classical studies and his contribution to the revival of Neostoicism in the later sixteenth century. He was known for his edition of and commentary on the writings of the Roman historian Tacitus, which helped to initiate the vogue of Tacitism in European political thought. His treatise of moral philosophy, *De constantia in publicis malis* (*On Constancy amidst Public Evils*) (1584), became widely popular as an exposition of a Christianized Neostoicism that recommended an ethic of suppression of emotions, personal detachment, and imperviousness to external conditions. It made a particular appeal to educated people unhappy at being forced to live in an era of bitter religious division, rebellion, and civil war, who wished to achieve an interior transcendence of confessional conflicts. A subsequent influential work of his on politics, *Politicorum sive civilis doctrinae sex libri* (*Six Books of Politics or Civil Doctrine*) (1589), expounded a doctrine of reason-of-state that had some affinities with Machiavellianism. Born a Catholic, Lipsius was educated by Jesuits in the Catholic University of Louvain. After spending some time in Rome as secretary to Cardinal Granvelle, the former adviser of Philip II in the Netherlands, he taught by turns at Louvain, the Lutheran University of Jena, and the Calvinist University of Leiden in Holland before finally returning to Louvain, where he ended his career. In each of these places he conformed to the official religion, finishing with the appearance of a devout Catholic. Actually, he was indifferent to all three denominations and belonged to a circle of humanists centered in Antwerp who were secretly affiliated with the Spiritualist sect of the Family of Love. While affirming his loyalty to Christ, he disliked religious disputes, cared nothing for creeds and rituals, and once said that all religions and no religion were the same to him. His attitude to the Netherlands rebellion was one of neutrality and noninvolvement but with a definite disposition in favor of established authority. As far as possible he strove to remain above the battle, whose violence he deplored, and to continue his work as a scholar and philosopher. Owing to his religious shifts and prudential conformism, some of his contemporaries looked upon him as a hypocrite and opportunist who cared only for his own safety. Although Coornhert admired his erudition, he thought of people like Lipsius as "still sitters" and "self-lovers."[25]

The controversy between the two arose from Coornhert's reaction to some comments on religion in Lipsius's book on politics. This work, a guide for princes filled with classical references and quotations, looked at its subject entirely from the standpoint of the prudential interests of the state. When he came to discuss religion, Lipsius limited himself to its political role. He stressed its vital importance to a country's welfare, since religion and the fear of God were the only bond that kept society together. The prince accordingly had a prime duty to supervise and protect religion. He further maintained that a state should permit only one religion, and that any attempt to change a country's religion was a capital crime meriting punishment because it led to disorder and revolts. In this connection he lamented the misery that religious dissensions had produced in Christian Europe, causing millions to perish on the pretext of piety. Not ignoring the problem of religious dissent, he distinguished between persons who differ publicly from the state religion and persuade others to do so, and those who differ privately. The first group, he thought, should be punished; he quoted Cicero to the effect that there was no place for mercy in such a case, as it was better to cut and burn one member than for the whole body to perish. The second group, however, should be left alone because force could not change belief, which was best done by teaching and persuasion. He also noted the possibility that the prince might be too weak to prevent religious innovation, and that repression might bring more damage than benefit to the commonwealth by provoking armed resistance. In that case he advised that it would be better for the prince to temporize and permit dissent rather than resort to methods that would create an even greater evil.[26]

Coornhert, who objected to some of these ideas, first exchanged several letters with Lipsius on the subject, charging that he wanted to suppress freedom of conscience and once more light the fires of heresy persecution. Lipsius answered that those who created disturbances to change religion were punishable because the magistrate wields the sword to maintain peace. Denying that he desired to rekindle the flames of persecution, he claimed that there would be no religious wars in Europe if his views were put into effect. He had no desire, though, to debate with Coornhert, whom he considered his intellectual inferior and an unlearned man. Their correspondence ceased when they failed to reach any understanding.[27] Coornhert, who described their dispute to a friend as "a mortal struggle to prevent the new murdering and burning,"[28] found it impossible to contemplate religion from a purely political standpoint. What concerned him most was the right of conscience to dissent and whether the religion enforced by the state was the true one, matters that did not interest Lipsius.

His reply to Lipsius constituted the first part of his *Trial of the Killing of Heretics and the Forcing of Conscience.*[29] It took the form of a courtroom debate between Lipsius as the state's prosecutor and himself as defender of the people and the public good striving to prevent the revival of persecution. He wrote it in Dutch, he explained, so that the people could judge the arguments for themselves. The fundamental issue at stake was the state's maintenance of a single religion, which Coornhert opposed as a violation of religious freedom. It was for the sake of this freedom that he wished to keep the state and religion apart. Lipsius had never said which particular religion the prince should support (apparently it made no difference to him), and Coornhert attacked him on this crucial point. He would not accept that a false religion could preserve the state, or that the prince should protect religion without knowing whether it was true or perhaps supposing it true even though it was false. He had little confidence in the wisdom of princes in any case. He also disagreed that concord based on a false religion was better than discord and verbal disputes. Because no one could find salvation in a false religion, he preferred what he called "salutary discord" if it led to the true religion. Christ himself had sowed discord for the sake of truth. This was a reiteration of his earlier position in the *Synod* in behalf of free discussion and criticism.

He went further in his argument, though, because he was altogether against Lipsius's mixture of civil with ecclesiastical jurisdiction. Calling the two as different as heaven and earth, he contended that the prince had no authority in religious matters or the judgment of heresy; the church could be protected only by spiritual weapons and with the sword of the apostles Peter and Paul, not with the sword of Augustus or Nero. That the state should recognize one religion and ban all others was anathema to him. The only role he would assign it in the supervision of religion was to assure tolerance and pluralism. Unlike Lipsius and so many others of his time, he placed no value on uniformity as such. For him the real cause of religious disturbances and unrest was the forcing of conscience. Instead of being a danger to the state, he was convinced that religious freedom and pluralism were conducive to its peace and unity. It was no wonder that he intimated that Lipsius was on the side of Spanish oppression, and that the Inquisition and persecution were the inevitable consequences of his teaching.

The second part of Coornhert's *Trial* was a plea against the injustice of killing heretics, using arguments that resembled Castellio's. The States of Holland—believing, of course, in the magistrate's control of religion—disliked his book and forbade its

further publication.[30] Lipsius published an abusive reply to it in
1590 in his *De una religione* (*On One Religion*), explaining and defending the statements on religion in his political treatise.[31] Just
before his death in 1590, Coornhert managed to write a short
answer to this attack, which was published posthumously in the
following year.[32] In the same year Lipsius left Leiden permanently
for a professorship in the Catholic University of Louvain in Brabant in the southern Netherlands.

Coornhert was a great and brave advocate of religious freedom.
His works show how easily the distinction between toleration and
freedom of religion could be eroded, for he was unable to conceive of one without the other. One of the most striking features
of his thinking was his dedication to the principle of untrammeled
discussion, argument, and inquiry in religious matters with the
hope of serving truth. For many years he fought against Calvinist
dogmatism and the intolerance of the Reformed Church, which
would gladly have seen him silenced. While he remained a somewhat isolated voice during his lifetime, he was by no means forgotten and exerted a continuing influence in the Dutch struggle for
toleration in the first decades of the seventeenth century.[33]

THE GREAT QUARREL: ARMINIANS,
CALVINISTS, AND TOLERATION

The theological quarrels of four centuries ago may now seem
strange, if not utterly incomprehensible, and no longer of the
slightest interest. We wonder but perhaps fail to understand how
nations could be so troubled, how turmoil could arise, and how
people could attack, imprison, and kill their fellow human beings
over disagreements on such recondite, speculative matters as predestination, the Trinity, or the nature of Christ's presence in the
Eucharist. If we keep in mind, however, that the Christian religion
and churches were omnipresent in Western society in the sixteenth and seventeenth centuries; that they still claimed to regulate many parts of human life and to represent mankind's highest

spiritual goals; that their influence and values permeated culture, education, and the thoughts of human beings, to whom God, sin, the devil, heaven, and hell were very real; and finally, that they were a powerful instrument of social control, closely bound up with government and politics—then the puzzle of the significance and relevance of theological quarrels may disappear, since they could arouse strong passions and affect society profoundly.

The great quarrel that shook the Dutch Republic in the first twenty years of the seventeenth century, with significant consequences for toleration, was the conflict between Arminians and orthodox Calvinists. The main issues dividing the two parties were dual and interconnected: the doctrine of predestination and the relationship between the state and the public Reformed Church.

Jacobus Arminius (1560–1609), a distinguished minister and theologian of the Reformed Church, was the thinker from whose name the term "Arminianism" derived. It designated a religious movement that first developed in the Netherlands within Calvinism itself as a dissent from the doctrine of predestination and the dogmatism of the Reformed Church. Although Calvin had stressed the importance and benefits of this doctrine that posited God's eternal and arbitrary election of sinful men to salvation and damnation, Beza and other theological successors gave it an even greater emphasis and development.[34] It was seen as an essential part of Protestant orthodoxy, even though the denial of Christian free will to cooperate with God's grace had always met with criticism from some non-Calvinist Protestants. Becoming a force in the early years of the seventeenth century, however, Arminianism delivered a major blow against this vital Calvinist conception and all its implications; in doing so, it presented the broadest, most formidable intellectual challenge to Calvinism that had thus far appeared in Protestant Europe.

After studying in Marburg, Leiden, Italy, and in Geneva under Theodore Beza, Arminius was called in 1588 to the ministry of the Reformed Church in Amsterdam.[35] By 1590, if not earlier, he had become dissatisfied with the doctrine of predestination. When he was assigned the task of refuting Coornhert's heterodox

Engraved portrait of Jacob Arminius, Dutch Protestant minister, theo-
logian, and noted critic of the intolerance and dogmatism of the Calvinist
Dutch Reformed Church. Reproduced from a copy in *The Works of James
Arminius*, 1825.

opinions, it is reported that he found himself instead persuaded
by them.[36] In 1593, a fellow minister accused him of heresy for
disagreeing with the Belgic Confession of Faith and the Heidelberg Catechism, the official doctrinal formularies of the Dutch
Reformed Church, but the charges were dropped. His reputation
grew, and while his tone remained moderate, his writings and

preaching indicated his deviation from the Calvinist teaching on predestination. Among other points of disagreement he questioned the Calvinist denial of free will, suggested that predestination made God the cause of sin, and concluded that the elect could fall from grace, and that Christ died for all sinners and not only for the elect.[37]

Despite reports of his unorthodoxy, Arminius was named in 1603 to the very important position of professor of theology at the University of Leiden. It was a controversial appointment, brought about largely through the influence and management of Johan van Oldenbarnevelt, the advocate, or highest official, of the States of Holland and the leading statesman of the Dutch Republic in the first years of its independence. Although he was a member of the Reformed Church, Oldenbarnevelt was never a thorough Calvinist. An Erastian in his view of the relation between state and church and quite tolerant in his religious outlook, he disliked any kind of zealotry or clerical pretensions.[38] Arminius's tenure as professor was marked by disputes with the other Leiden theology professor, Francis Gomarus, an orthodox Calvinist, who attacked the heterodoxy of his opinions. As a result of the conflict between Arminians and Gomarists, tensions developed not only within the university but in the Dutch church as a whole. Along with their disagreement about predestination, Arminius held that the orthodox party was lacking in charity toward differences and disturbed the peace of the church by making salvation depend on the acceptance of every minute point of dogma.[39] In 1605, in a discourse delivered to Leiden University on the reconciliation of religious differences among Christians, he revealed his tolerant position very clearly. This statement contained a penetrating analysis of the causes and nature of religious divisions, their harmful psychological effects upon the contending parties, and their consequences in hatred and persecution. Deploring the spirit of dogmatism, Arminius expressed the hope of agreement on essential articles of faith. As a means to this end, he envisaged the possibility of a religious council to be convened by the supreme magistrate in which complete freedom of discussion would prevail. Above the portal to the building where it met would be inscribed the motto "Let no one enter without a desire for truth and peace." If the council failed to achieve mutual consent and agreement on some articles, then those on the opposing sides should part in friendship, treat each other thereafter with charity and tolerance, and promise to abstain from all bitterness and evil-speaking while they preached the truths they deemed necessary with gentleness and moderation. But according to Arminius, even those articles that the council accepted unanimously should not be forcibly imposed upon others, as it was always possible for such a body itself to commit an error in judgment.[40]

The irenic acceptance of doctrinal divergences that Arminius proposed depended on the distinction between essential and nonessential parts of the Christian faith, an acknowledgment of human fallibility, and a consequent abandonment of dogmatism on disputed doctrines within the Reformed Church. His opponents, of course, could see nothing admirable in his point of view. For them predestination was a keystone of Protestant orthodoxy and absolutely necessary for salvation; to tolerate those who rejected it meant tolerating heresy and the subversion of the church. There was yet a further fundamental difference between the parties. The Arminians were deferential to civil authority, agreeing with the regents on the civil magistrate's right to oversee the public church and its teachings. The orthodox Calvinists insisted instead on the public church's autonomy with respect to doctrine and its freedom to discipline its heterodox ministers without the magistrate's interference.

By the time Arminius died in 1609, the Reformed Church had become bitterly divided between the Arminians and their adversaries, with considerable repercussions on domestic politics. The religious leaders of the Arminian party were now the two ministers Jan Uytenbogaert, a close associate of Oldenbarnevelt, and Simon Episcopius, who became theology professor at Leiden in 1612. In 1610 the Arminians put forward their famous Remonstrance drafted by Uytenbogaert, a manifesto stating their doctrinal position against predestination in five major articles.[41] Thenceforth the Arminian party was also known as the Remonstrants. Its adversaries, the strict Calvinists, replied in the following year with a declaration of their own position, whose adherents were thereafter called Counter-Remonstrants. The Remonstrants looked for protection and support to the States of Holland, which, led by Oldenbarnevelt, ordered the church to assure the charitable toleration of the views of the Remonstrants. The latter also called upon the States General to summon a national synod in which the Dutch Reformed Church's confession of faith and catechism would be amended. This was a major bone of contention with the Counter-Remonstrants, who were unwilling to see any change in the church's formularies. They, too, wanted a synod, but only if it would reaffirm the orthodox position and expel the heretical ministers who rejected the church's teachings. They considered it a tyrannical infringement on the church's freedom for the civil magistrate to compel the toleration of the Arminians and dictate the conditions for a national synod.

As further incidents after 1610 intensified the conflict, it spread throughout the republic, affecting all classes, provoking dissensions in every province, and inciting disturbances among the artisans and workers of the manufacturing towns, who were mostly partisans of the Calvinists and the princely house of Orange-Nassau. The Remonstrants' main bastion of defense was the Holland regents and Oldenbarnevelt, the political head of the Arminian party. He considered that the Counter-Remonstrants were guilty of the oppression of conscience, and that their attitude toward civil authority in the matter of doctrine was a menace to public peace. He refused to permit a national synod unless the Counter-Remonstrants would consent to a revision of the church's confession and catechism. A widely unpopular politician, he had many enemies, the most formidable of whom was the stadholder Prince Maurice of Nassau, the republic's military commander. In 1609 Oldenbarnevelt had successfully concluded the drawn-out negotiations for the Twelve-Year Truce between the Dutch and Spain. This had cost him the friendship of Prince Maurice, who was against the truce and suspected Oldenbarnevelt of disloyalty and complicity with the enemy. Further differences between them in the next years increased their estrangement.

In 1618, the religious and political strife in the republic finally reached its climax in a dispute pitting Prince Maurice against Oldenbarnevelt and the Holland regents over the issue of provincial sovereignty and the control of the country's armed forces. Maurice, who supported the Counter-Remonstrants, mobilized his troops and easily gained the upper hand against his opponents and their allies in the other provinces. His victory led to the fall of Oldenbarnevelt, who was arrested and imprisoned in August 1618 with several of his colleagues. After a lengthy trial, the seventy-two-year-old statesman was executed for treason in May 1619. Following his arrest, the prince and Counter-Remonstrants proceeded to carry out a purge of Arminians in the republic's governing bodies and town councils. In November 1618, the long-awaited national synod of the Dutch Reformed Church, summoned by a compliant States General, met in the town of Dort (Dordrecht). With not only Dutch delegates present but also representatives from England, Scotland, Switzerland, and several German Calvinist states, the synod was a significant event in international Calvinism. It condemned the Arminian Remonstrants as heretics and disturbers of church and state, reaffirmed the doctrine of predestination in the strictest terms, and confirmed the authority of the church's confession of faith and catechism.[42] In its aftermath, Episcopius and Uytenbogaert left the country, while some two hundred other Remonstrant ministers who refused to submit to the synod's decrees were expelled from the church. About eighty of the group were also banished from the republic.[43]

Despite this crushing defeat, the Remonstrants survived as a religious society. Now a persecuted minority, they carried on for some years in underground congregations and as exile churches in several neighboring countries. In 1621 they issued their own confession of faith. Following the death of Prince Maurice in 1625, Episcopius and Uytenbogaert returned to Holland, and the Remonstrants were gradually able to resume worship in some Dutch cities without being molested. After the Synod of Dort, they no longer strove to remain within the public church but evolved over the following decade into a separate religious body with its own ministry. They thus became another Protestant denomination, or sect, in the Dutch Republic and occupied an important place in its religious and intellectual life throughout the seventeenth century.

Although Arminius and his Remonstrant successors stood for religious toleration, their understanding of this concept was at first somewhat restricted: it did not pay much heed to questions of tolerance or religious freedom for Christians and sects outside the public church. Broadly speaking, in their rejection of the orthodox doctrine of predestination, their aim prior to the Synod of Dort was to persuade the Reformed Church to become tolerant and comprehensive by recognizing the legitimacy of dissenting opinions on disputed questions. They also wished to moderate Calvinism's dogmatic certainty partly by separating the fundamentals of faith from nonessential doctrines on which differences could be tolerated without rancor. Arguing on these lines, they likewise defended the right of private judgment and individual conscience within the public church. It was perhaps a paradox—but one explained by their coalition with the Holland regents who supported their cause—that the Arminians were also inclined toward Erastianism and therefore did not seek to reduce the state's authority in religion. Instead, they looked to the civil magistrate to enforce comprehension and toleration in the public church. The Arminian conception of the church-state relation accordingly assumed that God had given the supreme magistrate wide authority over the church, including the duty of watching over doctrine; this entailed the power not to determine doctrine but to mediate and prohibit doctrinal quarrels in the church that caused discord and division among subjects. Such was the view that Uytenbogaert expressed in a treatise of 1610 on the Christian magistrate's authority in ecclesiastical affairs.[44] The Dutch Calvinists, on the other hand, while they did not, of course, believe that the church was independent of the state in secular matters, could not abide Erastianism. Hence they insisted on the church's authority to enforce the orthodox faith against dissenting ministers and members, and on the magistrate's duty to ratify and cooperate with its judgments.

HUGO GROTIUS AND SIMON EPISCOPIUS

After Arminius, the two principal thinkers on the Arminian side of the Dutch toleration controversy of the early seventeenth century were Hugo Grotius and Simon Episcopius. Grotius (1583–1645), a member of the regent class, showed his astonishing intellectual gifts at a very young age. He studied at Leiden and achieved a European reputation as an outstanding classical scholar, a Christian humanist and disciple of Erasmus, a renowned theologian, jurist, and professional lawyer, and a prolific author of enormous erudition. His greatest fame was due to his treatise *De iure belli ac pacis* (*The Law of War and Peace*) (1625), a foundational work in the development of modern international law. Another of his most popular writings, translated into many languages, was *De veritate religionis Christiani* (*The Truth of the Christian Religion*) (1622), in which he presented the Christian faith founded on the simple teachings of the New Testament as a creed superior to other religions. Grotius was a legal consultant to the Dutch East India Company and held office as legal adviser to the city of Rotterdam. As one of Oldenbarnevelt's main associates, he was arrested with him in 1618 and later sentenced to life imprisonment, but managed with the help of his wife to escape from captivity in 1621 and make his way to France. Never permitted to live in his own country again, he spent his remaining years as an exile in France, where he continued his intellectual work and acted as Sweden's ambassador to the king of France during the last decade of his life.[45]

Although Grotius was a strong believer in freedom of conscience and adhered to a relatively undogmatic Christianity, he was also consistently Erastian in his attitude to the church and religion.[46] This was one of the reasons that he admired the Church of England, a state church that recognized the monarch as its supreme head.[47] He maintained that the sovereign authority of the

ROIT HORA.

HVGO GROTIVS,
Reginæ Regnique Suedici Consiliarius, eorundemque ad
Regem Christianissimum Legatus ordinarius. quondam
Syndicus Roterodamensis, ejusdemque Urbis in Conventu
Ordinum Hollandiæ & Westfrisiæ Delegatus.

Engraved portrait of Hugo Grotius. Famed throughout Europe as a scholar, theologian, and one of the founders of modern international law, Grotius adhered to a tolerant, undogmatic type of Protestantism, which made him a leading adversary of Calvinist orthodoxy in the Dutch Republic. Reproduced from Grotius, *De iure belli ac pacis*, 1670 edition. Courtesy of the Law Library, University of Virginia.

state necessarily and properly included the government and supervision of the church, a thesis he expounded in a philosophical
work written around 1614–1616 on the relationship of church
and state and not published till after his death.[48] In 1614 he
drafted the decree of the States of Holland ordering mutual tolerance in the Reformed Church between Remonstrants and
Counter-Remonstrants and a cessation of their public debate. Two
years later he defended this decree in a speech to the magistrates
of Amsterdam. He based the claim to tolerance on the double
nature of all dogmas. Some were such that every person who
reached the age of discretion understood and embraced them
as necessary to salvation. These, he said, were a small number of
articles called fundamental and accepted by all the Protestant
churches as associated with the promise of salvation to everyone
who believed them. Other points of doctrine, not fundamental,
were merely a superstructure. Likening the two kinds of dogmas
to gold and silver and hay and straw, he held that those who
wanted to build a superstructure of hay and straw on the foundation of silver and gold would also be saved, and that their infirmities ought to be tolerated and not judged until the day came
that revealed the truth. He described as contrary to the spirit of
Christ the papal practice of condemning and persecuting people
as heretics in regard to articles of faith. He also recalled that
many differences had existed in the early church on articles of
faith, yet it remained the universal church and preserved complete concord.[49]

In these and other statements, although Grotius was more concerned about toleration within the public church than about freedom of religion in general, the wider implications of his position
as a way of reconciling differences are evident.[50] A short work of
1611 entitled *Meletius,* the name of a tolerant-minded sixteenth-
century bishop of the Greek Orthodox Church, contained a further expression of his dedication to toleration. Written in the form
of a letter to a friend who had told him about Meletius, its main
theme was the points of agreement that, according to Meletius,
united Christians in spite of their divisions. Grotius called these

divisions a disease caused by making dogmas rather than ethical precepts the most essential part of religion. The remedy for them, he said, was to limit "the number of necessary articles of faith to those few that are most self-evident." The other articles could be a subject of inquiry under the guidance of Scripture, without prejudice and preserving charity. And if people should err even on matters of importance, then "the only thing we can do is not to accuse them with hateful incrimination for . . . their unintended error, but to relieve the misery of their ignorance by a kindly explanation." With this he quoted in conclusion the words of the fifth-century Christian writer Salvian that those who are heretics are unwittingly so and should be treated with patience because they also presume to have the truth.[51]

Grotius was always in favor of a public church and never departed from the conviction that the church was subject to the sovereignty of the state. Two of the enduring marks of his religious thought, however, were his broad tolerance, which condemned the enforcement of belief, and his antipathy to the spirit of dogmatism as an obstacle to Christian concord. He opposed the persecution of heretics, and in his annotations on the Gospel of Matthew, he interpreted the parable of the tares as an injunction against persecution. Magistrates and leaders of the church, he said, should be foremost in imitating Christ by showing patience and mercy, and the church should proceed with moderation and gentleness even in the case of seeming error.[52] His reduction of the Christian faith to a small number of essential beliefs was an irenic attempt to bridge differences. He honored Erasmus as the first to distinguish between essential and nonessential articles of faith.[53] Beside his friendly attitude toward both Catholics and Socinians, he supported toleration for the Jews, although with some restrictions on their freedom of worship and a prohibition banning the conversion of Christians and polemics against Christianity.[54]

In his famous treatise *The Law of War and Peace*, Grotius reduced true religion, common to all ages, to four universal principles. They were that God exists and is one; that he is invisible and more exalted than visible things; that he cares for human affairs and

judges them most righteously; and that he created all things besides himself. All four principles, Grotius stated, were contained
in the Ten Commandments, and out of them arose the opinions
that God is to be honored, loved, worshiped, and obeyed.[55] He
also explained that war could not be justly waged against those
unwilling to accept the Christian religion or who err in their interpretation of the divine law. On this account he barred the punishment of heretics.[56] The common beliefs Grotius discerned among
mankind pointed to an underlying unity both among Christians
and between Christianity and other religions. He always particularly lamented the divisions and religious warfare in Christian Europe. For years he cherished the project of reuniting the churches
and in later life wrote various works in furtherance of this cause.[57]
His Calvinist critics saw his ideas as a deadly danger to orthodox
religion. Some considered him an atheist, a rationalist, a Socinian,
a deist, and even a concealed Catholic.[58] As a celebrated and
widely read thinker, however, he exemplified a liberal type of
Christianity that exerted a continuing influence during the seventeenth century in favor of toleration through its conciliatory view
of religious difference and opposition to dogmatic orthodoxy and
the coercion of belief.

Simon Episcopius (1583–1643), who studied at Leiden and was
a disciple of Arminius, was the principal leader of the Remonstrant Church until his death. In 1618 he spoke in behalf of the
Arminians at the Synod of Dort and later wrote the Remonstrant
Confession of Faith. After returning to Holland from exile, he
served as a Remonstrant minister in Amsterdam and as rector and
theology professor in the newly established Remonstrant College.
A major figure in the debates of the later 1620s between the Remonstrants and their Calvinist opponents, he made a singular contribution in extending the Arminian theory of religious toleration
well beyond its previous limits.[59]

Like all the Dutch Arminians, he argued that the beliefs necessary for salvation were clearly stated in the Bible and accepted by
all Christians. In the distinction between the fundamentals and

nonessentials of faith, he found a basis for mutual tolerance. Most theological disputes, he believed, sprang from disagreements on nonessentials. His conception of the relationship of church and state, as outlined in his *Theological Disputations* (1622), *Apology for the Remonstrant's Confession* (1629), and other writings, recognized the state's and ruler's supremacy over the church and also presupposed the existence of a public church.[60] While it attributed numerous functions and powers to the sovereign magistrate in his care of the public church, including the appointment of ministers and the times and places of worship, it withheld from him authority over the substance of religion and Christian doctrine, which belonged to the church itself. More strikingly, it separated membership in the polity from affiliation with the public church. Episcopius maintained that religious creed was not a sign of loyalty, and that all should be free to express their religious beliefs and to belong to other churches. He consistently condemned all force in religion: religion was free; it was love and could only be voluntary. The magistrate accordingly had no power to compel conscience or to forbid religious expression or assemblies outside the public church. Within the latter, discipline could not be coercive, and dissenters from the church were to be left free to practice their faith.

Episcopius thus advocated a latitude of toleration that made religious freedom into a requirement of all churches and a basic feature of public life. Denying that anyone had authority to determine what was heresy, he would have prohibited no religious opinion but blasphemy. He held that liberty of conscience greatly benefited both religion and the commonwealth by promoting reform and preventing the hypocrisy resulting from compulsion. For him the freedom of sects and religious inquiry was not a regrettable necessity but morally valuable. His *Free Worship of God* (1627), a dialogue between a Remonstrant and a Counter-Remonstrant, offered a revealing statement of the breadth of his commitment to toleration.[61] Here the Remonstrant maintains that freedom of worship for all churches is good for society, because the state's enforcement of a single religion breeds anger, resentment, and hypocrisy; citizens are therefore happier and more contented when conscience and religious practice are free from coercion. Episcopius defended religious freedom not only for Protestants but for Catholics as well, provided they took an oath promising loyalty to the Dutch Republic. He believed that if Catholics were allowed to worship freely, they would become better subjects of the republic and less sympathetic to Spain.[62]

The Arminians' theological dissent from the dogmatic orthodoxy of the Reformed Church gave rise in the Dutch Republic to a major controversy over toleration during the earlier part of the seventeenth century. In this controversy, which was noted in other Protestant countries, the Arminians argued in behalf of liberty of conscience in the public church and an attitude of mildness and conciliation toward differences on what they deemed nonessentials in religion. Through their criticisms and subsequent influence, they helped to weaken the theological ascendancy of Calvinism and to promote the development of religious and, indirectly, also of intellectual freedom in parts of Protestant Europe. Episcopius as one of their foremost spokesmen propounded a concept of religious toleration that, while it envisaged a public church subject to the authority of the state, also affirmed the full right of existence of other churches.[63] He approved and welcomed religious pluralism as a positive good. What most concerned him was the removal of every form of coercion in religion. In a tolerant society such as he conceived it, individual Christians would be assured of complete liberty of conscience and the right to the free practice of their faith.

BENEDICT SPINOZA

By the mid–seventeenth century, and with the waning of the persecution of the Remonstrants, the Dutch Republic was the most tolerant country in Europe and was so regarded by both natives and foreigners. A land of religious pluralism, hospitable to Protestant refugees who came to seek asylum, receptive to new ideas in science and philosophy, the seat of a very large book trade and printing and publishing industry, the home of great schools of painters—the republic was one of the foremost cultural, artistic, and intellectual centers in Europe. Nevertheless, the Reformed Church remained a powerful institution, and the Dutch acceptance of toleration, due principally to the attitude and policy of the regents, was always limited by a fear of ideas that appeared to threaten the foundations of Christianity or religion itself. For this reason, despite the religious coexistence that the inhabitants of the republic enjoyed, the public church and political authorities were always watchful to silence persons and groups who propagated subversive doctrines. Among them were members of certain sects who rejected the doctrine of the Trinity, like the Socinians and some of the Anabaptists, Quakers, and Collegiants; these last were an offshoot of the Remonstrants who called their religious communities "colleges" and had neither a confession of faith nor a ministry. In a concerted campaign against Antitrinitarianism during the 1650s, the government in Holland and other provinces prohibited conventicles of Socinians and similar groups and forbade the sale of Antitrinitarian books.[64]

The career of Benedict, or Baruch, Spinoza (1632–1677) coincided with this period in the history of the Dutch Republic, a time of considerable religious freedom and artistic-intellectual efflorescence, but also one in which the expression of ideas opposed to the Christian religion as then understood was subject to censorship and condemnation. Spinoza had no connection with the Remonstrants, nor did he take any part in the Dutch toleration controversy waged very largely between Christian ministers and theologians. A Jew by birth and one of the preeminent philosophers of the seventeenth century, he was the son of a merchant family of Amsterdam whose immediate forebears had emigrated from Portugal to the Netherlands to escape the Inquisition's persecution of Judaism. Among the thinkers discussed in this chapter, he made a unique contribution to the understanding of the concept of religious toleration by situating it within the broader framework of freedom of thought and expression in general.

Natus Amsteled·
M.DC.XXXII
24 Novemb·

Denatus Hag Com·
M.DC.LXXVII
21 Febru·

BENEDICTUS DE SPINOZA.
Cui natura, Deus, rerum cui cognitus ordo,
Hoc Spinofa ftatu confpiciendus erat.
Expreffere viri faciem, fed pingere mentem
Zeuxidis artifices non valuere manus,
Illa viget fcriptis: illic fublimia tractat:
Hunc quicunque cupis nofcere, fcripta lege·

Spinoza Opera

Engraved seventeenth-century portrait of Baruch, or Benedict, de Spinoza, Jewish philosopher of the Dutch Republic, who extended the concept of toleration into a call for the broadest intellectual freedom. Reproduced from a copy in Spinoza, *Opera*, 1925.

Raised as an observant Jew, Spinoza worked in his father's business, but from around the age of twenty he was in friendly communication with freethinking non-Jews through whom he became acquainted with many unorthodox ideas. A considerable influence upon him was his Latin teacher Franciscus van Den Emden, a highly educated ex-Jesuit and man of radical opinions in religion and politics who probably exposed him to a variety of philosophic doctrines. He also read Descartes, whose philosophy, with its rigorous method of thinking, strongly impressed him. His mental independence and intellectual development brought him into open conflict with Judaism, as a result of which he was excommunicated from the synagogue in 1656 at the age of twenty-four. The decree of excommunication named his "evil opinions and acts" and his "abominable heresies" as the grounds for casting him out from the people of Israel. By then he had renounced his interest in the family business, which was heavily in debt. Resolved to dedicate himself completely to philosophy, he lived thereafter for his intellectual vocation while earning his livelihood as a lens maker for optical instruments. A number of friends and disciples supported his work, and by the time he died at the age of forty-five, his fame as a philosopher was well established and continued to spread. His reputation, however, made him appear a dangerous thinker, an atheist, and an enemy of Christianity and religion.[65]

After his excommunication, which he seems never to have regretted, Spinoza did not affiliate himself with any religious body, although he had friends among the Collegiants, Quakers, and other sects. In his radical departure from the principles of organized religion held in common by both the Christian churches and orthodox Judaism, he was one of the boldest minds of the seventeenth century. Not even his contemporary Thomas Hobbes, another philosopher accused of atheism, went as far in questioning the tenets of conventional religion. Although Spinoza expressed a very exalted conception of God and was a highly moral thinker, it is easy to understand why he was reputed to be an atheist. The philosophy he propounded in his *Ethics*, his most important treatise,[66] and in other writings, was based on a complete monism that conceived of God and nature as one and the same power. His system recognized no personal deity or divine providence concerned with human affairs. Nature, or God, determined all phenomena by an absolute and intrinsic necessity. God's decree consisted of the universal laws of nature, from which there were no exceptions. Miracles did not exist, and belief in them was a superstition: nothing could violate the regularity of the order of nature, which was identical with God. Philosophy and faith were completely independent of each other; philosophy, founded exclusively on reason, had truth alone as its object, while the sole object of faith was obedience or compliance with the moral precepts of religion, such as love of neighbor. The Jewish prophets in their visions were men not of intellect but of great imagination. The Scriptures were not a divinely revealed body of truths, and their purpose was to teach faith and therefore obedience, not to convey information or knowledge about nature. The Jews were not God's chosen people except temporarily and in circumstances that had long passed away. Moses could not have written the first five books of the Old Testament, and the Hebrew Scriptures were impossible to understand or interpret without a historical knowledge of their various authors and times of composition and an exact grasp of the Hebrew language and vocabulary. Professing complete independence of authority, Spinoza strove to be guided exclusively by *ratio*, or reason. In his view, the highest life for a human being was one that, conquering all irrational desires and passions, aspired to know and love God. He was also a republican in his political outlook and, despite his contempt for the superstition and unintelligence of the masses, considered democracy as the best form of government.

Such were some of the conceptions that made his philosophy seem a danger to many and posed a challenge to the fundamental religious assumptions of his time. Spinoza wrote all his books in Latin and expressed his understanding of toleration principally in his *Tractatus theologico-politicus* (*Theological-Political Treatise*), one of his few writings printed during his lifetime. It was published anonymously in Amsterdam in 1670, under a false printer's name and alleging Hamburg as the place of publication. Other clandestine editions followed, but the book was under threat from the start. In 1674 the States of Holland ordered its suppression together with other "Socinian and blasphemous books," including Thomas Hobbes's *Leviathan*. These works were condemned and their printing, sale, and dissemination forbidden on the ground that they were contrary to the Christian Reformed religion and overflowed with "blasphemies against God, his attributes and admirable Trinity, against the divinity of Jesus Christ and his true blessedness."[67] French and English translations of the *Tractatus* followed in the 1670s, and the book attained a wide diffusion notwithstanding the measures against it.[68] Despite its anonymity, Spinoza was certainly known as the author, though he suffered no physical harm because of this fact.

The full title of the *Theological-Political Treatise* declares that its aim is to show not only that "liberty of philosophizing" is consistent with piety and the peace of the commonwealth, but that the latter cannot exist without it.[69] In the preface Spinoza commented, perhaps not altogether sincerely, on the good fortune of living "in a commonwealth where freedom of judgment is fully granted to the individual citizen and he may worship God as he pleases, and where nothing is esteemed dearer or more precious than freedom." He considered therefore that the task he had undertaken in his book was beneficial to this freedom. The preface further explained that superstition was the product of fear, and that despotic governments used the cloak of religion to keep their subjects in a state of deception. Spinoza wanted to liberate men from religious superstition, which sprang from fear and kept their minds in error. His main targets were the ministers and theologians, of whom he spoke scathingly as men ambitious for power and prominence who despise the light of reason, teach irrational dogmas, and bitterly persecute those who do not share their opinions. He made clear that he was addressing the learned reader, since he had no hope that the common people could be freed from their fears and superstition; hence, he said, he does not invite them to read his book.[70]

Most of the treatise is concerned with the interpretation of Scripture through an examination of parts of the Hebrew Old Testament; of its twenty chapters, only the last five deal with the relation between religion and politics and the necessity of freedom of thought and opinion. The philosopher devoted so much

space to the Bible in order to expose the misconceptions and perversions due to religious superstition. By explaining with numerous examples how to read and interpret the Bible correctly, he
intended to demonstrate that it had nothing to do with philosophy or reason and taught only virtue, morality, and charity; that
its teachings were simple and few and its writings adapted to the
aim of persuading men to embrace them willingly; and that the
sole end of faith was obedience to these teachings.[71] Spinoza's application of critical reason and historical method to the Bible was
an epoch-making development, one of whose purposes was to ex-
tricate the Bible's moral message from its less than rational context and show that it is concerned not with natural knowledge or
truth but with inculcating an ethic of love, justice, and obedience.
In the fourteenth chapter he associated faith with pious rather
than true dogmas and reduced the universal faith contained in
the Bible to seven dogmas. The seventh of them states that God
forgives repentant sinners, and that the person who believes this
has Christ in him. What God really is, however, "is irrelevant to
faith." It is possible to have many beliefs about God, but all that
matters is obedience to divine law, which is the essence of faith.[72]
He acknowledged that reason could give no justification for the
authority of the Scriptures, which was dependent on the authority
of the prophets; but he nevertheless maintained that by inculcating obedience, they taught mankind the way to salvation.[73]

The political principles set forth in the treatise's final five
chapters describe the natural right that men possess in the state
of nature. Spinoza always equates natural right with power, the
two being coextensive, and he explains how individuals create political society by transferring their power to the community, whose
laws everyone is obliged to obey. He praises democracy as the
freest polity and most natural form of state, which does most to
keep men within the bounds of reason so that they live in peace
and harmony. Although he emphasizes the duty of obedience to
the law and the sovereign, which has full power over religious
matters, he likewise stresses that it is impossible for subjects to
transfer all their natural rights to the sovereign, and equally im-

possible for any government to completely control its people's thoughts or actions.[74]

This brings him finally to the discussion of the desirability of letting all think as they please and say what they think, as is the case, he says, in a free commonwealth. After first distinguishing thoughts from actions, he points out that no one is able to give up the freedom to think and judge, and that thinking and judging cannot violate the sovereign's right. Attempts to suppress thought and speech hurt good men but fail to restrain the wicked; they produce nothing but hypocrisy, sycophancy, and corruption, while persecution of belief through legislation has led to innumerable divisions in the Christian churches and drives men to resistance. Spinoza's essential claim is thus that it is in the sovereign's interest to permit freedom of judgment and to govern so that subjects will live peacefully together despite differing opinions. This is the best kind of government, he maintains, because most in accord with human nature and nearest to democracy, in which people need not think alike to act and decide in common by majority vote. As an example that men need not harm each other even though their opinions are in conflict, he cites the renowned city of Amsterdam, whose prosperity is one of the fruits of its freedom of belief. There "men of every race and sect live in complete harmony," all are treated equally in a court of law, and none are denied the protection of the civil authority. The conclusions of Spinoza's argument are double: first, as long as men refrain from acts that contravene the laws, freedom of thought and expression are fully consistent with the right and authority of the sovereign; second, this freedom is not detrimental to public peace or the welfare of the state, which, indeed, cannot be preserved without it.[75]

The *Theological-Political Treatise* is a highly original work, one of whose most remarkable features is the unprecedented significance it gives to freedom of thought and expression. Spinoza does not posit this freedom as a right, and indeed his equation of power and right is a claim that raises many difficulties.[76] Rather, he champions such freedom as politically desirable and both appropriate and necessary in a free commonwealth. While toleration in religion is, of course, important in his discussion, he subsumes it in the wider category of the freedom to believe, speak, and write, and this meant the right of individuals to publish thoughts that were contrary even to the Christian religion and theology or to prevailing political assumptions.[77] He was more concerned with freedom of the mind for the individual than with freedom of religion. The "liberty of philosophizing" for which he contended thus went beyond the removal of constraints upon the philosopher; it pointed to a political environment of intellectual freedom in which ideas of every kind could be exchanged without danger and none were prevented from voicing their beliefs and opinions on religion, politics, or other subjects whether in speech or in writing. It is essential to emphasize, however, that Spinoza was not a political rebel. He believed firmly in obedience to the government and law as a moral duty. Although the freedom of thought and expression he commended in the *Theological-Political Treatise* is a type of negative liberty, for him, as his *Ethics* makes clear, the freedom of the individual consists above all in conformity to reason. He made no provision for any right of resistance to the sovereign authority other than to observe that the power of all governments is ultimately limited, and that misrule and persecution are understandably likely to provoke revolt.

Before his death, Spinoza was engaged on another work, left unfinished, entitled *Tractatus politicus* (*Political Treatise*) and concerned with politics and forms of government. This book, which never reached the subject of democracy, manifests the author's preference for an aristocratic republic as superior to monarchy and "more suitable for the preservation of freedom."[78] Here with regard to religion in an aristocratic polity, he endorses the existence of a public church recognized by the state. He recommends that the patricians who rule the republic share the same faith in order to avoid splitting into sects; he also suggests that the state churches should be large and magnificent. Although dissenters should be free to build as many churches as they wish, these structures should be small and located far apart from one another.[79] In an aristocratic republic, Spinoza therefore approved of a state religion along with complete toleration for other religious bodies.

Although Spinoza's radical critique of religion became one of the major sources of the European Enlightenment and enlisted many followers in the Dutch Republic, Germany, and elsewhere who were advocates of toleration and freedom of thought, his writings were fiercely attacked after his death. The Leiden consistory of the Reformed Church in 1679 condemned his *Opera posthuma* as a book "which perhaps since the beginning of the world . . . surpasses all others in godlessness and endeavors to do away with all religion and set impiety on the throne." Shortly afterward an edict of the States of Holland banned the work and all reprints, summaries, or extracts from Spinoza's writings or any restatement of them, with heavy penalties for authors, editors, printers, publishers, and booksellers who offended in this matter.[80] Anti-Spinozism was a prominent strand of late-seventeenth-century philosophy and religion. Not only orthodox theologians and ecclesiastics but even thinkers of a liberal cast of mind in Holland and England denounced him as an impious, irreligious, atheist philosopher.[81] His *Theological-Political Treatise* was a milestone in the history of the idea of toleration. It was a pioneer, even a visionary work in the breakthrough it made in extending the rationale of tolerance beyond the domain of freedom of religion to encompass freedom of thought and expression on behalf of the individual as an intrinsic part of political freedom.

CHAPTER 6

The Great English Toleration
Controversy, 1640–1660

&◊&

The English Reformation did not originate as a widespread popular movement of discontent with Catholicism. It began as the work of the state and monarchy, which initiated, imposed, and enforced it. In the 1530s, Henry VIII (1509–1547) broke England's ties of obedience to the papacy for political reasons and assumed the title of supreme head of the English church. His son Edward VI (1547–1553), a child who governed through his advisers, made England Protestant by law. Edward's successor Mary I (1553–1558) restored Catholicism and England's submission to the papacy, but in 1559 her half sister and heir Elizabeth I (1558–1603) once more established Protestantism as the state religion. Thereafter England remained a Protestant country whose laws affirmed the royal supremacy over the Anglican Church.[1] The English Protestant regime was Erastian, with church and religion subordinated to the political control and interests of the state in the person of the monarch, whom God had entrusted with power over both secular and religious matters. It was also thoroughly intolerant. The Anglican Church, governed by bishops appointed by the crown, was the only religious institution permitted to exist; the only licit form of worship was the one prescribed in the Book of Common Prayer, the official Anglican service book. The church's doctrines were formulated in the Thirty-nine Articles, which all clergy were required to acknowledge as in accord with the word of God. The law ordered that everyone attend Anglican services on Sundays and holy days, with penalties for noncompliance. Although the government did not conduct investigations into the consciences of subjects to ascertain their orthodoxy, it demanded conformity to the state church and religion. Catholicism was banned, and Catholics were subject to various disabilities. Their persecution worsened after the pope excommunicated Queen Elizabeth in 1570 and authorized her subjects to depose her. In the later years of her reign celebrating Mass became a crime, it was made treasonable to reconcile anyone to the Catholic Church, and a Jesuit or priest ordained abroad after 1559 who was found in England was liable to the death penalty. The queen's government executed about 189 Catholics as traitors, although most of them were in reality religious victims who died for their faith. When she began her rule, Catholicism was still the religion of a large majority of the English people. By the early seventeenth century, persecution plus Protestant evangelism had reduced the number of English Catholics to a minority.[2]

The English government and ecclesiastical authorities also punished Protestant dissenters and heretics who separated from the Anglican Church to form their own religious communities. Separatists denied that the state church was a true church of Christ and rejected the royal supremacy in religion. Three of the best known of them in the later sixteenth century were Henry Barrow, John Greenwood, and Robert Browne, the last of whom gave his name to the word "Brownists," often used as a general term for sectarians and schismatics. Six Anabaptists and Antitrinitarians were burned for heresy, and eight other Separatists, including Barrow and Greenwood, were hanged for sedition under Elizabeth. Her successor James I (1603–1625) burned two more Antitrinitarians in 1612, the last persons to be executed in England for the crime of heresy.[3] Persecution drove some of the Separatist churches of King James's reign to emigrate to the Dutch Republic, where they were allowed freedom of worship. Another Separatist congregation, the so-called Pilgrim Fathers, after first moving to Holland, emigrated to Massachusetts, where they founded the Plymouth Colony in 1620.

Other than Catholicism, the predominant form of religious dissent in England before 1640 was Puritanism. This was a movement of zealous Protestants, both clergy and laity, in the Anglican Church who contended that it was insufficiently reformed and demanded further reformation. The Puritans were themselves intolerant, hating Catholicism and also opposed to Separatist sects. They were not against a compulsory national church but considered some of the Anglican Church's ceremonies to be popish and wanted either to abolish bishops or to reduce much of their power. In place of bishops, the more radical Puritans called for an autonomous Presbyterian Church governed by assemblies of ministers and lay elders. They maintained that this form of church government, which resembled the Calvinist model in Geneva, was the only one authorized in Scripture. From the 1570s to the 1630s Queen Elizabeth, James I, and Charles I (1625–1649) all took various measures to break up the organized Puritan movement and to penalize and silence Puritan ministers and advocates who refused to conform. Persecution failed to weaken the vitality and tenacity of Puritanism, however, which, through the Puritan ministry's preaching and pastoral counsel, affected thousands of laypeople and had grown by the early seventeenth century into a strong and distinctive Calvinist subculture in English Protestantism. This subculture was well represented within the gentry of landed society and the urban classes of merchants and artisans in London and other towns. Puritans were noted as the most godly and pious of Protestants. They were apt to be keen readers of the Bible, diligent attenders at sermons and prayer meetings, rigorous observers of the Sabbath, and moralists who reproved swearing, drunkenness, and lewd behavior. Given to examining the condition of their souls, many of them experienced a spiritual conversion that gave them the assurance of being among the elect whom God had predestined for salvation. They

were a people who never abandoned the hope of a further reformation of the church and religion.[4]

Until the 1640s the Christian theory of persecution prevailed
almost universally, and scarcely any advocates of religious toleration could be found in England. A handful of exceptional thinkers
in the first decades of the seventeenth century, such as Francis
Bacon, William Chillingworth, John Hales, and Lord Falkland—
all of them loyal to the national church but opposed to zealotry
and dogmatism—expressed a tolerant attitude toward religious
differences. Bacon (d. 1626), the best known of them, a leading
English statesman and one of the foremost philosophers of the
seventeenth century, was a consistent proponent of moderation
in religion. In "Of Unity in Religion," included in his famous collection of essays, he deplored religious controversies and warned
against attempts to achieve unity by methods that "deface the laws
of charity" and "sanguinary persecutions to force consciences."[5]
Chillingworth, the author of *The Religion of Protestants* (1638), and
Falkland were both liberal and latitudinarian Anglicans who
stressed the role of reason in religion and were influenced by the
Arminian Grotius and the Erasmian tradition. Hales, who shared
the same tradition, had broken with Calvinism and disapproved of
its intolerance and all religious persecution.[6] None of these men,
however, brought into question the relationship between the English state and religion or dealt with the fundamental problem of
dissent and freedom of conscience.

The only approach to a genuine principle of toleration prior to
1640 came from Separatists, particularly those who belonged to
the illegal Baptist churches founded in the reign of James I.[7] As
voluntary congregations of Christians who subscribed to believers'
baptism, the Baptists held that religious persecution was contrary
to the spirit of Christ, and denied that the prince or magistrate
had any rightful authority over the church and religion. These
were some of the main themes in the writings of several Baptist
ministers of the time.[8] One of them, Leonard Busher, addressed
a tract to the king in 1614 entitled *Religions Peace*, which pleaded
for liberty of conscience for all Christians. In it he also proposed

that all, including Jews and papists, should be free "to write, dispute, confer and reason, print and publish any matter touching religion, either for or against whomsoever," so long as they neither slandered nor reproached others and alleged only the Scripture as proof.[9] Such writings by the Baptists, however, who were only a small sect on the fringes of English Protestantism, were little noticed at this period.

THE ENGLISH REVOLUTION

In 1640 England entered an era of revolution against the rule of Charles I that affected all three kingdoms of the British monarchy. By then Scotland was already in revolt, and before the end of 1641 rebellion also broke out in Ireland. Although the three movements differed in very essential ways, each of them was the product of a crisis produced by opposition to the royal government's tendencies toward absolutism and its religious, political, and fiscal policies, which created a host of grievances. In England in the autumn of 1640, Charles I summoned the famous Long Parliament, so named because it lasted thirteen years, to deal with the crisis. After passing a number of measures to restrict the monarch's powers, it demanded further political and religious changes, which he refused to concede. Unresolved differences between him and Parliament, and the latter's determination to reform the church and fetter the king's power in new ways, led to the outbreak of civil war in England in the summer of 1642. On one side were the Parliamentarians, the forces supporting Parliament, which had authorized resistance against the king; on the other were the Royalists, who were loyal to Charles I and the state church.

Parliament's conflict with the king opened an era of unprecedented experiment and revolutionary change in England's history. As the revolt against the Stuart monarchy expanded, it swept away ancient institutions, including the Anglican state church, and gave birth to radical new conceptions of religious, political, and social freedom. Traditional authority in religion and politics disintegrated, creating an explosion of thought and discussion that challenged many inherited assumptions and beliefs. Revolution generated a new level of political consciousness among the English people and brought a new and much wider public into being. Many Puritans were filled with the highest expectations of religious renewal in the early 1640s. The press, released by the collapse of royal censorship, poured forth an unprecedented quantity of books, pamphlets, newspapers, and manifestos dealing with religion, politics, and current affairs.

Early in its meeting the Long Parliament promised a further reformation, and a bill was introduced calling for the abolition of episcopacy in the national church. Considerable disagreement existed in Parliament, however, on what should replace the traditional ecclesiastical order. In the summer of 1643 it convened a synod composed mostly of Puritan clergy, the Westminster Assembly, to advise it on the intended reformation of the church. A large majority in the assembly favored a national Presbyterian Church governed by committees and synods of ministers and lay elders. This was also the desire of most English Puritans and of a majority of the members of Parliament. The latter, however, unlike many of the Puritan ministers, wanted to make the national church ultimately subject to Parliament's control. But even if it were answerable to Parliament, such a reformed church, Calvinist in its organization and discipline, would have imposed compulsory conformity, prohibited any dissent or separation, and subjected everyone to its jurisdiction in both doctrine and morals. It would also have brought England into closer union with Scotland, where the Scottish rebels, the Covenanters, on gaining power, had already got rid of bishops and established a Presbyterian state church. In August 1643 the Scots, rigid Presbyterians who were eager to achieve religious uniformity between the two countries, made an alliance with the English Parliament, the Solemn League and Covenant, which provided for Scotland's assistance in the war against the king. The Scots were then able to use their military aid as a means of pressure on Parliament to introduce a Presbyterian church order in England.

By this time, however, English Puritans were becoming increasingly divided. Some of them, while not necessarily opposed to a national Presbyterian Church, were against its compulsory, centralized character, preferring that every individual congregation within it should be autonomous rather than subordinate to any external authority. The minority who held this position were known as Independents, or Congregationalists, in opposition to the Presbyterians.[10] In December 1643 five well-known Independent ministers, all members of the Westminster Assembly, published a declaration, *An Apologeticall Narration*, which, while disavowing any favor toward sectarianism, contended for the right of each congregation to govern itself.[11] This statement signified an open breach with the Presbyterians and gave further impetus to the controversy over church government and toleration that was being heatedly waged in both the pulpit and the press. Meanwhile, moreover, new sects of Baptists and other Separatist bodies were springing up, uneducated laymen and even women were preaching in public to newly formed congregations, and heresies were spreading. All of these dissenting groups, who looked to the Independents for support, insisted on their right to practice their faith freely. The Presbyterians responded to these developments with fear and horror, convinced that they were leading to religious anarchy, and called for the suppression of sects. Among the Independents, on the other hand, many held a charitable view of the sects, supporting the right to form voluntary congregations and advocating tolerance for the tender consciences of Protestant dissenters who refused to be part of a national church. The parliamentary army that was fighting the king's party was itself infected by Independency and sectarianism. Among the Independents in the army was one of its ablest commanders, Oliver Cromwell, a Puritan gentleman and member of Parliament steadily rising in reputation, who believed in freedom for the sects. The acute disagreements between the Presbyterians on the one hand and the Independents and sects on the other, in which toleration was a central issue, became one of the main causes of the growing stresses undermining the unity of the parliamentary coalition against the king.

In 1645, Parliament, after formally abolishing episcopacy, voted to institute a Presbyterian Church. The following year the civil war ended with the king's defeat. The Presbyterians then strove to reach a political compromise with him that would have included his agreement to a Presbyterian national church. This move was blocked by the Independents in Parliament and the army, who fought a second civil war in 1648 to prevent it. They then proceeded to forcibly expel the Presbyterian members from Parliament, and in January 1649 they executed the king for treason against his people. Following this unprecedented act, Parliament, which was now dominated by the Independents, abolished the monarchy and House of Lords and proclaimed England a republic founded on the sovereignty of the people. Despite this claim, the English republic, or Commonwealth, in which the army's general Oliver Cromwell played a leading role, represented only a dwindling minority. It was maintained in power, however, by its victorious army and provided an exceptional degree of toleration for nearly all Protestants during its tenure. The governments of the interregnum survived for eleven years (1649–1660) in the face of increasing unpopularity. Although they went through several changes, moving closer to kingship in 1654 when Cromwell assumed the position of head of state with the quasi-royal office and title of Lord Protector, they never succeeded in winning legitimacy in the eyes of most of the English people. In 1660, two years after Cromwell's death, the English revolution finally ended in failure with the recall and restoration of the Stuart monarchy in the person of Charles II. This was followed by the reinstatement of the dispossessed Anglican state church and the return of a regime of religious intolerance and persecution.[12]

During its twenty years of revolution, England became a fiercely contested ideological battleground in religion and politics. The civil war and other conflicts of the period generated a rich variety of political writings; these included theories of natural rights, demands for the widespread extension of the suffrage and democratic representation in Parliament, projects of social reform, depictions of utopian societies, and notable defenses of republicanism. The revolution also provoked the widest, most searching and intense debate on toleration since the beginning of the Protestant Reformation. To select from the mass of writings that appeared on the subject is not an easy task. In the remainder of this chapter, however, I will discuss a number of works and authors that seem to me to be of major importance in the arduous struggle for toleration and religious freedom that took place during this period.[13]

ROGER WILLIAMS

It is difficult to exaggerate the fear and rage with which Presbyterians of the 1640s confronted the sudden upsurge of sects and heresies. It seemed to them as though the cherished Puritan dream of a new dawn of reformation had vanished in a nightmare of religious chaos. Appalled by these developments, Presbyterian authors compiled catalogs of the errors and heresies that were polluting the nation, and recitals of the misdeeds committed by Separatists and prophets of the newly hatched sects. They blamed the Independents and liberty of religion for bringing confusion on the nation by opening the door to an array of false and dangerous doctrines, schism, Antinomianism, social disruption, and sexual license. Committed to the Calvinist theory of persecution, which emphasized the God-ordained duty of the magistrate to maintain truth and punish heresy and blasphemous opinions by death, they demanded the rigorous repression of heresy and sectarianism.[14]

Roger Williams's *The Bloudy Tenent of Persecution* was published in London in July 1644 amid the mounting controversy over toleration.[15] It was not only the most sweeping indictment of religious persecution thus far written by any Englishman but one of the most comprehensive justifications of religious liberty to appear during the seventeenth century. His work called for the complete separation of churches and religion from the state, a position he defended on religious grounds perhaps more fully than any previous thinker.

THE
BLOVDY TENENT,
of P ers e cution, for caufe of
Conscience, difcuffed, in

A Conference *betweene*
TRVTH and PEACE.

VVho,
In all tender Affection, prefent to the High
Court of *Parliament,* (as the *Refult* of
their *Difcourfe*) thefe, (amongft other
Paffages) of *higheft confideration.*

Printed in the Year 1644.

Title page of New England minister Roger Williams's anonymously published
The Bloudy Tenent of Persecution, 1644. This work by Williams, the founder of
the colony of Rhode Island, was one of the great pleas for religious freedom
for Christians and members of all faiths. Courtesy of The Albert and Shirley
Small Special Collections Library, University of Virginia Library.

Williams (ca. 1604–1683) was one of the towering personalities
in early American history.[16] A London merchant's son educated
at Cambridge University, after ordination to the ministry he became a chaplain in 1627 in the household of a Puritan gentry
family in Essex. Unhappy with the Anglican Church, he joined the

Puritan migration to Massachusetts, where he arrived in 1631 and was offered the ministry of the church in Boston. The Massachusetts Bay Colony, founded the previous year under the auspices of the Massachusetts Bay Company, was then led by its governor, John Winthrop, and consisted of people who wanted a more reformed religion and church order than was possible in England under the repressive rule of Charles I and his bishops. Between 1630 and 1640, nearly thirty thousand people emigrated to the colony. Although the New England churches professed to be part of the Anglican Church, their distance from episcopal supervision enabled them to introduce various innovations in their worship and ecclesiastical organization, which was based on a congregational discipline; their church polity is best characterized as a non-Separatist Congregationalism.[17] Massachusetts was a Puritan theocracy in which church and state were closely linked; the civil power was the custodian of both Tables, a reference to the two Tables of the Law delivered by Moses in the Ten Commandments, the first containing religious, the second secular ordinances. This meant that Governor Winthrop and the General Court, the colony's legislative body, exercised a broad supervision over the churches and religion in a system that permitted neither dissent nor separation.

When Williams reached New England, he may already have been a Separatist; if not, he shortly became one. In search of a true church of regenerated Christians, he insisted that the colony's churches should make a complete and open separation from the impure and anti-Christian Anglican Church. Because they failed to do so, he rejected spiritual communion with them. The Massachusetts authorities tried to dissuade him from disseminating this view, but he persisted, contending that the civil power had no jurisdiction over religion. Their principal spokesman in their quarrel with him was the Reverend John Cotton, a Puritan luminary and pastor of the Boston church.[18] Williams created further friction by denying the colony's right to occupy the lands belonging to the native Indians. Challenging the validity of the royal charter of Charles I to the Massachusetts Bay Company that granted it this right, he maintained that kings lacked authority to take away the property of others. Understandably, his arguments were seen as a threat to the unity, if not the existence, of the newly founded Puritan society.

In 1635, the General Court finally banished Williams for his dangerous opinions. Forced to depart in the harsh winter season, he made his way with a few companions to the territory of the Narragansett Indians south of Massachusetts, with whom he formed a close and friendly relationship. Purchasing land from them, in the following year he became the founder of the town of Providence and the colony of Rhode Island, which was based on freedom of conscience. Although he underwent rebaptism in Rhode Island in 1639, he was apparently never a member of a Baptist church. Except for two visits to England, he spent the rest of his very active career in America, occupied with the affairs of the new colony. For several years he was governor of Rhode Island. When the new sect of Quakers made their appearance in the later 1650s, despite his disagreement with them he refused to have anything to do with the persecution to which they were subjected in England and in neighboring Massachusetts. All of his life he remained an extreme religious individualist, one who, while much in sympathy with the Baptists and other voluntary religious societies, did not believe in any visible church. In this he resembled Sebastian Franck, the great German Spiritualist of the previous century, who held that since the time of the apostles no visible church of true Christians had existed anywhere in the world.[19]

During the civil war Williams traveled to his mother country in order to secure a charter from the English Parliament giving legal recognition to the Rhode Island colony. While crossing the Atlantic, he wrote *A Key into the Language of America*, published in 1644, which dealt with the language and life of the native Americans whom he had come to know in New England. He always held that the English and the Indians shared the same blood, and was profoundly opposed to the latter's forced conversion. In England, where he was successful in obtaining his charter, he probably met the poet John Milton and other proponents of toleration. Before returning home at the end of 1644, he wrote *The Bloudy Tenent of Persecution.* Although well aware of the intolerance of the Presbyterians, he composed this work primarily as a critique of the Massachusetts theocracy and their apologist John Cotton, who were responsible for his banishment. It takes the form of a dialogue between the characters of Truth and Peace, which is less an exchange of views than an exposition of Williams's own position in more than 130 chapters. It brought a reply from Cotton in 1647, a tediously detailed chapter-by-chapter answer to all of Williams's arguments.[20] Although an able and learned opponent, Cotton held entirely different assumptions; he could not conceive that the magistrate had no authority over religion, or that heresy was not a punishable offense. In 1652, while on a second visit to England, Williams published a similarly detailed seriatim rejoinder to Cotton in defense of his previous arguments, and he was also the author of several other writings on toleration.[21] *The Bloudy Tenent*, however, remains his essential treatment of the subject. It is difficult to determine the sources of his ideas. He was undoubtedly indebted to some of the earlier English Baptist writers against persecution and could also have read the work of Castellio, with whom he had a number of affinities.[22] Although he inevitably shared some of his conceptions with other champions of religious liberty, *The Bloudy Tenent* is in many ways an original work which spelled out the fundamental beliefs and arguments that inspired his dedication to freedom of conscience as an absolutely inviolable Christian principle.[23]

He addressed his book to Parliament, which he praised for its wisdom and courage in vindicating England's laws and liberties, while also noting that it had not yet relieved the oppression of souls and consciences.[24] As we should expect, his thinking was steeped in the Bible, and he dealt with the question of toleration predominantly from a religious and theological standpoint. In spite of his strong humanitarian hatred of its cruelty, bloodshed, and injustice, his greatest reason for condemning religious persecution was the harm it inflicted on religion itself and the small number of true Christians, the children of the living God, whose

consciences ought to be free from all compulsion. Political considerations, while also vital to his argument, were ancillary to his over-
arching religious view. Cotton had maintained that it was the duty
of the civil magistrate and church to punish blasphemers of the
truth who obstinately adhered to their false and wicked beliefs.
He had also declared that a person shown the truth who still persisted in his error was guilty not of an erring conscience but of
sinning against conscience, a deservedly punishable offense.[25]
Against these claims, Williams advanced the fundamental thesis
that Christ had ordained a complete distinction between the civil-
political and the religious-spiritual domains, and hence that the
magistrate was excluded from all power over the church and religion. The principal significance of *The Bloudy Tenent* lay in its systematic development of this thesis.

Williams grounded his position in a scriptural typology entail-
ing the widest possible contrast between Moses and Christ and
their respective kingdoms. He gives an early hint of this typology
when he observes that "Persecutors seldom plead Christ but Moses
for their author."[26] Later he expounds it at length at different
places in his work, and it provides the indispensable theological
cornerstone for his theory of toleration.

Typology was a form of biblical interpretation centered on the
relationship between the Old and New Testaments in terms of
their correspondences, continuity, and discontinuity. Read in a
Christian typological perspective, the Old Testament allegorically
or symbolically foreshadowed or prefigured in various ways the
dispensation in the New, while the New Testament depicted in
various ways the consummation and also the partial supersession
or negation of the Jewish dispensation in the Old. Typology thus
treated specific persons, events, and actions in the Old Testament
as not merely literally true but as types or symbolic figures whose
full historical and spiritual meaning was disclosed only through
their relationship to other persons, events, and actions in the New.
Some degree of typology was inherent in any attempt by Christian
theologians to relate the two Testaments, and many Protestant
theologians used this method in their exegesis of particular parts

of Scripture. What distinguished Williams from nearly all the others was the extent to which it permeated his thought and the inferences he derived from it as a justification for complete toleration.[27]

According to his understanding, the theocratic kingdom and national church of the Jews described in the Old Testament was the type of which Christ's kingdom and church in the New Testament constituted both the fulfillment and the antitype. Moses and Christ were "the two great Prophets and Messengers from the living God, the one the type or figure of the later." This meant that Christ at his coming had abolished the Jewish national state and church founded through Moses in the land of Canaan, which united civil and religious authority. He instituted instead a purely spiritual church for which he appointed only spiritual governors, denying power to the civil ruler over church and worship. While the kings of Israel had been given charge of both Tables of the Law—that is, of the religious as well as the moral and civil duties prescribed in the Ten Commandments—this had ceased to be the case under the gospel.[28] Williams recurs repeatedly to the great typological divide between the Jewish national church and Christ's spiritual church in order to show how the union of civil and religious authority in the one had come to an end in the other. This basic dichotomy, in which Israel appears as the "Figure" or "Shadow" and Christ as the "unmatchable" antitype whose followers are the true Israel of God, operates continuously throughout his thought.[29] It provides the explanation of his Separatism, because God's church as he conceived it consists only of spiritual Christians, "the Regenerate or Newborne," who can take no part in the promiscuous parish assemblies of a state or national church that submits to the magistrate's authority in religion.[30] He likewise employs it to indict the ecclesiastical polity in New England as an "implicit" state church that imitates Moses and denies Christ by its confusion of civil with spiritual power in granting the magistrate custody of both Tables of the Law.[31] And it serves also as a conclusive argument against compulsion and persecution in religion, because Christ, the sole ruler over conscience, has strictly forbidden the use of the civil sword in spiritual and soul matters.[32]

The implications for the disputed question of toleration that Williams drew from his typological interpretation of Scripture were far-reaching. Christ's decree that conscience should be free debarred the Christian magistrate thereafter from exercising any control over religion or worship, which were matters of personal belief belonging to the realm of conscience. By confounding the church with the state, Williams said, "the unknowing zeale" of Constantine and other Christian Roman emperors did greater harm to Christ's crown and kingdom than "the raging fury of the most bloody Neroes." They had made "the Garden of the Church, and the Field of the World to be all one," thereby giving rise to the reign of religious persecution.[33] The distinction between the world as a field and the church as a garden composed exclusively of spiritual Christians is one of Williams's most cherished metaphors. He uses it in his discussion of the parable of the tares (Matt. 13:30–38) to complain of those who have labored to extend "this Field of The World into the Garden of the Church."[34] His explanation of this classic text in the toleration controversy, a refutation of Cotton's reading, interpreted it in conformity with his Separatism as a justification of toleration. The tares, or weeds, were not false doctrines or corrupt practices in the true church; rather they symbolized the false worshipers, idolaters, and anti-Christians in the field of the world who were opposed to Christ's kingdom; the good seed, on the other hand, represented the true spiritual disciples and members of Christ and his church. The former must be tolerated and left alone in their worship and consciences until the time of harvest at the Last Judgment.[35]

Convinced as he was that "the doctrine of persecution necessarily and commonly falls heaviest upon the most godly persons," it was especially for their sake that Williams would have deprived the magistrate of jurisdiction over religion.[36] Nor did he shrink from the most extreme consequences of his adherence to the principle of toleration, which he extended universally to call for freedom of religion not only for God's people and Protestants but equally for Catholics and other faiths as well. Because God had enlightened believers and could open anyone's eyes to the truth, Christians, he declared, were obliged to be gentle and merciful, tolerating Jews, Turks, anti-Christians, and even pagans. As we shall see, some of the most prominent Protestant supporters of toleration in seventeenth-century England rejected religious freedom for Catholics, arguing that their allegiance to Rome and the papacy made them a danger to the state. Williams was a rare exception on this point, consistently affirming that Catholics should enjoy liberty to practice their religion as long as they give "good assurance . . . of civill obedience to the civill state."[37]

The political theory Williams associated with his tolerationist doctrine was the correlative of his typologically based dichotomy between state and religion in a Christian society. It held that the ends of the state were exclusively secular, consisting of civil justice and peace, the defense of individuals, property, families, and liberties, "and the suppressing of uncivill or injurious Persons and actions by . . . civill punishment." Its power no longer extended to "spirituall and Soul-causes" now that all nations under Christ had become "meerly civill" and without the "typicall holy respect" that had pertained to Israel as a national church-state.[38] It was in this sense that he interpreted the famous passages in chapter 13 of Saint Paul's letter to the Romans on the Christian's duty of obedience to the higher powers. Williams held that this injunction pertained to obedience only in civil things, not in matters of worship and faith.[39]

Since he denied the magistrate's power in religion and advocated liberty for all denominations and faiths, he was obliged to confront the familiar objections that religious differences were likely to cause rebellion, that a state divided in religion could not stand, and that the magistrate was duty-bound to protect the true religion by suppressing its adversaries. One of his fundamental claims, accordingly, was that religious pluralism and civil peace were compatible. The "*pax civitatis*," or peace of the city, he stated, depended on a "civill way of union" that could remain safe and unbroken amid religious diversity. He compared a society of worshipers or a church to particular corporations within the city, such as the College of Physicians or the East India Company of London.

All of these bodies were separate from the city and could suffer disputes, divisions, and even dissolution while the city's peace remained intact. Thus notwithstanding the existence of "spirituall oppositions in point of . . . Religion," no breach of civil peace need result "if Men keep but the bond of Civilitie."[40] Of course, he knew very well that religious differences could and did provoke civil dissension. But he blamed this fact on the policy of persecution itself, when the state, in suppressing doctrines and practices whose expression does no harm to the civil peace, resorts to "weapons of wrath and blood," the usual means "by which men are commonly persuaded to convert Heretickes, and to cast out unclean spirits." He condemns such methods as both evil and entirely ineffectual, because nothing but "the mighty power of The Spirit in the Word" and "Light from the bright shining Sunne of Righteousness" could conquer religious error, heresy, and blasphemy in the souls and consciences of men.[41]

The concept of conscience as a spiritual faculty subject only to Christ plays a crucial role in Williams's argument. He makes much of the observation that all consciences are equal and alike in their subjective conviction of certainty and rightness. Rebutting Cotton's assertion that the fundamentals of religion are so clear that any person who refuses to acknowledge them is guilty of willful sinning against conscience, he maintains that Christians may well differ about fundamentals, and that those who disagree with Cotton might with the same right persecute him as a sinner against conscience.[42] As he reflected on the many disputes among Christians concerning the church, ministry, worship, and who is truly religious, Williams doubted that any authoritative judge existed to decide these controversies. Since the civil magistrate was incapable of judging them, the only way to avoid plunging the world into endless bloodshed was to leave each person's conscience free to decide for itself.[43] Hence he attached great weight to the fact that someone holding a belief that others call heresy was nonetheless conscientiously persuaded of its truth. Just as Cotton believed in the truth of his own religion and worship, so other people thought that theirs was true although opposed to Cotton's. What reason of justice or peace was there, then, he asked in *The Bloody Tenent of Persecution Yet More Bloody*, "why Master Cottons conscience and ministry must be sustained by the sword, more than the conscience and Ministeries of his other fellow subjects? Why should he be accounted (I mean at the bar of civill justice) a soul Saviour, and all other Ministers of other Religion and consciences, soul-murtherers, and so be executed or forced to temporize or turn from their Religion. . . ?"[44] To Williams it was obvious that all persecutors were guilty of self-partiality. They all said, "We are holy, we are Orthodox and godly," while others are "Heretickes, Apostates, Seducers, Idolaters, Blasphemers, starve them, imprison them, banish them, yea hang them, burn them, with fire and sword pursue them."[45] He denounced the forcing of conscience caused by such partiality as "spirituall and soule-rape" and alluded frequently to England's "sinful shame" in its repeated changes of religion during the sixteenth century in accordance with its change of rulers and under the dictate of the strongest power. The civil sword, he said, "may make a Nation of Hypocrites and antichristians, but not one Christian."[46] He accused Cotton of failing to treat others as he wished to be treated himself, and of condemning Catholic persecution while endorsing persecution by Protestants.[47]

Williams stands out in his life and work as a deeply religious and even prophetic personality whose greatest care was for God's people and conformity with Christ. It is thus paradoxical that his theory of toleration, developed chiefly in the interests of religion and the truly spiritual Christian, should have issued in such a completely secularized conception of the political order. In the view he advanced, the church ceased to be coterminous with society and regime, as was still almost universally the case in Christian Europe. Instead, it became merely one kind of private and voluntary association among many others, whose ministers were to subsist on freely given contributions rather than compulsory tithes. It could claim no exceptional immunities or privileges from the civil power nor exercise any authority over nonmembers. Against members its only sanctions were spiritual, with expulsion as the ultimate weapon, "Corporal killing in the [Jewish] Law, typing out Spirituall killing by Excommunication in the Gospel."[48] Governments, whose ends were purely civil, were obliged to refrain from all coercion of conscience and permit absolute freedom of religion and worship to everyone, Catholic as well as Protestant, Christian and non-Christian, so long as they were law-abiding citizens.[49] In insisting on separation between the state and religion, Williams was adamant that "a false Religion and Worship will not hurt the Civill State, in case the worshippers broke no civill Law . . . and the civill Lawes not being broken, civill Peace is not broken."[50] While churches were to be autonomous and free from state interference, citizenship and political membership were completely divorced from creedal allegiance and religious affiliation. He often stressed the difference between the moral and civil goodness that fitted a person to be a citizen or magistrate and the spiritual or supernatural gifts and goodness marking the real Christian. For the needs of the state he considered that the first was sufficient. Like other Puritans, he perceived the essential difference among Christians to consist in the distinction between the regenerate and elect of God and the unregenerate. At the same time, though, he recognized that the unregenerate might include many people with excellent gifts for civil employments, and therefore rejected the proposition that only true Christians could be trusted in civil affairs. For the same reason he denied that the church and commonwealth must be joined like twins who always go together. No thinker went further in disengaging the civil polity from the religious order, and he did not hesitate to admit that states could flourish without a true church, since the latter's existence did not in any way depend upon the state.[51]

Williams may have been a contentious character, but his references to Cotton throughout their controversy were courteous and unmarred by personal aspersions. He understood that "Mr Cotton speakes and writes his Conscience"; his prayer, however, was that "the Father of Lights" would show Cotton that the tenet of persecution he defended and strove to wash white was "black and abominable, in the most pure and jealous eye of God."[52] Soon after its publication, the House of Commons ordered the burning of Williams's book for its dangerous opinions. Three years later a declaration subscribed by fifty-two Presbyterian ministers of London cited it together with several other publications as evidence of the prevalence of heresy and blasphemy.[53] I do not think *The Bloudy Tenent* has generally been estimated as highly as it deserves to be. It is a work of exceptional courage, vision, and consistency; and although it is somewhat repetitive and not well organized, it contains a considerable amount of independent thought on its contested subject. A historical landmark by a man who was among the shapers of American civilization at its beginnings, it provides an exceptional revelation of the strong religious roots that lie at the origins of toleration and liberty of conscience in both the United States and England.

THE INDEPENDENTS: JOHN GOODWIN AND JOHN MILTON

The conflict between the Independents and Presbyterians dominated the religious and political history of the English revolution during most of the 1640s. Among the Independents, a number of authors joined in the battle against the Presbyterians over the burning question of toleration. One of the more prominent was Henry Robinson, a merchant by profession, who published a series of able pamphlets between 1643 and 1646 attacking Presbyterian intolerance in behalf of liberty of conscience.[54] The two most important thinkers to align themselves with the Independents, however, were John Goodwin and John Milton. Both were unorthodox Puritan Protestants, congenital nonconformists, and consistent supporters of the Independent party in Parliament. While Goodwin was a clergyman and pastor of souls, Milton was a humanist scholar and one of England's greatest poets. Both men threw themselves wholeheartedly into the struggles of their time, the first as a minister of the gospel, the second as a revolutionary intellectual. Although Goodwin's contemporary influence was considerably larger than Milton's, the latter's lasting fame as a writer and poet has given his commitment to tolerance and religious freedom a heightened importance.

After attending Cambridge University, Goodwin (ca. 1594–1665) served as a minister in several different places before moving to London in 1633 as vicar of Saint Stephen's, Coleman Street, one of the city's parish churches.[55] There he became known as a popular preacher with a large congregation of London citizens. He was a prominent political writer as well as a theologian and religious controversialist. When the civil war began, he immediately saw it as a crusade for liberty and religion against the political and spiritual tyranny of king and bishops. Rallying support for Parliament's cause, he published an incendiary pamphlet urging resistance to the king as the people's right.[56] Seven years later, following the execution of Charles I, he defended the justice of this act of regicide and the people's right to change their government.[57] When the monarchy was restored in 1660, his revolutionary record might have cost him his life. Although spared from execution, he was incapacitated from ever holding any public office, and his book in justification of regicide was publicly burned.

Goodwin owed the greatest part of his reputation to his writings as an Independent in defense of toleration. A prolific publicist and skilled debater, during the 1640s he was the best-known, most formidable adversary of the Presbyterians and their repressive church order. Much less sympathetic to the principle of a national church than other leading Independent ministers, he favored the Congregationalist ideal of a voluntary, or gathered, church composed only of true believers.[58] Around 1643 he established such a church alongside his parish congregation at Saint Stephen's; when he was forced in 1645 to quit his position at the latter, his gathered church met at his house in Coleman Street.[59] From an early time he manifested his unorthodoxy by straying from the Calvinist doctrine of predestination. Eventually he embraced the idea of general redemption in the conviction that God would save everyone who believed in and sought him according to their knowledge and ability.[60] He extended the possibility of salvation even to pagans who had never heard of Christ. Among the influences upon him was the sixteenth-century tolerationist writer Acontius.[61] It is possible that he knew Roger Williams, who mentioned him favorably in *The Bloudy Tenent*.[62] A continual target of Presbyterian attacks, Goodwin was almost entirely a controversialist who, as he himself said, had "to contend in a manner with the whole earth."[63] He was not merely a negative critic of the Presbyterians, however, but stood positively for the principle of an open and inquiring mind in the search for truth.[64]

One of his most effective tracts in favor of toleration was his *Theomachia: or The Grand Imprudence of Men Running the Hazard of Fighting against God*, published in 1644. This was an enlargement of two of his sermons based on Acts 5:27–39, which relates how Gamaliel, a wise and learned Pharisee, warned the Jewish authorities in Jerusalem against harming Peter and the other apostles, lest—if the latter's work proceeded from God—the Jews be found "even to fight against God." Goodwin used this text against Presbyterian intolerance to explain that many people who think they are fighting for God would be found, when the truth was known, to have been fighting against him. Observing that to suppress "any Doctrine, practice, or way which is from God" is to fight against God, he condemned the attempt by either civil or ecclesiastical power to silence the publishing, practice, or debating of different religious ways, doctrines, judgments, or consciences. Those who seek to do so, he declared, need a great many proofs and demonstrations to be sure they are not acting against doctrines derived from God. Since they lack such proofs, they are mad to run the risk of resisting God when they cannot know whether the teachings they want to suppress derive from God.[65]

All of these arguments, aimed at Presbyterian dogmatism, were part of Goodwin's effort to affirm what he called "the Independent Way" of gathered churches and voluntary congregations as very possibly the "Way of God." He demanded freedom for these churches as an essential requirement of a "Nationall Reformation." Replying to various objections to Independency, or Congregationalism, he denied that the toleration and liberty of gathered

ΘΕΟΜΑΧΙΑ;

OR

THE GRAND IMPRUDENCE

of men running the hazard of

FIGHTING AGAINST GOD,

In suppressing any Way, Doctrine, or Practice, concerning which they know not *certainly whether it be from God or no.*

Being the substance of two Sermons, Preached in *Colemanstreet*, upon occasion of the late disaster sustain'd in the West.

With some necessary Enlargements thereunto.

By JOHN GOODVVIN, *Pastor of the Church of God there.*

HEB. 10. 31.
It is a fearefull thing to fall into the hands of the living God.

MAT. 21. 44.
Whosoever shall fall on (or, stumble at) *this stone, shall be broken in pieces.*

Imprimatur.   *John Bachiler.*

LONDON;
Printed for *Henry Overton,* and are to be sold at his Shop entring into *Popes-head-*Alley out of *Lumbard-street.*
1644.

Title page of John Goodwin's *Theomachia,* 1644, one of numerous writings by which Goodwin, a prominent London minister and publicist, gained renown as a leading advocate of the principle of religious toleration during the English revolution. Courtesy of the Folger Shakespeare Library.

churches would cause divisions or tumults. Christians could peaceably choose to attend different churches and hear different ministers in the same manner that citizens of London who resided within the same parish could nevertheless belong to different companies and guilds, like the Grocers or Merchant Taylors. He also denied that the Independent Way opened the door to all kinds of errors and heresies. Only truth, he argued, could overcome error, and by encouraging the search for truth and light, the Independent Way rejoiced in possessing the right method of combating errors and heresies.[66] These considerations led him to his most important thesis, the denial of the civil magistrate's authority to persecute or use compulsion in religion. He cited various reasons why the secular power's punishment of heresy and other spiritual evils was both unchristian and ineffective in preventing the spread of heresy. Nothing but the sword of the spirit, he insisted, could slay the enemies of Christ; prisons, swords, and force "are no Church-officers."[67]

In this and his other writings Goodwin mustered a number of arguments against religious coercion and the state's power in religion. He believed in the Independent Way because he was opposed to any church maintained, as he said, by "the kingdoms of the world."[68] Like Roger Williams, he held that the Christian magistrate did not possess the authority in religion which the Jewish kings of the Old Testament were allowed to exercise. When the civil power punished spiritual offenses, it assumed an infallibility to judge religious truth that it did not possess. It should therefore tolerate all peaceable dissenters and sects; and even if the latter were considered in error, they should not be suppressed, imprisoned, banished, or killed but refuted by preaching, persuasion, and instruction.[69] He assailed the dogmatism of the Presbyterians, who, pretending to a full knowledge of religious truth, tried to make their own interpretations of Scripture binding on everyone. One of his frequent observations was that no one's judgment is infallible; truth revealed itself progressively and at first to only a few.[70] He prized toleration so highly in part because it permitted freedom of inquiry and discussion. It was "a marveilous bewtie, benefit, and blessing," he believed, to willingly "cast away even long-endeered . . . opinions" when the light of truth "discovered them to be but darknesse." Even the great Protestant reformers were not infallible, and just as America was once unknown, so many truths likewise remained to be discovered in Scripture. In the treatment of theological and religious differences, the only way to truth, he held, was through peace and tolerance.[71]

Concerned very largely with the Presbyterians' intolerance of Congregationalists, sects, and dissenters, Goodwin said little about the right of Catholics to practice their religion freely. He left unclear how completely he would have separated the church and religion from oversight by the state. The entire weight of his thought, however, was directed against the magistrate's establishment of a compulsory church system, such as Presbyterianism, and in opposition to persecution and the state's right to impose any religious belief and enforce it with penalties. For him toleration equated with religious freedom and pluralism. His critique of dogmatism in religion, insistence on human fallibility, and faith in free inquiry as a religious virtue distinguished him as one of the most forceful and liberal proponents of toleration during the revolutionary era.

The poet John Milton (1608–1674) was even more of a religious individualist than Roger Williams. A thinker of incomparable intellectual pride and self-regard, he refused to be confined by any orthodoxy. He evolved from the Puritanism of his adolescence and youth to a form of personal Christianity that detached him from every visible church. By middle life he had come to embrace a number of notorious heresies: Antitrinitarianism; belief in free will against the Calvinist doctrine of predestination; and mortalism, the idea that the soul dies with the body and remains dead until the final resurrection. Born in 1608 and educated at Cambridge, he grew to manhood with a unique sense of having been chosen by God to become an immortal poet and teacher of nations. His early poems written in his

Gul. Faithorne ad Vivum   Delin. et sculpsit

Joannis Miltoni Effigies Ætat: 62.
1670.

Engraved portrait of John Milton by William Faithorne. The poet Milton was a dedicated proponent of religious toleration and freedom of conscience but was unwilling to extend this freedom to Roman Catholics. Courtesy of the National Portrait Gallery, London.

twenties gave proof of his rare literary talent. Intending at first to be a minister, he renounced this aim in the later 1630s on account of his dissatisfaction with the Anglican Church. By good fortune he never had to earn a livelihood or seek a literary patron. Owing to the liberality of his father, a prosperous London businessman who generously supported his son's gifts and left him economically well provided, he was always in a position of financial independence.

Milton is the first instance in English history of a great writer and man of letters who dedicated himself to the cause of revolution and of religious and political freedom. After the assembling of the Long Parliament in November 1640, he joined passionately in the struggle against the king and established church. For the next two decades, he wrote comparatively little poetry, devoting the greater part of his literary efforts to pamphleteering in support of religious and political reformation and liberty. By the 1650s a worsening eye disease made him completely blind. He became a strong republican in these years, publishing a succession of works that justified the people's right to change their government and defending the revolutionary regime against its critics. In 1649, as a result of his defense of regicide, he was appointed Latin secretary of the new English republic. He served the latter and then the government of Lord Protector Oliver Cromwell as an official and publicist through most of the 1650s. The restoration of Charles II in 1660 brought him in danger of execution, but friends and his literary reputation helped to save his life. The return of monarchy put an end to his political activity, leaving him morally isolated in the postrevolutionary climate but free to devote himself entirely to poetry. His great epic, *Paradise Lost*, and his other major poems, *Paradise Regained* and *Samson Agonistes*, appeared in the years thereafter. Almost the final work to come from his pen was a brief tract urging toleration, *Of True Religion*, published in the year before his death.[72]

Milton made his debut as a revolutionary publicist in 1641–1642 with five tracts against episcopacy that allied him with the Presbyterians. An idealistic plea for the national reformation of religion and a severe indictment of the institution of bishops, they called for a Presbyterian national church as the only one in accord with Scripture.[73] He soon abandoned his Presbyterian allegiance, however, which hardly fitted his character and was due to his political naïveté and inexperience. This change was connected with the four pamphlets he next wrote between 1643 and 1645 dealing with divorce, a subject he took up in response to his own miserable personal situation as a recently married man whose wife had deserted him. Under existing law, divorce in England was extremely difficult and possible only for adultery. Milton's divorce pamphlets were reasoned and courageous arguments in favor of permitting divorce on the ground of the spouses' incompatibility of mind and temper.[74] They had to wrestle with the words of Jesus forbidding divorce and offered a high conception of marriage, claiming that its primary purpose was conjugal love and intimate companionship, not procreation or relief of sexual desire. One of the fundamental concepts Milton asserted in propounding his view was that "the great and only commandment of the Gospel, is to command nothing against the good of man, and much more no civil command against his civil good."[75] Another such concept was that of "Christian liberty," a spiritual freedom deriving from the gospel that emancipated man from legal literalism and made charity the rule.[76] Both concepts, of course, had significant implications for the cause of toleration. Milton was reconciled with his wife in 1645, but his alienation from the Presbyterians was hastened by their denunciation of his divorce writings as immoral. He had already begun to diverge from them, and by 1644 he regarded Presbyterianism as a despotic system that sought to replace episcopacy with a new and equally harsh religious yoke imposed on the English people. Thenceforth he associated himself permanently with the Independents and some of their leaders, like Cromwell, as the party of liberty and toleration.

Areopagitica, published in November 1644 in the midst of the civil war, was his first work relating to toleration.[77] The most famous of his prose writings, some of its passages resembled a prose poem in their rich imaginative imagery and elevated language. It was occasioned by Parliament's revival of censorship by an ordinance in July 1643 for the suppression of seditious and libelous books and pamphlets, which required that appointed censors approve and license all writings prior to their publication.[78] A firm believer in "free speaking" and "free writing,"[79] Milton undertook

AREOPAGITICA;

A SPEECH

OF

Mr. JOHN MILTON

For the Liberty of VNLICENC'D PRINTING,

To the PARLAMENT of ENGLAND.

Τὲλδ'θεερν δ' ἐκεῖνο, εἴ τις θέλῃ πόλᾳ
Χρηςὸν τι βύλδμ' εἰς μέσον φέρειν, ἔχᾳν.
Καὶ ἰαῦθ' ὁ χρηζων, λαμπρῴς ἐϑ', ὁ μὴ θέλων,
Σιγᾷ, τί τύτων ἐςῖν ἰσκίτιερον πόλᾳ;

Euripid. Hicetid.

This is true Liberty when free born men
Having to advise the public may speak free,
Which he who can, and will, deserv's high praise,
Who neither can nor will, may hold his peace;
What can be juster in a State then this?

Euripid. Hicetid.

LONDON,
Printed in the Yeare, 1644.

Title page of Milton's *Areopagitica*, 1644, his most famous prose work, which argued against press censorship and in favor of toleration of religious differences among Protestant denominations and sects. Courtesy of the Folger Shakespeare Library.

this work primarily to discredit the policy of prepublication censorship, an aim that also involved him in questions of intellectual and religious freedom and hence had a direct bearing on the subject of toleration. He addressed his tract to Parliament, modeling it on the form of a classical oration to the ancient Athenian council of elders, the Areopagus.

The heart of his argument was that literary censorship was an obstacle to the pursuit of truth, a discouragement to learning, and an offense to authors and independent minds. He traced the practice back to the Catholic Inquisition, which was then borrowed, he claimed, by the bishops of the Anglican Church, and since continued by the English Presbyterians, the authors of a new spiritual tyranny.[80] He opposed book licensing in the name of both freedom and reason as the twin foundations of virtue. Although the professed aim of censorship was to protect people from contamination by evil, God had endowed human beings with reason, which consisted of the freedom to choose, and no one could choose good without being exposed to evil. He poured scorn on the notion that virtue lay in ignorance or could be attained under legal compulsion. True virtue consisted in the ability freely to choose the good based on the knowledge of evil in a world in which good and evil were always intermingled. The person who could see and consider vice with all its allurements and seeming pleasures and nevertheless abstain was "the true warfaring Christian." "I cannot praise a fugitive and cloistered virtue," he wrote in a celebrated passage, "unexercis'd and unbreath'd, that never sallies out and sees her adversary, but slinks out of the race where the immortal garland is to be won, not without dust and heat." What purifies individuals "is triall, and triall is by what is contrary."[81]

He expressed a profound confidence in the ever increasing revelation of knowledge and truth, which could only be hindered by the practice of censorship. If the two were to progress and reformation advance, human beings needed to be free to publish their thoughts and make them heard. Like virtue, which must prove itself through combat with evil, truth could be tested only in battle with falsehood. Truth needed no licenser to assure her victory, for she could never be defeated by her adversary in a free and open encounter.[82] Milton deplored the conformity that led people passively to accept the beliefs of their ministers and teachers. He required independent thinking and personal judgment in religion. "A man may be a heretick in the truth," he said, "if he beleeves things only because his Pastor says so, or the [Westminster] Assembly so determines, without knowing other reason, though his belief be true, yet the very truth he holds, becomes his heresie."[83]

In the unprecedented outburst of public discussion and controversy provoked by the revolution, Milton saw proof that the English had become a people of truth-seekers whom God had chosen to lead the way to a new reformation. Intent on persuading Parliament to abolish book licensing, he reminded the Lords and the Commons of the greatness of the nation they governed, of its keen intelligence and piercing spirit, "acute to invent, suttle and sinewy to discours, not beneath the reach of any point the highest that human capacity can soar to." His country, he exulted, had cast off the old skin of corruption and become young again, entering "the glorious waies of Truth and prosperous vertue." His vision turned to gaze upon the vast city of London of which he was himself a native: a city he described as the "refuge" and "mansion house of liberty" in its support of Parliament, where many minds were searching out new thoughts in homage to the approaching reformation and gave their assent "to the force of reason and convincement" while reading and testing all things.[84] In this glowing image of his regenerated country, he found room for the sects whose emergence the Presbyterians found so alarming. Sure that new knowledge remained to be discovered, he criticized the latter for their intolerance in making it "such a calamity that any man dissents from their maxims." He blamed their pride and ignorance as the real cause of disturbance, because instead of hearing reason and trying to convince, they were determined to suppress those who disagreed with them. He scoffed at the "fantastic terrors of sect and schism," seeing in the sects a sign of "the earnest and zealous thirst after knowledge and understanding which God hath stirr'd up in this City." He called for charity and forbearance in a fraternal search for truth and the renouncing of "this Prelaticall tradition of crowding free consciences and Christian liberties into canons and precepts of men." Differences, he pointed out, were inevitable in the construction of the temple of the Lord, whose symmetry and perfection would consist in a harmony of "many moderat varieties and brotherly dissimilitudes that are not vastly disproportionate."[85] Milton allowed for the coexistence of diverse religious societies on the assumption that they would be in accord on the fundamentals of the Christian faith. While he did not define these fundamentals, he maintained that, aside from them, Christianity left many things indifferent in religion in which individuals should be free to believe or not as their reason and conscience directed. "[I]f all cannot be of one mind," he commented, "as who looks they should be? this doubtles is more wholesome, more prudent, and more Christian that many be tolerated rather then all compell'd."[86]

Areopagitica was as much a plea for freedom of conscience and the right of private judgment as it was for free speaking and writing in the search for truth. But to these freedoms Milton also laid down certain limits. First, he refused freedom to "Popery, and open superstition," and likewise to what was "impious or evil absolutely either against faith or maners." His support for toleration therefore extended only to "those neighboring differences, or rather indifferences . . . whether on some point of doctrine or discipline . . . which though they be many, yet need not interrupt the unity of Spirit, if we could but find among us the bond of peace." This criterion excluded Catholicism, which, according to Milton, should be extirpated because it was guilty of trying to extirpate "all religions and civill supremacies." It would also have excluded those Antinomian sects whose members considered themselves freed from obedience to the moral law by their inward possession of the spirit. Second, while he would have freed the press from prepublication censorship, he did not oppose its regulation following publication. Recognizing the power of books, he maintained that it was right for the church and commonwealth "to have a vigilant eye" how they "demeane themselves, as well as men; and thereafter to confine, imprison, and do sharpest justice on them as malefactors."[87] Practically speaking, this made authors accountable for what their works contained and approved the burning or destruction of books that were found mischievous and harmful to morals. Milton was not inconsistent with himself in taking this position. Although he prized freedom very highly, he never saw it as an end in itself; for him it was inseparable from morality and must be united with virtue to be justifiable. Without virtue freedom became license, and it was part of his lifelong creed that those in thrall to their passions and vices were not qualified to be free and deserved to become subjects of tyrants.[88] It must be emphasized, nevertheless, that as an author himself he urged the greatest caution in the punishment of books, observing that a good book was "the pretious life-blood of a master spirit, imbalm'd and treasur'd up on purpose to a life beyond life," so that to destroy it was almost like killing a man or reason itself.[89]

Areopagitica was a well-reasoned, learned piece of advocacy that offered an eloquent and powerful argument for religious in association with intellectual freedom. The limitations Milton placed on this freedom were outweighed by the entire spirit of the work, with its penetrating critique of censorship, its praise of independent thought, its welcoming of plurality of sects and divergent religious views, and its call for tolerance and charity toward differences in the quest for truth. Representative of Milton in his most hopeful frame of mind, it was written while he was still an idealistic believer in the English people's fitness for freedom and the prospects of reformation. The events of the following years were to make him increasingly disillusioned about both.[90] The contemporary impact of *Areopagitica* was negligible, and it apparently made little impression upon the general discussion of press freedom or toleration. It was nevertheless a very significant composition not only as a brilliant product of the poet's mind but as a unique testimonial to the great range of ideas provoked by the contemporary debate.

During the following years Milton continued to regard the Presbyterians as the principal domestic enemies of religious and intellectual freedom. In a poem of 1646 against their coercion of conscience, he said of them that "New Presbyter is but Old Priest writ large."[91] His dislike became even stronger when they condemned the execution of Charles I and aligned themselves with the opponents of the English republic. In his prose writings of 1649 and later, he was occupied mostly with the defense of revolution and regicide, republican liberty, and the Cromwellian government. About 1658 he began to write *De doctrina Christiana* (*Christian Doctrine*), a treatise on the teachings of the Christian religion based exclusively on Scripture, on which he labored for many years. Beside the light it sheds on his personal faith and the heresies he adopted, it contained a discussion of the basic conceptions that sustained his belief in toleration, including Christian liberty, the right and necessity of private judgment, and the church as a purely voluntary society over which the state has no authority. This work remained unknown in Milton's time, however, and was not printed until 1825.[92] We may therefore leave it aside in order to look at his fullest public statement in behalf of toleration. Addressed to Parliament, it was entitled *A Treatise of Civil Power in Ecclesiastical Causes* and published in February 1659, the year before the English revolution expired.[93]

In *Areopagitica* Milton had ignored the problem of the relationship of the state to religion, perhaps because he had not yet fully made up his mind on the subject. It is clear, however, that in the following years he became completely opposed to any state establishment of religion, the state's appointment of ministers, and compulsory payments of tithes for the support of the ministry.[94] *A Treatise of Civil Power* addressed the question of church and state, invoking the principle of Christian liberty against any tendency toward the introduction of a state church and government control of religion. Written in a plain, unadorned style, the work relied only on Scriptural texts, which it quoted abundantly. Several of its ideas resembled those of Roger Williams, who might have influenced Milton somewhat.[95] Beginning with the proposition that Protestants embrace God's word in Scripture as the only Rule of Faith, he took this Protestant conviction to its extreme by maintaining that the individual's conscience is the sole and final arbiter in religious matters. Like Williams, he held that no earthly judge, and certainly no visible church or the civil power, could determine the meaning of Scripture. The understanding of the latter must therefore be left to the personal conscience of each Christian guided by the Holy Spirit. Like Williams also, he treated conscientious persuasion in religion as an ultimate fact that must be respected and renders the believer immune from religious coercion. It followed from these considerations that neither the civil magistrate nor church governors had any right to employ force against conscience.[96]

Milton reviewed Saint Paul's famous injunction on the duty of obedience in his letter to the Romans (Romans 13), only to conclude that "this most wrested and vexd place of scripture" allowed the magistrate no power over the church or spiritual things. Christ was the sole governor of the church, ruling a spiritual kingdom concerned entirely with the inner man. To compel conscience was thus not only wicked but futile; it was to "compell hypocrisie" rather than advance religion. Christ's kingdom did not need the help of state coercion, for it subdues the world by its own spiritual power to reach the mind and conscience. Milton accused Protestants of violating their own basic principles when they persecuted others who founded their faith on Scripture. He rejected fears of heresy, blasphemy, and the spread of error as baseless. Taking heresy in its ancient Greek meaning to signify "no word of evil note" but merely the choice of an opinion, he claimed that no believer who held an opinion based on conscience and the best effort to understand the truth could be censured as a heretic. Indeed, those who followed their conscience in the understanding of Scripture, even if they contradicted the visible church and its doctors, were "not heretics, but the best protestants." Only Catholics, he suggested, were true heretics, because they alone clung to beliefs and traditions not probable according to Scripture.[97]

The effect of this reasoning was to strip the state of its authority over religion and the church. The gospel, Milton maintained, had ended the Jewish law's mixture of civil and religious powers, introducing an order of grace, faith, and freedom in which God severed the church from the state. Consequently, to employ force in religion was a violation of Christian liberty, "the fundamental privilege of the gospel."[98]

In *A Treatise of Civil Power* and elsewhere, Milton wrote as a devout Protestant to demonstrate that "the right of Christian and evangelic liberty" constituted a sufficient refutation of all arguments in favor of a state church or religious persecution.[99] He saw no difficulty, however, in agreeing that the magistrate should prohibit and punish blasphemy and idolatry.[100] As in *Areopagitica*, moreover, and in contrast to Roger Williams, he denied liberty to Catholics. For this exclusion he gave several justifications. As adherents of the pope's claim to universal dominion, Catholics were loyal to a foreign sovereign, and political reasons therefore dictated that the magistrate should not tolerate them. In addition, because they based their faith on the church, not Scripture, he claimed that their conscience was enthralled to man's law rather than God's and thereby forfeited its Christian liberty. He even went so far as to say that Catholics had "almost ... no conscience."[101] He remained constant to this position, reiterating it again in 1673 in his final work on toleration, *Of True Religion*, which urged freedom of religion for all Protestants and the suppression of Catholicism.[102]

His illiberal attitude to Catholics was motivated equally by political and religious bias. It is ironic that his intolerance toward them was so unremitting when we note that in 1649 the American colony of Maryland, which was founded and owned by English Catholics, proclaimed the principle of mutual toleration between Catholics and Protestants of every variety. In that year the Catholic Lord Baltimore, the proprietor, and the Maryland Assembly passed an act to punish abusive language against people's religious beliefs, which forbade any forcing of conscience as a danger to the colony's peace and unity.[103] Milton may never have known of this enlightened law, of course, and his refusal to extend freedom to Catholicism, an oppressed religion in England, is explained by his Puritan background and the legacy of religious hatreds left by the Reformation conflict from which he was unable to emancipate his mind.

THE LEVELLERS AND WILLIAM WALWYN

The Levellers have generally and rightly been perceived as "the first democratic political movement in modern history."[104] They were also among the most forceful, resolute, and clear-minded champions of religious freedom in the seventeenth century. A product of the English revolution, they emerged in 1646–1647 as an organized party that grew out of the increasing popular discontent with the inadequate fruits of Parliament's civil war victory over the king, which brought neither religious liberty nor the hoped-for redress of the many political, social, and economic grievances of which they complained. Their principal leaders and spokesmen, John Lilburne, Richard Overton, and William Walwyn, first became politically active as individuals in the fight for toleration against the Presbyterians. This struggle brought them together as inspirers and voices of an organized popular movement whose demands included freedom of religion, democratic reform of Parliament and the system of voting and representation, and other political and social changes. The Leveller party's name originated as a smear based on the false accusation that it aimed to level all distinctions of rank and property. It found its mostly urban supporters and sympathizers among the members of the gathered congregations and Separatist sects, the craftsmen, retailers, and merchants who suffered from the economic hardships and depression caused by the civil war, and in many of the common soldiers and some of the officers in the parliamentary army. The Leveller movement aimed at a revolution within the revolution. It had its own populist ideology and program, its party press and propaganda, its publicists, manifestos, and activists, and its meetings and mass petitions to Parliament. Its organization extended to some of the regiments of Parliament's army, in which the soldiers elected agents to represent them and their grievances. Between 1647 and 1649 it played a significant political role, first as allies of the Independents and Cromwell and then as their adversaries when the Independents refused to accept the Leveller proposals for democratic reform. The Levellers opposed the English republic because it failed to order elections for a new Parliament and depended for its survival on the power of Cromwell's army. Although the movement was largely broken in 1649, when the republican regime imprisoned its leaders and Cromwell executed some of its soldier supporters for mutiny, it created a remarkable body of democratic theories and ideas whose significance was not fully recognized until the twentieth century.[105]

John Lilburne, the Levellers' principal leader, a great popular agitator and pamphleteer, was a Separatist victim of persecution before 1640 who had been flogged and imprisoned for his religious beliefs. He joined in the battle against the Presbyterians' intolerance, which he associated with other burdensome grievances of the time. In a tract of 1645 for freedom of conscience, he wrote that "the Black-Coates," meaning the Presbyterian clergy, would "prove more cruell Task-masters then their dear fathers the Bishops." Opposed to censorship, he demanded that the press "be as open for us" as it was for Presbyterian authors. Like other Separatists, he held that Christ's kingdom was a purely spiritual one distinct from the powers of the world, and, accordingly, that neither parliaments, kings, nor magistrates had any authority over this spiritual kingdom or its subjects. Persecution of conscience, he declared, came from the devil and Antichrist. In a reply to the argument that the civil power had for centuries been involved in matters of religion, he asked to know by what right or authority based on the word of God it had exercised such power. In company with other proponents of religious freedom, he condemned tithes and all forced payments to ministers. His conclusion stated that he was not against Parliament's establishment of a state church provided it granted the freedom of conscience of those who refused to be part of it.[106] This position, as we have seen, was not uncommon on the part of some defenders of toleration in these years who were prepared to accept a state-supported church on condition that it remained voluntary and permitted freedom to dissenters.

Another prominent Leveller publicist was Richard Overton, once a printer and also a Separatist, who had been a member of a Baptist church. His religious unorthodoxy became apparent in 1643 when he published a notorious materialist work, soon to be denounced by Presbyterians as heretical, that affirmed the mortality of the soul until the general resurrection.[107] A clever controversialist who excelled at satire, he was one of the outstanding religious and political pamphleteers of the mid–seventeenth century. His best tract in behalf of religious liberty was *An Araignement of Mr. Persecution*, directed to the House of Commons, a satire depicting a mock trial against Presbyterian persecution, which appeared in 1645 under the pseudonym of Martin Mar-Priest.[108] Its allegorical characters bore names like Reason, Humanity, Sir Simon Synod, and Sir John Presbyter. The work advanced a variety of reasons to indict persecution for its many crimes, the blood it had shed, and the disunity it bred within nations. Overton attacked the intolerance of Protestants and Catholics alike, all of whom acted upon "this rotten & devouring principle of forcing the consciences of one another." If the members of the two faiths were only to know one another, he maintained, they would soon cease to hate and destroy each other and learn to live peaceably together as "all . . . Creatures of one God redeemed by one Lord Iesus Christ." He advocated religious freedom not just for Catholics but for Jews. His main opponents, though, were the Presbyterians, whom he assailed for their ambition for power, religious tyranny, and disobedience to Christ's command in the parable of the tares to let the weeds and good seed grow together until the harvest. "Toleration," he maintained, "is not against Nationall Loyalty, but may well stand with Nationall peace," as witnessed by many ancient and modern examples, including Holland and Poland. One of his arguments contended that religious persecution was contrary to the just liberty of English subjects; hence Independents, Baptists, and all Separatist bodies were entitled as loyal subjects to religious freedom. Near the conclusion, Reason informed Parliament that the people had entrusted it with authority in order to preserve

their just and native liberties, and that it betrayed this trust if it
used any coercive power against individuals to "subject any of their
consciences, persons, or estates to any Ecclesiastical Iurisdiction
whatsoever." Overton's work was thus a justification of universal
religious freedom, which he considered the English people could
claim as a fundamental right.[109]

The most important of the Leveller publicists in the controversy
over toleration was William Walwyn (1600–1680), an affluent
London merchant and man of exceptional urbanity and breadth
of mind.[110] Self-converted in earlier life from Calvinism and the
doctrine of predestination, he embraced a nondenominational
Protestantism founded on free justification through Christ to all
sinners, love and charity as the keystone of true religion, and inner
peace as one of its signs. Although lacking a university and classical
education, he was a wide reader who reported that his mind had
been shaped not only by the Bible and the books of various English Protestant divines, but by certain "humane authors" such as
the ancients Seneca, Plutarch, and Lucian, and the modern
French skeptics Montaigne and Charron. As an admirer of the
Catholic Montaigne and his famous essay on the cannibals who
lived according to nature, Walwyn advised his adversaries in the
contemporary Protestant churches to "go to this Papist, or to these
innocent Cannibals . . . to learn civility, humanity, simplicity of
heart; yea, charity and Christianity."[111] It was his conviction that
"nothing maintains love, unity and friendship in families; Societies, Citties, Countries, Authorities, Nations; so much as a conde-
scention to the giving, and hearing, and debating of reason."[112]
Dedicated to reason, truth, and the value of open, unconstrained
discussion, he refrained from prejudicial judgments against the
sects and heresies that caused such scandal among the orthodox.
His habit was therefore to examine all religions, churches, and
opinions with an open mind, and while sympathizing with some
of the sects, he identified himself with none. He expressed an un-
shakable belief in the right of private judgment and religious freedom as the doctrine of Christ and the conclusion of reason, a
belief reinforced by his recognition of the fallibility of human be-

ings, the impossibility of putting an end to all religious differences, and the triviality of many religious disputes.

Walwyn may have been the first author of the revolutionary era to speak out in favor of complete religious toleration. A short anonymous tract addressed to Parliament that he published in 1641, *A New Petition of the Papists,* was a plea in behalf of all "the afflicted brethren." Making no denominational distinctions, it urged that it would be to the good of the state and people "to tollerate all professions whatsoever, every one being left to his own conscience, none to be punished or persecuted for it." Toleration, it maintained, far from leading to confusion, would contribute to peace, harmony, and love. Walwyn was explicit that Brownists and other Separatists, Puritans, Socinians, Arminians, and Catholics, along with sects like the naked Adamites and the Spiritualist Family of Love, should all be free to worship according to their beliefs because all were servants of Christ. As long as all were "obedient to the State and temporall lawes," they should be allowed to follow their religion, and he was convinced that if this were the case, error would "in time appear . . . perish . . . and vanish as smoake."[113]

This remarkable statement was the prelude to a succession of further publications that Walwyn dedicated to the freedom of religion. All reflected the author's sometimes sharp but always civil and persuasory tone, which avoided any abuse of persons. They often expressed a marked strain of anticlericalism and presented a consistently moralized conception of religion in which Christ as the redeemer stood for love as the highest Christian virtue. One of the most notable of these works was *The Power of Love* (1643), whose opening asked its readers not to be afraid of opinions, whether Anabaptist, Brownist, or Antinomian, and not to trust any authority, but to inquire and think for themselves before coming to a conclusion on any doctrine. If they did this, Walwyn said, they would find "that scarcely any opinion hath beene reported truly to you." He was confident of Christ's love for all mankind, and because of this love, all Christians should be allowed to judge and speak their minds freely so that truth might come to light. Writing in the midst of the civil war, he cautioned against the ministers whose sermons sowed divisions on Parliament's side by inventing "a name of reproach for every particular difference in judgment." Religious differences were bound to exist, and love taught that everyone should bear with others' infirmities. "Such opinions as are not destructive to humane society, nor blaspheme the work of our Redemption," Walwyn affirmed, "may be peaceably endured, and considered in love." It was madness, moreover, to fight over petty opinions. He defended the Separatist sects from the false accusation that they were a danger to society, explaining that if their worship was not as decent as they would have liked, it was because they were "hunted into corners" and "not free to exercise their consciences." In passing, he also noted that governments arose from the consent and agreements of men, and that the learning acquired in the universities was often misused to advance tyranny. He had no esteem for a learned clergy, maintaining that any person who could read English only was just as competent to understand the Scriptures as a Hebrew, Greek, and Latin scholar.[114]

The fundamental ground of Walwyn's defense of religious freedom was an ethical Christianity. It was on this account that he stressed the sanctity of conscience based on each individual's personal persuasion of the truth in religion. In *The Compassionate Samaritane* (1644), which he addressed to the House of Commons, he recommended that in a time of the recovery of "the Common Liberties of England" the House should relieve the oppressed consciences of the Separatists. The main body of the work, entitled "Liberty of Conscience Asserted," offered a defense of Separatism and critique of persecution. The love of God, Walwyn said, which most appeared in people's doing good to others, required that all should enjoy liberty of conscience to worship God and perform Christ's ordinances in their own way, "and no man [to] be punished or discountenanced by Authority for his opinion, unless it be dangerous to the State." He pointed out that Separatists formed their religious opinions intelligently, and that individuals could not help but choose to adhere to their own judgment in

Title page of William Walwyn's anonymously published *The Compassionate Samaritane*, 1644. Walwyn, a London merchant, was one of the most effective spokesmen in behalf of religious toleration as well as a leader of the democratic movement during the English revolution. Courtesy of the Folger Shakespeare Library.

religion; force, moreover, was powerless to change conscience or beget religious unity. In a scathing criticism of the Presbyterian clergy and their vested interests, he accused them of aiming at power as did the bishops, whose repressive policies they continued. To make themselves great, they insisted on the distinction between clergy and laity, declaring that without their help the people could not understand the Scriptures. Walwyn rejected these claims, of course, and with them the tyranny of trying "to force men against their mind and judgment" to believe what ministers or synods concluded to be true. He regarded differences as unavoidable. "All times have produced men of severall wayes," he said, "and I beleive no man thinkes there will be an agreement of judgment as longe as this World lasts"; and if there were such an agreement, he added, it would have to proceed "from the power and efficacie of Truth, not from constraint."[115]

While recognizing the supremacy of the state in all civil matters, Walwyn denied that it had any rightful authority over religion. The people, he explained, in electing a Parliament could not confer on it more power than they justly possessed; they could not entrust it, therefore, with matters of religion and the worship and service of God, which pertained exclusively to individual conscience. And just as no man could bind himself without willful sin to act contrary to conscience and understanding, so no one could convey the power to compel others in religion, nor could Parliament or any assembly or council receive such a power.[116] To the Presbyterian heresy hunter, the Reverend Thomas Edwards, who had accused him of being a dangerous man, he replied in defense of the Separatists:

> [W]hen the question is of Liberty of Conscience, the Scripture tells me, everyone ought to be perswaded in his own mind, and that whatsoever is not of faith, is of sin: it tells me I must doe as I would be done unto: I would not be enforced to the Parish Congregations, then I must not force them to them, or from their owne. God onely perswades the heart: compulsion and enforcement may make a confused masse of dissembling hypocrites, not a Congregation of beleevers.[117]

One of his most succinct and general statements for religious freedom was *Tolleration Justified* (1646), a reply to a declaration of London Presbyterian ministers against toleration, Independency, and Separatism. It began by wondering why the Presbyterians, formerly the victims of episcopal persecution themselves, should not be satisfied with an equal freedom but strive to become the lords and masters of everyone's religion. It then went on to rebut each of the ministers' arguments, denying first of all that dissenting opinions and Separatism necessarily produced division. "Why should we not peaceably beare one with another," Walwyn desired to know, "till our sights grow better, and our light increase?" He rejected the Presbyterians' claim to possess the sole truth in religion and decide what was heresy and schism. No religion, he said, was qualified to be the final judge over another, and every sect and denomination had "a like . . . right to Freedome, or a Toleration." This right originated not in some particular opinion but in "the Equity of every mans being Free in the State he lives in," matters of opinion not being considered unless "they break out into some disturbance, or disquiet to the State." Walwyn held that even those whose minds were "so-far misinformed as to deny a Deity, or the Scriptures" were entitled to this freedom; he hopefully noted that errors like these could be overcome by "the efficacy and convincing power of sound reason and argument." It was the failure of the state to be "equall in its protection" of all religion, rather than toleration, he insisted, that was the cause of perpetual strife. In a comment on the ministers' call for the repression of dangerous opinions, he maintained that "it cannot be just, to set bounds or limitations to toleration, any further than the safety of the people requires."[118]

Walwyn's writings abounded in humanity and a charitable acceptance of religious diversity. He was very conscious of human fallibility as a reason for treating differences tolerantly. He saw the hallmark of the Christian not in churchgoing, fasting, and praying, which he called "the cheapest parts of Religion," but in such actions as resisting oppression, helping the poor, and feeding the hungry. The true Christian, he never doubted, was "the greatest enemy to compulsion or restriction that can be; affirming there is no sinne so unreasonable, or un-Christian, as for one man (especially one erring man) to persecute, punish, or molest another for matters of religion, or to make Lawes, concerning anything supernaturall."[119] What he called toleration was identical in his mind with universal religious freedom. He believed that the state was obliged for the sake of both peace and justice to grant equal protection to all religions, and that citizens must be completely free to practice their faith provided their opinions and actions in religion did not endanger the state.

The leaders of the Leveller party were highly effective popular publicists whose writings and petitions helped to create for a time a broad democratic movement. One of their goals, related to both religious and political freedom, was freedom of the press, which they often mentioned in their tracts. A Leveller petition of 1649 against censorship stated that an unlicensed press was "so essential unto Freedom, as that without it, its impossible to preserve any Nation from being liable to the worst of Bondage."[120] The Levellers also supported religious freedom for Catholics. In a declaration of 1649 they asked for the repeal of all penal statutes against "non-conformists in Religion," both papists and others, maintaining that Catholics were as much entitled to freedom of conscience as all other Christians.[121] Apart from their individual publications, the greatest contribution that the Levellers made toward the securing of religious freedom was their collective program for the reform and renewal of the state, contained in a document they named *An Agreement of the People*. The *Agreement* was a landmark in the history of constitutionalism. It was the first attempt in Western history to establish the state upon a written constitution that defined the powers and limits of free parliamentary government. Embodying the principle of the sovereignty of the people, it was in part a statement of the liberties that the people possessed as inherent natural rights. As its title indicated, it was designed to be submitted to all the people for individual subscription as the only legitimate authorization for the institution of a new political order in the aftermath of the civil war.[122]

The Leveller *Agreement* went through three successive versions in 1647, 1648, and 1649, the last of which was the longest and most comprehensive.[123] The text of all three declared both the powers that the people delegated to their representatives in Parliament and those they reserved to themselves as their native liberties. Beside ordaining such vital political changes as the democratic broadening of the voting franchise for elections to Parliament, equality of all persons before the law, and a number of other major reforms, it mandated complete religious freedom. In its first two versions, the *Agreement* withheld from Parliament the power to impose any form of religion or worship upon the people but permitted it to establish a public though noncompulsory way of instructing the nation. In the final version of 1649, drawn up mainly by Lilburne, Overton, and Walwyn, the possibility of a public church was omitted. The third *Agreement* simply stated that "we do not inpower or entrust our . . . representatives . . . to continue . . . or make any Lawes . . . to compel . . . any person in or about matters of Faith, Religion or Gods worship or to restrain any person from the profession of his faith, or exercise of Religion according to his Conscience." It also commanded Parliament to discontinue the grievance of tithes and compulsory payments to ministers, and prohibited it from disabling any person from holding office in the commonwealth for any religious opinion, except those who maintained the pope's or other foreign supremacy.[124]

The Levellers' hope of achieving religious freedom in their time went unrealized, of course. They left behind them, nevertheless, a significant body of thought that for the first time conceived freedom of conscience and religion not only as a Christian imperative but as a fundamental individual right proper to a free people.

THE ENGLISH REVOLUTION AND RELIGIOUS TOLERATION

Beside those who have been discussed above, there were a considerable number of other writers and thinkers during the revolution who stood on the side of toleration. They were both clergy and laymen who looked at the subject from various perspectives and ranged from moderate to radical in their understanding of reli-

gious freedom. Some were Independents; others belonged to the
Baptist churches: both denominations grew markedly and became
permanently established in England at this time. While each opposed compulsion in religion, the first had a more limited view of
toleration than the second. Thus most Independents as a rule did
not deny the authority of the civil power in religious matters or its
right to suppress heresy and idolatry, whereas the Baptists would
have made a separation between religion and the state.[125] There
were other sects too, as well as visionary individuals not associated
with any church, who utterly condemned persecution and desired
freedom of religion. Among them were the Socinians, who took a
rationalistic approach to religion and were persecuted for their
Antitrinitarianism; radical Spiritualists such as Gerrard Winstanley, a penetrating critic of all organized religion who denounced
spiritual and economic oppression and argued for common ownership of the land; and the new Spiritualist sect of Quakers, who
based their faith on the Inner Light. This religious movement led
by its prophet George Fox, which appeared in the 1650s, made
thousands of converts despite the severe persecution its members
suffered.[126] Another noted Spiritualist was Sir Henry Vane, Jr., a
leading politician and statesman of the Long Parliament and the
English republic, who was executed as a regicide after the restoration of kingship. A religious individualist of mystical tendencies
and a strong proponent of freedom of conscience, Vane wrote
several books which argued that the state had no power in religion
and spiritual matters.[127] In the Anglican Church, which the revolution overthrew, the Royalist clergyman Jeremy Taylor's *The Liberty
of Prophesying* (1647) expounded a liberal attitude of latitudinarian tolerance within the church in opposition to compulsion and
persecution in religion.[128] Theorists of republicanism in the 1650s
were also among the supporters of toleration. *Oceana* (1656), an
influential treatise by James Harrington, the outstanding republican thinker of the 1650s, pictured an ideal English republic that
had a national church but granted freedom to dissenters and
placed the clergy under strict government supervision in order to
ensure religious liberty.[129]

Although the years 1640–1660 resounded with the controversy over toleration, those who believed in tolerating religious diversity among Christians were never more than a minority. Within this minority, a much smaller number went so far as to advocate the separation of state and church. Most supporters of toleration refused to accept that the civil magistrate should have no responsibility or authority in religious matters. Nearly all of them were against freedom for Catholics and likewise drew the line at tolerating heresy or blasphemy. The toleration controversy may have contributed to undermining pretensions to infallibility in religion, yet among the sects, many who believed in tolerance were nevertheless dogmatically certain that they alone possessed the truth. None of the advocates of the removal of the state's control of religion ever envisaged their country as a secular society. They were religious people who assumed that England would always be a pious Christian nation in which faith and worship remained an essential part of personal and public life. In the name of Christianity, however, they argued for religious pluralism in the belief that the state should rightfully recognize freedom for the different churches and denominations and refrain from compulsion in religion.

Intolerance also had noteworthy representatives on its side. William Prynne, a learned lawyer, an Erastian, and a vehement partisan of the Presbyterians against the Independents, published numerous writings maintaining that the state must suppress dissent from the national church lest sectarian anarchy and civil disorder overwhelm the nation.[130] In 1649 Samuel Rutherford, a leading Scottish Presbyterian minister and theologian well acquainted with the English religious scene, published an able comprehensive treatise against freedom of conscience. A rigid Calvinist convinced beyond any doubt that his was the only true church of Christ, he upheld the right and duty of persecution against sects and heresies, making no concession whatever to the claims of conscience.[131] Thomas Hobbes, the foremost philosopher of the period, saw in religious division and clerical ambition a potent cause of political instability and civil war. His most famous work of political philosophy, *Leviathan* (1651), presented a carefully reasoned case to demonstrate that the maintenance of internal peace required the sovereign to possess sole control over religion and the church with the right to punish dissent from the doctrines sanctioned by the state.[132] The governments of the revolutionary era were frequently concerned with heresy and other religious offenses. An ordinance of the Presbyterian-dominated Parliament in 1648 to prevent the spread of heresy and blasphemy imposed the death penalty for the preaching, teaching, or publishing of a variety of prohibited theological beliefs, including Antitrinitarianism. Two years later under the republic, Parliament passed an act "against several Atheistical, Blasphemous and Execrable Opinions, derogatory to the honor of God, and destructive to humane Society," which was primarily intended to suppress the Antinomian doctrines of certain sects who held that they were free of sin and the moral law.[133]

Owing to the toleration struggle, the interregnum that followed the abolition of the monarchy in 1649 became the most tolerant epoch that England had thus far known. A major piece of legislation in 1650 for the relief of religious and peaceable people repealed the previous statutes that had made church attendance compulsory. It left England without a national church, either Anglican or Presbyterian, and gave freedom to individuals to attend religious services at the place of their choice.[134] While the governments of the republic and then of Oliver Cromwell as Lord Protector between 1654 and 1658 never relinquished control of religion and made various efforts to define the acceptable limits of doctrinal divergence, they allowed almost all Protestant denominations and sects to practice their faith without molestation. The Presbyterian system that Parliament had tried to impose in the previous decade remained unfinished and never became compulsory: Presbyterian churches were obliged to coexist with Independents, Baptists, and other sects in a relationship of mutual tolerance. Because Antitrinitarianism remained a heresy under the law, the repression of Socinians continued intermittently. Although Catholic worship was banned and two priests were executed in the 1650s, government policy nevertheless tended generally toward practical tolerance of Catholics. As a national leader and Lord Protector, Cromwell showed himself particularly solicitous to assure freedom of conscience for all the Protestant Christians, whom he considered the people of God though they belonged to different religious bodies. Undogmatic and lacking any inclination to persecute, he was also lenient toward Anglicans, who continued to hold private services throughout the period. He tried to mitigate the persecution of Quakers, which was due more to local initiative than to the government's policy. Sympathetic also to the Jews, he shared the philosemitism of some of the Puritans and favored their official readmission to England.[135] Not only did the revolutionary era give rise to a great body of tolerationist ideas; it produced a degree of religious pluralism impossible to eradicate after 1660, which made a substantial contribution in the long run to the achievement of religious toleration in English society.[136]

CHAPTER 7

John Locke and Pierre Bayle

༄༅

In the closing years of the seventeenth century and the first decades of the eighteenth, the fires of religious passions were slowly dying down in Europe, and the last age of faith in Western civilization springing from the Protestant Reformation was gradually expiring. Rationalist, deist, empiricist, and skeptical trends were making steady inroads in philosophy and theology and, together with the beginnings of the historical criticism of the Bible, were undermining orthodox religion and fostering free thought, indifference, and unbelief. These developments, whose growing effects were felt chiefly among members of the educated upper classes, intellectuals, and men of letters, marked the inaugural stage of the Enlightenment in Europe, an era that proclaimed the autonomy and supremacy of human reason.[1] Despite such significant cultural shifts, however, institutional religion remained a powerful force in Western society and intolerance a troubling problem. The only country where genuine toleration of religious denominations outside the state church existed was the Dutch Republic. In France under the regime of the Edict of Nantes, the Catholic monarchy permitted Protestants of the Reformed Church legal toleration of a limited character. Everywhere else religious minorities had been suppressed or were obliged to suffer penalties for their refusal to conform to the religion of the state or ruler.

In Protestant England after 1660, questions of religious difference remained acute during the reigns of Charles II (1649–1685) and his brother James II (1685–1688). The period of the Restoration, which returned the Stuart monarchy and the Anglican Church to power, was one of political and religious reaction in which England once more became a persecuting society. By this time, though, the situation was very different from the past owing to the fact that the main dissenting denominations to emerge during the revolution, the Presbyterians, Independents (or Congregationalists), and Baptists, had all become too well established to be suppressed. The Quakers, too, had grown in numbers in spite of persecution. At the time of his return from exile, Charles II published a declaration offering dissenters the hope of toleration. A conference also ensued between the Anglican bishops and leading dissenting ministers with the idea of making the Anglican Church more comprehensive by concessions designed to incorporate the Presbyterians in particular. Lack of flexibility on both sides, however, caused this conference to fail, so that neither comprehension nor toleration came to pass. Many Anglicans were determined to be revenged on Puritans and dissenters, whom they held responsible for overthrowing the church and engulfing the nation in twenty years of revolt and usurpation. In the decade of the 1660s a Parliament made up of Royalists and Anglicans enacted a body of legislation imposing heavy penalties on Protestant dissenters. These measures included a new act of religious uniformity in 1662 requiring all ministers of religion to be episcopally ordained, use only the Anglican Book of Common Prayer in church services, and declare their assent under oath to everything contained in the prayer book. Nearly a thousand clergy who had held parish ministries during the revolution, the majority of them Presbyterians, were ejected or left the Anglican Church because of their unwillingness to swear this oath. Other statutes barred dissenters from holding municipal office unless they took communion in the Anglican Church; prohibited meetings for worship attended by five or more persons not part of the household, unless conducted according to the Anglican prayer book; and forbade dissenting ministers to come within five miles of their former parish or any corporate town. Violation of these laws was punishable by fines, prison, and other penalties. An act of 1662 aimed specifically at Quakers caused hundreds of them to be imprisoned. Catholics were also persecuted. Besides the earlier penal legislation against them, the Test Act of 1673, renewed in 1678, compelled all holders of civil and military offices to sign a declaration against transubstantiation and take the Anglican communion or forfeit their places. In 1678, accusations of a Popish Plot to assassinate Charles II and set fire to London incited a national outburst of anti-Catholic feeling and further persecution of Catholics.[2]

On several occasions the king attempted to offer Protestant dissenters and Catholics some relief from the persecutory Anglican regime. He strove to accomplish this end by means of a Declaration of Indulgence suspending the operation of the penal laws, which he issued on his sole will as an exercise of the royal prerogative. Charles II, who inclined secretly to Catholicism and became a convert just before his death, twice promulgated such a declaration, first in 1662 and again in 1672. In each case, however, he was forced to withdraw it because Parliament challenged the king's authority to suspend the law. In 1687 James II, an avowed and open Catholic, issued another Declaration of Indulgence to suspend the penal laws against all dissenters, both Protestant and Catholic. His doing so, and other actions in behalf of Catholics that aroused the suspicion that he was planning to legalize Catholicism as a step toward making England Catholic, were among the causes that brought about his overthrow in the revolution of 1688.[3]

Anglican apologists advanced various arguments to justify the government's persecution of dissenters. They stressed the necessity of a national church and the harmfulness of religious disunity and schism. They charged dissenters with unreasonable separation from the Anglican Church merely over things indifferent in religion (i.e., neither commanded nor forbidden by Scripture), which the magistrate therefore had the right to regulate for the sake of order and uniformity. They maintained that while the mag-

istrate was powerless to deprive people of their liberty of judgment, he was entitled to restrain the expression of opinion if it
did harm. They also made wide use of Saint Augustine's defense of
religious coercion in his writings against the Donatists.[4] Although
agreeing that force could not compel or change belief, they defended its employment as legitimate and useful on the ground
that it could help to produce a receptive frame of mind, induce
those in error to reconsider their opinions, and thus serve indirectly to bring them to the truth.[5]

In France, relations between the Catholic state and the Huguenots, or Protestants of the French Reformed Church (which Catholics called the Pretended Reformed Religion), were regulated by
the Edict of Nantes issued by Henry IV in 1598. This royal decree
was supposed to be valid in perpetuity and carried a pledge that
it would never be revoked. While it assured Protestants legal toleration with certain political guarantees for their security, it also subjected the exercise of their religion to a number of restrictions
that placed them on a much less than equal footing with Catholics.
Rather than a recognition of the principle of liberty of conscience,
the edict was an act of expediency to which at the time there
seemed no alternative. It froze the religious situation as it was in
1598, so that under its terms the Reformed Church could neither
change nor expand. The Protestants possessed freedom of worship in a number of designated towns and localities. They also had
a political organization, which the government abolished in 1629
after the suppression of several Huguenot revolts. In the succeeding decades, the Protestants became notable for their strong
support of the authority and absolutism of the French monarchy,
which was also supposed to be the protector of their religious
rights. During the later seventeenth century there may have been
a million French Protestants in a nation of about twenty million
inhabitants. In the daily life of particular communities, peaceful
coexistence between Protestants and Catholics was often the case.
The physical proximity of members of the two religions plus family
ties and intermarriages among them contributed to mutual toler-

ance at the communal level. Henry IV's son Louis XIII (1610–
1643), however, and his grandson Louis XIV (1643–1715) were
hostile to the Protestants, as were the Catholic clergy and many
devout Catholics, who considered their presence an anomaly in a
Catholic state. In general, the spirit of Catholic renewal, which
was very active in France at this period, was strongly opposed to
the coexistence of Catholics with Protestants.

After 1661, when Louis XIV assumed personal control of his
government, the position of the French Protestants steadily deteri-
orated. The king, who ruled as an absolute monarch, created what
was for that time a highly centralized authoritarian regime. Reasons of state dictated his government's desire for religious uniformity because the existence of a Protestant minority in France
seemed incompatible with national unity. Becoming more devout
and bigoted in his later years, the king was also eager to eliminate
heresy among his subjects so that he could boast that France was
"toute Catholique." At first royal decrees and policy imposed new
restrictions on Protestants while also offering them financial rewards as an incentive to conversion. In a continuing process of
repression came further measures impairing their religious liberty, such as the demolition of their churches and the removal of
Protestant children from their parents and their rearing as Catholics. The government justified some of its actions against the Protestants as the strict enforcement of the letter of the Edict of Nantes
against illegal violations. From 1681 it also resorted to the notorious *dragonnades*, the brutal system of quartering dragoons on Protestant households in which these soldiers perpetrated all sorts of
outrages. During this same period Louis XIV was also persecuting
the Jansenists, a rigorist movement within French Catholicism. His
mistreatment of his Protestant subjects, however, was far worse.
The persecution of the latter culminated in October 1685 with
the revocation of the Edict of Nantes, based on the claim that
since Protestantism no longer existed in France, the edict was ob-
solete. The decree of revocation banned Protestant worship and
called for the destruction of all Protestant churches. It ordered
the banishment of pastors who refused to convert and forbade lay

people to leave the country or remove their property. Despite this prohibition, 200,000 or more Protestants left France to find refuge abroad in the Dutch Republic, England, parts of Germany and Switzerland, the American colonies, and elsewhere.[6]

The revocation of the Edict of Nantes was an event of great significance in European Protestantism and had considerable international repercussions. France, then the preponderant military power in Europe, had already manifested its ambition for aggrandizement by territorial annexations plus a series of aggressive wars against the Spanish Netherlands and the Dutch Republic. Particularly among the Dutch and in England the revocation aroused wide public anger, concern, and opposition to Louis XIV's government as a menacing union of political absolutism and Catholic religious tyranny.

As a manifestation of cruel religious persecution and the suffering it caused, the revocation also made an indelible impression on the Englishman John Locke (1632–1704) and the Frenchman Pierre Bayle (1647–1706). Both men were then living as exiles in Holland, where they could witness the flood of Protestant refugees coming from France. Bayle himself, moreover, was a Huguenot who had left France a few years before to escape persecution. Aside from Spinoza, Locke and Bayle were the most important thinkers to deal with the problem of toleration in the later seventeenth century. Locke was one of the foremost philosophers of his time; Bayle was not only a philosopher but an enormously erudite scholar and antiquarian. Both were among the main precursors of the European Enlightenment. With the writings of these two powerful minds, the early modern debate over religious toleration, begun in the sixteenth century after the advent of the Protestant Reformation, may be said to have reached its final stage in the cumulative creation of a rich, broad, and strong rationale. The work of a succession of writers beginning with Castellio, it undermined and discredited the Christian theory of persecution and demonstrated the rightness and necessity of religious freedom and pluralism in a Christian society.

Portrait of the philosopher John Locke by Sylvester Brounouwer, ca. 1685. Locke's *Epistola de tolerantia* (*Letter concerning Toleration*), 1689, remains the best-known defense of religious toleration by any English thinker of the seventeenth century. Courtesy of the National Portrait Gallery, London.

LOCKE'S EARLY WRITINGS ON TOLERATION

Locke was the son of a Puritan family in the west of England whose religion was Calvinism. His father, a small landowner who fought on the side of Parliament in the civil war, was a supporter of Presbyterianism. After attending the famous Westminster School in London, Locke proceeded to Oxford in 1652 as a member of Christ Church College. Following his graduation and an M.A. degree, he became a Student (fellow) of Christ Church in 1658, a position he held until 1684 when he was expelled from his fellowship for political reasons. He once asserted, "I had no sooner found myself in the world than I perceived myself in a storm." He lived a very eventful life, growing up amid the turmoil, political and religious debates, and violent conflicts of the English revolution, and later taking part in the fierce political dissensions of the Restoration era in the 1670s and 1680s that climaxed in the revolution of 1688. At Oxford, if not earlier, he would certainly have thought about the problem of toleration. The head of Christ Church and vice-chancellor of Oxford during the 1650s, the Reverend John Owen, an eminent Independent minister and one of Oliver Cromwell's advisers, was an advocate of liberty of conscience. So was Locke's college friend Henry Stubbe, with whom he corresponded on the subject and who in a work of 1659 urged toleration for all religious bodies, including Anglicans, Catholics, and Quakers.[7]

Locke was a versatile and original thinker. In later life he achieved an enduring reputation for his influential philosophical treatise, *An Essay concerning Human Understanding* (1689); his defense of the right of revolution and foundational contribution to the formation of modern liberalism, *Two Treatises on Government* (1689); and his *A Letter concerning Toleration* (1689). His lesser works included *Some Thoughts concerning Education* (1693) and *The Reasonableness of Christianity* (1695). He studied medicine and was the friend of such leading scientists as Robert Boyle, Dr. Thomas Sydenham, and Isaac Newton. He was active in public affairs as a close personal adviser to the earl of Shaftesbury, one of the most prominent political figures in the reign of Charles II. Never married, he traveled in Germany and France, and in 1683, when his involvement in opposition politics made it unsafe for him to remain in England, he went to the Dutch Republic to live as an exile for the next five years.[8] Returning home after the revolution of 1688, he held a post as one of the commissioners on the British government's Board of Trade and published several tracts on economic subjects. Locke was a deeply religious Christian, although unorthodox in various respects in his later years. Like Newton he became an Antitrinitarian and was in sympathy with the Socinians. Despite his abandonment of the doctrine of predestination, he never shed the Calvinistic Puritan ethic that was at the root of his moralism and belief in the necessity of work, self-discipline, and obedience to God as mankind's creator. A thinker with an impressive range of intellectual interests and achievements, he possessed a keen understanding of politics, large knowledge of the world, and great practical experience and wisdom. His dedication to the principle of toleration was something he came to gradually and only after close reflection and observation.

The issue of toleration in England as it presented itself after the Restoration involved the existence not only of Catholics but of the large minority of Protestant dissenters of various denominations outside the Anglican Church who demanded freedom to practice their religion. The worst persecuted of them were the Quakers, but all were oppressed by the penal laws prohibiting their worship and imposing disabilities for their nonconformity to Anglicanism.

Locke first addressed the question of toleration in two tracts of 1660–1661 that he never published. Similar in content, the first was in English, the second in Latin.[9] It is evident from these works that at this stage in his intellectual development he cared much less about religious liberty than about the stability of government and the maintenance of its authority. In them he deplored the English revolution and hailed the happy return of Charles II. With the memory of the revolution fresh in his mind, he feared that people would use the claim of religious freedom not, as he put it, in order to be Christians but "so as not to be subjects" and to engage their country "in perpetual dissension and disorder."[10] The point on which both tracts focused was the power of the magistrate in indifferent things, the subject of a previous work by Edward Bagshawe, also a Student of Christ Church College, to which the first of Locke's tracts was a direct reply.[11] We need only consider this reply to understand his position at this time.

Indifferent things in religion, as I have noted earlier, were those which were thought to be neither forbidden nor commanded in Scripture. The concept, which Christian theologians designated by the Greek term *adiaphora*, went back to statements in Saint Paul's letters about what believers in Christ were free to do or not to do. Protestant theologians usually discussed it in connection with the doctrine of Christian liberty, as Calvin did, for example, in his exposition of freedom in "things indifferent" on which the Christian conscience was left free.[12] Indifferent things in religion covered matters like rites and ceremonies, ecclesiastical organization, clerical vestments, foods and fasts, church ornaments, and other aspects of external worship and observance. Insofar as they were in themselves neither morally good nor evil, God left indifferent things to be used or omitted in accordance with human discretion. One of the troublesome complications of this concept, however, was the possibility of disagreement on whether something was indifferent. This was among the main points of dispute between the Anglican Church and dissenters of different denominations; the latter, who took a much more restrictive view of the scope of indifferency, could not conscientiously accept as indifferent certain ceremonies, practices, and forms of church government that the law enjoined and to which political and religious authority therefore required conformity as a duty.[13]

It was Bagshawe's contention that indifferent things relating to religion fell within the realm of Christian liberty and should be left entirely to individual conscience; hence the magistrate ought to have no authority to determine for any other Christian whether or how indifferent things in religion should be used. Locke's answer to this tolerant position was a clear-cut denial springing from his conception of political society. In whatever way magistracy may have originated, he said, when men placed themselves under government for the sake of peace and security, they had to part with their natural freedom. They therefore resigned to the magistrate the right and power to determine what should be done regarding indifferent things. Because the magistrate was empowered to make law and command what any subject could lawfully do, he also had the right to impose the use of indifferent things in religion, which subjects were obligated to obey. Locke's case was basically a political one with overtones resembling the absolutist ideas

of the philosopher Thomas Hobbes. Refusing to separate indifferent things in religion from those that pertained to the civil
order, he insisted that the magistrate's authority must extend to
both alike if peace and security were to exist. He showed no sympathy for the earlier Puritan cause and its complaints against
superstitious Anglican ceremonies as a violation of conscience.
The specious plea of religion and the call for reformation, he
noted, had been repeatedly used in Europe as a justification for
rebellion. Recalling that in England "a liberty to tender consciences" was the first cause of "all those confusions" that had
overwhelmed the nation, he blamed the civil war on "overzealous
contentions" about small, indifferent religious matters. He
warned against the danger of allowing the multitude the free and
unrestrained exercise of religion. If the individual conscience
were permitted to hold sway in indifferent things, he wondered
how religious sectarians could be compelled to pay tithes to the
state church, and Quakers be made to remove their hats in due
respect to the magistrate. He was convinced that should the people ever believe that government lacked authority to enjoin things
indifferent in religion, they would apply this view to civil actions
as well. For Locke indifferent things were to be treated the same
whether they pertained to civil or religious matters. His essential
claim, therefore, was that the ends of political society made the
magistrate's power over indifferent things in religion both legitimate and necessary.[14]

Locke's tract made clear his support for a regime of religious
uniformity defined and enforced by the magistrate. Besides its
main thesis, one other element is of interest in this early work.
Locke stressed that while the magistrate was powerless to compel
belief, he could affect individuals' actions by rewards and punishments. Accordingly, in the realm of indifferent things in religion,
"rigour which cannot work on internal persuasion may notwithstanding [produce] an outward conformity," which was all that
was necessary.[15] The distinction Locke thus made between mental
states like belief or assent, on the one hand, and outward actions,
on the other, resembled a similar argument by Hobbes, who had

stated in *Leviathan* (1651) that while "Internall Faith" was invisible and exempt from all human jurisdiction, words and actions fell under the sovereign's authority.[16] Locke's view also aligned him with Anglican opponents of the dissenters in the 1660s, who, as noted above, maintained that the conformity demanded of the latter restrained only their external practices, not their liberty of conscience or judgment. Replying to this type of Anglican argument, John Owen, speaking as a prominent dissenter, maintained that conscience could not be free without freedom of action, and that imposed conformity was an attempt to force assent.[17] The Quaker William Penn similarly declared that liberty of conscience was not a mere freedom to believe "but the exercise of ourselves in a visible way of worship" as the necessary expression of belief that, if neglected, would "incur sin and divine wrath."[18]

Locke next took up the question of toleration in 1667 in *An Essay concerning Toleration*, which substantially altered his previous authoritarian position on the magistrate's power in religion. In this work, which he likewise never published, he tried to marshal with considerable precision the reasons that justified a large degree of toleration to dissenters. What accounts for this striking change of view is unclear. It may have had to do with some of his reading at that period and with his perception of the unjust hardships inflicted on dissenters. Probably one of the principal causes was his new association with Lord Ashley, later made earl of Shaftesbury, whom he first met in 1666. Shaftesbury (1621–1683), whose public career had begun during the English revolution, became one of Charles II's most important ministers of state after the Restoration. He was an astute and sophisticated politician, an outstanding speaker, and a talented man of business who served the king in a number of high offices. Subscribing to liberal religious views, he was in favor of a national state church with freedom for dissenters. Locke became his physician and in that capacity saved his life by an operation. A close relationship developed between them, which led Locke to join the nobleman's household and act thereafter as his aide and adviser.[19] The 1667 *Essay* reads like a brief or position paper that Locke drafted to assist Shaftesbury in influencing government policy in the direction of toleration for dissenters.[20] It also gives the definite impression that its author is a member of the Anglican Church. Locke's conceptions of both government and religious knowledge shaped this document, which fell broadly into two parts, one containing general observations, the other dealing with their application to England's situation.[21]

Again his starting point was political, based on the assumption that the magistrate was entrusted with power solely for the good, preservation, and peace of the people placed under his rule. These ends, according to Locke, ought to be the standard of all law and government. He then proceeded to distinguish three categories of opinions and actions in reference to toleration: (1) opinions and actions that did not concern society because they were purely speculative and related to the performance of divine worship; (2) those neither good nor evil in their nature, but that concerned society and the dealings of human beings with each other: these were practical opinions and acts in themselves indifferent; and, finally, (3) opinions and actions that concerned society and were intrinsically good or bad, hence moral virtues or vices. With this classification as a framework, he went on to argue that the things in the first category had "an absolute and universal right to toleration." Purely speculative opinions, like belief in the Trinity, purgatory, and transubstantiation, he held, deserved complete freedom because they pertained only to men's relationship to God, not to their actions as members of society. Besides speculative opinions, the determination of ways of worship also deserved complete toleration because, being unable to harm others or the community, they were beyond the scope of politics and government. As the magistrate was not infallible and could not affect the interest of individuals in a future world, he should refrain from prescribing anything to them to do with worship. Nor should he presume to force others to follow his own way of going to heaven, because men did not give him the power to choose their way of salvation for them. On this point Locke also stressed that religion was not susceptible to compulsion and could be changed only by the inward constraint of the spirit.[22]

The second category, which comprised indifferent actions and opinions, was more complicated. As examples of what it included, Locke mentioned practical things like deciding times of rest and work, the rearing of children, and arrangements for the disposition of estates, but its range, of course, was indefinitely wide. He continued to hold, as he had in the earlier *Two Tracts*, that the magistrate had power over all indifferent things tending to the peace and security of the people. He likewise maintained that everything in this category had "a title to toleration" as long as it did not lend itself to disturbances of the state. This meant that the magistrate should not interpose his authority in this domain except as it conduced to the people's safety and welfare. Locke pointed out that opinions on indifferent matters could not claim toleration as a matter of conscience, because the subject's conscience could not possibly be the measure by which the magistrate framed his laws. Trying to indicate the degrees and limits of the restraints the magistrate could use against acts and opinions in themselves indifferent, he allowed that the magistrate could prohibit the publication of any opinions tending to the disturbance of government, and could also forbid actions flowing from these opinions. But while the magistrate had to be the judge in such matters, Locke warned that he must avoid making laws or imposing restraints unless the state's or people's welfare required them, and that God would hold him to account should he abuse his power and oppress his subjects. He also explained that if government commanded men to act contrary to their conscience in this domain, they ought to follow their conscience but without violence by submitting to the law's penalty for their disobedience. Subjects who disobeyed for this reason, however, must be sure that their conscience hadn't deceived them to think something unlawful or unnecessary which was not. Since "liberty of conscience" was "the great privilege of the subject," Locke declared, and "the right of imposing was the great prerogative of the magistrate, they ought the more narrowly to be watched that they do not mislead either magistrate or subject" to do wrong.[23]

The third category, made up of actions considered good or bad in themselves, included the moral duties in the second table of the Ten Commandments and the moral virtues of the philosophers. Locke judged that these had little relevance to disputes over toleration. Moreover, so far as they pertained to people's souls and hopes of a future life, they were of no concern to the magistrate, whose interest in them was only in their effect on relations in society.[24]

In some further remarks he also took note of the fact that some religious opinions and organized religious groups could be dangerous to society's peace and safety. In such a case, he did not doubt that the magistrate would be justified in suppressing them. At the same time he rejected the objection commonly made against toleration that to permit the existence of different religions in one country would cause disorders, conspiracy, and sedition against the government. In his view, toleration was a much better safeguard of peace than repression, especially if all religious bodies received fair treatment.[25]

Having laid down what he called "the limits of imposition and liberty," Locke next turned to England to decide whether "toleration or imposition" was the best means to promote its peace and welfare. At the outset he excluded Catholics from the benefits of toleration because some of their religious opinions were destructive to all governments but the pope's, and because they practiced persecution themselves whenever they had the power. It always remained his view that a religion that refused to tolerate other beliefs should not be tolerated itself. Concerning Protestant dissenters, however, he made a major shift from his earlier position. Toward them he urged a policy of charity and toleration. He deplored labeling them "fanatics," a name, he said, that should be laid aside. His main reason for proposing to grant them toleration was the wrongfulness and folly of attempting to achieve religious uniformity by force. Persecution not only tended to drive its victims to resistance but could not possibly change their minds and had never prevented the growth of dissent. That persecutors considered themselves right, he pointed out, could not justify persecution, since all people thought their own beliefs were right. After thus demonstrating the futility and dangers of religious oppression, Locke closed with some brief practical comments and suggestions of topics for discussion intended to show that "toleration and latitudinism" would contribute significantly to English unity, economic prosperity, and power.[26]

Locke produced several versions of this 1667 essay, in the last of which he liberalized his views still more. Revising his treatment of things indifferent, he now came to the striking conclusion—a total reversal of his previous opinion—that in matters of religion and worship nothing was indifferent. For him to concede this meant looking at religious practices and worship from within the subjective standpoint of the persons who believed in them, and to whom, therefore, none of these things could be indifferent. While this change of perspective did not alter his conviction that the magistrate necessarily possesses power to regulate things indifferent—an idea that remained a permanent part of his thought, it did mean that the magistrate's authority should not encompass religion and worship, because on Locke's latest understanding, the concept of indifference did not apply to them.[27] With this concession, he provided a rationale for a broad and permissive policy of religious tolerance and freedom.

Although Locke often spoke of the preservation of the people's lives and safety as the magistrate's prime duty, the natural rights of individuals, which were to constitute a key concept of his political philosophy, did not figure in the theory of toleration he sketched in the 1667 essay. Two features in particular gave this work its distinctive and original character. The first was its analysis of indifferent things and the several categories of opinions and actions. This led Locke to conclude that in the main religious beliefs and worship, since they were directed toward God, didn't affect and couldn't injure society and should therefore be immune from government action. The second was its argument that the magistrate was not empowered to choose the religion or way of salvation of his subjects, and was incapable of doing so anyway, because he was not infallible. Both features tended to conceive the state as an exclusively secular institution separate from religion. They also clearly implied that individuals had to be their own judges of the way to heaven without any interference by the state. Other reasons Locke advanced in favor of toleration were based on both pragmatism and principle. He now condemned compulsion in religion because it was morally wrong, powerless to change belief, and likely to incite resistance. He also stressed the benefits of toleration in augmenting the nation's trade and riches. While he left it to the magistrate to decide whether a religious opinion was so dangerous to society that it should be suppressed, the main thrust of his work was to exempt belief and worship from the magistrate's authority.

Since Locke never published the 1667 *Essay*, its thoughts merely stand as a record of his intellectual evolution and a forerunner of his main and fullest statement on the subject of toleration written some years later. In 1669, however, he collaborated with Shaftesbury in drafting the constitution of the North American Carolina colony, of which the nobleman and several of his associates were the proprietors. Although the religious arrangements laid down in this document reflected Shaftesbury's convictions, they were similar to the ideas expressed in Locke's previous *Essay*. They ordained that the Anglican Church should be the colony's state church, supported by public funds, but also granted liberty of religion to dissenters, Jews, and others in order to maintain "civil peace . . . amidst diversity of opinions." Any seven or more persons were free to form a church and worship as they determined. Membership in a church was made a condition of receiving the protection of the law and holding any office of profit or honor. The constitution prohibited abusive language against the religion of any church and any molestation or persecution of a person for "his speculative opinions in religion . . . or way of worship."[28]

LOCKE'S *A LETTER CONCERNING TOLERATION*

There was probably never a time in which the problem of toleration was far from Locke's mind. The issue was impossible to avoid in the conflicts of his age between the defenders of Anglicanism

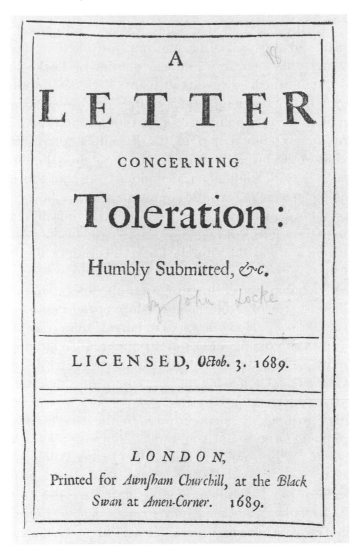

A

LETTER

CONCERNING

Toleration :

Humbly Submitted, &c.

by John Locke

LICENSED, Octob. 3. 1689.

LONDON,
Printed for Awnsham Churchill, at the Black
Swan at Amen-Corner. 1689.

Title page of the anonymously published English edition of 1689 of Locke's *Letter concerning Toleration.* Courtesy of the Folger Shakespeare Library.

and dissenters. In 1670, *A Discourse of Ecclesiastical Polity* by the Anglican clergyman Samuel Parker, a chaplain of the archbishop of Canterbury, affirmed the civil magistrate's authority over the religion and conscience of subjects in a fierce attack against dissenters and the claim to toleration. Parker's influential book, which achieved a great deal of notoriety, provoked a number of replies, including some brief critical queries by Locke that remained unpublished.[29] Locke read many Anglican authors over the years. Some of them were irenic thinkers known as latitudinarians, the advocates of a policy of religious comprehension through measures of accommodation to the dissenters on indifferent things that would bring them back into the national church. In 1680–1681 Edward Stillingfleet, an eminent Anglican churchman and theologian who had favored comprehension, published a sermon and a book that denounced the dissenters' unwillingness to conform to the Church of England as a violation of the peace and unity of religion and the church. Locke was one of the host of critics who responded to Stillingfleet's arguments, writing an unpublished detailed answer that supported the toleration of different religions and of Protestant worship outside the national church.[30] Locke's personal library contained numerous publications by advocates of toleration and exponents of an antidogmatic Christianity. Among them were several books by Castellio—including *Contra libellum Calvini,* his attack upon Calvin's defense of the killing of heretics—Acontius's *Strategmatum Satanae,* the works of Coornhert, writings by Socinians and by the Dutch Arminians Episcopius and Grotius, the Anglican Chillingworth's *The Religion of Protestants,* Milton's political tracts, the Quaker William Penn's book of 1670, *The Great Case of Liberty of Conscience,* Spinoza's *Tractatus Theologico-Politicus,* and Pierre Bayle's treatise on toleration, *Commentaire philosophique sur ces paroles de Jésus Christ, "Contrains-les d'entrer",* published three years prior to Locke's own *A Letter concerning Toleration.*[31]

During the late 1670s Locke was associated with Shaftesbury when the earl became the leader of an opposition movement that developed in Parliament and the country as a result of growing fears that England was moving toward a union of absolutism and Catholicism like that of Louis XIV's government in France. The focal point of the conflict was the campaign of persuasion and intimidation Shaftesbury and his allies launched to exclude Charles II's Catholic brother and next heir, James, duke of York, from the succession to the throne. The struggle led to a political crisis from which Charles II emerged in 1681 with his authority strengthened by the defeat of the opposition movement. His brother James II, who succeeded him in 1685, pursued the trend toward absolutism, which included his effort to legalize Catholicism by suspending the penal laws, until his overthrow. Shaftesbury, his life in danger in England, had to flee for political refuge to Amsterdam, where he died in January 1683. Fearful for his own safety, Locke also took refuge in Holland in the autumn of 1683. He returned to England five years later, following the revolution against James II that replaced him with William and Mary as sovereigns.

Locke's *Epistola de tolerantia* (*A Letter concerning Toleration*) dates from his period of exile. While he always presented himself as a member of the Anglican Church, the ideas in this work were the product not only of his liberal and sympathetic attitude toward the existence of religious dissent, but of his association while in the Dutch Republic with thinkers of highly tolerant views. Among the closest friends he made there were Philip van Limborch, a distinguished Arminian theologian of the Remonstrant church in Amsterdam, and the freethinking English Quaker merchant and bibliophile Benjamin Furly, in whose house in Rotterdam he lived for two years. Beyond these circumstances, *A Letter concerning Toleration* was also written at a time when he had matured the revolutionary political theses presented in his *Two Treatises of Government* and the philosophy of mind contained in *An Essay on Human Understanding*, both published in 1689, the same year as the *Letter.* The former in its exposition of natural rights and justification of the right of revolution made no mention of toleration or religious freedom. The latter, however, touched directly and indirectly on toleration at several points. Its emphasis on the limitations of human knowledge and the distinction between faith and reason, leading to the conclusion that religious differences could not be definitively resolved, was conducive to toleration. Its long discussion of the imperfections and ambiguities of language included some observations on the difficulties and uncertainties in the interpretation of texts like the Bible, which made disagreements inevitable. Hence Locke admonished that "it would become us to be charitable to one another in our Interpretations or Misunderstanding of those ancient Writings." In a chapter on the degrees of assent, he also pointed out the unavoidable uncertainty of many of the beliefs people held, which he took as a ground to urge the necessity of mutual toleration and "the common Offices of Humanity, and Friendship, in the diversity of Opinions."[32]

A *Letter concerning Toleration* was written in Holland in 1685 against the dark background of the revocation of the Edict of Nantes in France and the Catholic reign of James II in Britain. Locke wrote it in Latin for his friend Limborch. The latter then published the work in 1689, and an English translation printed in London appeared in the same year.[33] Although it had some basic points in common with Locke's earlier writings on toleration, it also contained a number of fresh or more fully developed ideas. It began with the new and remarkable claim that toleration was "the chief distinguishing mark of a true church." This was a further move in the direction of a profound moralization of Christianity that placed great emphasis on its ethical-humanitarian character. Love, charity, and goodwill, according to Locke, were the true meaning of the Christian religion, and persecution was therefore contrary to the gospel. He described persecutors as wicked hypocrites actuated by pride and lust for power who masked their unchristian cruelty under the pretext of the advancement of religion and care for the commonwealth. Both reason and the gospel, he held, mandated the toleration of different opinions in religion, and it seemed to him monstrous that men were blind to so obvious a truth. Beside censuring the practice of persecution among Christians, he also deplored the persecution of pagans and idolaters and the forcible conversion of Indians in America. The incompatibility of religious intolerance with the spirit and teaching of Christ was one of his major themes.[34]

He then proceeded to propound his fundamental thesis, which was continuous with that in his earlier works. "I regard it as necessary above all," he stated, "to distinguish between the business of civil government and that of religion, and to mark the true bounds between the church and the commonwealth." While the commonwealth was a society of people established solely to preserve and advance their civil goods—life, liberty, bodily health, and property—religion was concerned with a future life and the care of the soul. The jurisdiction of the civil magistrate was accordingly limited to securing subjects in the civil goods of their earthly existence, for which end compulsion was a necessary means. Religion, on the other hand, was a matter exclusively for the individual, who was incapable of abandoning his concern for his salvation by adopting under compulsion a faith that the ruler or some other person prescribed. God had not given authority to anyone to compel others to embrace his own religion, nor could men give such a power to the magistrate. Locke apparently considered it to be a conceptual truth about belief that it could not be compelled. He therefore commented that "no man, even if he would, can believe at another's dictation." Yet even if force could change belief, he pointed out, this would not help to achieve the salvation of souls, because the doctrines imposed by the princes and laws of different countries might be far from the true religion. Only faith, moreover, was efficacious for salvation; to manifest conformity in belief or worship without a full inward persuasion was thus hypocrisy and contempt of God, which were obstacles to being saved.[35]

It followed from these considerations that the magistrate had no responsibility for souls and therefore no right to impose articles of faith, doctrines, or forms of worship by law. This was the case because the force of law consisted in its penalties, which were ineffective to convince the mind. Locke's systematic elaboration of the consequences flowing from the basic difference between religion and government, and from the primacy of personal and subjective conscientious conviction in everything relating to the former, was the pillar sustaining his justification of toleration. A consequence of this view was his definition of the church as a "free and voluntary society" of people who joined in public worship in a manner they believed acceptable to God for the salvation of their souls. So conceived, a church, even if the magistrate belonged to it, could exercise no jurisdiction over other churches. In this connection he noted the speciousness of the claim that the orthodox church had power over other churches. Every church, he pointed out, "is orthodox to itself and erroneous or heretical to others"; whatever each believed, it believed to be true, and no earthly authority but only God could judge between them. As a voluntary society, a church possessed no sanctions against its members or others except exhortations, appeals to conscience, and excommunication as a last resort; not even the last, however, could entail any civil punishment or deprive persons of their liberty or rights as citizens. Locke also reviewed the duties of the clergy to show that the absolute distinction between the church and commonwealth prohibited them from exercising any authority in civil affairs. They had no power to punish persons not of their church or faith by taking away their lives, freedom, or goods on account of religion. Not only must they abstain from persecution, but they were obliged by their calling to show goodwill to all and treat those who differed from them with charity, meekness, and toleration.[36]

Of central importance for Locke was the argument that each person had no choice but to be responsible for his own soul. He seemed to regard this, too, as a conceptual truth about religion, or at least the Christian religion. Everyone must be his own judge of the way to salvation. The magistrate was not better qualified than others to decide which was the right way. No one should be forced to follow the magistrate's way, because if it proved to be wrong, the magistrate could not recompense the individual for loss of the kingdom of heaven. Although the magistrate might impose not his own personal judgment but that of his church, churches, too, were fallible and had often erred and changed their doctrines, as had the English church a number of times during the sixteenth century. While one could grow rich, Locke observed, by methods one disliked, or be cured by remedies one distrusted, "I cannot be saved by a religion I distrust, or by a worship I dislike." God would not accept outward appearance but required faith and inward sincerity.[37]

Locke's conception thus made it obligatory for the magistrate to tolerate all religious societies that did not impede the ends of civil government. And with regard to indifferent things, while the state's legislative power extended to them, anything that was indifferent ceased to be in the magistrate's jurisdiction if it was made part of religion and worship, because then it no longer had any connection with civil affairs. By means of these principles he outlined a very wide area of religious freedom and pluralism exempt from interference or imposition by the state. At the same time, however, he made it clear that certain practices, like infanticide or sexual promiscuity, that were illegal according to human law could not become lawful by their use in religion. The rule he proposed in this matter was that if something was lawful in the commonwealth, then it could not be prohibited in the church. Conversely, things harmful in the commonwealth and forbidden in ordinary life because opposed to the common good could not be permitted in the church.[38]

Locke urged complete liberty for speculative doctrines in religion and articles of faith, neither of which had any connection with the ends of government. Conduct and moral actions, however, since they were related to both religion and civil life, had to concern the magistrate. Because men had mutually contracted to create civil society out of a common need for security and the goods of earthly life, the magistrate ought always to aim at the common good in making laws. When conscience in religion conflicted with the civil law—although Locke thought this would seldom happen if the magistrate governed in good faith—then the individual should not comply with the law but should accept the punishment decreed. Unwilling to undermine the authority of government, Locke commented that "the private judgment of any person concerning a law enacted in political matters, and for the public good, does not take away the obligation of that law, nor does it deserve toleration." He went on to some further clarifications that had much in common with the second of his *Two Treatises on Government*. If subjects believed that a law did not pertain to the purpose of civil society or exceeded the magistrate's authority, they were not obliged to obey it. And although the magistrate might think it was for the public good, he had no right to impose laws in religion. If he did so and his subjects disagreed, the only judge between them was God, who would decide by giving all their just deserts at the Last Judgment. Locke was also clear that doctrines incompatible with human society or contrary to good morals should not be tolerated. While he did not refer to them by name, he approved the refusal of toleration to Catholics because of their allegiance to a foreign sovereign (the pope) and their subversive doctrine that their church could depose kings and break faith with heretics. He also held that atheists had no right to toleration. The reason he gave for this view (a very questionable one, needless to say) was that neither promises, oaths, nor covenants could obligate those who did not believe in God.[39]

Although Locke's work never directly referred to English affairs, in its immediate context it was in part a plea for the religious freedom of Protestant dissenters. Writing as an Anglican, he denied that dissenting sects, conventicles, and religious meetings would present a danger to the state if tolerance prevailed. Only "one thing gathers people for sedition," he declared, "and that is oppression. . . . Take away the unfair legal discrimination against [the sects], change the laws, take away the penalties they have to endure, and everything will be safe and secure." His view of the effects of religious persecution paralleled the political defense of the right of revolution in his *Two Treatises of Government*. Unwillingness to tolerate diversity, he maintained, was the cause of most of the disputes and civil wars over religion in the Christian world. Leaders of the church, moved by avarice and lust for power, had always used all means to incite both the magistrate and the common people against the unorthodox, heretics, and schismatics. If men were persecuted and delivered up as prey for their religion, it was no wonder that they would finally consider it lawful to resist force with force and take up arms to defend "the rights which God and nature have granted them." The commonwealth's security would consequently be much greater if all good subjects, whatever their church, enjoyed "the same favour of the prince and the same benefit of the laws, without any distinction on account of religion." The logic of Locke's theory of toleration thus led him to envisage freedom of worship as a right of all churches and sects irrespective of their differences, and he likewise insisted that this freedom be extended also to pagans, Muslims, and Jews, none of whom should be excluded from the commonwealth because of religion.[40]

Although Locke's *Letter* was not a long work, as a synthesis of reasons to justify toleration and religious freedom it had no counterpart in the previous tolerationist literature. Certain of its ideas could, of course, be found in preceding writers going back to Castellio and including those like Roger Williams and Milton who insisted on the separation of church and state; but as a whole it was an original work of exceptional intellectual force in spelling out the rationale for religious pluralism. To argue in 1689 that the civil magistrate had no rightful authority in matters of religious belief and worship was still a very daring act. Few of Locke's contemporaries were ready to accept such a radical position. In calling for the separation of the state and religion, however, he made a very considerable effort to analyze and explain how the two differed in their nature and ends, and to define the relationship and boundaries between them. He may have been the first Christian thinker to maintain that toleration was one of the marks of a true church. It was certainly significant that he conceived of toleration as a major Christian duty and religious freedom as a natural right of subjects. Never questioning that there was only one true religion leading to salvation, he also provided for the right of conscience by arguing that every Christian must sincerely decide for himself which religion this was; neither the magistrate by compulsion nor anyone else could do this for him. The limits Locke set on toleration excluded immoral opinions harmful to society, atheists, and Catholics. His explanation for excluding atheists was not defensible, since it ought to have been obvious that their lack of belief in God would not necessarily cause them to feel no obligation to abide by their promises, oaths, and covenants; Locke knew perfectly well, moreover, that plenty of Christians, despite their theism, were guilty of oath- and covenant-breaking. When he touched upon Catholics, it is noticeable that he did not name them but spoke only of their dangerous political tenets. I believe this shows that he would probably have been willing to tolerate their religion and worship if they abandoned these tenets.

Locke's work involved him in a lengthy controversy with an Anglican cleric at Oxford, Jonas Proast, a strong opponent of toleration. Although taken together, his three successive rejoinders to Proast's critiques were much longer than his original *Letter*, they added little to his theory of toleration.[41] The main issue between him and Proast was the use of compulsion in religion. While Proast admitted that compulsion was powerless to change belief, he nevertheless held that a moderate amount of force could contribute to religion by causing dissenters to give due consideration to the objections to their own mistaken beliefs. His general thesis was similar to the one Saint Augustine had propounded centuries earlier to justify compulsion against Donatist heretics, but neither he nor Locke mentioned this fact, and most modern commentators on the controversy have also overlooked it. Locke was successful, I think, in refuting Proast's position by arguing that the likeliest effect of force would be to harm religion by arousing the hatred of the people punished for their opinions. He also affirmed in the strongest terms that to compel dissenters to hear the arguments of their opponents was plain persecution, immoral, and unjust.[42] Proast made the further claim that the magistrate had the right and duty to employ force in behalf of the true religion; he had no doubt, of course, that the true religion was his own Anglicanism. In answer, Locke pointed to the distinction between knowledge and belief or faith: while the magistrate might believe that his was

the true religion, this could not be a matter of certain knowledge.[43] Locke's reply suggests that he saw no practical difference
from a moral and policy standpoint between belief in a religion
and belief in the true religion; given that every believer considered
his own religion to be the true one, mutual tolerance remained
the only alternative to endless conflict.[44]

Immediately following the completion of the revolution of
1688 that deposed James II, the Toleration Act of 1689 at last
freed Protestant dissenters from the Anglican Church from some
of the most burdensome penal laws that had been passed against
them. By this statute, and in order to "ease scrupulous consciences
in the exercise of religion," Parliament granted dissenters who
believed in the Trinity (which was nearly all of them) freedom
of public worship, preaching, and teaching. It did not, however,
remove any of their civil disabilities, such as their exclusion from
public office, and Catholicism remained a prohibited religion. Yet
even though it provided only a limited toleration, this legislation
was significant as the first political recognition and acceptance in
England of religious pluralism, and it opened a new era in the
history of dissent.[45] Although Locke, who was back in England
when the Toleration Act was passed, did not find it satisfactory, he
nevertheless regarded it as a notable step forward. He made the
appropriate comment on it in a letter to Limborch: "Toleration
has now at last been established by law in our country. Not perhaps
so wide in scope as might be wished for by . . . those . . . who are
true Christians. . . . Still, it is something to have progressed so far.
I hope that with these beginnings the foundations have been laid
of that liberty and peace in which the church of Christ is one day
to be established."[46]

PIERRE BAYLE, PHILOSOPHER AND PUBLICIST

In 1681, Louis XIV abolished the Protestant Academy of Sedan
in eastern France, where Pierre Bayle (1647–1706) had been professor of philosophy since 1675. Anticipating this event and the

loss of his employment, Bayle joined the French emigration to the Dutch Republic, where he settled in Rotterdam in 1681 for the rest of his life. He had been offered a post there as professor of philosophy and history in a newly founded institution, the École Illustre, established by the civic government. Rotterdam was a fortunate choice for Bayle. It was a tolerant environment of Protestant diversity and home to a number of booksellers and publishers. The flow of educated French Huguenots who sought refuge in the city made it an intellectual center of a lively Francophone culture. Bayle never married, and his teaching position provided him with the time and means to write. After coming to Rotterdam, he embarked on a career of great literary productivity that made him one of the foremost intellectuals in Europe.

Prior to 1681 his life had been that of a wandering scholar. Born in a remote village in the south of France adjoining the Pyrenees, he was the younger son of a poor Protestant pastor. Although he was a voracious reader with an incessant appetite for knowledge, his family's poverty forced him to defer his education while his older brother Jacob was being trained for the Protestant ministry. He had access to his father's books and a local school, and at the age of twenty-one, after several unsatisfactory months at a Huguenot academy, he went to Toulouse and entered the Jesuit College as an external Protestant student. The result was his conversion to Catholicism, to the grief of his family. It was only a short-lived intellectual conversion, however, and in 1670 further examination led him to return to the Calvinist Protestant faith. Since it was a serious crime in France for a convert to renounce his Catholicism, Bayle left his country for Geneva, where he pursued his theological and philosophical studies at the Protestant Academy. Exposure in Geneva to the philosophy of Descartes made him a keen Cartesian, while later he was also strongly influenced by the philosophy of Malebranche, a major French thinker in the Cartesian tradition. For two years he worked as a tutor in a nobleman's family near Geneva, after which, returning to France incognito in 1674, he spent some months as a tutor in Normandy and Paris. The following year, at the age of twenty-eight, he won a com-

Tel fut l'illustre *Bayle*, honneur des beaux esprits
Dont l'élégante plume en recherches fertile,
Fait douter qui des deux l'emporte en ses écrits,
De l'agréable ou de l'utile.

D. L. M.

Portrait engraving of the great French thinker, scholar, and publicist Pierre Bayle, whose *Commentaire philosophique*, 1686, was one of the ablest, most original and controversial defenses of toleration and religious freedom of the seventeenth century. Reproduced from Pierre Bayle, *Dictionnaire historique et critique*, 1734 edition. Courtesy of The Albert and Shirley Small Special Collections Library, University of Virginia Library.

petition for a philosophy professorship at the Protestant Academy of Sedan. There his patron, friend, and fellow professor was Pierre Jurieu (1637–1713), ten years his senior, an orthodox Calvinist and noted Protestant theologian, who also accompanied him to Rotterdam and held a post at the École Illustre. Jurieu was later to become his greatest personal enemy and intellectual adversary.

Bayle taught at Sedan for six years until the government's suppression of the school, a time in which he read very widely in philosophy, theology, and other subjects. To a considerable extent he was a self-educated prodigy, and by the time he moved to Rotterdam in 1681, he was already an erudite and independent thinker. One of the most grievous blows he suffered during his first years in Rotterdam was the loss of his brother Jacob, who died in 1685 in a French prison where he had been held for months in very bad conditions for refusing to convert to Catholicism. Jacob's death, together with the sight of Huguenot refugees pouring into the Dutch Republic, only strengthened Bayle's hatred of religious persecution and his belief in the necessity of toleration.

Bayle was a complex and paradoxical thinker: a great rationalist and critical doubter who insisted on the complete disjunction between reason and faith; a mind much influenced by the skeptical philosophy of ancient Pyrrhonism, which questioned the possibility of establishing indubitable truth; an ironist and acute dialectician who poked holes in bad arguments, which he found in great numbers; a bold reasoner who followed ideas through to their conclusions; a fideist and believer whose religion was founded on faith in the supernatural truth of the Christian revelation, which reason could not justify, and who after his brief lapse into Catholicism remained a lifelong member of the Calvinist Reformed Church. In his political theory, in contrast to Locke, he always rejected the notion of a reciprocal contract between sovereigns and people, denied that subjects had a right of rebellion, and consistently upheld the duty of obedience and nonresistance to kings.[47]

The succession of writings that came from Bayle's pen in Rotterdam brought him international renown. Among the first to appear were *Lettre sur la comte* (1682) (*Letter on the Comet*), followed the next year by a larger work on the same subject, *Pensées diverses sur la comte* (*Miscellaneous Reflections on the Comet*), which was occasioned by the comet that had appeared in the skies over Europe in 1680.[48] This composition, an attack on religious superstition as a worse enemy to religion than atheism, stressed natural causation as an explanation and proved with a number of arguments that celestial phenomena could not be miraculous warnings sent by God. Among its most striking conceptions was the suggestion that morality was independent of religion, that atheists could be more virtuous than Christians, who were guilty of many crimes, and that a society composed of atheists was a viable possibility.[49] Between 1684 and 1687 Bayle also wrote and edited *Nouvelles de la république des lettres* (*News of the Republic of Letters*), one of the earliest intellectual periodicals to appear in Europe, whose pages contained reviews of a large number of recent books in many diverse fields and provided a medium of communication and discussion for learned men of different countries.

Bayle's most lasting achievement as an author was his *Dictionnaire historique et critique* (*Historical and Critical Dictionary*), published in 1697 and in a larger four-volume edition five years later. Originating as a project to correct the factual errors in a previous dictionary, the *Dictionary* was a vast collection of articles on various persons ancient and modern, many of whom were little known. Its discussion of religious, philosophical, historical, and many other subjects was crammed with references, dense notes, and digressions often much longer than the main text at the top of its pages. One of its curious aspects was the obscene anecdotes included in some of the articles. Its longest entry was devoted to Spinoza, whose philosophy Bayle opposed as "systematic atheism." Another article, on the biblical King David, was notorious for its critical treatment of the Hebrew ruler's actions. Bayle's monumental compilation combined encyclopedic erudition with corrosive criticism of various opinions and beliefs, which made it one of the seminal books of the eighteenth century. Its character and others of Bayle's writings persuaded some contemporary and later readers that the author was a covert atheist, a libertine, and an unbeliever.[50] The contents of the first edition caused the consistory of the Reformed Church in Rotterdam to charge Bayle with scandalizing the faithful by some of the things he had written. As a consequence he was obliged to add several "Clarifications" in the second edition and to remove a number of offending passages from the article on David, which the publisher subsequently restored.

BAYLE AND RELIGIOUS TOLERATION: THE *PHILOSOPHICAL COMMENTARY*

Bayle was a believer in toleration from an early time, as uncompromisingly opposed to Protestant as to Catholic intolerance. He voiced his revulsion against religious persecution in a number of publications, including some of the articles in his *Historical and Critical Dictionary.* When he came to write in defense of toleration in 1686, he was undoubtedly familiar with the works of earlier French authors on the subject like Michel de L'Hopital and Castellio, as well as with the tolerant, charitable attitude Montaigne expressed in his *Essais.* Through his residence in Holland, if not before, he would also have been acquainted with some of the Socinian and Arminian literature in favor of toleration. Although he was aware of the great number of works on toleration published in England in the seventeenth century, it is unlikely that he knew any of them at first hand since he did not read English.[51] He met Locke in Rotterdam during the latter's exile, and the two men later expressed respect for one another's works. Locke's *A Letter concerning Toleration,* of which he sent Bayle a copy of the original Latin edition, appeared after the publication of Bayle's main work on the subject. Locke had read Bayle's *Nouvelles de la république des lettres* and *Lettre sur la comte* in Holland, and his library contained both the latter's *Dictionary* and his treatise on toleration.[52] Even though Bayle and he shared the same values in their common affirmation of the principle of tolerance and religious pluralism, their theories of toleration differed in various ways and developed independently of each other.

Bayle mentioned several of his conceptions relating to toleration in two publications of 1682 and 1684, but it was not until after the revocation of the Edict of Nantes that he undertook his principal work on the subject.[53] It was published anonymously in Rotterdam in 1686 with the long title *Commentaire philosophique sur ces paroles de Jésus Christ, Contrain-les d'entrer; ou l'on prouve, par plusieurs raisons demonstratives, qu'il n'y a rien de plus abominable que de faire des conversions par la contrainte: et ou l'on réfute tous les sophismes des convertisseurs à contrainte, & l'apologie que St. Augustin a faite des persécutions* (*Philosophical Commentary on These Words of Jesus Christ, Compel Them to Come In, Where It Is Proven by Several Demonstrative Reasons That There Is Nothing More Abominable Than to Make Conversions by Force: And Where Are Refuted All the Convertists' Sophisms for Constraint and the Apology That St. Augustine Made for Persecution*).[54] The title alerts the reader to the fact that the author was writing as a philosopher, not a theologian. The main object of the commentary, a mixture of rationalism and skepticism, was to demonstrate the falsity of a literal interpretation of Jesus' words in the parable of the feast (Luke 14:23), "Compel them to come in," which Saint Augustine had invoked in the fifth century to justify the use of force against heretics.[55] Bayle was not the first writer, of course, to deny that this biblical text authorized coercion in religion; the importance of his work lay chiefly in the character and novelty of some of his arguments.

The *Philosophical Commentary* was a sustained work of controversy, a lively discussion marked by repeated polemical thrusts, which presented an array of thoughts in an informal, personal style. Throughout its pages Bayle frequently condemned the persecution of the Protestants of France, a subject that was never absent from his mind as he wrote. The "Preliminary Discourse" contained a scathing attack on the "abominable doctrine" authorizing forced conversion and on the Catholic Church's defense and practice of intolerance and persecution. It called the perpetrators of forced conversions "Convertists," explaining that the term was synonymous with "dishonest man," "persecutor," and "anything else injurious." Citing the many religions and the diversity of opinions that coexisted in pagan Greece and Rome, it ridiculed "the absurdity of those who accuse toleration of causing dissension in countries," and asserted that "toleration . . . is the very source of peace and intolerance the source of confusion and conflict." Bayle concluded this opening section with the striking comment that the growth of deism and freethinking in the present century was not surprising in view of the ravages, extinction of virtue, crimes, and hypocrisy religion had produced in the world for its own temporal interests as a result of its intolerance.[56]

The remainder of the work consisted of two parts whose chapters centered on the injunction "Compel them to come in" in the Gospel of Luke. The author revealed the heart of his philosophy in the first chapter when he declared that his was a new kind of commentary containing principles more general and infallible than anything that the study of languages, criticism, or books of biblical commonplaces could provide. He then propounded the fundamental principle of the "natural light" as the one that should guide the interpretation of the Scriptures in all matters of morality. This principle proved that "any literal interpretation which carried an obligation to commit iniquity was false." Bayle conceived the "natural light" as identical with reason and logic; it was an interior illumination of the mind manifested in incontrovertible propositions such as that the whole is greater than its parts and contradictories cannot both be true. Not even Scripture could authorize the contrary of these true propositions or prevail "against the true light of reason," for in such a case no one would believe it. On this account, he made the bold countertraditional statement that philosophy, not theology, was the queen of the sciences. Reason, speaking through the axioms of the natural light, was the supreme tribunal, judging without appeal whatever was proposed to the human mind. God himself had determined that this should be so by endowing men with the natural light as the means of infallibly distinguishing truth from falsehood. This resource enabled the right understanding of the great number of passages in

Scripture whose literal sense conveyed the lowest imaginable conception of God. Although Bayle immediately limited the cognizance of the natural light so that it did not extend to speculative truths like the Trinity or the Incarnation, he insisted that it most certainly applied to all questions of morality. His Cartesianism is evident in his description of the natural light as a clear and distinct conception in every attentive mind, and he also terms it "a natural revelation from God."[57] The rule that he then formulated for scriptural interpretation was that any dogma contained or advanced in Scripture or otherwise proposed was false if "repugnant to the clear and distinct notions of natural light, principally in regard to morality."[58]

The following chapters of the first part undertook to refute the literal sense of "Compel them to come in" as contrary to the natural light. They consisted of demonstrations of the irrationality and immorality of compulsion in religion in its opposition to the spirit of Christ and the gospel. One of its prominent themes is the author's humane horror of persecution. Bayle described religion as a persuasion of the soul that produces love, fear, and reverence toward God. Force cannot inspire this state of belief and is thus opposed to the common principles of reason. Because it is a mistaken means of establishing religion, God could not have commanded in his word that force should be used to make men embrace the gospel. The passage which seemed to say that God did command such a thing must therefore be either corrupted or understood figuratively. Bayle further explains that the gospel represents the highest expression of morality, all of Jesus' precepts being intended, in conformity with reason, to subdue passions, moderate anger, and thereby unite men with God. The supposition that he approved torture and duress to compel the profession of Christianity was accordingly false, and nothing could be more impious or injurious to Christ than to think that he ordered his followers to make conversions by constraint.[59]

Bayle further maintained that the Catholic Church's literal interpretation of "Compel them to come in" removed the boundaries between justice and injustice and confused virtue with vice

to the ruin of societies. The church defended itself, he noted, by
the principle that "a thing which would be unjust if not done in
the name of true religion becomes just by being done for the true
religion." This doctrine was in his view the most outrageous and
abominable affront to Christ because it approved every crime
committed in the name of the true religion. Jesus, however, who
would have foreseen the appalling consequences of the literal interpretation of his saying, never intended it to justify the use of
force in religion, which would permit even the killing and deposi-
tion of kings should their subjects be of a different faith.[60]

It is unnecessary to review all the proofs Bayle produced in
the first part of his work to refute the literal interpretation of
Christ's words in the Gospel of Luke. The main device he employs
in his discussion is that of the *reductio* in order to expose the
unwelcome far-reaching consequences of the doctrine of compulsion. It is apparent throughout that he regards this doctrine as not
only morally reprehensible but entirely opposed to reason in its
assumptions. If the literal sense were true, he observed, then infidels would be right to exclude and expel Christians from
their domains because of the latter's readiness to use force against
the infidels' beliefs. It would likewise justify the force the Muslims
employed to spread their religion, and it would also allow the persecution of the first Christians by the pagans. It would throw
all the churches and sects of Christianity into continual war,
since each of them believed it was orthodox and the true church.
Impartial reflection, he stated, shows that all religious parties say,
"I have truth on my side, therefore my violences are good works;
so-and-so errs, therefore his violences are criminal." Such futile
reasonings, he considered, merely begged the question of truth
while perpetuating the evils of persecution and persecuting the
truth as well.[61]

In several remarks in part 1 against the injustice of Louis XIV's
persecution of the French Protestants, Bayle alluded for the first
time to the right of conscience, which was to become the central
subject of his commentary. Sovereigns, he contended, had no authority to make laws that obliged people to act against their con-

science, an opinion he based on the claim that conscience in each person was the voice and law of God and recognized as such. Since to act against the law of God was to show hatred and contempt of God, a command to act against conscience was the same as commanding hatred and contempt of God. That God could have conferred authority upon sovereigns for such a purpose was absurd and impossible, nor could the people, in surrendering their liberty to the sovereign, have ever given him a right over their conscience. "From here," Bayle declared, "I draw a new and demonstrative proof against the literal sense of the parable," because if it were true, it would justify the right of princes to enact laws compelling subjects to profess a religion repugnant to the light of their conscience, which meant that they could make laws for the hatred and contempt of God.[62]

Part 2 of the commentary comprised Bayle's replies to a number of objections that could be made against his previous demonstrations. One of the most interesting addressed the objection that the purpose of violence in religion was not to force conversion but to overcome people's obstinacy and make them examine the truth. This, as we have seen, was the excuse for coercion given by Saint Augustine in the case of the Donatists and similar to the claim made by the Reverend Jonas Proast in his critique of Locke's *A Letter concerning Toleration*. In his answer, Bayle first pointed out how necessary it was, as everyone agreed, that the mind should be calm and free of passion or prejudice when sifting a question to find the truth. This state of mind, he observed, was unattainable when someone was forced by persecution to examine the differences between two religions. In such circumstances the persecutor made himself the judge of the persecuted, who knew that he stood to gain relief from his pain and other temporal advantages if he acceded to the persecutor's beliefs. Under coercion, some persecuted people would be perplexed, others yield, and some would adhere to their own beliefs after hearing all the arguments. Although persecutors insisted that those persons who refused to heed their arguments were obstinate, how could they know that this was so, Bayle inquired, when they were incapable of seeing into people's hearts? He went on to point out that victory in argument was not a sign of truth: "It is not a mark of falsehood in any religion, to see that all who profess it are not capable of answering every difficulty which learned Convertists of the opposite side may suggest." Evidence, moreover, was a relative feature, and except for common principles, "what appears evident to ourselves" may not "likewise appear so to others." Bayle therefore concluded that to charge someone with obstinacy for failing to agree led only to endless disputes; and in the matter of persecution it amounted to saying that the reason of the strongest was the best, and that "you are obstinate because I uphold the truth." What was highly characteristic in this response was Bayle's focus on the fallacious question begging and circular reasoning that he perceived as sustaining the case for religious persecution.[63]

Bayle's condemnation of the theory of persecution integrated moral judgment with the principle of the natural light. Responding to the objection that God might use persecution to accomplish his ends, he called it a gross illusion of persecutors that God used their iniquities to enlighten those in error. God did not approve of iniquities for any purpose, and it was not possible that Jesus should have chosen intrinsically evil actions contrary to natural equity and the gospel as an instrument for the salvation of men. In this connection he also made the point that "constraint and threatened punishment have the very same effect against the true as against a false religion." If the literal sense of "Compel them to come in" were true, God would have authorized every Christian sect to persecute the others in the hope that God would convert them by these means.[64]

Like Locke and other theorists of toleration, Bayle denied that toleration would breed confusion and disunity harmful to Christianity. It seemed clear to him that the opposite was true: the cause of disorder and disunity lay in lack of tolerance and in persecution, while the effect of toleration would be peace and the harmonious coexistence of differences. He acknowledged that religious innovators should not be tolerated if they incited seditions and civil wars, but nevertheless held that princes ought to tolerate heretics and all who differed from the state religion, provided they expressed their beliefs peacefully. No one, he maintained, should ever be condemned for speaking according to conscience. Reason showed, moreover, that it was "humanly inevitable that men in different ages and countries should have different sentiments in religion." This fact should be less shocking to Christians than the torture and burning of a person who disagreed with another's religion. The horror of such acts would be evident, he said, when it came to be understood that "there is an eternal law forbidding us to betray our conscience." Accepting that differences of opinion were an inherent infelicity of the human condition, he suggested that the best way to reduce this evil to its narrowest possible limits was "by mutually tolerating each other."[65]

In his replies to objections, Bayle admitted that abolishing religious compulsion would lead to universal toleration and unlimited pluralism. This was a conclusion he enthusiastically embraced and defended wholeheartedly. It had to be "all or nothing," he was convinced, because if there were a reason to tolerate one sect, then the same reason applied equally to all, including Muslims and Jews. He had no patience for those he described as "half-tolerationists," who, though willing to tolerate some inessential differences in religion, excluded blasphemers and had killed the Spaniard Servetus as a blasphemer. The "half-tolerationists" to whom he alluded were the Calvinists of both the past and his own time, like his colleague the minister Pierre Jurieu, men who execrated universal tolerance as giving free rein to deadly heresy and irreligion.[66] To them he pointed out that definitions of blasphemy differed; hence a blasphemer deserved punishment only if he blasphemed according to his own religion, not according to the persecutor's. Christians who disbelieved in the Trinity, persuaded in their conscience that three persons could not each be God, were not blasphemers by the lights of their own religion. The half-tolerationists refused to tolerate such people because they destroyed the foundations of faith; but this accusation, Bayle said, only begged the question by arguing, "Such a thing appears fundamental to me, therefore it is," which he called very poor reasoning.[67]

BAYLE AND THE RIGHTS OF THE
ERRONEOUS CONSCIENCE

Bayle's commentary reached its culmination in its four concluding chapters (pt. 2, chaps. 8–11), which contained his most exceptional and provocative arguments. The question at issue in this crucial part of his discussion concerned the right of conscience, of which he gave an unprecedented analysis. Countering the objection that violence was justified when used in behalf of the truth, he declared that every exercise of violence in religion was against the cause of truth, and that an erroneous conscience had the same rights as an enlightened conscience. He proceeded to formulate the latter thesis as follows: "[E]verything a well-enlightened conscience allows us to do for the advancement of truth, an erroneous conscience permits for what we believe to be the truth." Bayle's defense of this position rested on a basic proposition concerning the nature of conscience which he believed was indisputable: that everything done against conscience is sin, because everyone who is not an atheist agrees that conscience judges an action as good or bad according to whether or not it conforms to God's law and pleases God. Conscience was thus the arbiter in decisions concerning whether an act is good or bad, and the supreme obligation of the Christian is never to act against the promptings of conscience. A person who willingly performed an action contrary to conscience did evil and was guilty of sin because he chose to transgress the law of God. It then followed that the worst sin anyone could commit was to act against the light of conscience; moreover, an incontestably good action like giving charity, if done against the dictates of conscience, was worse than an incontestably bad action done in accord with the dictates of conscience; and finally, something called evil, if done in conformity with a conscience that was really erroneous, was much less evil than another action called good but done against the dictates of a conscience supposedly conformed to truth.[68]

Bayle's thesis attributed the same rights to the conscience in error as to the conscience in possession of the truth, and it did so by treating actual knowledge of the truth and the erroneous conviction that one knows the truth as equivalent from a religious and moral point of view. He went on to state that

> if the Eternal Law or any positive Law of God, requires that a man who is convinced of the truth employ fire and sword to establish it in the world, then all men ought to employ fire and sword for the establishment of their own religion.

This principle has been well named "the reciprocity argument."[69] Not only did it apply, Bayle said, to everyone to whom such a law of God was revealed, but it would be a transgression against God for them to disobey it. Since every church was indispensably obliged to practice whatever God commands the true church to do, if God commands the enforcement of the truth by persecution, every church must do so. Accordingly, by an unavoidable necessity, "everything which would be permitted to truth against error becomes likewise permitted to error against truth." Everyone, the heretic included, should, of course, search for the truth; but if people believed they possessed it, they had no alternative but to act on it.[70]

This conception proved, as Bayle put it, that "an action done in consequence of a false conviction is as good as if done in consequence of a true belief." One of the examples he gave to illustrate this point was that of the woman who admits an impostor to her bed because she honestly thinks he is her legitimate husband; had she refused to sleep with him, she would have been as blameworthy as if she had refused to sleep with her real husband.[71] Since every church believed it was the true church, his logic supported the shocking conclusion that if God commanded the true church to enforce the truth by persecution, then every church was obliged to persecute. Heretics accordingly had as much right to persecute the orthodox as the orthodox had to persecute heretics. But Bayle, of course, was utterly opposed to persecution, whose evil and irrationality he sought to demonstrate. He quite justifiably denied that his argument destroyed his claim that persecution was an abomination, because what he had shown was that the literal sense of "Compel them to come in" was false, impious, and absurd, and that Christ therefore did not command violence. In other words, the consequences of the literal sense were such that it could not be true. To the objection that his arguments would likewise permit murder and other crimes if done with a good conscience, he replied that the magistrate, who had the duty of protecting society, was not obliged to regard the conscience of criminals. He also insisted that his reasoning did not license atheism, because the atheist was not able to appeal to conscience, which comes from God, in behalf of his belief.[72]

Bayle fortified his defense of the rights of the erroneous conscience by contending in his penultimate chapter that no distinction could be made in religion between truth and reputed truth. If God willed that truth obligates men to follow it, he said, then this law could not be promulgated to mankind "without its authorizing not only the truth itself, but also reputed truth as well." He further observed that while God required men to search diligently for the truth, his infinite wisdom also took into account all the human defects due to rearing, education, worldly cares, passions, and habits that made the pursuit of truth so difficult. God therefore demanded not absolute truth from Christians but only that which was reputed true after sincere and faithful inquiry; this was the most that could be asked of conscience, since men could not know with infallibility. Although Bayle seemed here to be treading perilously close to a general skepticism about truth and knowledge, this was not the case. As he explained, he was not speaking of things like the properties of numbers or the first principles of metaphysics, where one could establish absolute and genuine truth, but of the particular truths of religion. Because in the case of the latter God was satisfied to require no more than sincere and diligent search, men were obliged to have the same regard for a reputed as for a real truth. Even here Bayle applied this conclusion only to speculative truths in religion like transubstantiation and Christ's nature, which were the ones that divided Christians, not to moral truths. He saw no solution to such divisions. The Scripture itself did not provide one, for even though Christians believed that all of Scripture was true, they interpreted it differently and could not agree which interpretation was the true one.[73]

At the close of his commentary, Bayle summed up what he thought he had accomplished. He believed his discussion of the rights of conscience had exposed "the deepest roots" of the falsity of the persecutors' justification for persecution and the chicaneries that propped it up. If the literal sense of the injunction "Compel them to come in" were true, then the partisans of falsehood could persecute truth with the same right with which the partisans of truth persecuted falsehood. This would open the door, he warned, to a thousand dreadful conflagrations in which the partisans of truth would suffer most without legitimate cause for complaint.[74]

BAYLE AND LOCKE

In 1687 the Swiss exile Jean Le Clerc wrote in his *Bibliothque universelle et historique*, the famous periodical published in Amsterdam of which he was the founder-editor, that toleration was "a matter of such importance in the time in which we live" that "almost nothing else is spoken of today."[75] Although in the aftermath of the revocation of the Edict of Nantes Bayle was only one of a number of French Protestants in the Dutch Republic who published works in support of toleration, his *Philosophical Commentary* was by far the most significant.[76] Nothing in the previous literature of the toleration controversy resembled it in the philosophical character of its affirmation of religious liberty and pluralism founded on the right of conscience. In his basic perspective and many of his arguments Bayle was as strongly religious and Christian as other notable champions of toleration in the sixteenth and seventeenth centuries. He was convinced that tolerance was a great and necessary Christian moral virtue, and one of his most powerful motivations was the certainty that persecution was absolutely contrary to the spirit and teachings of Christ. But some of his central arguments were directed against the irrationality of religious persecution, its inconsistencies, logical fallacies, and question-begging evasions, while others derived their force from epistemological considerations connected with conscience and the difficulties of discerning religious truth. In his *Suplement* to the *Philosophical Commentary*, he declared that had relied in his work on a "manner of reasoning called *reductio ad absurdum* . . . which has always been considered supremely efficacious in disabusing people who permit themselves to be prejudiced by a false principle."[77]

Earlier tolerationist authors such as Castellio and Roger Williams had touched on the toleration due to a sincerely convinced, even if erroneous, religious conscience. Castellio had also argued that while the moral truths of Christianity were simple and clear, the obscurity of parts of Scripture and the uncertainty of doctrines over which divisions arose constituted a strong reason for Christians to tolerate differences. A number of writers, including Locke, had pointed out that each church thinks itself orthodox, and that what it believes is true. Locke had likewise said in his *Essay concerning Toleration* that "in speculative opinions and worship every man hath a perfect uncontrollable liberty which he may freely use without, or contrary to, the magistrate's command, without any guilt or sin at all, provided always that it all be done sincerely out of conscience to God according to the best of his knowledge and persuasion." In a subsequent essay on error, he had also pointed out that "he that examines, and upon a fair examination embraces an error for a truth, has done his duty more than he who embraces the profession of the truth (for the truths themselves he does not embrace) without having examined whether it be true or no. For, if it be our duty to search after truth, he certainly that has searched after it, though he has not found it, in some points has paid a more acceptable obedience to his Maker than he that has not searched at all."[78] Although all these observations might be considered as moves toward Bayle's position, no one before him had followed the concept of the erring conscience to its utmost consequences in such a systematic way in the context of the problem of toleration.

Bayle's discussion of the erring conscience placed the case for universal toleration and pluralism on epistemological grounds. If conscience was the arbiter of religious truth and of what the law of God willed, and if it was not possible to be certain whether or not any conscience had the truth, then every conscience that diligently sought the truth had an equal right to toleration. This justification of tolerance, which appalled orthodox Calvinists like Pierre Jurieu, became one of the main causes of his breach with Bayle. An able, prolific author and determined adversary of toleration, Jurieu maintained that the Christian prince, in his supreme duty of upholding the glory of God, was obligated to silence heretics and defend the truth in religion. He accused Bayle of atheism and called his *Philosophical Commentary* "the most pernicious book . . . ever . . . written in support of Pyrrhonism." The doctrine of the erring conscience, he charged, was an attempt to establish "a tolerance and general indifference of all sects and even of all religion." It was not just their conflict over toleration that divided the two former friends, but bitter political disagreements as well. Bayle was completely opposed to Jurieu's widely circulated writings that justified the revolution of 1688 in England deposing the Catholic James II, and that defended the right of resistance against a Catholic sovereign. In the long controversy between them, which continued to the end of Bayle's life, Jurieu succeeded in having Bayle deprived of his professorship in the £cole Illustre in 1693 and later instigated the proceeding against him in 1697 by the consistory of the Reformed Church in Rotterdam on the charge of causing scandal to the faithful.[79]

While rationalism and skepticism were both vital elements in Bayle's advocacy of universal toleration, he was first and foremost a rationalist rather than a skeptic. In putting philosophy above theology, the *Philosophical Commentary* was largely a tribute to rationalism based on the comprehensive claim that reason, or the natural light, was the sole judge of truth, and that in Scripture God himself did not contravene its principles. His main ground for holding that the literal sense of "Compel them to come in" was false was its failure to conform to the natural light, which showed that God and Christ could not command anything contrary to equity and justice. One scholar has suggested that Bayle's skepticism in his discussion of the right of the erring conscience was so extreme that it placed a strain on his entire position and threatened to destroy his own arguments.[80] There were many things, however, about which Bayle was not a skeptic. For instance, he was certain of the truth of the principles of reason in mathematics and fundamental metaphysical propositions like the whole is greater than its parts. He was certain that the rules of logic held universally and could expose common fallacies. Furthermore, as his *Historical and Critical Dictionary* showed, he believed in the veracity of historical facts and their ability to explode falsehood and misconceptions.[81] Finally, he was certain of the truth of the moral teachings of the Gospels. With respect to the Christian religion, it was theological doctrines such as the Trinity, the Incarnation, the nature of Christ, and other dogmas about which he believed that the truth was uncertain and open to legitimate doubt. His skepticism on this score compelled him to relativize the truths of religion to each individual's conscience and knowledge. This made the conclusion unavoidable that it was impossible to know for certain what was orthodoxy and what was heresy. In the matter of toleration it showed that every religious conscience that sought the truth deserved scrupulous respect and the right to liberty.

When comparisons are made between Bayle and Locke, the former's conception of religious toleration has often been considered wider or "more 'absolutistic' and universalist," as one writer has put it.[82] Certain scholars who wish to distinguish between liberty of conscience and toleration because the former is more comprehensive have maintained that Bayle represents the first principle and Locke the second.[83] Elizabeth Labrousse has commented that while the views of the two philosophers were very similar as far as practice was concerned, their reasons were appreciably different, Locke's being based on the rights of the individual, Bayle's on the right of God.[84]

Whatever differences we may perceive between Bayle's and Locke's theories of toleration, we ought not to exaggerate them, because on this subject the two were in accord in so many respects. Both spoke of toleration, or *tolérance*, without distinguishing it from liberty of conscience. Like Bayle, Locke attributed a unique value to the Christian conscience and the sincerity of its conviction. Both believed in tolerance toward the Jewish people and toward Muslims. Neither thought atheists should be tolerated, and for similar reasons. While Bayle, however, would have tolerated Catholicism, Locke was unwilling to do so. His refusal was not a sign of bigotry but due to political considerations that, though mistaken, are historically quite understandable in light of England's long conflict with the papacy, and with Catholic plotters and powers ever since the days of Elizabeth I. Locke and Bayle were alike in their hatred of religious persecution, which each condemned for its cruelty and violation of the ethical teachings of Christ. Although both wrote in a Christian framework, one of the foremost grounds for Bayle's advocacy of toleration and pluralism was the duty of Christians to act in conformity with conscience in religious matters and the corresponding duty of the magistrate to refrain from compulsion lest he force subjects to disobey what they believed in their conscience to be God's law. Locke, by contrast, based the claim to toleration especially on the recognition that subjects had a natural right to religious liberty rooted in the fundamental distinction, to which he devoted careful analysis, between the nature and purposes of religion and religious associations, on the one hand, and of the state and political association, on the other. Bayle, too, however, held that the magistrate's care and functions pertained exclusively to the preservation of civil peace and order, and was in complete agreement with Locke that no Christian government rightfully possessed authority to impose any religious belief on its subjects or to ban or persecute religious societies that dissented from the state religion. Both were among the most influential of tolerationist authors, much read in the eighteenth century. Each delivered a powerful indictment of persecution and made an outstanding contribution to the collective achievement of the courageous minds of the sixteenth and seventeenth centuries who created the intellectual and moral foundations for the long-term development of religious tolerance, freedom, and pluralism in Western culture.

CHAPTER 8

Conclusion: The Idea of Religious Toleration in the Enlightenment and After

✦

I n the battles over religious toleration that were so bitterly and widely waged in the sixteenth and seventeenth centuries, the idea of toleration was itself very largely inspired by religious values and was fundamentally religious in character. The proponents of toleration, whether Anabaptists, Sebastian Franck, and other sectarians, or Castellio, Socinians, Dutch Arminians, Roger Williams, Milton, and others of similar mind, might have been seen by their Catholic and orthodox Protestant adversaries as either dangerous heretics or doctrinally deviant, but there could be no question that they were nevertheless profoundly Christian in their thought and ideals. It is only stating the obvious to say that in advocating a policy of peace and tolerance toward religious differences, their supreme concern was the welfare of religion itself. They acted from the primary conviction that persecution was contrary to the mind of Christ and a terrible evil which did great harm to Christianity. When they maintained that princes and civil magistrates had neither a right nor a duty to punish heresy, nor any responsibility for the care of religion, they were striving to put an end to coercion in enforcing religious belief or church affiliation, but they certainly did not intend to banish religion from the polity or common life. Such a thought could hardly have occurred to them, nor could they ever have imagined as a proper setting for religious freedom a completely secular society in which the Christian religion had ceased to be a dominant public presence and a pervasive force in morals and conduct and was largely relegated to the realm of personal and private belief.

With John Locke and Pierre Bayle, we reach a point of transition in the concept of toleration, for, as we have seen, they stood between the age of faith that was passing and the age of the Enlightenment that was dawning. Although both were deeply affected by the Calvinist Protestant environment in which they grew up and remained genuinely religious thinkers, they emancipated themselves from doctrinal dogmatism and religious intolerance, coming to support religious pluralism in the hope of a world in which the Christian state favored no church and left religion free. In the years following their death the two held a prominent position among the Enlightenment's culture heroes not only for their commitment to tolerance but, in the case of Locke, also for his sensationalist philosophy, with its critique of the existence of innate ideas and his conception of a reasonable Christianity, and, in Bayle's case, for his critical rationalism, skepticism, and antipathy to superstition.

The Enlightenment in Europe spanned the intermediate decades of the eighteenth century until the beginning of the French Revolution. It was a cultural-intellectual movement fed by many tributary streams of unorthodox thought in the preceding era. Highly cosmopolitan and yet also inflected by marked national differences, it nonetheless stood for certain general attitudes, beliefs, and values. Its significance for its contemporaries was summed up near its end in the notable work of 1784 by the German philosopher Immanuel Kant, *What Is Enlightenment?* Kant defined it as humanity's release from self-imposed tutelage to external authority and readiness to use its independent reason: "Dare to know. Have courage to use your own reason—that is the motto of enlightenment."[1]

The carriers and disseminators of the Enlightenment on the European continent comprised a great variety of thinkers and writers, some of whom the French called *philosophes,* a term that denoted not professional philosophers but persons with broad general interests and ideas on many different subjects who addressed themselves mainly to a public of members of the middle and upper bourgeoisie and aristocracy. Among them were men of letters, scientists, statesmen and government officials, scholars, and journalists, as well as an underground of radical authors producing irreligious publications that circulated clandestinely in defiance of censorship. The most famous of them was Voltaire, the preeminent *philosophe* of the age, a thinker and writer of extraordinary versatility. All these people formed a small but increasingly influential intellectual minority in France and other countries.

The Enlightenment stood for a constellation of themes that marked something of a break with the past. They included confidence in the power of untrammeled reason and denial of original sin; a critical attitude toward traditional authority; the idea of progress; contract and consent as the origins of government; the oneness of human nature; humanitarianism and opposition to slavery and torture; the beneficence of science; and an image of the universe ruled by natural laws such as were exemplified in Newton's discovery of the laws of motion. High among these tenets was also the principle of religious toleration. In the course of the eighteenth-century Enlightenment, many of Europe's foremost intellectuals, those in the vanguard of the thought of their time, arrayed themselves against the Christian theory of persecution and endorsed the idea of toleration in one form or another. Under the influence of Enlightenment ideas, a number of rulers of the later eighteenth century—such as Frederick the Great, king of Prussia, and the emperor Joseph II of Austria—promoted the growth of toleration in their kingdoms.[2]

The ultimate importance of the Enlightenment lay in its long-run contribution to the gradual secularization and liberalization of Western society. Secularization in the eighteenth and nineteenth centuries meant chiefly the decline of the dominance of the Christian religion and churches over individual minds and in political and social life. It also meant the displacement of Christian otherworldliness by the values of earthly happiness, pleasure, and utility. The thinkers of the Enlightenment were on the whole more critical and destructive than constructive. Many were deists, devotees of natural religion, and freethinkers who could not accept the Christian faith; some were philosophical materialists and atheists. Of all the forces that they combated, what they most detested was supernatural religion, ecclesiastical authority and dogmas, persecution, priestcraft, fanaticism and superstition, clerical tyranny and obscurantism, religious censorship—in a word, everything in the Christian religion and established churches that seemed unjust and antithetical to reason. In France, the center of the Enlightenment, the *philosophes* made the Catholic Church a prime object of their criticism for its promotion of superstition and its history of persecution. Although they believed in enlightened government and the rule of law, they were not democrats, and some among them even agreed with the age-old idea that religion and superstition were necessary for preserving social order and keeping the lower classes in quiescent subordination to rulers and superiors. Their dedication to enlightenment and the sovereignty of reason pointed nevertheless in the direction of a humane and liberal society based on freedom of thought, the dissolution of orthodox religion as a coercive power, the rule of law, and political and religious liberty.[3]

It was in this context that some of the thinkers of the Enlightenment carried on the struggle for toleration. Their writings on the subject contained little that was original. In their hands, however, the concept of toleration underwent considerable secularization. During the eighteenth century it became largely separated from its religious roots and thus drained of the religious inspiration and vital preoccupation with the spiritual welfare of the Christian religion that had provided the most powerful motive in the earlier defense of toleration since the advent of the Protestant Reformation. The concept of toleration was now frequently extended to unite religious with intellectual freedom. This was a quite novel move, for while the tolerationist literature of the sixteenth and seventeenth centuries did sometimes encompass the necessity of freedom of thought and debate—as seen, for instance, in some of the writings of Castellio and Coornhert, the praise of free discussion in Milton's *Areopagitica,* and Spinoza's emphasis upon the principle of intellectual freedom—its understanding of toleration was for the most part limited to the demand for acceptance of freedom to differ in religion. Locke, for instance, while he would have been averse to any type of ecclesiastical or other censorship and was wholly committed to freedom of worship, had little to say in his *Letter concerning Toleration* in behalf of freedom of thought in general.[4] Toleration and freedom of the religious conscience also came to be more and more justified during the Enlightenment primarily as a natural right associated with other natural rights. These developments infused the idea of toleration with an increasingly secular character.

VOLTAIRE AND TOLERATION

There were many noted advocates of toleration during the Enlightenment. In England they included deists and freethinkers like John Toland, Matthew Tindal, Anthony Collins, and Tom Paine, and radical religious dissenters such as Joseph Priestley and Richard Price. In Germany one of the greatest beside Kant was the poet, dramatist, critic, and philosopher Gotthold Lessing. In France Montesquieu, Voltaire, Turgot, Diderot, Rousseau, Condorcet, and other prominent thinkers were in favor of tolerance and pluralism in religion. A great blot on the tolerant outlook of some of them, however, which must not be overlooked, was their anti-Semitism.[5] One of these, unhappily, was Voltaire, who, though he believed in toleration for the Jews, reviled their religion and detested them collectively as a fanatical, avaricious people who hated all other nations and were hated by them.[6] On the other hand, certain major figures of the Enlightenment, like Toland and Lessing, were philosemites whose disposition toward the Jews was sympathetic and liberal. Toland published a pamphlet in 1714 to support the granting of naturalization and rights of citizenship to the Jews in Britain. He called his work "a defence of the Jews against all vulgar prejudices in all countries"; it was intended to encourage "affection" for the "Jewish Nation."[7] Lessing was a close friend of the Jewish philosopher Moses Mendelssohn, a leading contributor to the Enlightenment in Germany. Lessing's humanity embraced the Jews equally with people of other religions, as all engaged in a common search for truth, and his famous play *Nathan the Wise* (1779), whose principal character was a Jew, was a plea for general tolerance.[8]

At the forefront of the Enlightenment movement for religious toleration stood Voltaire (1694–1778), the head of "the party of humanity," a writer renowned throughout Europe and its most celebrated opponent of intolerance. The son of a bourgeois family, he was born in Paris and educated by the Jesuits. While still in his twenties, he won literary and social success for his poems and plays, and he was reputed for many years to be the best dramatist in France. A deist who believed in an unknowable Supreme Being, Voltaire disliked metaphysics and theology. He deprecated speculation into remote, useless truths and was often biting and irreverent toward supernatural religion. His well-known battle cry, "écrasez l'infame" (crush the infamous thing), expressed his undying enmity toward religious fanaticism, superstition, and persecution. For him the essence of religion was morality. Although a humanist who spoke for the rights of the free intelligence and reason, he was also conscious of the limitations of the human mind. His erudition, skepticism, wit, charm, worldliness, variety, and humor, his easy style and accessibility, and his basic seriousness of purpose made a profound and lasting impression on his own and subsequent generations. He was an endlessly prolific author, a satirist and fighter against persecution, many of whose works contributed directly or indirectly to further the cause of toleration.[9]

His *Lettres philosophiques* or *Lettres anglaises* (*Philosophical Letters* or *Letters on England*), which he published in 1734 after being forced to leave France and spending nearly three years in England, has been called the first bomb thrown at the *ancien régime*. A partial account of various aspects of English life, which it tacitly compared with France, it praised England for its free political institutions and the broad religious tolerance visible in the peaceful coexistence of its many denominations. England, Voltaire wrote in it, "is the land of sects. An Englishman, as a free man, goes to heaven by whatever route he likes."[10] His *Dictionnaire philosophique* (*Philosophical Dictionary*) of 1763 contained a number of articles relating to toleration, including the ones on Antitrinitarianism, fanaticism, freedom of thought, the Inquisition, and persecution. This book, whose tone was reasonable, moderate, and conversational, and which often made use of sharp, witty dialogue, was thoroughly destructive of orthodox Christianity.[11] In its article on toleration, a virtue Voltaire called "the prerogative of humanity," he deplored the intolerance of Christians and stated that "of all religions, the Christian is undoubtedly that which should instill the greatest toleration, although so far the Christians have been the most intolerant of all men." Stressing how far present-day Christians were from the teachings of Jesus, he pointed out that "the Parsee, the Jew, the Mohammedan, the Chinese deist, the Greek Christian, the Roman Christian, the Protestant Christian, the Quaker Christian trade with each other in the stock exchanges of Amsterdam, London, Surat, or Basra; they do not raise their daggers against one another to win souls for their religions." "Why then," he asked, "have we butchered each other almost without interruption since the Council of Nicaea?" He appealed for kindness and charity between people and declared that every person who persecuted another because the two disagreed was a monster. "We are all steeped in weaknesses and errors," he said; therefore "let us forgive one another's follies, it is the first law of nature."[12]

Voltaire's *Traité sur la tolérance* (*Treatise on Toleration*) was his most sustained discussion of this subject. After its first appearance in 1763, it went through a number of French editions, one of which in 1764 also contained a French translation of Locke's *A Letter concerning Toleration* with a preface recommending this work by the "celebrated John Locke" for upholding "the utility of universal toleration."[13] It was the notorious Calas case that prompted Voltaire to write this treatise. After the revocation of the Edict of

Nantes, there were still many Protestants remaining in France during the eighteenth century who, though their religion had no legal existence, adhered to it secretly in the face of persecution. In 1762 Jean Calas, a Protestant cloth merchant in Toulouse, was atrociously executed after being convicted on the false charge that he had murdered his son to prevent him from converting to Catholicism. The son had actually committed suicide. Persuaded to take up Calas's cause as a matter of justice, Voltaire pursued it so effectively that in 1765 Louis XV's Council of State reversed the verdict of the Toulouse judges and affirmed his innocence. Although the *Treatise on Toleration* included an account of *l'affaire Calas*, it was mainly concerned with toleration in its general aspects and advanced a plea for freedom of thought as well as for religious toleration of the Protestants and other minorities.[14]

Voltaire argued with historical examples that toleration was in the interest of the state, and that persecution was wicked and immoral. Toleration was also necessitated, he believed, by the advance of European civilization. Reason had been making progress owing to the spread of fine literature; manners were more gentle and so was society. "The whole face of Europe had changed" in the past fifty years, as "the influence of reason," growing stronger, smothered discord, affirmed virtue, and made obedience to law agreeable without coercion. This, of course, was a considerable idealization, but as an instance he cited the treatment of the Catholics in England, who, other than paying double taxes, he said, enjoyed the rights of citizens. He also mentioned the toleration prevailing in the Ottoman Turkish Empire and in China, as well as in the American colonies of Carolina and Pennsylvania. While tolerance had never caused civil war, he noted, intolerance had covered the earth with blood.[15]

In a very short chapter, he explained toleration as a "human right" founded on natural law, the universal principle of both being the rule "Do unto others what you would have done unto yourself." In light of this principle, Voltaire found it impossible to understand how one man could tell another, "Believe that which

I believe and you cannot believe, or you will die." If everyone acted in accord with the latter doctrine, the Japanese, Chinese, Indians, Mongols, Hindus, Persians, and Turks would all hate each other and also hurl themselves against the Christians, who had been killing one another for a very long time. Therefore, he concluded, any law sanctioning intolerance was "absurd and barbaric," since it was a law of wild animals but even more horrible, because animals killed only to eat, whereas men have exterminated each other over verbal formulae.[16]

Voltaire's fundamental position was that "each individual citizen . . . be permitted to believe" and "to think only what his reason . . . may dictate," whether correct or mistaken.[17] To those who were horrified by this proposal, he declared that it was very necessary as long as no one disturbed the civil order, since everyone was expected to respect the laws of his country. But if it were thought a crime not to believe the dominant religion, then the persons who held this view also accused their ancestors, the first Christians, and justified the latter's persecutors who delivered them to execution. He took note of the answer of those who would insist that there was a complete difference between the Catholic and other religions, because the first was the work of God. To such people he put the question of whether they wished in good faith that the Catholic religion, because it was divine, should rule by means of hatred, ferocity, prisons, tortures, and murders. If God founded it, he assured them, God would preserve it, "while intolerance begets either hypocrites or rebels." Did Catholics therefore "want to maintain by executioners the religion of a God who died at the hands of executioners and preached only gentleness and patience?"[18] It was always "la douceur" (gentleness) that Voltaire ascribed to Christ; he devoted a chapter to showing that Jesus was tolerant, and that his command in the parable in the Gospel of Luke, "Compel them to come in," did not authorize intolerance or persecution. Because tolerance was the divine law, he advised those "who want to be like Jesus Christ" to be martyrs, not hangmen.[19]

In the midst of his treatise, Voltaire inserted a discussion of the question of whether it was useful to keep the people in superstition. His answer was that "mankind always needs a bridle," and that the human race was so perverse and weak that it was better for it to be subjugated by superstitions, provided they weren't murderous, than to live without religion. Thus it was more reasonable for men to adore fantastic images and hold false ideas of divinity than to be atheists. But once they had come to embrace a pure and holy religion, then superstition became not only useless but very dangerous. He went on to note instances of superstition in Christian practices and the decline of superstition in France owing to the progress of reason, which "daily seeps into tradesmen's shops" and "into the grand mansions of the nobility." The worst, most dangerous of all superstitions, he said, was the one that demanded that "we hate our neighbor on account of his opinion." Rather than persecute one's brother, it was indeed more reasonable to adore the holy navel and the milk and robe of the Virgin Mary.[20]

The high point of Voltaire's work was an appeal for "universal toleration." Not only should Christians tolerate one another, but "we ought to regard every man as our brother," meaning the Turk, the Chinese, the Jew, the Siamese, and all others. This was certain without a doubt, he maintained, for "aren't we all children of the same Father and creatures of the same God?" His sarcasm was never sharper than when, after asking his Christian readers to picture the Day of Judgment, he inquired whether they were sure God would send to hell wise and virtuous men like Confucius, Solon, Pythagoras, Socrates, Plato, and other famous pagans who were models of mankind, while bestowing eternal bliss upon the Catholic assassins who murdered Henry IV and attempted the life of Louis XV.[21] He followed these exhortations with a prayer beseeching God that all men should love each other as brothers and hold in horror the tyranny of persecution.[22]

Voltaire's *Treatise on Toleration* said nothing about the rights of the erring conscience and avoided discussion of the relationship between the state and church or religion. Assuming a Catholic state in France, it sought to overcome Catholic resistance to toleration. In collaboration with the efforts made by others, its discussion of the case of Jean Calas and condemnation of persecution bore some fruit in 1787, when Louis XVI issued an edict of toleration to those who did not profess the Catholic religion. This decree restored the civil status of France's Protestants by granting them liberties that were said to derive from nature: the right to marry, to hold and inherit property, to exercise their occupations, and to have their children born in legitimacy. It did not, however, give them freedom of worship.[23] Voltaire urged the toleration of Christian religious minorities and non-Christian peoples in the name of both reason and morality. One might wonder whether it was his ridicule of superstition and persistent skepticism toward Christian dogma or his moral condemnation of persecution that had the greater effect in inculcating the principle of toleration. He endeavored through satire and argument to expose the injustice and inefficacy of intolerance. While he invoked the ethic of the gospel and the example of Christ to persuade his readers to treat religious differences with charity, he conceived of toleration fundamentally as the natural right of individuals to express their minds and opinions freely in matters of religion. By grounding the concept of toleration in natural right and natural law, he helped to give it a universality which associated it with other natural rights that justified men's freedom.

THE PROGRESS OF RELIGIOUS TOLERATION FROM THE END OF THE EIGHTEENTH CENTURY TO THE PRESENT

The development of religious toleration in the modern age from the Enlightenment onward was a long, complicated, and tortuous process that was nevertheless marked by the steady growth of the idea in Western consciousness, and by the expanding recognition of toleration as a right to be afforded all human beings and religions. Its gradual progress and realization in law and institutions were part of the evolution of most of western and central Europe and the Americas in the direction of political freedom, democracy, and—in the widest, least doctrinaire sense—toward a liberal society protective of individual rights. This process, which involved many national variations in church-state relationships, was, of course, always imperfect; it was never complete or final or without local contradictions, exceptions, and calamitous retrogressions in particular countries. Nor was it identical on the psychological and social plane with the elimination of prejudice and hateful attitudes toward other religions on the part of individuals, miscellaneous groups, and political organizations and parties. Anti-Protestantism, anti-Catholicism, and anti-Semitism have all flourished at different times in the nations of Western society, although they also greatly declined during the later twentieth century, certainly in their public expression. Over the long term, therefore, the advance of religious toleration has constituted one of the main lines of change and progress within Western society in the past two centuries. This advance took the form of the undermining of the confessional or denominational state, which existed everywhere in Europe in the seventeenth and eighteenth centuries, and its slow replacement by the full recognition of religious pluralism and, in many instances in the later twentieth century, by the separation of church and state.

The growth of toleration suffered a hideous reverse in the first half of the twentieth century through the coming to power of one-party totalitarian and authoritarian regimes of political and religious intolerance and persecution in Soviet Russia, Italy, Germany, and some other countries of Europe and Latin America. The phenomenon of modern anti-Semitism based on doctrines of racial difference and inferiority, a further development in the centuries-old anti-Judaism and hatred of the Jews fostered by the Catholic and other Christian churches, reached its height in Germany under Nazi rule after 1933. Its monstrously inhuman culmination occurred during the Second World War when the Nazi regime put into effect the policy of genocide aiming at the total destruction of the Jewish people. As a result, however, of the defeat of fascism and Nazism in the Second World War, the containment of communism in the ensuing Cold War, and the ultimate collapse of the Soviet communist system and empire in Europe at the end of the twentieth century, religious toleration has become a universal value with global impact and is seen as one of a number of basic rights and freedoms to which human beings are entitled.

In the progress of the idea of religious toleration toward its current status in Western society and its present worldwide significance, certain milestones point the way, and I shall note some of the most important of them in bringing this work to a conclusion.[24]

Developments in colonial America and the early United States were of great significance in the history of toleration and contributed to making the United States in the course of time the most religiously diverse and tolerant country in the world. In the seventeenth century, the colonies of Maryland, Rhode Island, and Pennsylvania, founded respectively by Catholics, Baptists, and Quakers, introduced legal regimes of freedom of conscience and worship for differing religious beliefs.[25] During the eighteenth century the principle of religious toleration became rooted in the concept of natural rights, the doctrine that inspired the American Declaration of Independence of 1776. The ordaining of religious freedom in the Pennsylvania state constitution of 1776 stated that "all men have a natural and unalienable right to worship Almighty God according to the dictates of their own consciences and understandings," and prohibited all compulsion in religion or deprivation of the civil rights of any citizen on account of religious belief or mode of worship.[26] Most notable was the Virginia Statute for Religious Freedom, drafted by Thomas Jefferson in 1777 and passed by the Virginia legislature in 1786 through the efforts of James Madison and the pressure of the dissenting sects led by the Baptists. Madison's *Memorial and Remonstrance against Religious Assessments*, which he wrote in 1785, preceded its passage as a major elaboration of the view that freedom of religion was an inalienable right of nature existing prior to civil society. It asserted that the "free exercise of . . . Religion according to the dictates of conscience is held by the same tenure with all . . . other rights," and that religion was exempt from the authority of the civil magistrate.[27] Both Jefferson and Madison were men of the Enlightenment whose ideas on toleration were strongly influenced by Locke's *Letter concerning Toleration.*[28] Always conscious of the danger of ecclesiastical tyranny, both were opposed to any state church. The Virginia Statute disestablished the Anglican Church as the state-supported church in Virginia. Its text was a memorable expression of the claim to freedom of religion as a part of the freedom of the mind and as a natural right derived from God. Denying that the ruler or legislator was empowered to impose his religion upon other men, it provided for complete freedom of religious opinion, belief, and worship. Its concluding clause, which declared that the religious freedoms previously enumerated were "the natural rights of mankind," contained the warning that if any future legislature should ever revoke the statute, it would be guilty of violating natural right.[29]

Reinforcing the natural-rights ideology were the conditions of American life in the later colonial period and earlier nineteenth century, which were highly conducive to the growth of religious freedom. The de facto limitations on formal authority in America due to the great distances and spread of settlement; the weakness of ecclesiastical authority and organization; the ability of dissident religious communities to move on to other parts of the country where they were free of control; and the continual arrival of growing numbers of immigrants of different religious affiliations—all these factors created a fluid situation favorable to the emergence of new religious bodies and popular movements and caused the United States to become "a free market of religion."[30]

Religious freedom was enshrined as a fundamental American principle in the federal constitution of the United States ratified in 1789. Article VI of the Constitution barred all religious tests as a qualification for holding any office or public trust under the United States. Two years later, the Bill of Rights proposed by James Madison, which comprised the first ten amendments incorporated in the Constitution, provided for complete freedom of religious belief and practice.[31] The First Amendment declared that the Congress of the United States "shall make no law respecting

An ACT *for eſtablishing* RELIGIOUS FREEDOM, *paſſed in the aſſembly of Virginia in the beginning of the year* 1786.

WELL aware that Almighty God hath created the mind free ; that all attempts to influence it by temporal punishments or burthens, or by civil incapacitations, tend only to beget habits of hypocriſy and meanneſs, and are a departure from the plan of the Holy Author of our religion, who, being Lord both of body and mind, yet choſe not to propagate it by coercions on either, as was in his Almighty power to do ; that the impious preſumption of legiſlators and rulers civil, as well as eccleſiaſtical who, being themſelves but fallible and uninſpired men, have aſſumed dominion over the faith of others, ſetting up their own opinions and modes of thinking as the only true and infaillible, and as ſuch endeavouring to impoſe them on others, hath eſtablished and maintained falſe religions over the greateſt part of the world, and through all time : That to compel a man to furnish contributions of money for the propagation of opinions which he disbelieves, is ſinful and tyrannical ; that even the forcing him to ſupport this or that teacher of his own religious perſuaſion, is depriving him of the comfortable liberty of giving his contributions to the particular paſtor whoſe

First page of the Virginia Statute for Religious Freedom, drafted by Thomas Jefferson and passed by the Virginia legislature in 1786. Courtesy of The Albert and Shirley Small Special Collections Library, University of Virginia Library.

an establishment of Religion, or prohibiting the free exercise thereof." It is significant that the amendment linked these provisions to other rights by also barring Congress from making a law abridging freedom of speech, the press, and the people's right to assemble peaceably and to petition the government for redress of grievances. The newly born United States of America was thus unique as the first Western country whose basic law contained in its Constitution excluded any state-supported national church.[32]

The conception of religious freedom as a natural right, of which no authority, church, or government could justly deprive any human being, gave the struggle for toleration a new character. Henceforth it was commonly demanded as a right, often along with other rights, as a condition of freedom. This change, exemplified by the American Constitution, was also reflected in contemporaneous developments in France after the beginning of the French Revolution in 1789. The Declaration of the Rights of Man and Citizen, adopted in August 1789 by the revolutionary French National Assembly, was premised on the proposition that "men are born and remain free and equal in rights." It proclaimed liberty, property, security, and resistance to oppression as "natural, inalienable, and sacred rights of man." On the subject of religion, it did not speak of religious liberty but affirmed that "no one is to be disquieted because of his opinions, even religious, provided their manifestation does not disturb the public order established by law."[33] In other actions, the National Assembly opened all civil and military offices to non-Catholics and extended the rights of citizenship to the Jews of France. The Constitution of 1791, the first written constitution in France's history, guaranteed various natural and civil rights to French citizens, including freedom to speak, write, print, and publish their opinions without being subject to any prepublication censorship, and to worship as they pleased.[34] In contrast to the separation of church and state in the United States, the French Revolution destroyed the old religious order in France through the Civil Constitution of the Clergy in 1790, which placed the Catholic Church completely under the national state's control. The church's property was confiscated by the state, while bishops and priests became salaried officials of the government and were persecuted if they refused to accept their new status. Catholicism continued to be the state religion, but with toleration for other religions and civil liberty and equality for non-Catholics.[35]

The spread of the doctrines of the revolution, which was aided by France's territorial expansion under the first French Republic and the subsequent conquests of Napoleon Bonaparte as French emperor, was among the factors that helped to undermine the institutions of the *ancien régime* in Italy, Germany, Spain, and other parts of Europe. The coupling of the ideas of political and religious freedom in the nineteenth century led to the gradual removal of legal disabilities upon religious denominations outside the state churches, the growing acceptance of religious pluralism, and the recognition of religious freedom as a right of citizens. During this period, and especially in the pontificate of Pope Pius IX (1846–1878), the papacy and Catholic Church remained steadfastly opposed to the principle of religious toleration and to any compromise with growing political liberalism and aspirations to democratic government. Within the church, nevertheless, a significant movement of liberal Catholicism emerged in the earlier nineteenth century that protested against the split between the church and the modern world. Represented by such well-known Catholic thinkers as Montalembert and Lamennais in France and Lord Acton in England, it advocated political and religious liberty in opposition to the church's ideological conservatism, intolerance, and support of reactionary governments.[36]

In England toleration prevailed in the course of the eighteenth century, with both Protestant dissenters from Anglicanism and Catholics left free in the main to practice their faith. In 1828 the British Parliament finally repealed the Test and Corporation Acts, the last remaining penal laws against the dissenters, and in the following year it removed the disabilities against the Catholics.[37] The English philosopher John Stuart Mill's famous *On Liberty*, published in 1859, was one of the strongest, most influential statements by any thinker of the nineteenth century urging the widest

possible extent of individual freedom, political, religious, and intellectual. Mill recognized not only the close interrelationship of
the three but the debt that the struggle for political and intellectual freedom owed to the earlier struggle for religious freedom.
It was on "the [religious] battlefield, almost solely," he wrote,

> that the rights of the individual against society have been as
> serted on broad grounds of principle, and the claim of soci
> ety to exercise authority over dissentients openly contro
> verted. The great writers to whom the world owes what liberty
> it possesses, have most asserted freedom of conscience as an
> indefeasible right, and denied absolutely that a human being
> is accountable to another for his religious belief.[38]

The late eighteenth century and the nineteenth also saw the
political emancipation of the Jews of western Europe, which began
with the French Revolution. Their former pariah status as an oppressed alien people within Christian society came to an end as
they were gradually accorded full legal equality and the rights of
citizenship in England, France, and other European countries. In
the United States, Jews, although long liable to prejudice and discrimination, always enjoyed civil equality and citizen rights. Jewish
emancipation meant deliverance not only from the ghetto and
legal intolerance but also from the bonds of the traditional religious community and the strict mandates of orthodox observance.
It coincided with the increasing dissemination of Enlightenment
and secular values in Jewish life and resulted in gradual Jewish
assimilation into the wider cultures of the nations of which they
were part. In the process they became French, Americans, English,
Italians, Germans, Austrians, and the like. Such assimilation,
though it never led to their complete acceptance by Christian society in the nineteenth and earlier twentieth centuries, entailed
their departure from the ancestral religious beliefs and practices
that had held them together as a people; this was the price they
paid for emancipation.[39]

By the end of the twentieth century the principle of religious
tolerance and freedom, even if by no means always honored in

practice, had come to be seen throughout Western society as a basic legal and human right. In almost every country except Great Britain, moreover, its acceptance was accompanied by the constitutional separation of church and state. The war of 1939–1945 against fascism and Nazism and the conflict of the second half of the century with Soviet communism confirmed the Western world's belief in religious freedom as one of its supreme values. The same period also witnessed the increasing penetration of the concept of political, religious, and other rights within non-Western societies throughout the globe. These rights were commonly designated as human rights. Two major events in particular must be reckoned as the outstanding symbols of the extraordinary ascent of human rights, including those pertaining to religion, to their preeminent normative position on a global scale in the later twentieth century. One was the United Nations General Assembly's adoption in 1948 of the Universal Declaration of Human Rights; the other was the Declaration on Religious Freedom in 1965 by the Second Vatican Council of the Catholic Church.

When the United Nations created its Commission on Human Rights in 1946, the new body had a broad membership representing a number of countries of different cultures and political systems. The main work in drafting the Universal Declaration was done by the commission's American chair, Eleanor Roosevelt, the widow of President Franklin D. Roosevelt, and a small group of United Nations delegates who were among the members of the commission. These were a Chinese diplomat, writer, and Confucian scholar, P. C. Chung; a Lebanese Christian professor and philosopher, Charles Malik; a French Jew, distinguished jurist, and future Nobel Peace Prize laureate, Jean Cassin; and an Indian legislator, nationalist, and Hindu, Mrs. Hansi Mehta. In its concept of human rights, the Universal Declaration included not only civil, political, and religious, but social, economic, and cultural rights as well. Beside rights, its other fundamental concepts were the dignity of man and the basic unity of the human race. In his speech presenting the final document to the General Assembly of the United Nations in December 1948, Malik described the

Universal Declaration of Human Rights as a "composite synthesis" of all existing rights traditions; he said it had been designed on an international basis in which "no regional philosophy or way of life was permitted to prevail." The General Assembly accepted it unanimously, with eight abstentions.[40]

Its preamble began with this statement: "The inherent dignity and the equal and inalienable rights of all members of the human family [are] the foundation of freedom, justice and peace in the world." It also referred to the famous Four Freedoms that had been outlined by President Roosevelt in 1941: freedom of speech and belief, freedom from fear and from want. Going on to articulate the body of rights to which all human beings were entitled, the Universal Declaration pronounced in Article 18 that "[e]veryone has the right to freedom of thought, conscience and religion; this right includes freedom to change his religious belief, and freedom, either alone or in community with others and in public or private, to manifest his religion or belief in teaching, practice, worship and observance." The following article provided for freedom of opinion and expression in all forms and all media.[41] These two articles, particularly the first, may be considered a summation of all that the advocates and champions of toleration and religious freedom had collectively striven for over the past four hundred years. Of course, the Universal Declaration of Human Rights is only words. It has no provision for enforcing its principles and is not legally binding on the member states of the United Nations. At the beginning of the twenty-first century, religious tolerance and freedom are sadly lacking in various parts of the world. The Universal Declaration serves nevertheless as a standard for international organizations, governments, and great numbers of people everywhere. Many experts believe that it has become part of international customary law and provides a moral, political, and quasi-legal framework to which countries belonging to the United Nations have an obligation to adhere.[42]

The Second Vatican Council of the Roman Catholic Church, which met in 1962, was convened by Pope John XXIII and was continued after his death in 1963 by his successor Pope Paul VI.

The council's Declaration on Religious Freedom bears the subtitle "On the Right of the Person and of Communities to Social and Civil Freedom in Religious Matters." When debated, it met with considerable resistance from some Vatican officials and a number of bishops.[43] It drew inspiration, however, from John XXIII's well known encyclical of 1963 on world peace and justice, *Pacem in Terris*, which spoke of "universal, inviolable, inalienable rights and duties" and used the phrase "the dignity of the human person" over thirty times.[44] Among its chief intellectual sponsors and promoters was the American Jesuit philosopher John Courtney Murray, who was called to Rome during the council's proceedings to serve as one of its theological experts. Having written extensively on religious freedom, Murray was convinced of the need for the church to update its teachings on the subject in the light of twentieth-century insight. In an essay circulated to the American bishops on the right of the human person to religious liberty, he characterized the opposing view in the Catholic Church in recent times as "intolerance wherever possible, tolerance wherever necessary."[45]

In December 1965, the Second Vatican Council passed the Declaration on Religious Freedom, also known from the opening words of its Latin text as *Dignitatis humanae personae*, by an overwhelming majority. Of all the council's documents, this was the only one addressed to the entire world and all faiths. After referring in its exordium to the increasing contemporary consciousness of the dignity of the human person and to the church's scrutiny of its sacred tradition and doctrine in order to draw forth new things in harmony with the old, it stated that "the human person has a right to religious freedom." In defining this freedom, it asserted that "all men are to be immune from coercion" by individuals, social groups, or "any human power," so that "in matters religious no one is forced to act in a manner contrary to his own beliefs. Nor is anyone to be restrained from acting in accordance with his own beliefs, whether privately or publicly, whether alone or in association with others, within due limits." It perceived the foundation of this right in "the very dignity of the human person" as known through "the revealed word of God and by reason itself."

The one limit the Declaration placed on the free exercise of religion was "the just requirements of public order." In the case of particular countries that recognized a state religion, it pointed out the imperative obligation to secure all citizens and other religious bodies in their right to religious freedom. Looking at religious freedom in the light of revelation, it affirmed that God created man to enjoy freedom, and that Christ and the apostles had appealed only to conscience, never using force to compel belief. It took note of the importance of the rights of the Catholic Church in a pluralistic society, emphasizing the church's own need of freedom to perform its spiritual mission. The Declaration also acknowledged that in "the vicissitudes of history," the church had acted at times in ways "which were less in accord with the gospel and even opposed to it." In its conclusion, finally, it stressed the necessity of universal religious freedom "in the present condition of the human family," in which the different nations, cultures, and religions of the world were coming together in closer relationships.[46]

The Catholic theologian John Courtney Murray said of this document that "in all honesty it must be admitted" that the church was "late in acknowledging the validity of the principle" of religious freedom.[47] Indeed, it was very late. Moreover, the document was far from confronting with complete candor the Catholic Church's long history of cruel intolerance and far from expressing any contrition or apology for its record of religious persecution. In spite of these faults, the Declaration on Religious Freedom was an accomplishment of world importance. It signified a complete reversal of the Catholic Church's former inimical attitude to toleration and announced its adherence to religious freedom as a universal principle and contemporary obligation and necessity.

In his work on the political theory of justice and liberalism, the distinguished American philosopher John Rawls has observed that one of the most important roots of the liberal society lay in "the long controversies over religious toleration in the sixteenth and seventeenth centuries." It was then, he notes, that "something like the modern understanding of liberty of conscience and freedom of thought began."[48] As I have assumed and often pointed out in this book, the ideas of toleration and religious freedom are ultimately not separable. Wherever tolerance has been recognized as more than a temporary expedient, wherever it has been advocated for religious, moral, and humanitarian reasons, it has also had a relation to and tended to develop in the direction of religious freedom. The succession of thinkers and publicists who conceived and worked out the theory of religious toleration in early modern Europe all had some concept of religious freedom in their minds as they strove to deliver Christian dissenters from persecution at the hands of the representatives of the Catholic and Protestant state churches. The poet Goethe once wrote, "What you have inherited from your fathers / You must work on, that you may possess it."[49] During the twentieth century, religious freedom and pluralism became largely a reality in Western society and inseparable from political and other freedoms. We in the Western world, especially if we are at all conscious of the long hard struggle that lies behind the achievement of our religious and other freedoms, can never permit ourselves to take them for granted and must always strive to protect them. We must also hope that despite the many adverse signs at present, we shall in time, and with the help of Western example, see the right to the free exercise of religion, together with political freedom and freedom of thought and expression, accepted and embraced in those places—including considerable parts of the Islamic world and the few remaining communist countries—where they do not exist today.

NOTES

%&%

Chapter 1
Religious Toleration: The Historical Problem

1. Historians today usually think of medieval Europe as a persecuting society, in the phrase used by R. I. Moore, *The Formation of a Persecuting Society: Power and Deviance in Western Europe, 950–1250* (Oxford: Blackwell, 1987). In several recent essays, however, Cary J. Nederman and John Christian Laursen have challenged this judgment as a myth and caricature, and Nederman has attempted to show the existence of ideas of tolerance in medieval political theory and in such thinkers as the twelfth-century John of Salisbury and the fifteenth-century Nicholas of Cusa; see Cary J. Nederman and John Christian Laursen, "Difference and Dissent: Introduction," and Cary J. Nederman, "Liberty, Community, and Toleration: Freedom and Function in Medieval Political Thought," in *Difference and Dissent: Theories of Toleration in Medieval and Early Modern Europe*, ed. Cary J. Nederman and John Christian Laursen (Lanham, Md.: Rowman and Littlefield, 1996); Cary J. Nederman, "Introduction: Discourses and Contexts of Tolerance in Medieval Europe," and "Toleration, Skepticism, and the 'Clash of Ideas': Principles of Liberty in the Writings of John of Salisbury," in *Beyond the Persecuting Society*, ed. John Christian Laursen and Cary J. Nederman (Philadephia: University of Pennsylvania Press, 1998); Cary J. Nederman, "*Natio* and the 'Variety of Rites': Foundations of Religious Toleration in Nicholas of Cusa," in *Religious Toleration*, ed. John Christian Laursen (New York: St. Martin's Press, 1999). Despite their commendable efforts, I have not found their arguments and claims convincing. While we may see some strains of tolerance in John of Salisbury's praise of liberty of thought and speech and in Nicholas of Cusa's irenicism and belief in dialogue between different faiths and nationalities, neither in these nor in other medieval writers do we find anything resembling a theory of religious toleration. The critical test of such a theory in Christian and Catholic Europe is its attitude to heresy and heretics and hence its willingness to argue against the long-standing Christian theory of religious persecution and to support coexistence and concord between rival Christian confessions and

different religious faiths. It was not until the religious conflicts generated in the sixteenth century by the Protestant Reformation and in the actual struggle against persecution that genuine theories of religious toleration first made their appearance in Europe. On the medieval persecution of heresy and the theory that sustained it, see below, chap. 2.

2. Voltaire, *Philosophical Dictionary* (1st French ed. 1764), ed. Theodore Besterman (Harmondsworth: Penguin, 1983), s.v. "Tolérance: Toleration."

3. It was not until 1965 that the Catholic Church finally embraced the principle of toleration in its fullest meaning in the Second Vatican Council's authoritative Declaration on Religious Liberty; see below, chap. 8, for a discussion of this document.

4. Here and elsewhere in this book, the reader should note that I use the terms "freedom" and "liberty" interchangeably, since the meanings of the two are identical.

5. On the absence of a concept of toleration in Roman society and the extent of religious toleration in the Roman world, see Peter Garnsey, "Religious Toleration in Classical Antiquity," in *Persecution and Toleration*, ed. W. J. Sheils (Oxford: Blackwell, 1984), and J. A. North, "Religious Toleration in Republican Rome," *Proceedings of the Cambridge Philological Society*, n.s., no. 25 (1979): 85–103.

6. On the Roman persecution of Christianity and tolerance of Judaism, see Garnsey, "Religious Toleration in Classical Antiquity," and the accounts by G.E.M. de Sainte Croix, "Why Were the Early Christians Persecuted?" in *Studies in Ancient Society*, ed. M. I. Finley (London: Routledge and Kegan Paul, 1974), and Robin Lane Fox, *Pagans and Christians* (New York: Knopf, 1987), chap. 9.

7. D. D. Raphael, "The Intolerable," in *Justifying Toleration: Conceptual and Historical Perspectives*, ed. Susan Mendus (Cambridge: Cambridge University Press, 1988), p. 139. For some recent theoretical discussions of the meaning of toleration, see the essays in this work and in *Aspects of Toleration*, ed. John Horton and Susan Mendus (London: Methuen, 1985); Preston King, *Toleration* (New York: St. Martin's Press, 1976); *On Toleration*, ed. Susan Mendus and David Edwards (Oxford: Clarendon Press, 1987); *Toleration: An Elusive Virtue*, ed. David Heyd (Princeton: Princeton University Press, 1996); *Philosophy, Religion, and the Question of Tolerance*, ed. Mehdi Amin Razavi and David Ambuel (Albany: State University of New York Press, 1997).

8. W. K. Jordan, *The Development of Religious Toleration in England*, 4 vols. (Cambridge: Harvard University Press, 1932–1940); Joseph Lecler, *Toleration and the Reformation* (1st French ed. 1955), 2 vols. (New York: Association Press, 1960). Lecler comments in his preface (I:x) that "the verb 'to tolerate' had been used for a long time in connection with religious freedom," and cites as a precedent for this the discussion in Thomas Aquinas's *Summa theologia* (IIa IIae, qu. 10, art. 2), on whether the worship by infidels may be tolerated. In his introductory remarks in vol. 1, Jordan observes that toleration, as a refraining from persecution, consists of "a limited and conditional freedom" but constitutes nonetheless "one of the most significant advances the human race has ever achieved" (p. 17). He also notes, however, that in its finest conception, it presumes an attitude that gives a charitable and sympathetic hearing to the views of

other persons and concedes their right to retain and practice contrary religious beliefs (p. 16). Although he comments that religious toleration had to be achieved before religious liberty became possible (p. 19), as his work goes on to the treatment in his final volume of the controversy over toleration in the mid-seventeenth-century English revolution, the difference between toleration and religious liberty tends to become increasingly blurred and the two appear more and more alike.

9. Henry Kamen, *The Rise of Toleration* (New York: McGraw-Hill, 1967), p. 7.

10. Johannes Kuhn, "Das Geschichtsproblem der Toleranz," in *Autour de Michel Servet et de Sébastien Castellion*, ed. Bruno Becker (Haarlem: Tjeene Willink & Zoon, 1953).

11. *Religiöse Toleranz. Dokumente zur Geschichte einer Forderung*, ed. Hans R. Guggisberg (Stuttgart-Bad Cannstadt: Frommann-Holzboog, 1984), p. 10. Elsewhere Guggisberg remarks that at first toleration and religious liberty or liberty of conscience did not mean the same thing, but he goes on to say that "toleration creates religious liberty"; "The Defence of Religious Toleration and Religious Liberty in Early Modern Europe: Arguments, Pressures, and Some Consequences," *History of European Ideas* 4, no. 1 (1983): 36.

12. Philip Benedict, "*Un Roi, Une Loi, Deux Fois*: Parameters for the History of Catholic-Reformed Co-existence in France, 1555–1685," in *Tolerance and Intolerance in the European Reformation*, ed. Ole Peter Grell and Bob Scribner (Cambridge: Cambridge University Press, 1996), pp. 67–68.

13. See John Edwards, "Mission and Conversion among Conversos and Moriscos in Spain 1250–1550," in Sheils, *Persecution and Toleration*; Angus MacKay, "The Hispanic-*Converso* Predicament," *Transactions of the Royal Historical Society*, 5th ser., 35 (1985); and the detailed account by Yitzhak Baer, *A History of the Jews in Christian Spain*, 2 vols. (Philadelphia: Jewish Publication Society, 1961).

14. See John Lynch, *Spain under the Habsburgs*, 2 vols. (Oxford: Blackwell, 1965–69), vol. 1, chap. 7; 2:42–51.

15. See the discussion of these reasons in Jordan, *The Development of Religious Toleration in England*, 1:15–19, and in Ole Peter Grell's introduction to Grell and Scribner, *Tolerance and Intolerance in the European Reformation*, pp. 1–3.

16. Most of the intellectual trends I have mentioned are discussed in the classic study by Paul Hazard on the prehistory of the Enlightenment, *The European Mind* 1680–1715 (1st French ed. 1935) (New York: New American Library, 1963), and Jonathan I. Israel, *Radical Enlightenment: Philosophy and the Making of Modernity*, 1650–1750 (Oxford: Oxford University Press, 2001). Developments in philosophy are surveyed in *The Cambridge History of Seventeenth-Century Philosophy*, ed. Daniel Garber and Michael Ayers, 2 vols. (Cambridge: Cambridge University Press, 1998), which includes full bibliographies. For the advances in science during the seventeenth century, see A. R. Hall, "The Scientific Movement," in *The New Cambridge Modern History*, 13 vols. (Cambridge: Cambridge University Press, 1957–1979), vol. 5, chap. 3, and A. C. Crombie, "The Scientific Movement and the Diffusion of Scientific Ideas, 1688–1751," ibid., vol. 6, chap. 2. This subject is discussed below, chap. 8.

17. See René Pintard, *Le libertinage érudit dans la première moitié du XVIIe siècle*, new rev. ed. (Geneva: Slatkine, 1983), passim, and Perez Zagorin, *Ways of Lying: Dissimulation, Persecution, and Conformity in Early Modern Europe* (Cambridge: Harvard University Press, 1990), pp. 321–24.

18. Herbert Butterfield, *Toleration in Religion and Politics* (New York: Council on Religion and International Affairs, 1980), pp. 4–8.

19. On the Peace of Augsburg, see Hajo Holborn, *A History of Modern Germany: The Reformation* (New York: Knopf, 1959), pp. 243–46.

20. Henry IV had been a Protestant and a leader of the Protestant cause. He became a Catholic in 1593 in order to secure his succession to the French throne and to help bring peace to his country.

21. The Edict of Nantes was mostly a codification of the provisions of prior temporary edicts of pacification that the French crown had issued during the religious civil war. On the problem of toleration in sixteenth-century France and the religious pacification of the Edict of Nantes, see Lecler, *Toleration and the Reformation*, vol. 2, pt. 6, chap. 5. Roland Mousnier, *The Institutions of France under the Absolute Monarchy* 1598–1789, 2 vols. (Chicago: University of Chicago Press, 1979–1984), vol. 1, chap. 2, contains an account of the Edict of Nantes and the deteriorating situation of the Protestants in the reigns of Henry IV's successors that culminated in its revocation. See also the discussion by Philip Benedict of the religious settlement in France in *Handbook of European History* 1400–1600, ed. Thomas A. Brady, Jr., Heiko A. Oberman, and James D. Tracy, 2 vols (Leiden: E. J. Brill, 1995), vol. 2, chap. 14.

22. The breakdown of the Peace of Augsburg and outbreak of the Thirty Years War are described by Holborn, *A History of Modern Germany*, chaps. 10–12.

23. See Bob Scribner, "Preconditions of Tolerance and Intolerance in Sixteenth-Century Germany," in Grell and Scribner, *Tolerance and Intolerance in the European Reformation*, p. 29; Randolph C. Head, "Introduction: The Transformations of the Long Sixteenth Century," in Laursen and Nederman, *Beyond the Persecuting Society*, pp. 97, 104.

24. See the discussion by Benedict in Grell and Scribner, *Tolerance and Intolerance in the European Reformation*, and below, chap. 7, for the significance of the revocation of the Edict of Nantes.

Chapter 2
The Christian Theory of Religious Persecution

1. Acton first reviewed Creighton's book in the *English Historical Review* in 1887, and a correspondence between the two men then followed. Acton's review, his letter to Creighton, and the latter's answer are reprinted in Lord Acton, *Essays in the Study and Writing of History:Selected Writings of Lord Acton*, ed. J. Rufus Fears, 3 vols. (Indianapolis: Liberty Classics, 1985), 2:365–92; the passage quoted is on p. 381.

2. For Acton's statement of this position, see his letter in ibid., pp. 378–88, and his "Inaugural Lecture on the Study of History," delivered upon his ap-

pointment as Regius Professor of History at Cambridge University, in Lord Acton, *Lectures on Modern History*, ed. J. N. Figgis, and R. V. Laurence (London: Macmillan, 1918). I have discussed Acton's view in my essay "Lord Acton's Ordeal: The Historian and Moral Judgment, *Virginia Quarterly Review* 74, no. 1 (1998): 1–17.

3. Printed in Lord Acton, *Selected Writings*, 2:389.

4. See Peter Nicholson, "Toleration as a Moral Ideal," in *Aspects of Toleration*, ed. John Horton and Susan Mendus (London: Methuen, 1985).

5. Cited in W. K. Jordan, *The Development of Religious Toleration in England*, 4 vols. (Cambridge: Harvard University Press, 1932–1940), 1:25

6. Henry C. Lea, *A History of the Inquisition of the Middle Ages*, 3 vols. (New York: Macmillan, 1922), 1:234.

7. Jordan, *The Development of Religious Toleration in England*, 1:24.

8. On heresy and its history, there is a good discussion in *Encyclopedia Britannica*, 11th ed., s.v. "Heresy." The long article on the subject in *Dictionnaire de théologie catholique*, s.v. "Hérésie, Hérétique," is much more legal and technical than historical in its treatment and includes extensive citations from Catholic authorities. Edward Peters presents a useful brief survey of the background and emergence of the concept of heresy in the church in *Heresy and Authority in Medieval Europe* (Philadelphia: University of Pennsylvania Press, 1980), pp. 13–20. On the absence of a conception of heresy in Judaism analogous to that which appeared in early Christianity, see *The Jewish Encyclopedia*, s.v. "Heresy and Heretics," and *Encyclopedia of Religion and Ethics*, s.v. "Heresy (Jewish)." Although the Jewish religion of the first century C.E. had sects like the Sadducees, Pharisees, Essenes, and others, which differed in their various beliefs, it had no single authority that could define orthodoxy, and indeed lacked any concept of orthodoxy to be contrasted with heresy.

9. See Hobbes's chapter on the history of heresy in the appendix of the Latin version of *Leviathan* (1668), which is printed in an English translation in Thomas Hobbes, *Leviathan* (1651), ed. Edwin Curley (Indianapolis: Hackett, 1994), pp. 521–36. Hobbes also wrote *An Historical Narration concerning Heresy, and the Punishment Therof*, which was posthumously published in 1680 and is printed in *English Works*, ed. Sir William Molesworth, 11 vols. (London, 1839–1845), vol. 4.

10. The word is related to the Greek verb *haireomai*, "a choosing"; see Liddell and Scott's *Greek-English Lexicon*, s.v.

11. See Lewis and Short, *Latin Dictionary*, s.v.

12. All references to the English translation of the Bible are to the King James, or Authorized, Version of 1611, unless otherwise stated. The later Revised Standard Version of 1952 translates *haireseis* in this passage as "factions." The King James translators, however, lived in a period when the conception of heresy continued to be widely accepted in the Protestant churches, and their rendering of the term as "heresies" with all its disparaging associations is therefore historically pertinent.

13. In Acts of the Apostles we find the word *hairesis* used pejoratively to refer to the Jewish sects of Sadducees and Pharisees (Acts 5:17, 15:5). The Authorized Version translates the term as "sect."

14. The numerous writings against heresy are surveyed in the encyclopedic treatment of the Christian literature of the first four centuries by Johannes Quasten, *Patrology*, 4 vols. (Utrecht: Spectrum Publishers, 1964–1966). Texts illustrating some of these heresies that concern the person of Christ are included in *Documents of the Christian Church*, ed. Henry Bettenson, 2d ed. (London: Oxford University Press, 1967), pp. 35–39.

15. The term "heresy" appears in Ignatius's letter to the Christians of Tralles, one of his seven epistles; see *Encyclopedia Britannica*, 11th ed., s.v. "Heresy."

16. See Henry Chadwick, *The Early Church* (Harmondsworth: Penguin, 1982), pp. 41–45, and Adolph von Harnack, *History of Dogma*, 3d ed., 7 vols., (1900; reprint, Gloucester, Mass.: Peter Smith, 1976), vol. 2, chaps. 1–2.

17. Edward Gibbon, *The History of the Decline and Fall of the Roman Empire* (1776–1788), ed. David Womersley, 3 vols. (London: Allen Lane, 1994), 1:778.

18. I cite these statements in Irenaeus's *Adversus omnes haereses* from the selections printed in Carl Mirbt, *Quellen zur Geschichte des Papsttums und des Römischen Katholizismus*, 6th ed., 2 vols. (Tübingen: J.C.B. Mohr, 1967), 1:35; Quasten discusses Irenaeus's work in *Patrology*, 1:287–313.

19. Tertullian, *De praescriptione haereticorum*; my comments in the text are based on the selections from this work in Mirbt, *Quellen*, 1:40–42; see also the account in Quasten, *Patrology*, 2:269–72.

20. Quoted from Tertullian's *Apologeticus* and *Ad Scapulam* by Peter Garnsey, "Religious Toleration in Classical Antiquity," in *Persecution and Toleration*, ed. W. J. Sheils (Oxford: Blackwell, 1984), p. 14.

21. On Hippolytus's *Refutation of All Heresies*, or *Philosophoumena*, see Quasten, *Patrology*, 2:166–68. Mirbt, *Quellen*, prints a selection from this work attacking the Monarchian heresy of Noetus and Sabellius, 1:30–31.

22. On Eusebius, see Quasten, *Patrology*, 3:314–15.

23. On Epiphanius's *Panarion*, see ibid., pp. 387–88.

24. See the detailed account of the conversion and religious policy of Constantine by A.H.M. Jones, *The Later Roman Empire*, 2 vols. (Norman: University of Oklahoma Press, 1964), 1:80–93, and Robin Lane Fox, *Pagans and Christians* (New York: Knopf, 1987), chap. 12. On the Christianization of the empire, see also Ramsay MacMullen, *Christianizing the Roman Empire* (New Haven: Yale University Press, 1984), who notes as part of the process of Christianization the relentless suppression of paganism and conversion by coercion. The Nicene Creed is printed in Bettenson, *Documents of the Christian Church*, p. 25.

25. Jones, *The Later Roman Empire*, 1:164.

26. Ibid., pp. 165–66; see also the illuminating discussion in Charles Norris Cochrane, *Christianity and Classical Culture*, rev. ed. (London: Oxford University Press, 1944), chap. 9, from which the passages in the text are quoted, and the excellent recent account of Theodosius's persecution of heresy and paganism by Stephen Williams and Gerard Friell, *Theodosius: The Empire at Bay* (London: Batsford, 1994), chaps. 4, 9. The edict of 380, which was issued in the name of Theodosius I and his imperial colleagues Gratian and Valentinian II, is printed in Bettenson, *Documents of the Christian Church*, p. 22.

27. Quoted from Symmachus's *Relatio* in Samuel Dill, *Roman Society in the Last Century of the Western Empire*, 2d ed. rev. (London: Macmillan, 1919), pp. 30–31.

28. Cochrane, *Christianity and Classical Culture*, pp. 332–34; Jones, *The Later Roman Empire*, 1:285–86, 2:950–54.

29. On Donatism and its history and doctrines, see W.H.C. Frend, *The Donatist Church: A Movement of Protest in Roman North Africa*, 3d ed. (Oxford: Clarendon Press, 1985), and Yves M.-J. Congar's introduction to Saint Augustine, *Traités anti-donatistes*, 5 vols., in *Oeuvres de Saint Augustin*, 4th ser. (Paris: Desclée de Brouwer, 1963–1968), vol. 1; for the Circumcellions, so-called because they lived "around the shrines" (*circum cellas*), see the particulars in Frend, *The Donatist Church*, pp. 172–78. The quotation from Bishop Donatus is in ibid., p. 171.

30. On Augustine's dealings with Donatism and the Donatists and his view of coercion, see the well-documented account by Herbert A. Deane, *The Political and Social Ideas of St. Augustine* (New York: Columbia University Press, 1963), chap. 6; Frend, *The Donatist Church*, chap. 15; the perceptive discussion by Peter Brown, "St. Augustine's Attitude to Religious Coercion," in Peter Brown, *Religion and Society in the Age of Saint Augustine* (New York: Harper & Row, 1972); Congar, introduction, pp. 22–25, "Position d'Augustin sur l'usage de la contrainte."

31. Congar, introduction, p. 22.

32. Saint Augustine, *Letters*, 5 vols. (New York: Fathers of the Church, 1951), 1:131 (letter 34 to Eusebius, undated, but probably written before 400).

33. Ibid., p. 182 (letter 43 to Glorius et al.).

34. Ibid., 2:73–74 (letter 93 to Vincent).

35. For this work I use the parallel Latin and French texts in Saint Augustine, *Contra epistulam Parmeniani*, in *Traités anti-donatistes*, vol. 1.

36. Ibid., pp. 239–43, 245–52 = bk. 1.8.13–14, 9.15, 10.16, 11.17.

37. Ibid., pp. 421–23 = bk. 3.2.13.

38. In his treatise *On the Priesthood*, written ca. 386, Saint John Chrysostom, a contemporary of Augustine, interpreted the parable of the tares similarly as meaning that Christ approved the repression and silencing of heretics but forbade killing them; see Joseph Lecler, *Toleration and the Reformation*, 2 vols. (New York: Association Press, 1960), 1:60.

39. Saint Augustine, *Letters*, 2:57, 59 (letter 93, dated 408).

40. Ibid., pp. 60–61.

41. Ibid., p. 72.

42. See the comments of Brown, "St. Augustine's Attitude," pp. 269–70.

43. *Letters*, 4:152 (letter 185); cf. the passage in *Letter to Catholics about the Donatist Sect* (*Epistula ad catholicos de secta donatistarum*), ca. 401, in *Traités anti-donatistes*, 1:659 = 20.53, in which, defending the repression of the Donatists, Augustine states, with a citation from Psalm 100:5 (Psalm 101 in the Authorized Version), that not all persecution is culpable, and gives examples of good persecution.

44. *Letters*, 4:154, 160.

45. Ibid., pp. 161–62.

46. Ibid., pp. 163–66.

47. Ibid., pp. 74–75, 80–81 (letter 173 to a Donatist priest, ca. 416).

48. Ibid., 2:205 (letter 105 of 409).

49. Frend, *The Donatist Church*, pp. 263–65, 273.

50. *Letters*, 2:141–42 (letter 100 of ca. 408); ibid., vol. 3 (letter 133 of 412 to Marcellinus).

51. See Frend, *The Donatist Church*, chap. 19.

52. Congar, introduction, pp. 24–25.

53. *Letters*, 2:203 (letter 105 of 409).

54. Brown, "St. Augustine's Attitude," pp. 260, 277.

55. For a summary of the origins, chronology, and nature of these medieval popular heresies, see the introduction by Walter L. Wakefield, "Historical Sketch of the Medieval Popular Heresies," in Walter L. Wakefield and Austin P. Evans, *Heresies of the High Middle Ages* (New York: Columbia University Press, 1969). There is a very large body of historical scholarship on the growth of medieval heresy and its persecution. Beside the work by Wakefield and Evans, which contains valuable historical information together with a large selection of documentary sources and rich bibliographical references, among the writings I have found useful are the following, some of which include bibliographies of both the older and more recent literature: Ernest W. Nelson, "The Theory of Persecution," in *Persecution and Liberty: Essays in Honor of George Lincoln Burr* (New York: The Century Co., 1931); Lord Acton, "The Protestant Theory of Persecution," in *The History of Freedom and Other Essays*, ed. J. N. Figgis and R. V. Laurence (London: Macmillan, 1909); Lea, *A History of the Inquisition*, vol. 1, chap. 5, "Persecution"; Lecler, *Toleration and the Reformation*, vol. 1, chap. 4, "The Middle Ages"; Gordon Leff, *Heresy in the Later Middle Ages*, 2 vols. (Manchester: University of Manchester Press, 1969); Jeffrey B. Russell, *Religious Dissent in the Middle Ages* (New York: John Wiley, 1971); *The Concept of Heresy in the Middle Ages* (11th–13th C.), ed. W. Lourdaux and D. Verhelst (Louvain: Louvain University Press, 1976); Peters, *Heresy and Authority*, chaps. 2–10; R. I. Moore, *The Origins of European Dissent* (London: Allen Lane, 1977), and the same author's *The Formation of a Persecuting Society: Power and Deviance in Western Europe 950–1250* (Oxford: Blackwell, 1987), which deals not only with the persecution of heretics but also with that of Jews and lepers; Malcolm Lambert, *Medieval Heresy*, 2d ed. (Oxford: Blackwell, 1992); Heinrich Fichtenau, *Heretics and Scholars in the High Middle Ages 1000–1200* (University Park: Pennsylvania State University Press, 1998), pt. 1.

56. Lambert, *Medieval Heresy*, p. xi; on the Lollard and Hussite movements, see the account in Leff, *Heresy in the Later Middle Ages*, vol. 2, chaps. 8–9.

57. See Annie Brenon, "Christianisme et tolérance dans les textes cathares et vaudois du bas moyen âge," in *Naissance et affirmation de l'idée de tolérance XVIe et XVIIIe siècle*, ed. Michel Perronet (Montpellier: Université Paul Valéry, 1987).

58. *Decretum magistri Gratiani*, pt. 1 of *Corpus iuris canonici*, ed. Emil Friedberg and Emil Richter, 2d ed., 2 vols. (1879; reprint, Graz: Akademische Druck, 1955), vol. 1. For the legal and juridical conception of heresy in the Middle Ages, see the discussion and references in Othmar Hageneder, "Der Häresie-Begriff bei den Juristen des 12. und 13. Jahrhunderts," in Lourdaux and Verhelst, *The Concept of Heresy in the Middle Ages* (11th–13th C.), and Winfried Trusen, "Rechtliche Grundlagen des Häresiebegriffs und des Ketzerverfahrens," in *Ketzerverfolgung im 16. und frühen 17. Jahrhundert*, ed. Silvana Seidel Menchi, Hans R.

Guggisberg, and Bernd Moeller (Wiesbaden: Harrassowitz, 1992). The subject is dealt with on a large scale by Ruggero Maceratini, *Ricerche sullo stato giuridico dell'eretico nel diritto romano-cristiano e nel diritto canonico classico (da Graziano ad Uguccione)* (Padua: CEDAM, 1994).

59. *Decretum*, pt. II, C. XXIV, qu. III, cc. xxvi, xxviii–xxix, xxxi = cols. 997–98.

60. Ibid., C. XXIII, qu. IV, cc. xxxvii–xliii = cols. 916–23.

61. ibid., C. XXIII, qu. V, c. xliii = col. 943.

62. Russell, *Religious Dissent*, p. 125; Mirbt, *Quellen*, 1:274, 275.

63. *Corpus iuris canonici*, pt. II, *Decretalium collectiones*, Gregory IX, bk. V, tit. VII, "De haereticis," c. ix = cols. 780–82.

64. English translations of the statement of the Third Lateran Council and the papal decree *Ad abolendam* are included in Peters, *Heresy and Authority*, pp. 168–75.

65. *Corpus iuris canonici*, *Decretalium collectiones*, Gregory IX, bk. V, tit. VII, "De haereticis," c. 10 = cols. 782–83.

66. Ibid., c. xiii = cols. 787–89; English translation in Peters, *Heresy and Authority*, pp. 173–77.

67. These texts are taken, respectively, from the Ordinary Gloss to the *Liber extra*, or decretals, of Pope Gregory IX, issued in 1234, and from commentaries by the two canonists Goffredo da Trani and Tancred, both of the first half of the thirteenth century, quoted in Latin by Hageneder, "Der Häresie-Begriff," pp. 45–47, and in English translation by Edward Peters, *Inquisition* (New York: The Free Press, 1988), pp. 62–63.

68. Quoted in Peters, *Inquisition*, p. 42.

69. For the contribution of the legislation of secular rulers in creating a general system of persecution of heresy including the death penalty, see Lea, *A History of the Inquisition*, 1:220–21, 319–24; Nelson, "The Theory of Persecution," pp. 14–15; and the account and some of the documents in Peters, *Heresy and Authority in Medieval Europe*, chap. 6.

70. On the founding, organization, and procedure of the medieval Inquisition, see Lea, *A History of the Inquisition*, vol. 1, chaps. 7–14, and the concise account in Peters, *Inquisition*, chap. 2.

71. On these inquisitors' handbooks and the use of dissimulation by suspected heretics under questioning, see, for example, the manual *The Conduct of the Inquisition of Heretical Depravity*, written ca. 1323 by the Dominican Bernard Gui, a learned theologian, administrator, and inquisitor in the diocese of Toulouse, excerpts from which are printed in English translation in Wakefield and Evans, *Heresies of the High Middle Ages*, pp. 373–445, and Perez Zagorin, *Ways of Lying: Dissimulation, Persecution, and Conformity in Early Modern Europe* (Cambridge: Harvard University Press, 1990), pp. 64–66.

72. Saint Thomas Aquinas, *Summa theologiae*, IIa–IIae, qu. x, 8; qu. xi, 3–4. I cite these passages, respectively, from Bettenson, *Documents of the Christian Church*, pp. 133–35, and Lecler, *Toleration and the Reformation*, 1:87–88.

73. R. I. Moore, "Heresy as Disease," in Lourdaux and Verhelst, *The Concept of Heresy in the Middle Ages* (11th–13th C.).

Chapter 3
The Advent of Protestantism and the Toleration Problem

1. The best and fullest modern work on the Reformation and the problem of toleration is the Catholic historian Joseph Lecler's *Toleration and the Reformation*, 2 vols. (New York: Association Press, 1960), which includes a good bibliography. Henry Kamen, *The Rise of Toleration* (New York: McGraw-Hill, 1967), contains a short discussion of the subject in chaps. 2–3. The collection of essays *Tolerance and Intolerance in the European Reformation*, ed. Ole Peter Grell and Bob Scribner (Cambridge: Cambridge University Press, 1996), provides a partial survey.

2. See Paul Oskar Kristeller's account of humanism as a cultural movement in *The Cambridge History of Renaissance Philosophy*, ed. Charles B. Schmitt and Quentin Skinner (Cambridge: Cambridge University Press, 1988), chap. 4, "Humanism."

3. See the discussion of Nicholas of Cusa's *The Peace of Faith* by Ernst Cassirer, *The Individual and the Cosmos in Renaissance Philosophy* (New York: Harper Torchbooks, 1963), pp. 29–31, and the latest account by Cary Nederman, *Worlds of Difference* (University Park: Pennsylvania State University Press, 2000), chap. 6, which stresses Nicholas's recognition of religious and national differences.

4. See Lecler, *Toleration and the Reformation*, 1:110–13.

5. Jean Bodin, *Colloquium of the Seven* (*Colloquium heptaplomeres*), ed. M. L. Kuntz (Princeton: Princeton University Press, 1975). This work, a dialogue between spokesmen for Catholicism, Protestantism, Judaism, Islam, natural religion, and skepticism, remained unpublished until the nineteenth century, but manuscript copies circulated widely during the seventeenth century and the Enlightenment. See the discussion of the book in Kuntz's introduction; Perez Zagorin, *Ways of Lying: Dissimulation, Persecution, and Conformity in Early Modern Europe* (Cambridge: Harvard University Press, 1990), pp. 285–88; Gary Remer, *Humanism and the Rhetoric of Toleration* (University Park: Pennsylvania State University Press, 1996), pp. 211–27.

6. The following may be consulted as useful and perceptive accounts of the life and work of Erasmus and More, on both of whom a large body of scholarship exists: J. Huizinga, *Erasmus of Rotterdam* (London: Phaidon, 1952); Margaret Mann Phillips, *Erasmus and the Northern Renaissance* (London: English Universities Press, 1964); Cornelis Augustijn, *Erasmus: His Life, Works, and Influence* (Toronto: University of Toronto Press, 1991); James D. Tracy, *Erasmus of the Low Countries* (Berkeley and Los Angeles: University of California Press, 1996); Richard Marius, *Thomas More* (New York: Vintage Books, 1985); Peter Ackroyd, *The Life of Sir Thomas More* (New York: Doubleday, 1998).

7. On the meaning of Erasmus's philosophy of Christ, see the discussion in Phillips, *Erasmus and the Northern Renaissance*, chap. 2, and Augustijn, *Erasmus*, chap. 7.

8. The title of this work, a volume of almost a thousand pages, was *Novum instrumentum.* For Erasmus's work as a biblical scholar and his edition of the Greek New Testament, see Augustijn, *Erasmus*, chap. 8; *The Cambridge History of*

the Bible: The West from the Reformation to the Present Day, ed. S. L. Greenslade (Cambridge: Cambridge University Press, 1963), pp. 56–61, 79–81; Rudolf Pfeiffer, *History of Classical Scholarship* (Oxford: Clarendon Press, 1976), chap. 7.

9. Quoted in Augustijn, *Erasmus,* p. 89.

10. See the summary and quotations in Phillips, *Erasmus and the Northern Renaissance,* pp. 77–81.

11. See his comments on Reuchlin in his letter to Cardinal Wolsey, *The Correspondence of Erasmus,* 11 vols. to date (Toronto: University of Toronto Press, 1974–), 6:368 (letter 967 of May 1519). In further references this work is cited as *CE.*

12. Ibid., 7:49 (letter 1006 of August 1519). On Erasmus's attitude toward the Jews, see *Religiöse Toleranz. Dokumente zur Geschichte einer Forderung,* ed. Hans R. Guggisberg (Stuttgart-Bad Cannstadt: Frommann-Holzboog, 1984), p. 71; Augustijn, *Erasmus,* pp. 80–81; Heiko A. Oberman, *The Roots of Anti-Semitism in the Age of the Renaissance and Reformation* (Philadelphia: Fortress Press, 1984), pp. 38–40, which documents Erasmus's hatred of the Jews. For the controversy over Reuchlin and Hebrew books and Erasmus's involvement, see Augustinjn, *Erasmus,* pp. 110–12, and Oberman, *Roots of Anti-Semitism,* pp. 24–31.

13. *CE,* 7:126 (letter 1039 to Jan Slechta, secretary of the king of Bohemia, of 1 November 1519).

14. In his letter of 1518 to Abbot Paul Volz, which was the preface to a new edition of the *Handbook of a Militant Christian,* Erasmus criticized the logic chopping and endless commentaries and definitions of the theologians. Invoking the philosophy of Christ, he declared that Christ wished his way "to be accessible to all men, not beset with impenetrable labyrinths of argument but open to sincere faith, to love unfeigned, and their companion . . . hope"; *CE,* 6:74–75 (letter 858 of 14 August 1518).

15. Historians who discuss Erasmus's attitude to toleration rarely if ever distinguish the periods before and after the beginning of the Lutheran revolt in his writings. For an exploration of some of the major themes in his work conducive to tolerance in religion, see Lecler, *Toleration and the Reformation,* 1:120–29, and Remer, *Humanism,* chap. 1. Other discussions of his view of toleration include Robert H. Murray, *Erasmus and Luther: Their Attitude to Toleration* (London: Society for Promoting Christian Knowledge, 1920); W. K. Ferguson, "The Attitude of Erasmus toward Toleration," in *Persecution and Liberty: Essays in Honor of George Lincoln Burr* (New York: Century Co., 1931); Augustijn, *Erasmus,* pp. 176–79; Tracy, *Erasmus of the Low Countries,* chap. 12.

16. Sir Thomas More, *Utopia,* ed. Edward Surtz (New Haven: Yale University Press, 1964).

17. Ibid., pp. 130–35.

18. For discussions of religion and toleration in More's *Utopia,* see Lecler, *Toleration and the Reformation,* 1:134–38; Marius, *Thomas More,* chaps. 11–12; G. R. Elton, "Persecution and Toleration in the English Reformation," in *Persecution and Toleration,* ed. W. J. Sheils (Oxford: Blackwell, 1984), pp. 165–68.

19. Amid the huge amount of historical writing devoted to Luther's life, religious development, and ideas, Roland Bainton's *Here I Stand: A Life of Martin Luther* (New York: Abingdon Press, 1950) remains a reliable and accessible biog-

raphy. More recent studies include Martin Brecht, *Martin Luther,* 2 vols. (Philadelphia: Fortress Press, 1985–1990); Heiko Oberman, *Luther: Man between God and the Devil* (New Haven: Yale University Press, 1989); Richard Marius, *Martin Luther* (Cambridge: Harvard University Press, 1997). Luther's Ninety-five Theses on indulgences, his excommunication by the pope, and other documents pertaining to his break with the church are printed in *Documents Illustrative of the Continental Reformation,* ed. B. J. Kidd (Oxford: Clarendon Press, 1911), pt. 1. His three major works of 1520, *An Address to the Christian Nobility of the German Nation concerning the Reform of the Christian Estate, The Babylonian Captivity of the Church,* and *The Freedom of a Christian Man,* are printed in English translation in Martin Luther, *Three Treatises* (Philadelphia: Fortress Press, 1960).

20. Luther's first surviving letter to Erasmus was sent in March 1519; he expressed great deference in it, addressing Erasmus as "my glory and my hope"; *CE,* 6:281 (letter 933). Two years earlier, however, he wrote to a friend that "every day my regard for Erasmus decreases. I am pleased that he exposes and attacks the ignorance of the monks and priests, but I fear that he does not sufficiently promote Christ and the grace of God. . . . Human things carry more weight with him than divine things"; quoted by Steven Ozment, *The Age of Reform* 1250–1550 (New Haven: Yale University Press, 1980), p. 290. On 30 May 1519 Erasmus replied to Luther in a friendly letter, which made clear, however, his intention to remain uncommitted between the reformer and his adversaries; *CE,* 6:392 (letter 980).

21. Augustijn, *Erasmus,* chaps. 10–12, summarizes the relationship between Erasmus and Luther and their dispute concerning the freedom of the will; for Erasmus's loyalty to the consensus of the church, ibid., p. 152, and see also J. K. McConica, "Erasmus and the Grammar of Consent," in *Scrinium Erasmianum,* ed. J. Coppens, 2 vols. (Leiden: Brill, 1969), vol. 2.

22. *CE,* 7:111, 112, 115 (letter 1033 of 19 October 1519).

23. Ibid., 8:116, 117, 118 (letter 1167 of 6 December 1520).

24. Ibid., 10:80–81 (letter 1384 of 31 August 1523 to the Swiss reformer Zwingli); see also M. Gielis, "Erasme, Latomus et le martyre de deux augustins luthériens à Bruxelles en 1523," in *Erasmus of Rotterdam: The Man and Scholar,* ed. J. Sperna Weiland and W.Th.M. Frijhoff (Leiden: Brill, 1988).

25. See his statement to Luther's close colleague Philip Melanchthon that "the theologians supposed that if they burned two or three in Brussels, the rest would mend their ways; and that death made many new Lutherans"; *CE,* 10:385–86 (letter 1496 of 6 September 1524).

26. Ibid., pp. 457, 459 (letter 1526 of 12 December 1524 to Duke George of Saxony).

27. Quoted in Ferguson, "Attitude of Erasmus," p. 179.

28. *CE,* 10:186 (letter 1422 of 21 February 1524).

29. Ibid., 9:252, 257 (letter 1334 of 5 January 1523). This letter was the dedicatory preface to Erasmus's edition of the works of Saint Hilary of Poitiers.

30. On this conference, which took place in Valladolid and ended inconclusively, see Augustijn, *Erasmus,* pp. 155–58; Erika Rummel, "Erasmus and the Valladolid Articles: Intrigue, Innuendo, and Strategic Defense," in Weiland and Frijhoff, *Erasmus of Rotterdam: The Man and Scholar;* and the detailed account in

Marcel Bataillon, *Erasmo y España* (Madrid: Fonda de Cultura Economica, 1979), pp. 242–78. Besides censuring his comments on heresy, which derived from his *Paraphrase of Saint Matthew*, Erasmus's Spanish critics also charged him with unorthodoxy with respect to the dogma of the Holy Trinity.

31. *Apologia adversus articulos aliquot per monachos quosdam in hispaniis exhibitos* (Basel, 1529), printed also in Erasmus's *Opera omnia*, ed. Jean Le Clerc, 10 vols. (Leiden, 1703–1706), 9:1015–94. My summary above is based on the German translation of some passages from this work in Guggisberg, *Religiöse Toleranz*, pp. 74–76, and on the account by Rummel, "Erasmus and the Valladolid Articles."

32. Quoted in Ferguson, "Attitude of Erasmus," p. 178; for Erasmus's comparison of the Anabaptists with anarchists, see *CE*, 10:32 (letter 1369 of June 1523 to Bishop Cuthbert Tunstall).

33. See his letter to Martin Bucer, who had become a Protestant, *Opus epistolarum Desiderii Erasmi Roterodami*, ed. P. S. Allen and H. M. Allen, 12 vols. (Oxford: Clarendon Press, 1906–1958), 7:231.50–51, 65–102 (letter 1901 of 11 November 1527). This work is cited hereafter as Allen.

34. Ibid., p. 362.17–25 (letter 1976 of 19 March 1528 to Herman Wied, archbishop of Cologne).

35. See the discussion in Augustijn, *Erasmus*, pp. 178–81.

36. Allen, 6:311.107–12 (letter 1690 of 16 April 1526 to Joannes Faber).

37. Ibid., 8:450.79–82 (letter 2328 of 24 June 1530).

38. Ibid., 9:15.37–38, 53–55 (letter 2366 of 18 August 1530). In this letter, the word Erasmus uses for toleration is *sinerentur*, rather than any form of the verb *tolero*.

39. See the comments on this work in Augustijn, *Erasmus*, pp. 180–81.

40. Tracy, *Erasmus of the Low Countries*, p. 163; the role of the idea of religious concord as an alternative to that of toleration in the sixteenth century is discussed by Mario Turchetti, *Concordia o tolleranza? François Baudouin (1520–1573) e i "moyenneurs"* (Geneva: Droz, 1984); see also François Rigolot, "Tolerance et condescension dans la littérature française du XVIe siècle," *Bibliothèque d'Humanisme et Renaissance* 62, no. 1 (2000): 25–47.

41. On Cassander, Baudouin, and the persistence of the Erasmian tradition of religious conciliation, see Lecler, *Toleration and the Reformation*, vol. 1, chap. 6, 2:63–64, and Turchetti, *Concordia o tolleranza?*; for Erasmus's influence in the Netherlands and England in the earlier seventeenth century, see H. R. Trevor-Roper, "The Great Tew Circle," in *Catholics, Anglicans, and Puritans: Seventeenth Century Essays* (Chicago: University of Chicago Press, 1988), and "Hugo Grotius in England," in *From Counter-Reformation to Glorious Revolution* (Chicago: University of Chicago Press, 1992).

42. A. G. Dickens, *The English Reformation* (New York: Schocken Books, 1969), chap. 4, contains a concise account of the early English Lutherans and Protestants.

43. For an account of More's response to the growth of heresy in England, his activity as a royal official in the persecution and suppression of heresy, and his English works in defense of Catholicism, see Marius, *Thomas More*, chaps. 18–

22, 25, and Alistair Foxe, *Thomas More: History and Providence* (New Haven: Yale University Press, 1983), chaps. 4–8.

44. Saint Thomas More, *A Dialogue concerning Heresies*, ed. Thomas M. C. Lawler, Germain Marc'hadour, and Richard C. Marius, 2 pts., in *The Complete Works of St. Thomas More*, 15 vols. (New Haven: Yale University Press, 1963–1986), vol. 6.

45. It should be noted that More, like Erasmus, was in favor of vernacular versions of the Bible. What worried him was the production of heretical translations that in his view perverted the Christian faith and encouraged the tendency he attributed to the common people of disputing over things in Scripture about which they knew nothing; see ibid., pp. 337–39.

46. Ibid., pp. 37–38, 266, 409, 416.

47. Ibid., pp. 405–6, 430.

48. Ibid., pp. 122–23.

49. Foxe, *Thomas More*, chaps. 4–8, passim; W. K. Jordan, *The Development of Religious Toleration in England*, 4 vols. (Cambridge: Harvard University Press, 1932–1940), 1:44.

50. For these statements in More's writings, see the summary and quotations in Jordan, *The Development of Religious Toleration in England*, 1:44, 45.

51. See the text in Kidd, *Documents Illustrative of the Continental Reformation*, p. 78: "Haereticos comburi, est contra voluntatem Spiritus."

52. The evolution of Luther's attitude toward the use of force in religion is one of the themes of the well-informed discussion of Luther and toleration by W. J. Cargill Thompson, *The Political Thought of Martin Luther* (Brighton: Harvester Press, 1984), chap. 9.

53. On Luther's conception of the territorial church and its analogy, in spite of many significant differences, with the Catholic idea, see the classic discussion of Ernst Troeltsch, *The Social Teachings of the Christian Churches*, 2 vols. (London: Allen & Unwin, 1931), 2:477–85.

54. On the Peace of Augsburg, see my discussion above in chap. 1, and the account in Lecler, *Toleration and the Reformation*, vol. 1, chap. 5.

55. Luther, *Address to the Christian Nobility*, pp. 89, 91.

56. Luther, *The Babylonian Captivity of the Church*, pp. 145–46.

57. Martin Luther, *Of Secular Authority and How Far It Should Be Obeyed*, in *Martin Luther: Selections from His Writings*, ed. John Dillenberger (Garden City, N.Y.: Anchor Books, 1961), pp. 383, 385–87, 389, 391. For similar expressions at this period of Luther's opposition to the use of force against heresy, see his comment on the parable of the tares from a homily of 1525, quoted by Lecler, *Toleration and the Reformation*, 1:152; see also his Wittenberg sermons of 1522, in which he opposed his followers' forcible abolition of the Mass and smashing of Catholic altars and images and urged that these changes should be accomplished by the persuasion of hearts through the power of the word; printed in *Martin Luther*, ed. E. G. Rupp and Benjamin Drewery (New York: St. Martin's Press, 1970), pp. 100–102.

58. Luther, *Of Secular Authority*, p. 385.

59. See above, chap. 2.

60. *The Freedom of a Christian Man*, pp. 309–10.9

61. Steven Ozment, "Martin Luther on Religious Liberty," in *Religious Liberty in Western Thought*, ed. Noel B. Reynolds and W. Cole Durham, Jr. (Atlanta: Scholars Press, 1996), p. 77.

62. See Oberman, *Luther*, pp. 292–95, and *The Roots of Anti-Semitism in the Age of the Renaissance and Reformation*, chaps. 14–18.

63. See Luther's letter of November 1525, quoted in Lecler, *Toleration and the Reformation*, 1:157.

64. Ibid., pp. 157–58, quoted from a letter of February 1526.

65. See Marius, *Martin Luther*, pp. 474–75, and the detailed account by G. R. Potter, *Zwingli* (Cambridge: Cambridge University Press, 1976), chaps. 12–13.

66. See Bainton, *Here I Stand*, pp. 375–78.

67. "Ich kan auch nit bedenken, daß einiche ursach vorhanden sey, die gegen got die tollerantz möchte entschuldigen"; quoted by Winfried Schulze, " 'Ex Dictamine Rationis Sapere.' Zum Problem der Toleranz im Heiligen Römischen Reich nach dem Augsburger Religionsfrieden," in *Querdenken. Dissens und Toleranz im Wandel der Geschichte. Festschrift zum 65. Geburtstag von Hans R. Guggisberg* (Mannheim: Palatium Verlag 1996), pp. 225–26.

68. There are numerous studies of Calvin's life and character, religious conceptions, and work in Geneva. See, among others, John T. McNeill, *The History and Character of Calvinism* (New York: Oxford University Press, 1954); Georgia Harkness, *John Calvin: The Man and His Ethics* (New York: Henry Holt, 1931); T.H.L. Parker, *John Calvin: A Biography* (Philadelphia: Westminster Press, 1975); François Wendel, *Calvin: The Origins and Development of His Religious Thought* (Durham: Labyrinth, 1987); William J. Bouwsma, *John Calvin: A Sixteenth-Century Portrait* (New York: Oxford University Press, 1989). E. G. Rupp presents a concise account of Calvin's role in the Reformation in Geneva in *The New Cambridge Modern History*, 13 vols. (Cambridge: Cambridge University Press, 1957–1979), vol. 2 (2d ed., 1990), chap. 4. Calvin's *Ecclesiastical Ordinances* for the church of Geneva are printed in Kidd, *Documents Illustrative of the Continental Reformation*, pp. 589–603.

69. See some of the works mentioned in the previous note and Zagorin, *Ways of Lying*, chap. 4.

70. John Calvin, *Institutes of the Christian Religion*, ed. John T. McNeill, 2 vols. (Philadelphia: Westminster Press, 1960), bk. 3, chap. 19; the quotation is in bk. 3, chap. 19.15.

71. Ibid., bk. 4, chap. 12.

72. Ibid., bk. 4, chap. 20.2–3, 9.

73. Ibid., bk. 4, chap. 2.5

74. *Defensio orthodoxae fidei de Sacra Trinitate contra prodigiosos errores Michaelis Serveti . . . ubi ostenditur haereticos jure gladii coercendos esse . . .* (Geneva, 1554), printed in John Calvin, *Opera*, ed. W. Baum, E. Cunitz, and E. Reuss, 59 vols. (Brunswick, 1863–1896; reprint, 1964), vol. 8, cols. 461–81; *Déclaration pour maintenir la vraye foy . . . de la Trinité . . . contre les erreurs détestables de Michel Servete . . . ou il est aussi monstré, qu'il est licite de punir les hérétiques. . . .*

75. This section is entitled "Whether Christian Judges May Lawfully Punish Heretics" ("An christianis judicibus hereticos punire liceat").

76. My account of Calvin's justification of the punishment of heretics is based on the Latin *Defensio* and the summary of the French version with numerous quotations in Emile Doumergue, *Jean Calvin*, 7 vols. (Lausanne, 1899–1927; reprint, Geneva: Slatkine, 1969), vol. 6, bk. 3, chap. 3. The passages I have quoted above are from the French version as reproduced in Doumergue, pp. 412, 413, 414, 415. Summaries of Calvin's argument based on the French version are also given in J. W. Allen, *A History of Political Thought in the Sixteenth Century,* 3d ed. (London: Methuen, 1951), pp. 81–89, and Lecler, *Toleration and the Reformation,* 1:333–35. See also the discussion of Calvin's intolerance in Harkness, *John Calvin,* pp. 105–13.

77. See Brian P. Levack, *The Witch-Hunt in Early Modern Europe* (New York: Longmans, 1987).

78. See the outstanding work by G. H. Williams, *The Radical Reformation* (Philadelphia: Westminster Press, 1962).

79. See the extensive discussion of Anabaptism in ibid., and the account by James Stayer in *The New Cambridge Modern History,* 2d ed., vol. 2, chap. 5, "The Anabaptists and the Sects."

80. On the Anabaptist revolt in Münster, see Williams, *The Radical Reformation,* pp. 362–86, and Stayer,"The Anabaptists and the Sects," pp. 124–39.

81. See Hubmaier's tract, "Von Ketzern und ihren Verbrennern," in the selection printed in Guggisberg, *Religiöse Toleranz,* pp. 77–80.

82. See the selection from Menno Simons, "On the Ban: Questions and Answers," printed in *Spiritual and Anabaptist Writers,* ed. G. H. Williams and A. M. Mergal (Philadelphia: Westminster Press, 1957); on the ban, see also Williams, *The Radical Reformation,* pp. 394–98.

83. Spiritualism is extensively discussed by Williams, *The Radical Reformation,* passim, and concisely analyzed in its several forms in his introduction to Williams and Mergal, *Spiritual and Anabaptist Writers,* pp. 31–35.

84. On Franck's life, works, and ideas, see Alfred Hegler, *Geist und Schrift bei Sebastian Franck; Eine Studie zur Geschichte des Spiritualismus in der Reformationszeit* (Freiburg, 1892); Williams, *The Radical Reformation,* pp. 264–67, 457–65, and passim; Lecler, *Toleration and the Reformation,* 1:166–76; Roland Bainton's introduction to Sebastian Castellio, *Concerning Heretics: Whether They Are to Be Persecuted* (New York: Octagon Books, 1965), pp. 93–104; Steven Ozment, *Mysticism and Dissent: Religious Ideology and Social Protest in the Sixteenth Century* (New Haven: Yale University Press, 1973), chap. 6.

85. Franck expressed these ideas in such works as his *Chronicle of World History* (*Chronica, Zeytbuch und Geschichtsbibel* [Strasbourg, 1531, and later eds.]), which Ozment, *Mysticism and Dissent,* p. 141, calls "an exposé of human perversion from the very beginning of the world until the present (which . . . was very near the end for Franck)."

86. Sebastian Franck, "A Letter to John Campanus," printed in Williams and Mergal, *Spiritual and Anabaptist Writers,* pp. 148–51, 160.

87. Sebastian Franck, *Chronica, Zeytbuch und Geschichtsbibel*, from the selection printed in Guggisberg, *Religiöse Toleranz*, pp. 82–83.

88. Quoted from Franck's *Chronica* and his *Paradoxa ducenta octoginta* (1534), in Lecler, *Toleration and the Reformation*, 1:175, 176.

89. Quoted from Franck's *Das verbütschierte mit sieben Sigeln verschlossene Buch* (1539), in Lecler, *Toleration and the Reformation*, 1:175.

90. On the religious conferences in Germany, see Franz Lau and Ernst Bizer, *A History of the Reformation in Germany to* 1555 (London: A. & C. Black, 1969), chaps. 6–7, and Ozment, *The Age of Reform*, pp. 405–6; for the colloquy of Poissy, see N. M. Sutherland, "Persecution and Toleration in Reformation Europe," in Sheils, *Persecution and Toleration*, pp. 157–58; selections from the discussion at these conferences are printed in *Great Debates of the Reformation*, ed. Donald Ziegler (New York: Random House, 1969).

91. See Ozment, *The Age of Reform*, pp. 406–9, and Marvin R. O'Connell, *The Counter Reformation* 1559–1610 (New York: Harper Torchbooks, 1974), chap. 3.

92. See Edward Peters, *Inquisition* (New York: The Free Press, 1988), chap. 4.

93. See J. H. Elliott, *Imperial Spain* 1469–1715 (London: Edward Arnold, 1963), pp. 204–10.

94. William Monter, "Heresy Executions in Reformation Europe, 1420–1565," in Grell and Scribner, *Tolerance and Intolerance in the European Reformation*, p. 49. These figures cover eight countries: Germany and the Holy Roman Empire, Switzerland, the Netherlands, France, England and Scotland, Spain, and Italy, including Sicily. There were, of course, many executions for heresy after this date; in the Netherlands alone, about eleven hundred people were put to death between 1567 and 1574 by the Spanish governor, the duke of Alva, for the related crimes of heresy, iconoclasm, sedition, and rebellion; ibid, p. 49. On this subject, see also Brad S. Gregory, *Salvation at Stake: Christian Martyrdom in Early Modern Europe* (Cambridge: Harvard University Press, 1999), chap. 3.

95. G. R. Elton, *England under the Tudors* (London: Methuen, 1975), p. 220.

96. See Geoffrey Parker, *The Dutch Revolt* (London: Allen Lane, 1977), pp. 57–64; Gerhard Güldner, *Das Toleranz-Problem in den Niederlanden im Ausgang des 16.Jahrhunderts* (Lübeck: Matthiesen Verlag, 1968), pp. 32–35, 175, which includes figures; J.H.M. Salmon, *Society in Crisis: France in the Sixteenth Century* (London: Ernest Benn, 1975), pp. 84–89.

97. On the role of Calvinist Protestantism in the genesis of the religious civil war in France and the Netherlands rebellion, see Salmon, *Society in Crisis*, chap. 6; Parker, *The Dutch Revolt*, chap. 1; Perez Zagorin, *Rebels and Rulers* 1500–1660, 2 vols. (Cambridge: Cambridge University Press, 1982), vol. 2, chaps. 10–11.

98. On the Saint Bartholomew massacre, see Salmon, *Society in Crisis*, pp. 186–88.

99. My account is based on the selections from L'Hopital's speeches printed in *Les premiers défenseurs de la liberté religieuse*, ed. Joseph Lecler and Marius-François Valkhoff, 2 vols. (Paris: Les Editions du Cerf, 1969), 1:66–76; the quotation from his address to the French bishops is on pp. 72–73. I have also used the excellent discussion and quotations in Malcolm C. Smith, *Montaigne and Religious Freedom: The Dawn of Pluralism* (Geneva: Droz, 1991), chaps. 1–2. See also the

discussion in Lecler, *Toleration and the Reformation*, vol. 2, chap. 2, and the essay by Marie-Dominique Legrand, "Michel de L'Hopital: Elements pour une poétique de la liberté de la conscience," in *La liberté de la conscience (XVI–XVII siècles)*, ed. Hans. R. Guggisberg, Frank Lestringant, Jean-Claude Margolin (Geneva: Droz, 1991). Besides the statements by the chancellor L'Hopital, there were other expressions at this time in favor of religious coexistence, which are discussed by Lecler and Smith. One of the most striking was the anonymous tract, *Exhortation aux princes et seigneurs du conseil privé du roy (Exhortation to the Princes and Lords of the King's Privy Council)* (1561), of which selections are printed in Lecler and Valkhoff, *Les premiers défenseurs de la liberté religieuse*, 1:56–64.

100. See Smith, *Montaigne and Religious Freedom*, pp. 47–50.

101. See the summary of the January 1562 edict in ibid., p. 40, and the account in Lecler, *Toleration and the Reformation*, 2:67–70.

102. See Sutherland, "Persecution and Toleration," pp. 159–60.

103. La Boétie expressed his opposition to toleration in his *Mémoire sur la pacification des troubles*, ed. Malcolm C. Smith (Geneva: Droz, 1983), written at the end of 1561. I have used the summary and discussion of his point of view in Smith, *Montaigne and Religious Freedom*, chap. 3. For the evolution of Montaigne's attitude, see ibid., chaps. 4–6. La Boétie's and Montaigne's positions are also discussed by Lecler, *Toleration and the Reformation*, 2:168–77.

104. See Smith, *Montaigne and Religious Freedom*, pp. 41–44, and the account by Philip Benedict, "*Un Roi, Une Loi, Deux Fois*: Parameters for the History of Catholic-Reformed Co-existence in France, 1555–1685," in Grell and Scribner, *Tolerance and Intolerance in the European Reformation*, pp. 70–81.

105. See above, chap. 1.

Chapter 4
The First Champion of Religious Toleration: Sebastian Castellio

1. Earl M. Wilbur, *A History of Unitarianism: Socinianism and Its Antecedents* (Cambridge: Harvard University Press, 1945, chap. 12, and Roland H. Bainton,- *Hunted Heretic: The Life and Death of Michael Servetus 1511–1553* (Boston: Beacon Press, 1964), chaps. 10–11, contain accounts of Servetus's trial and execution. In addition to these, I have consulted the documents pertaining to his trial printed in John Calvin, *Opera*, ed. W. Baum, E. Cunitz, and E. Reuss, 59 vols. (Brunswick, 1863–1896; reprint, 1964), vol. 8, cols. 725–831.

2. On Servetus's theological conceptions, see Wilbur, *A History of Unitarianism*, chaps. 5, 9, 10; Bainton, *Hunted Heretic*, chaps. 2–3, 7; G. H. Williams, *The Radical Reformation* (Philadelphia: Westminster Press, 1962), pp. 269–72, 311–16, 322–23, 609–12, and passim; Jerome Friedman, *Michael Servetus: A Case Study in Total Heresy* (Geneva: Droz, 1978). The essays in *Autour de Michel Servet et de Sébastien Castellion*, ed. Bruno Becker (Haarlem: Tjeenk Willink & Zoon, 1953), contain discussions of various aspects of Servetus's work.

3. For Servetus's arrest and trial by the Inquisition in Vienne, see Wilbur, *A History of Unitarianism*, chap. 11, and Bainton, *Hunted Heretic*, chap. 8.

4. Bainton, *Hunted Heretic*, pp. 144–45.

5. Wilbur, *A History of Unitarianism*, pp. 15–56; Bainton, *Hunted Heretic*, pp. 150–57.

6. The document sentencing Servetus is printed in Calvin, *Opera*, vol. 8, cols. 827–31; excerpts are quoted in Bainton, *Hunted Heretic*, pp. 207–9.

7. On sixteenth-century martyrs, martyrdom, and martyrologies, see Brad S. Gregory, *Salvation at Stake: Christian Martyrdomn in Early Modern Europe* (Cambridge: Harvard University Press, 1999).

8. Lord Acton, "The Protestant Theory of Persecution," in *The History of Freedom and Other Essays*, ed. J. N. Figgis and R. V. Laurence (London: Macmillan, 1909), pp. 184, 185.

9. For the immediate reaction of Protestant opinion to Servetus's arrest and execution, see the account by Ferdinand Buisson, *Sébastien Castellion*, 2 vols. (Paris, 1892; reprint, 1964), vol. 1, chap. 11, and Hans R. Guggisberg, *Sebastian Castellio 1515–1563* (Göttingen: Vandenhoeck & Rupprecht, 1997), chaps. 5–6.

10. *Historia de morte Serveti* was first printed as an appendix to the first edition of Castellio's *Contra libellum Calvini* (Gouda, 1612) (*Against Calvin's Book*); for its contents and authorship, see Uwe Plath, *Calvin und Basel in den Jahren 1552–1556* (Basel: Helbing und Lichtenhahn, 1974), pp. 86–93, 270–78, who summarizes the tract, discusses its sources of information, and presents evidence showing that Castellio was probably the author; see also the account in Guggisberg, *Sebastian Castellio*, pp. 83–84.

11. For the facts in the following account of Castellio's history, I have depended on the biographies by Buisson and Guggisberg. The first, written from the standpoint of liberal Protestantism, is the most detailed treatment and remains of great value despite additions to knowledge of Castellio since its publication in 1892. The second, by the foremost Castellio scholar of the last generation, is the most up-to-date study and stands with Buisson's work as a major account of Castellio's life and thought. The bibliography of this work includes a list of Guggisberg's articles on Castellio.

12. See above, chap. 3.

13. Buisson, *Sébastien Castellion*, 1:173, describes this work as "a veritable manual of moral and civic instruction" that "inculcated a hatred of tyrants and mistrust of the worldly great, false judges, and persecuting priests."

14. Printed in Buisson, *Sébastien Castellion*, 1:239.

15. Printed in ibid., pp. 198–99.

16. On the Basel printers and publishers in the sixteenth century, see Peter G. Bietenholz, *Basle and France in the Sixteenth Century* (Geneva: Droz, 1971); Castellio is discussed in chap. 5.

17. Sebastian Castellio, *Biblia, interprete Sebastione Castalione, una cum eiusdem annotationibus*, published by Oporinus (Basel, 1551); Sebastian Castellio, *La bible nouvellement translatée . . . avec des annotations sur les passages difficile. Par Sebastian Chateillon*, published by Herwagen (Basel, 1555). Guggisberg reproduces the title pages of the two translations. On Castellio's work as a biblical translator, see Buisson, *Sébastien Castellion*, vol. 1, chap. 10; Guggisberg, *Sebastian Castellio*, chap. 4; and the comments in *The Cambridge History of the Bible: The West from the Reformation*

to the Present Day, ed. S. L. Greenslade (Cambridge: Cambridge University Press, 1963), pp. 71–72, 83, 116, 120.

18. Guggisberg, *Sebastian Castellio*, pp. 70–71.

19. See the summary and quotations from Castellio's dedication of his Latin Bible to Edward VI in Buisson, *Sébastien Castellion*, 1:304–8.

20. For bibliographies of Castellio's publications, see Buisson, *Sébastien Castellion*, 2:341–80, and Guggisberg, *Sebastian Castellio*, pp. 332–36.

21. German and French translations, neither of them made by Castellio, were also published in due course bearing the date 1554; see Guggisberg, *Sebastian Castellio*, pp. 105–6. Among the differences between the Latin and French editions was the inclusion in the latter of an additional short dedication to Willam, count of Hesse, the son-in-law of Christophe, duke of Württemburg, the original dedicatee.

22. On the question of Castellio's authorship and the possibility that he had the assistance of Celio Secundo Curione and Lelio Sozzini (two of the Italian exiles in Basel), David Joris (a Dutch Anabaptist who lived in Basel under an assumed name), and perhaps others as well, see Roland H. Bainton's edition and translation of *Concerning Heretics* (New York: Octagon Books, 1965), pp. 5–11; Buisson, *Sébastien Castellion*, vol. 2, chap. 13; Guggisberg, *Sebastian Castellio*, pp. 103–6; Delio Cantimori, *Eretici italiani del cinquecento e altri scritti* (Turin: Giulio Einaudi, 1992), p. 165.

23. In the following discussion of *De haereticis*, I have used Bainton's editorial introduction and English translation and also consulted the facsimile 1554 edition of *De haereticis*, ed. Sape van der Woude (Geneva: Droz, 1954). For bibliographical details, see Bainton's introduction, pp. 3–6, and Guggisberg, *Sebastian Castellio*, pp. 104–6. Eugénie Droz, *Chemins de l'heresie*, vol. 2 (Geneva: Slatkine, 1971), pp. 325–72, has examined the history of the French translation, which likewise bore a false imprint and printer's name. The work's contents are discussed in Bainton's introduction; Buisson, *Sébastien Castellion*, vol. 1, chap. 12; Joseph Lecler, *Toleration and the Reformation*, 2 vols. (New York: Association Press, 1960), 1:336–47; Guggisberg, *Sebastian Castellio*, chap. 5.

24. Four of these sixteen were not in the Latin edition and were added in the French translation. Bainton's English version also prints the additional material in the French and German editions.

25. *Concerning Heretics*, pp. 127–28.

26. Ibid., pp. 202–3.

27. Ibid., pp. 212–16.

28. On the censorship of books in Basel, see Buisson, *Sébastien Castellion*, 2:pp. 57 and n., 106, and passim; Bietenholz, *Basle and France*, passim.

29. *Concerning Heretics*, pp. 121–22.

30. Ibid., p. 123.

31. Ibid., pp. 125–26.

32. Ibid., p. 126; "Neque vero haec ideo dico, quod haereticis faveam. Odi ego haereticos." *De haereticis*, p. 12.

33. Guggisberg, *Sebastian Castellio*, calls the sentence a "rhetorical flourish" and points out that it did not reappear in Castellio's following work, *Against Cal-*

vin's Book (Contra libellum Calvini); " 'Ich hasse die Ketzer.' Die Ketzerbegriff Sebastian Castellios und sein Situation im Basler Exil," in *Ketzerverfolgung im 16.
und frühen 17. Jahrhundert*, ed. Silvana Seidel Menchi (Wiesbaden: Harrassowitz, 1992), pp. 253, 259. Castellio did repeat this thought, however, in the book
he wrote against Beza, *De l'impunité des hérétiques*, which is discussed later in this
chapter.

34. *Concerning Heretics*, p. 127.

35. Ibid., p. 129.

36. Ibid, pp. 129–32.

37. Ibid., pp. 132–34.

38. Ibid., pp. 134–35.

39. Ibid., pp. 136–38.

40. Ibid., p. 138.

41. Ibid., pp. 216–21.

42. Ibid., pp. 222–25.

43. Ibid., pp. 226–28, 230, 232–33.

44. Ibid., pp. 235, 256–47, 248–50.

45. Ibid., pp. 251–53.

46. Bainton's introduction and Guggisberg, *Sebastian Castellio*, pp. 140–45, discuss Erasmus's and Franck's influence on Castellio. Castellio may have found a
model for his work in Franck's *Chronicle of World History*, which discusses the questions of what and who a heretic is and whether he should be punished, and
includes citations from various authors; see Sape van der Woude's introduction
to the facsimile ed. of *De haereticis*, p. xv.

47. Buisson, *Sébastien Castellion*, 2:57; Guggisberg, *Sebastian Castellio*, pp. 111–
12. The Basel censorship forced Castellio to suppress this note.

48. Buisson, *Sébastien Castellion*, 1:358–59; Guggisberg, *Sebastian Castellio*, pp.
107–8.

49. Besides its arguments and language that identify it as Castellio's, Buisson
found proof of his authorship in a part of a manuscript of the work in Basel
written in his hand; see Buisson, *Sébastien Castellion*, 2:32–33.

50. Ibid., pp. 30–32; Guggisberg, *Sebastian Castellio*, pp. 121–22. The full title
of the work is *Contra libellum Calvini in quo ostenditur conatur haereticos jure gladii
coercendos esse (Against Calvin's Book, in Which He Tries to Show That Heretics Should
Be Coerced by the Right of the Sword)*. I have not had access to the original Latin
edition and have used the recent French translation, Sébastien Castellion, *Contre
le libelle de Calvin dans lequel il tente de montrer que les hérétiques doivent être contraints
par le droit de glaive*, ed. and trans. Etienne Barilier (Carouge-Geneva: Editions
Zoé, 1998). Bainton's edition of *Concerning Heretics*, pp. 265–87, includes a translation of some selections from the work; its contents are discussed by Buisson,
Sébastien Castellion, vol. 2, chap. 14; Lecler, *Toleration and the Reformation*, 1:350–
56; Guggisberg, *Sebastian Castellio*, pp. 116–22.

51. *Contre le libelle de Calvin*, pp. 55–57.

52. Ibid., pp. 58–89.

53. Ibid., pp. 112, 120, 147.

54. Ibid., pp. 97–98.

55. Ibid., pp. 103–4.

56. Ibid., pp. 98–102.

57. Ibid., pp. 143, 144, 244, 245, 267.

58. Ibid., pp. 112–13, 239, 273–81; on Castellio's approval of the punishment of blasphemers, see the editor's comment, p. 239n.

59. Ibid., pp. 160–61.

60. Ibid., pp. 214, 219, 222–23, 245–47, 252–53.

61. Ibid., pp. 164–65, 199, 232–33.

62. For a critique of Castellio and his reply to Calvin, see the comments by Emile Doumergue, *Jean Calvin, les hommes et les choses de son temps*, 7 vols. (Lausanne, 1899–1927; reprint, Geneva: Slatkine, 1969), vol. 6, bk. 3, chap. 4.

63. For biographies of Beza, see the old but scholarly work by H. M. Baird, *Theodore Beza* (1899; reprint, New York: Burt Franklin, 1970), and Paul-F. Giesendorf, *Théodore de Bèze* (Geneva: Labor et Fides, 1949).

64. For this account of Beza's *De haereticis a civili magistratu puniendis*, I have used a microfilm of the edition printed in his *Theodori Bezae volumen primum tractationum theologicarum*, 2d ed. (Geneva, 1582), pp. 85–169, and have drawn also on the discussions in Bainton's introduction to Castellio's *Concerning Heretics*, pp. 107–9; Plath, *Calvin und Basel*, pp. 221–30; Guggisberg, *Sebastian Castellio*, pp. 122–27; the quotation is taken from Bainton's introduction, p. 108.

65. On the history of the work and the discovery of the original manuscripts of the Latin and French texts in the Remonstrants Library in Rotterdam, which led to its publication in 1971, see the editorial introduction in Sébastien Castellion, *De l'impunité des hérétiques. De haereticis non puniendis*, ed. Bruno Becker and M. Valkhoff (Geneva: Droz, 1971). The Latin edition is dated at the end (p. 197) 11 March 1555. Valkhoff, the editor of the French text, believes that Castellio was probably the translator. Both Guggisberg, *Sebastian Castellio*, pp. 127–33, and Plath, *Calvin und Basel*, pp. 230–43, give an account of the work. My discussion below is based on the French translation, which I have checked against the Latin.

66. Castellio's note at the head of the French text states that it should not be printed for nine years; *De l'impunité des hérétiques*, p. 217.

67. Ibid., pp. 217–23, 359; cf. p. 229, where Castellio asks Beza to "cease seeking our blood" and notes that the latter, too, had used pseudonyms to avoid execution by Catholic authorities.

68. Ibid., pp. 235, 243, 247–48, and passim.

69. Ibid., pp. 224–27.

70. Ibid., pp. 250–54, 258, 259, 264, 266–68, 281–82. Elsewhere Castellio says that doctrine has two parts. One, which is very easy to know, concerns man's duty to fear and obey God and consists of the commandments of piety in the Holy Scriptures; the other deals with "high and difficult things" like the Trinity, angels, and the state of souls after death, and makes people not better but more wise. About this second part he quotes Saint Paul's saying (1 Cor. 13:2), that if "I understand all mysteries, and all knowledge . . . and have not charity, I am nothing"; ibid., pp. 381–82.

71. Ibid., p. 271.

72. Ibid., pp. 240–42; the Latin text says "libera religio," ibid., p. 41.

73. Ibid., pp. 289–93, 392; cf. also the comments, p. 352, distinguishing the obedience due to the magistrate in "civil things" and the obedience due to God in "divine things."

74. Ibid., pp. 228, 269–70, 281, 300, 301–2.

75. Ibid., p. 285.

76. Ibid., pp. 314–24.

77. Ibid., pp. 325–28.

78. Ibid., p. 352.

79. Ibid., p. 347.

80. Ibid., pp. 391–401.

81. Guggisberg, *Sebastian Castellio*, pp. 154–55, 206; see also Sape van der Woude, "Censured Passages from Sebastian Castellio's *Defensio Suarum Translationum*," in Becker, *Autour de Michel Servet et de Sébastien Castellion*.

82. Ibid., pp. 156–58.

83. Buisson, *Sébastien Castellion*, pp. 125–30; Guggisberg, *Sebastian Castellio*, pp. 163–66. Castellio's reply was called *Harpago, sive defensio ad authorem libri . . . calumniae nebulonis*; the passages quoted are taken from the excerpt in Guggisberg, *Sebastian Castellio*, pp. 165–66.

84. *Dialogi IIII. De praedestinatione, De electione, De libero arbitrio, De fide*, 1578; the first edition bore a false imprint and was actually published in Basel by Pietro Perna; see Guggisberg, *Sebastian Castellio*, p. 238.

85. Castellio's theological views and his *Dialogi IIII* are discussed by Guggisberg, *Sebastian Castellio*, pp. 238–46, and examined at length in Carla Gallicet Calvetti's perceptive introduction to her book, *Sebastiano Castellion: Il riformato umanista contro il riformatore Calvino* (Milan: Università Catolica del Sacro Cuore, 1989), which contains an edition of the dialogues in Italian translation.

86. See above, chap. 3.

87. Sebastian Castellio, *Conseil a la France desolée*, ed. Marius F. Valkhoff (Geneva: Droz, 1967). The original edition had neither the author's name nor the place of publication. I cite this work in the English translation, *Advice to a Desolate France*, ed. Marius F. Valkhoff (Shepherdstown, W.Va.: Patmos Press, 1975).

88. Ibid., p. v.

89. On Michel de L'Hopital, see above, chap. 3.

90. Among the writings published in France on the eve of the civil war advocating the toleration of Protestantism, the closest in attitude to Castellio was the anonymous *L'exhortation aux princes et seigneurs du conseil privé du roy* (*Exhortation to the Princes and Lords of the King's Privy Council*), 1561; *Les premiers défenseurs de la liberté religieuse*, ed. Joseph Lecler and Marius-François Valkhoff, 2 vols. (Paris: Les Éditions du Cerf, 1969), 2:56–64, contains excerpts from this work. Castellio's *Advice*, p. 29, refers approvingly to the *Exhortation*.

91. The quotations are in *Advice*, pp. 28, 29, 47–48.

92. Sebastian Castellio, *De arte dubitandi et confidendi ignorandi et sciendi*, ed. Elizabeth Feist Hirsch (Leiden: Brill, 1981). I have used this edition, which includes a helpful introduction, and have also consulted the French translation, *De l'art de douter et de croire, d'ignorer et de savoir* (Geneva: Editions Jeheber, 1953).

All further references are to the Latin edition. Bainton's edition of *Concerning Heretics*, pp. 287–305, contains an English translation of selections from the work. Its contents are discussed by Buisson, *Sébastien Castellion*, 2:216–24; Lecler, *Toleration and the Reformation*, 1:357–59; Guggisberg, *Sebastian Castellio*, pp. 246–63.

93. *De arte Dubitandi*, pp. 13–15.

94. Ibid., pp. 49–51 = chap. 18.

95. Ibid., pp. 51–55 = chaps. 19–20.

96. Ibid., pp. 57–67 = chaps. 22–25. The quotations are on pp. 65–67.

97. See Calvin's *Institutes of the Christian Religion*, ed. John T. McNeill, 2 vols. (Philadelphia: Westminster Press, 1960), bk. 2, chap. 2, 12, and the editor's note, 1:270. This is only one of Calvin's numerous references to mankind's total depravity and the corruption of its understanding and natural endowments due to the Fall.

98. *De arte dubitandi*, pp. 69–74, 77–89 = chaps. 27–30, 32–33; the quotations are on pp. 72, 79, 83.

99. Ibid., bk. 2, pp. 84, 87–89 = chaps. 1–2.

100. Wilbur, the historian of Unitarianism, who devotes a chapter to Castellio's "struggle for toleration," speaks of him as "the real founder of liberal Christianity," (*A History of Unitarianism*, p. 208) but does not appear to be aware of his Antitrinitarianism.

101. Thus he holds that faith is an act of free will, not a gift of God; that men are not wholly and absolutely sinful, and that justification through faith is always available to them if they seek it; and that Christ excludes no one who seeks his mercy and forgiveness.

102. Ibid., pp. 181–82 = chap. 42.2

103. John Calvin, *Calumniae nebulonis cuiusdam adversus doctrinam Johannis Calvini ad eadem responsio* (1558), in *Opera*, vol. 9, cols. 313–14; Guggisberg, *Sebastian Castellio*, p. 255n, quotes the Latin text.

104. *De arte dubitandi*, introduction, p. 11.

105. On Agrippa, see Charles G. Nauert, Jr., *Agrippa and the Crisis of Renaissance Thought* (Urbana: University of Illinois Press, 1965). Richard H. Popkin, "Theories of Knowledge," in *The Cambridge History of Renaissance Philosophy*, ed. Charles B. Schmitt, Quentin Skinner, and Eckhard Kessler (Cambridge: Cambridge University Press, 1990), includes a discussion of the revival of skepticism in the sixteenth century.

106. See the account in Guggisberg, *Sebastian Castellio*, pp. 219–21. On Poland's emergence as a refuge from persecution during the reign of King Sigismund II, see Lecler, *Toleration and the Reformation*, vol. 1, bk. 5, chap. 1, and below, chap. 5.

107. Acontius, who belonged to the circle of Castellio's friends in Basel, arrived there in 1557 and left around 1559 for England, where he remained. His *Satan's Stratagems* was published in Basel in Latin and French editions by Pietro Perna, who also published works by Castellio. The Latin text is printed in Jacobus Acontius, *Strategmatum Satanae libri VIII*, ed. Giorgio Radetti (Florence: Vallechi, 1946). An English translation appeared in 1651 under the title *Darkness Discovered. Or the Devils Secret Stratagems Laid Open*, with a commendatory preface by

John Goodwin, a leading fighter for toleration in England who is discussed below, chap. 6; it is available in a facsimile reprint (Delmar, N.Y.: Scholars Facsimiles & Reprints, 1978). A modern English translation of the first four books also exists: *Satan's Stratagems*, ed. Paul Radin (San Francisco: California State Library, 1940). Among the main themes Acontius shares with Castellio in their common opposition to persecution is the need for rationality, logic, moderation, respect for opponents, and charity toward religious differences in the conduct of religious argument. Another is the distinction between what is necessary and not necessary to know in order to attain salvation. For discussions of Acontius and his work, see W. K. Jordan, *The Development of Religious Toleration in England*, 4 vols. (Cambridge: Harvard University Press, 1932–1940), 1:303–65; Jean Jacquot, "Acontius and the Progress of Tolerance," *Bibliothèque d'Humanisme et Renaissance* 16 (1953): 192–206; Lecler, *Toleration and the Reformation*, 1:369–76; Cantimori, *Eretici italiani*, passim; Gary Remer, *Humanism and the Rhetoric of Toleration* (University Park: Pennsylvania State University Press, 1996), chap. 2.

108. On Mino Celsi and his treatise *In haereticis coercendis quatenus progredi liceat* (*On How Far It Is Lawful to Proceed in Coercing Heretics*), see Wilbur, *A History of Unitarianism*, p. 207, and Peter Bietenholz, "Mino Celsi and the Toleration Controversy of the Sixteenth Century," *Bibliothèque d'Humanisme et Renaissance* 34, no. 1 (1972): 31–47.

109. Coornhert's contribution in the toleration controversy is discussed below, chap. 5.

110. See Guggisberg, *Sebastian Castellio*, chap. 11, for a discussion of Castellio's posthumous influence; Lecler, *Toleration and the Reformation*, 2:258–59, notes the popularity of his writings in the Dutch Republic both in the original and in translation.

Chapter 5
The Toleration Controversy in the Netherlands

1. On the meaning of the term *politique* and the role of the *politiques* in the French wars of religion, see Joseph Lecler, *Toleration and the Reformation*, 2 vols. (New York: Association Press, 1960), vol. 2, bk. 6, passim.

2. See above, chaps. 1, 3.

3. See the account of the spread of the Reformation in Poland by R. R. Betts, "Poland, Bohemia and Hungary," in *The New Cambridge Modern History*, 13 vols. (Cambridge: Cambridge University Press, 1957–1979), vol. 2, *The Reformation 1520–1559*, ed. G. R. Elton, 2d ed., pp. 213–22. For Poland as a refuge of heretics and on the development of Antitrinitarianism in Poland in the late sixteenth and early seventeenth centuries, see Lecler, *Toleration and the Reformation*, vol. 1, bk. 5, and E. M. Wilbur, *A History of Unitarianism* (Cambridge: Harvard University Press, 1945), chaps. 20–36.

4. It was considered idolatrous because, according to the then Protestant view, Catholics turned the Mass into an idol that they worshiped and also made idols of the images and relics of saints.

5. For the revolt of the Netherlands, its antecedents, and the developments mentioned in the following paragraphs, see Jonathan Israel, *The Dutch Republic: Its Rise, Greatness, and Fall 1477–1806* (Oxford: Clarendon Press, 1995), chaps. 5–11; Geoffrey Parker, *The Dutch Revolt* (London: Allen Lane, 1977); Perez Zagorin, *Rebels and Rulers,* 1500–1660, 2 vols. (Cambridge: Cambridge University Press, 1982), vol. 2, chap. 11. On the toleration problem and controversy in the Netherlands and Dutch Republic, see Lecler, *Toleration and the Reformation,* vol. 2, bk. 7; Gerhard Güldner, *Das Toleranz-Problem in den Niederlanden im Ausgang des 16.Jahrhundert* (Lübeck: Matthiesen Verlag, 1968); Israel, *The Dutch Republic,* chaps. 16, 20, and the same writer's "The Intellectual Debate about Toleration in the Dutch Republic," in *The Emergence of Tolerance in the Dutch Republic,* ed. C. Berkvens-Stevelinck, J. Israel, and G.H.M. Posthumus Meyjes (Leiden: Brill, 1997); Andrew Pettegree, "The Politics of Toleration in the Free Netherlands 1572–1620," in *Tolerance and Intolerance in the European Reformation,* ed. Ole Peter Grell and Bob Scribner (Cambridge: Cambridge University Press, 1996).

6. "Paix de religion dans Les Pays-Bas"; I quote an excerpt from this document in English translation from *The Low Countries in Early Modern Times: A Documentary History,* ed. Herbert H. Rowen (New York: Harper & Row, 1972), p. 65.

7. See Israel, *The Dutch Republic,* chap. 16, for an excellent account of the different confessions in the early years of the republic.

8. On the nature and significance of Erastianism, see John Neville Figgis, *The Divine Right of Kings,* 2d ed. (Cambridge: Cambridge University Press, 1934), pp. 293–342.

9. On the regents as a social group, see the discussion in Israel, *The Dutch Republic,* pp. 341–44. For the condition of religion in the early Dutch Republic and the development of toleration, see ibid., chap. 16; M.E.H.N. Mout, "Limits and Debates: A Comparative View of Dutch Toleration in the Sixteenth and Early Seventeenth Centuries," in Berkvens-Stevelinck, Israel, and Meyjes, *The Emergence of Tolerance in the Dutch Republic;* Benjamin J. Kaplan, *Calvinists and Libertines* (Oxford: Clarendon Press, 1995), a valuable study of Dutch religion between 1578 and 1620 that combines illuminating general observations with a detailed account of religious developments and relations among confessions in the city of Utrecht.

10. "Discours sur la permission de liberté de religion . . . au Pais-Bas" (1579), attributed to the French Protestant author and adviser of William of Orange, Philippe du Plessis Mornay; I quote from the English translation in *Texts concerning the Revolt of the Netherlands,* ed. E. H. Kossmann and A. F. Mellink (Cambridge: Cambridge University Press, 1974), pp. 163, 164.

11. "Treaty of the Union, Eternal Alliance and Confederation" (1579), printed in ibid., art. 13, pp. 169–70. This article made an exception for Holland and Zeeland because in those two provinces Catholicism had already been suppressed.

12. The principal biography of Coornhert is H. Bonger's *Leven en Werk van D. V. Coornhert* (Amsterdam: G. A. Van Oorschot, 1978); see also Gerrit Voogt, *Constraint on Trial: Dirck Volckertsz Coornhert and Religious Freedom* (Kirksville, Mo.: Truman State University Press, 2000), and the biographical details in Güldner,

Das Toleranz-Problem, pp. 65–71. Both Bonger and Voogt contain surveys of his writings and ideas.

13. His collected writings appeared in a posthumous edition: *Wercken*, 3 vol. (Amsterdam, 1630).

14. Coornhert explained in this work that he wrote it out of concern that "due to the great variety of opinions in matters of religion . . . the common man, disgusted in reading so many warring pamphlets, might despair of coming to knowledge of truth, recklessly turn from all good morals, and entirely degenerate into libertine freedom and godless life"; quoted in Ethan Matt Kavaler, *Pieter Bruegel: Parables of Order and Enterprise* (Cambridge: Cambridge University Press, 1999), p. 290n.

15. On Coornhert's religious conceptions, the Family of Love and his relationship with it, and Calvin's attack on him as a libertine, see Güldner, *Das Toleranz-Problem*, pp. 71–80; Alastair Hamilton, *The Family of Love* (Cambridge: James Clarke, 1981), chaps. 2–5; Perez Zagorin, *Ways of Lying: Dissimulation, Persecution, and Conformity in Early Modern Europe* (Cambridge: Harvard University Press, 1990), pp. 78–80, 117–27; Voogt, *Constraint on Trial*, chaps. 3–5 and passim.

16. Quoted in Güldner, *Das Toleranz-Problem*, pp. 159–60. For Coornhert's ideas on religious toleration and Castellio's influence, see the discussion and references in ibid., pp. 71–118, 159–69, which contains the closest analysis; Lecler, *Toleration and the Reformation*, 2:271–86; James D. Tracy, "Erasmus, Coornhert and the Acceptance of Religious Disunity in the Body Politic: A Low Countries Tradition," in Berkvens-Stevelinck, Israel, and Meyjes, *The Emergence of Tolerance in the Dutch Republic*; Voogt, *Constraint on Trial*, chaps. 5–7 and passim.

17. Quoted by Voogt, *Constraint on Trial*, p. 65.

18. *About the Constraint of Conscience in Holland* (1579), printed in Kossmann and Mellink, *Texts concerning the Revolt in the Netherlands*, pp. 191–96.

19. Lecler, *Toleration and the Reformation*, 2:276; Güldner, *Das Toleranz-Problem*, pp. 76–77; a French translation of the petition is printed in *Les premiers défenseurs de la liberté religieuse*, ed. Joseph Lecler and Marius-François Valkhoff, 2 vols. (Paris: Les Éditions du Cerf, 1969), 2:72–77.

20. For Coornhert's remonstrance in behalf of the Leiden magistrates, see Lecler, *Toleration and the Reformation*, 2:277, and Güldner, *Das Toleranz-Problem*, p. 77; on the Reformed minister Caspar Coolhaes, see the account in Lecler, 2:263–69; the quotation is in Kaplan, *Calvinists and Libertines*, pp. 98–99, which contains some comments on Coolhaes's religious beliefs.

21. Acts 5:34–39 describes Gamaliel advising the Jews against killing the apostles because if the latter's "counsel or work be of men, it will come to nought: but if it be of God, ye cannot overthrow it; lest haply ye be found to fight against God."

22. I cite the text of the *Synod* in the modern French edition: Dirck Coornhert, *A l'aurore des libertés modernes. Synode sur la liberté de conscience* (1582), ed. Joseph Lecler and Marius-François Valkhoff (Paris: Les Éditions du Cerf, 1979); for the title page of the original edition, see pp. 55, 62.

23. Ibid., Sessions 10–19, pp. 161–297.

24. In the tenth session Gamaliel quotes from Castellio's preface to his French translation of the Bible addressed to Henry II of France; he does not name the author but refers to him as "a learned and pious man"; ibid, pp. 175–76.

25. Quoted in Güldner, *Das Toleranz-Problem*, p. 135. On Lipsius and his dissimulation in religion, see Zagorin, *Ways of Lying*, pp. 122–25; beside the references cited there, see also Mark Morford, *Stoics and Neostoics: Rubens and the Circle of Lipsius* (Princeton: Princeton University Press, 1991). For Coornhert's relationship with Lipsius and the controversy between them, see Güldner, *Das Toleranz-Problem*, chap. 4, and Voogt, *Constraint on Trial*, pp. 197–227.

26. Justus Lipsius, *Six Books of Politickes or Civil Doctrine* (London, 1594; reprint, Amsterdam: Theatrum Orbis Terrarum, 1970), bk. 4, chaps. 2–4.

27. The preliminary correspondence between Coornhert and Lipsius is discussed by Güldner, *Das Toleranz-Problem*, pp. 99–104, and Voogt, *Constraint on Trial*, pp. 209–12.

28. Quoted in Voogt, *Constraint on Trial*, p. 211.

29. My discussion of the first part of this work is based on the selection in Lecler and Valkhoff, *Les premiers défenseurs de la liberté religieuse*, 2:86–90, and the account in Lecler, *Toleration and the Reformation*, 2:281–84; Güldner, *Das Toleranz-Problem*, pp. 105–7; Voogt, *Constraint on Trial*, pp. 213–18.

30. Lecler, *Toleration and the Reformation*, 2:284.

31. See the accounts of his answer in Güldner, *Das Toleranz-Problem*, pp. 107–10, and Voogt, *Constraint on Trial*, pp. 217–19.

32. Dirck Coornhert, *Verantwoordinghe van t'Proces van den Ketteren Niet To Dooden*, published in Latin as *Defensio processus de non occidendis haereticis* (1591).

33. For indications of his influence, see Güldner, *Das Toleranz-Problem*, pp. 138–47.

34. John Calvin, *Institutes of the Christian Religion*, ed. John T. McNeill, 2 vols. (Philadelphia: Westminster Press, 1960), bk. 3, chaps. 21–24; R. T. Kendall, *Calvin and English Calvinism to 1649* (Oxford: Oxford University Press, 1981).

35. Many particulars concerning Arminius's life, religious conceptions, and Calvinist opposition to his theological opinions are contained in the introductory material of the English edition of his *Works*, ed. James Nichols, 3 vols. (London, 1825), vol. 1; see also the modern biography and survey of his religious thought by Carl Bangs, *Arminius: A Study in the Dutch Reformation* (Nashville, Tenn.: Abingdon Press, 1974). On Arminius and the Dutch Arminian movement, see A.H.W. Harrison, *The Beginnings of Arminianism to the Synod of Dort* (London: University of London Press, 1926); W. K. Jordan, *The Development of Religious Toleration in England*, 4 vols. (Cambridge: Harvard University Press, 1932–1940), 2:319–49; Lecler, *Toleration and the Reformation*, vol. 2, bk. 7, chap. 6; Kendall, *Calvin and English Calvinism*, chap. 10, discusses Arminius's treatment of predestination.

36. Jordan, *The Development of Religious Toleration in England*, 2:322.

37. These views appear in Arminius's comments on a work on predestination in 1598 by William Perkins, one of the most distinguished of English Calvinist theologians. His critique of Perkins was published posthumously in 1612; an English translation of the Latin original, *Modest Examination of a Pamphlet [by] Dr.*

William Perkins . . . on the Mode and Order of Predestination, is printed in *Works*, vol. 3. Bangs, *Arminius*, chap. 15, discusses Arminius's critique, as does Kendall, who states (*Calvin and English Calvinism*, p. 143) that he "radically modified the reformed doctrine" of predestination.

38. See Jan den Tex, *Oldenbarneveldt*, 2 vols. (Cambridge: Cambridge University Press, 1973), vol. 2, chap. 10, for a discussion of Oldenbarneveldt's religion and his part in procuring Arminius's appointment as Leiden theology professor.

39. See Jordan, *The Development of Religious Toleration in England*, 2:325.

40. James Arminius, "On Reconciling Religious Dissensions among Christians," *Works*, vol. 1; see pp. 422, 461–64.

41. The Remonstrants' Five Articles are printed in Philip Schaff, *The Creeds of Christendom*, 3 vols. (New York, 1884), 3:545–49.

42. The canons of the Synod of Dort are printed in ibid., 3:550–97.

43. On the political and religious conflict in the Dutch Republic connected with the controversy between the Remonstrants and Counter-Remonstrants and the defeat of the former at the Synod of Dort, see den Tex, *Oldenbarneveldt*, vol. 2, chaps. 10, 12–13, and Israel, *The Dutch Republic*, chaps. 18–20.

44. Jan Uytenbogaert, *Treatise on the Office and Authority of the Higher Christian Magistrate in Ecclesiastical Affairs* (The Hague, 1610), written in Dutch; see the characterization of its position by Israel, *The Dutch Republic*, p. 426, and the discussion of the work by Lecler, *Toleration and the Reformation*, 2:302–4, and Douglas Nobbs, *Theocracy and Toleration* (Cambridge: Cambridge University Press, 1938), pp. 35–49.

45. For Grotius's biography, see W.S.M. Knight, *The Life and Works of Hugo Grotius* (London: Sweet and Maxwell, 1925).

46. For several accounts of Grotius's religious views and writings on toleration, see Jordan, *The Development of Religious Toleration in England*, 2:344–48; Lecler, *Toleration and the Reformation*, 2:305–6, 312–14, 318–21; Israel, *The Dutch Republic*, chaps. 18–20, and "The Intellectual Debate about Toleration in the Dutch Republic."

47. See H. R. Trevor-Roper, "Hugo Grotius in England," in *From Counter-Reformation to Glorious Revolution* (Chicago: University of Chicago Press, 1992), which gives an account of Grotius's visit to England in 1613 and the contacts he made there.

48. Hugo Grotius, *De imperio summarum potestatum circa sacra*) (*The Sovereignty of the Highest Powers in Religious Matters*); this work is discussed by Lecler, *Toleration and the Reformation*, 2:312–13, and Nobbs, *Theocracy and Toleration*, pp. 62–91.

49. Hugo Grotius, *Discourse of Toleration before the Amsterdam City Council* (1616); I cite the selection from this work in Lecler and Valkhoff, *Les premiers défenseurs de la liberté religieuse*, 2:133–37.

50. Israel comments that Grotius cared more about the "unchallengeable ascendancy of the public Church" than about "freedom for confessional minorities to organize or the individual openly to dissent"; *The Dutch Republic*, p. 501; cf. also his characterization of Grotius as a restricted advocate of toleration in his essay "The Intellectual Debate about Toleration in the Dutch Republic," p. 12.

51. Hugo Grotius, *Meletius sive de iis quae inter Christianos conveniunt epistola* (*Meletius or Letter on the Points of Agreement between Christians*), ed. G.H.M. Posthumus Meyjes (Leiden: Brill, 1988), pp. 103–5, 132–34. This is the first publication of the text, which Grotius left unprinted in his lifetime, as well as the first English translation.

52. Hugo Grotius, *Annotationes in Matthaeum* (1630); I cite this work from the selection in Lecler and Valkhoff, *Les premiers défenseurs de la liberté religieuse*, 2:139–42.

53. See the editor's note in *Meletius*, p. 162.

54. Israel, *The Dutch Republic*, p. 502.

55. *The Law of War and Peace* (1646 ed.), in *Classics of International Law*, 2 vols. (Oxford: Clarendon Press, 1925), vol. 2 (English translation), pp. 510–11, 512 = bk. 2, chap. 20.45.1, 3. In a further section, he made certain distinctions among these principles and justified the punishment or restraint of those who denied the existence of God or gods; ibid., pp. 513–14 = bk. 2, chap. 20.46.

56. Ibid., pp. 516–17, 518–20 = bk. 2, chap. 20.49–50. On this last point Grotius quoted Plato's *Republic* that the sole "punishment of the erring is: to be taught."

57. See the essay by G.H.M. Posthumus Meyjes, "Hugo Grotius as an Irenicist," in *The World of Hugo Grotius (1583–1645)* (Amsterdam and Maarsen: APA-Holland University Press, 1984), an excellent discussion of Grotius's ideas about the reunion of the churches as well as on the relationship between church and state.

58. See the article on Grotius in Pierre Bayle, *Historical and Critical Dictionary*, ed. P. des Maizeaux, 2d ed., 5 vols. (London, 1736), s.v.

59. See the article on Episcopius in ibid., s.v., and in *Encyclopedia Britannica*, 11th ed., s.v. There is no modern biography of him. For interesting details about his appearance and speeches at the Synod of Dort, taken from the letters of John Hales, an English minister who was present as an observer, see John Tulloch, *Rational Theology and Christian Philosophy in England in the Seventeenth Century*, 2d ed., 2 vols. (Edinburgh, 1874), 1:176–86. Episcopius's statements caused Hales to cease to be a Calvinist and believer in predestination. He was reported to have said about the synod, "There, I bid John Calvin good night"; ibid., p. 190.

60. Episcopius's theological writings were published in his *Opera theologica*, 2 vols. (Amsterdam 1650–1665), and in a 2d ed. (London, 1665–1678).

61. Simon Episcopius, *Vrije Godesdienst* (n.p., 1627).

62. See the discussion of Episcopius's conception of toleration in Nobbs, *Theocracy and Toleration*, pp. 91–107; Israel, *The Dutch Republic*, pp. 501–5, and "The Intellectual Debate about Toleration in the Dutch Republic," pp. 18–20; Jordan, *The Development of Religious Toleration in England*, 2:338–44; Lecler, *Toleration and the Reformation*, 2:316–18.

63. Nobbs, *Theocracy and Toleration*, p. 95, describes Episcopius's theory as "Erastianism qualified by toleration."

64. Israel, *The Dutch Republic*, pp. 909–13.

65. For Spinoza's biography, see Steven Nadler, *Spinoza: A Life* (Cambridge: Cambridge University Press, 1999); chap. 6 contains an account of his excommu-

nication and prints the decree on p. 120; see also the discussion of Spinoza's life, intellectual associations, conceptions, and subsequent influence in the magisterial work by Jonathan I. Israel, *Radical Enlightenment: Philosophy and the Making of Modernity, 1650–1750* (Oxford: Oxford University Press, 2001), pt. 2.

66. Spinoza's *Ethics*, written in Latin, was first published in Amsterdam in his *Opera posthuma* in 1677–1678; this edition was clandestinely printed without the publisher's name or place of publication; see Israel, *Radical Enlightenment*, p. 290.

67. Quoted in Nadler, *Spinoza*, p. 322.

68. On the printing, publication, suppression, and diffusion of Spinoza's book, see Israel, *Radical Enlightenment*, chap. 16.

69. *Quibus ostenditur libertatem philosophandi non tantum salva pietate, & reipublicae pace: sed eandem nisi cum pace reipublicae, ipsaque pietate tolli non posse.* I use Samuel Shirley's English translation, which retains the Latin title: Baruch Spinoza, *Tractatus theologico-politicus* (Leiden: Brill, 1989). The Latin title page is reproduced in ibid., p. 46; the Latin text is printed in Benedict de Spinoza, *Opera*, ed. Carl Gebhardt, 4 vols. (Heidelberg: Carl Winters Universitätsverlag, 1925), vol. 3.

70. *Tractatus theologico-politicus*, pp. 50, 51–53, 56.

71. Ibid., pp. 53–55.

72. Ibid., pp. 224–25. In several places Spinoza speaks of Christ as the prophet nearest to God; see pp. 64, 65, 107.

73. Ibid., pp. 233–36.

74. Ibid., pp. 242–43, 252–53, 280, 286–88; see the entire discussion in chaps. 16–17, 19, of which this is a very condensed account.

75. Ibid., pp. 291–92, 293, 295, 297, 298–99.

76. His view that each person's natural right is as great as his power may even be incoherent: power is a fact, the fact of how far one person can compel another to comply with his will, while a right or natural right is a norm and an entitlement that imposes duties on others; hence to equate the two looks like a category mistake. We commonly and correctly think of power as limited by rights rather than coextensive with them.

77. See Israel's striking observations on Spinoza's conception of toleration, *Radical Enlightenment*, pp. 56–70, which also stresses its superiority to that of John Locke. In these remarks, I think, Israel fails to do Locke full justice. On Locke, see below, chap. 7.

78. Benedict de Spinoza, *Political Treatise*, trans. Samuel Shirley (Indianapolis: Hackett, 2000), p. 95. This work was first published in 1677 in Spinoza's *Opera posthuma*, and the Latin text is printed in Spinoza, *Opera*, vol. 3. See Nadler, *Spinoza*, pp. 342–49, for an account of the book.

79. *Political Treatise*, p. 118.

80. Israel, *Radical Enlightenment*, pp. 291–93.

81. For examples of the critical reaction to Spinoza's work, see Rosalie Colie, *Light and Enlightenment: A Study of the Cambridge Platonists and the Dutch Arminians* (Cambridge: Cambridge University Press, 1957), chaps. 5–6, and Israel, *Radical Enlightenment*, chap. 16 and passim.

Chapter 6
The Great English Toleration Controversy, 1640–1660

1. A. G. Dickens, *The English Reformation* (New York: Schocken Books, 1969), and G. R. Elton, *England under the Tudors*, 2d ed. (London: Methuen, 1975), contain a survey of the origins, development, and events of the English Reformation. Dickens's account emphasizes the popular character of the Reformation, but subsequent scholarship has modified this view; see J. J. Scarisbrick, *The Reformation and the English People* (Oxford: Blackwell, 1984); *The English Reformation Revised*, ed. Christopher Haigh (Cambridge: Cambridge University Press, 1987); Eamon Duffy, *The Stripping of the Altars* (New Haven: Yale University Press, 1992).

2. On the English government's treatment of Catholics and anti-Catholic legislation and persecution between 1559 and 1640, see W. K. Jordan, *The Development of Religious Toleration in England*, 4 vols. (Cambridge: Harvard University Press, 1932–1940), vol. 1, chaps. 2–3; vol. 2, chaps. 1–2; Jordan misleadingly describes the Elizabethan government's policy toward Catholics as moderate; see also Joseph Lecler, *Toleration and the Reformation*, 2 vols. (New York: Association Press, 1960), vol. 2, bk. 8, chaps. 4, 7, and John Coffey, *Persecution and Toleration in Protestant England 1558–1689* (Harlow: Longman, 2000), chaps. 4–5. Both Lecler, 2:363, 423, and Coffey, p. 90, give the number of Catholic martyrs for this period.

3. For details on the persecution of Separatism under Elizabeth and James I, see Jordan, *The Development of Religious Toleration in England*, 1:181–83; 2:44–47, and Coffey, *Persecution and Toleration in Protestant England*, pp. 96–104, 112–15. On the nature of Separatism and the early English Separatists and Anabaptists, see Champlin Burrage, *Early English Dissenters . . . (1550–1641)*, 2 vols. (Cambridge: Cambridge University Press, 1912); Jordan, *The Development of Religious Toleration in England*, 1:261–99, 216–314; B. R. White, *The English Separatist Tradition* (Oxford: Oxford University Press, 1971); Murray Tolmie, *The Triumph of the Saints* (Cambridge: Cambridge University Press, 1977), chaps. 1–4; Michael R. Watts, *The Dissenters* (Oxford: Clarendon Press, 1978), chap. 1.

4. For a selection of works on English Puritanism and the Puritan movement, the subject of a very extensive literature, see M. M. Knappen, *Tudor Puritanism* (Chicago: University of Chicago Press, 1939); William Haller, *The Rise of Puritanism* (New York: Columbia University Press, 1938); Christopher Hill, *Society and Puritanism in Pre-Revolutionary England* (London: Secker & Warburg, 1964); Patrick Collinson, *The Elizabethan Puritan Movement* (Cambridge: Cambridge University Press, 1967), and *Godly People* (London: Hambledon Press, 1983); Margo Todd, *Christian Humanism and the Puritan Social Order* (Cambridge: Cambridge University Press, 1987). Jordan discusses Puritan ideas on toleration, *The Development of Religious Toleration in England*, 1:239–61, 2:199–215.

5. Francis Bacon, *The Essays or Counsels Civil and Moral* (1625), in *Francis Bacon: A Critical Edition of the Major Works*, ed. Brian Vickers (Oxford: Oxford University Press, 1996), pp. 344, 346. For a detailed account of the ideas of Bacon, Chill-

ingworth, and Hales in relation to toleration, see Jordan, *The Development of Religious Toleration in England*, 2:377–412, 457–72; on Bacon, see also Perez Zagorin, *Francis Bacon* (Princeton: Princeton University Press, 1998), pp. 6, 141, 169, 171–73.

6. On Chillingworth, Falkland, and Hales, see Jordan, *The Development of Religious Toleration in England*, 2:371–412, who groups them under the heading of latitudinarians and moderates; John Tulloch, *Rational Theology and Christian Philosophy in England in the Seventeenth Century*, 2d ed., 2 vols. (Edinburgh, 1874), vol. 1, chaps. 3–5; Robert R. Orr, *Reason and Authority: The Thought of William Chillingworth* (Oxford: Clarendon Press, 1967): G.A.J. Rogers, "Locke and the Latitude Men: Ignorance as a Ground of Toleration," in *Philosophy, Science, and Religion in England 1640–1700*, ed. Richard Kroll, Richard Ashcraft, and Perez Zagorin (Cambridge: Cambridge University Press, 1992); Gary Remer, *Humanism and the Rhetoric of Toleration* (University Park: Pennsylvania State University Press, 1996), chap. 3. See also H. R. Trevor-Roper, "The Great Tew Circle," in *Catholics, Anglicans, and Puritans* (Chicago: University of Chicago Press, 1987), an essay on Falkland and the circle of his friends who gathered at his house at Great Tew in Oxfordshire in the later 1630s, which included both Chillingworth and Hales.

7. It should be noted that these Baptist churches were probably of native origin and not descended from the earlier English Anabaptist sects of the sixteenth century, which were the offspring of Continental Anabaptism; see the comments in White, *The English Separatist Tradition*, chap. 8. Unlike many Anabaptists of Germany and the Netherlands in the sixteenth century, the English Baptists of the early seventeenth century, who rejected the name "Anabaptists," recognized the legitimacy of the civil magistrate as an ordinance of God for the preservation of peace and the repression of evildoers.

8. On the Separatist and Baptist attitude toward toleration and the writings of these Baptist ministers, John Smyth, Thomas Helwys, John Murton, and Leonard Busher, see Jordan, *The Development of Religious Toleration in England*, 2:258–314; T. Lyon, *The Theory of Religious Liberty in England (1603–1639)* (Cambridge: Cambridge University Press, 1937), chaps. 4–5; H. Leon McBeth, *English Baptist Literature on Religious Liberty to 1689* (New York: Arno Press, 1980), chap. 1. For the Baptists, see also B. R. White, *The English Baptists of the Seventeenth Century* (London: Baptist Historical Society, 1983). It is worth noting that as far back as the mid–sixteenth century, a book attributed to an English Anabaptist, Robert Cooche, revealed the influence of Castellio's *De haereticis* against the killing of heretics. Cooche's work, written ca. 1557, has not survived but is known through an attack upon it in 1560 by the Scottish Calvinist reformer John Knox; it is discussed by Irwin B. Horst, *The Radical Brethren: Anabaptism and the English Reformation to* 1558 (Nieuwkoop: De Graaf, 1972), pp. 118–19.

9. Leonard Busher, *Religions Peace: or A Plea for Liberty of Conscience* (1614) (London ed., 1646), printed in *Tracts on Liberty of Conscience and Persecution 1614–1661*, ed. Edward B. Underhill (London, 1846), pp. 16, 17, 18, 24, 41, 50, 51.

10. On the Independents, see the account in Tolmie, *The Triumph of the Saints*, chap. 5.

11. On this document, see Jordan, *The Development of Religious Toleration in England*, 3:368–71.

12. The literature on the English revolution is enormous. For several accounts and explanations, not always in accord, of its origin and political and religious developments in the period 1640–1660, see Perez Zagorin, *The Court and the Country* (New York: Athenaeum, 1970); Conrad Russell, *The Causes of he English Civil War* (Oxford: Clarendon Press, 1990); Derek Hirst, *England in Conflict 1603–1660* (New York: Oxford University Press, 1999).

13. Jordan's discussion in *The Development of Religious Toleration in England,* vols. 3–4, which covers the two decades of the English revolution, remains indispensable for its comprehensive account of the government's policy with regard to toleration and the mass of contemporary writings on the subject.

14. See ibid., 3:267–346, for a discussion of the Presbyterians' alarmed response to the religious scene of the 1640s and their opposition to toleration. The best-known writer among these Presbyterians was the Reverend Thomas Edwards, whose notorious work *Gangraena,* published in three parts in 1646, was a sensational exposure of the heresies and sects of the time.

15. Roger Williams, *The Bloudy Tenent of Persecution, for Cause of Conscience Discussed in a Conference betweene Truth and Peace* (London, 1644); this work, which appeared without the author's name, is reprinted in *The Complete Writings of Roger Williams,* 7 vols. (New York: Russell & Russell, 1963), a facsimile of the Narragansett Club's edition of Williams's writings and letters, published in Providence, 1855–1874.

16. For biographies of Williams and surveys of his thought, see the excellent work by Edmund Morgan, *Roger Williams: The Church and the State* (New York: Harcourt Brace, 1967), and Edwin S. Gaustad, *Liberty of Conscience: Roger Williams in America* (Grand Rapids, Mich.: William B. Eerdmans, 1991).

17. See Perry Miller, *Orthodoxy in Massachusetts, 1630–1650* (Cambridge: Harvard University Press, 1933).

18. Cotton emigrated to Massachusetts in 1633. On his history and ideas as a major figure in the first generation of Puritan ministers of New England, see Larzer Ziff, *The Career of John Cotton: Puritanism and American Experience* (Princeton: Princeton University Press, 1962), and Everett Emerson, *John Cotton,* rev. ed. (Boston: Twayne, 1990).

19. On Franck, see above, chap. 3.

20. John Cotton, *The Bloudy Tenent, Washed, and Made White in the Bloud of the Lamb* (London, 1647; reprint, New York: Arno Press, 1972); Emerson, *John Cotton,* chap. 7, lists all of Cotton's writings in his controversy with Williams.

21. Williams entitled his rejoinder *The Bloody Tenent Yet More Bloody* (London, 1652), in *Complete Writings,* vol. 4. In behalf of religious liberty, he also wrote *Queries of Highest Consideration* (London, 1644) and *The Hireling Ministry None of Christs* (London, 1652), ibid., vols. 2, 7; several selections from Williams's writings are included in Hans R. Guggisberg, *Religiöse Toleranz. Dokumente zur Geschichte einer Forderung* (Stuttgart-Bad Cannstadt: Frommann-Holzboog, 1984), pp. 166–71.

22. See Hans R. Guggisberg, *Sebstian Castellio 1515–1563* (Göttingen: Vandenhoeck & Rupprecht, 1997), p. 281.

23. Jordan discusses Williams's ideas on toleration and religious liberty, *The Development of Religious Toleration in England*, 3:472–506; see also Perry Miller, *Roger Williams: His Contribution to the American Tradition* (New York: Athenaeum, 1962), and the acute account by Timothy Hall, *Separating Church and State: Roger Williams and Religious Liberty* (Urbana: University of Illinois Press, 1998), which discusses *The Bloudy Tenent* in chap. 3.

24. *The Bloudy Tenent*, pp. 5–9.

25. This is what Cotton had stated in answer to a Separatist critic's argument against persecution. Williams reprinted Cotton's remarks in *The Bloudy Tenent*, pp. 41–53.

26. Ibid., p. 58.

27. For the nature and history of typology, a hermeneutic method that went back to the early church and church fathers, see the introduction and essays in *Typology and Early American Literature*, ed. Sacvan Bercovich (Amherst: University of Massachusetts Press, 1972). The discussions of Williams by Jordan, *The Development of Religious Toleration in England*, and by William Haller, *Liberty and Reformation in the Puritan Revolution* (New York: Columbia University Press, 1955), ignore the importance of typology in his work. Perry Miller, a great scholar of American Puritanism, was apparently the first to recognize the large place it held in Williams's thought. He also supposed, however, that Williams was eccentric or unique in his typological vision, and that Calvinists and Puritans were strongly opposed to typological interpretation because it lent itself to the allegorical perversions they condemned in the Catholic treatment of Scripture; see, in particular, Perry Miller, "Roger Williams: An Essay in Interpretation," in *The Complete Writings of Roger Williams*, vol. 7. Miller was, of course, mistaken in this supposition, and subsequent scholars have corrected his view; see Bercovich's introduction and the essays by Thomas H. Davis, "The Tradition of Puritan Typology," and Richard Reinitz, "The Separatist Background of Roger Williams' Argument for Toleration," in *Typology and Early American Literature*. Protestant, Calvinist, and Puritan exegetes were in fact well versed in typology and used it frequently. Cotton himself relied upon it in his *A Brief Exposition of the Whole Book of Canticles* (1642), his exegesis of the Song of Songs; see Emerson, *John Cotton*, pp. 20–22.

28. *The Bloudy Tenent*, pp. 167, 181–82, 239–41.

29. Ibid., pp. 330, 347.

30. Ibid., p. 330.

31. Ibid., pp. 200, 221, 227–29, 233–34.

32. Ibid., pp. 77, 209–10.

33. Ibid., p. 184.

34. Ibid., p. 105. In a previous exchange with Cotton, Williams spoke of those who had "opened a gap in the hedge or wall of separation between the garden of the Church and the wilderness of the world," and that when that had happened, God had "made his garden a wilderness, as at this day"; *Mr Cottons Letter Lately Printed*, in *Complete Writings*, 1:392.

35. *The Bloudy Tenent*, pp. 107–18.

36. Ibid., pp. 200, 323–24.

37. Ibid., pp. 217–18.

38. Ibid., pp. 157–60, 250, 343. It should be noted that Williams held a conventional populist conception of the origin of government, which he traced to God's ordinance mediated by the free consent of the people, who may establish whatever form they deem best. The sovereignty of all civil authority, he said, "is founded in the consent of the People"; ibid., p. 214. In his subsequent *The Bloody Tenent of Persecution Yet More Bloody* (1652), he endorsed the execution of Charles I when he praised Parliament for its impartial justice on the greatest offenders; *Complete Writings*, 4:5. In the same work he noted that while magistrates derive their power from the people, the people cannot grant them spiritual power because they do not possess it themselves; ibid., p. 187.

39. *The Bloudy Tenent*, pp. 153–55.

40. Ibid., pp. 72–74.

41. Ibid., pp. 79–81.

42. Ibid., pp. 70–71.

43. Ibid., p. 214.

44. *The Bloody Tenent of Persecution Yet More Bloody*, p. 230.

45. Ibid., p. 425.

46. *The Bloudy Tenent*, pp. 126–37, 219.

47. Ibid., pp. 7–71, 205.

48. Ibid., p. 91.

49. In *The Hireling Ministry None of Christs* (1652), in *Complete Writings*, 7:174, William describes his position as "Absolute Freedom in matters meerly spirituall for all the consciences in the world."

50. *The Bloudy Tenent*, p. 198.

51. Ibid., pp. 245–47, 331–34.

52. *The Bloody Tenent of Persecution Yet More Bloody*, p. 493.

53. Gaustad, *Liberty of Conscience*, p. 85; Haller, *Liberty and Reformation*, p. 344.

54. On Henry Robinson and his involvement in the toleration controversy, see W. K. Jordan, *Men of Substance* (Chicago: University of Chicago Press, 1942), pp. 86–139. Robinson's anonymously published tract of 1643, *Liberty of Conscience*, was his main work in the controversy. It is reprinted in William Haller, *Tracts on Liberty in the Puritan Revolution*, 3 vols. (New York: Columbia University Press, 1934), vol. 3.

55. For a sketch of Goodwin's life, see *Dictionary of National Biography* [*DNB*], 22 vols. (Oxford: Oxford University Press, 1965), s.v. Despite his importance, there is no modern biography of Goodwin.

56. John Goodwin, *Anti-Cavalierisme* (London, 1642), reprinted in Haller, *Tracts on Liberty*, vol. 2.

57. John Goodwin, *Hubristodikai: The Obstructours of Justice* (London, 1649); on this and Goodwin's other political writings, see Perez Zagorin, *A History of Political Thought in the English Revolution*, new ed. (Bristol: Thoemmes Press, 1997), pp. 81–86.

58. See Geoffrey F. Nuttall, *Visible Saints: The Congregational Way 1640–1660* (Oxford: Blackwell, 1957), for a detailed discussion of the nature of the gathered church and its principle of voluntary membership.

59. On Goodwin and the formation of his gathered church, see Tolmie, *The Triumph of the Saints*, pp. 111–16, and Ellen More, "The New Arminians: John Goodwin and His Coleman Street Congregation" (Ph.D. diss., University of Rochester, 1980), and "John Goodwin and the Origins of the New Arminianism," *Journal of British Studies*, 22, no. 1 (1982): 50–70, an excellent account of Goodwin's Congregationalism and his religious ideas.

60. John Goodwin, *Redemption Redeemed* (London, 1651).

61. Goodwin was instrumental in the English translation of Acontius's *Strategmatum Satanae* in 1648 and 1651, and spoke of him as a man of much piety and worth who had fled to England for conscience's sake; see Jordan, *The Development of Religious Toleration in England*, 3:381n.

62. *The Bloudy Tenent*, p. 165.

63. Quoted from the dedication to his *Catabaptism* (London, 1655), in *DNB*, s.v. "John Goodwin."

64. Jordan, *The Development of Religious Toleration in England*, 3:376–412, presents one of the fullest discussions of Goodwin's ideas; see also Tolmie, *The Triumph of the Saints*; Arthur E. Barker, *Milton and the Puritan Dilemma 1641–1660* (Toronto: University of Toronto Press, 1942), passim, which contains insightful comments on Goodwin's religious conceptions and commitment to religious freedom; Haller, *The Rise of Puritanism*, passim, and *Liberty and Reformation*, passim.

65. John Goodwin, *Theomachia* (London, 1644), pp. 12–19, reprinted in Haller, *Tracts on Liberty*, vol. 2.

66. Ibid., pp. 22–23, 26–30, 31–33.

67. Ibid., pp. 34–36.

68. John Goodwin, *Independency Gods Veritie. or The Necessitie of Toleration* (London, 1647); printed in A.S.P. Woodhouse, *Puritanism and Liberty* (London: Dent, 1938), p. 186.

69. [John Goodwin], *M.S. to A.S. with a Plea for Libertie of Conscience* (London, 1644), pp. 50–55. Although this anti-Presbyterian work appeared without the author's name, most of it, beginning with p. 31, is clearly by Goodwin.

70. Ibid., pp. 56–58.

71. John Goodwin, *Imputatio Fidei, or, A Treatise of Justification* (London, 1642), quoted in Haller, *The Rise of Puritanism*, pp. 201–2.

72. The fullest modern biographies of Milton are W. R. Parker, *Milton: A Biography*, 2d ed., with additional notes and commentary, ed. Gordon Campbell, 2 vols. (Oxford: Clarendon Press, 1996), and Barbara K. Lewalski, *The Life of John Milton: A Critical Biography* (Oxford: Blackwell, 2000). Jordan surveys Milton's thought on toleration in *The Development of Religious Toleration in England*, 3:202–31. The number of studies of Milton's poetry and prose is second only to that on Shakespeare, and many of them include consideration of his religious, political, and other ideas. I have discussed his political conceptions and belief in toleration in my *Milton Aristocrat and Rebel: The Poet and His Politics* (London: Boydell & Brewer, 1992); see also Barker, *Milton and the Puritan Dilemma*, pt. 2, and the discussion in Haller, *Liberty and Reformation*, passim. The introductions and editorial matter in the successive volumes of *Complete Prose Works of John Milton*, ed.

Don M. Wolfe et al., 8 vols. in 10 (New Haven: Yale University Press, 1953–1982), contain accounts of the historical background and context of Milton's writings as a revolutionary publicist.

73. Milton's antiepiscopal tracts are printed in *Complete Prose Works*, vol. 1.

74. Milton's divorce tracts are printed in ibid., vol. 2.

75. John Milton, *Tetrachordon* (1645), ed. Arnold Williams, ibid., pp. 638–39.

76. Ibid., pp. 587–88.

77. John Milton, *Areopagitica* (1644), ed. Ernest Sirluck, printed in ibid.

78. On this licensing ordinance and its background, see the introduction to ibid., pp. 158–63.

79. Milton first used these phrases in reference to censorship in the second of his divorce tracts, *The Judgement of Martin Bucer*, published in July 1644, ibid., p. 479.

80. Ibid., pp. 487, 493, 505, 539, 541, 568–69.

81. Ibid., pp. 513–15, 527.

82. Ibid., pp. 549–50, 561–63.

83. Ibid., p. 543.

84. Ibid., pp. 551, 553–54.

85. Ibid., pp. 550, 554–55.

86. Ibid., p. 565.

87. Ibid., pp. 492, 565.

88. In a characteristic statement of this attitude, Milton wrote in his defense of regicide that "none can love freedom heartilie, but good men; the rest love not freedom, but licence; which never hath more scope or more indulgence then under Tyrants"; *The Tenure of Kings and Magistrates*, 2d ed. (London, 1650), printed in *Complete Prose Works*, 3:190. His view of the relationship between liberty and virtue is discussed in Zagorin, *Milton Aristocrat and Rebel.*

89. *Areopagitica*, pp. 492–93.

90. It is something of an irony that in 1649 the legislation of the English republic reaffirmed the licensing of books and that one of Milton's own official duties was that of licenser. In 1651, he approved the publication of the *Racovian Catechism*, an Antitrinitarian work that Parliament later ordered to be burned for its heresies. When called upon to explain his action, Milton said he was following his conviction in the tract he had written on the subject that men should refrain from forbidding books; see Zagorin, *Milton Aristocrat and Rebel*, p. 75. He probably never stopped a book from being published.

91. "On the New Forcers of Conscience."

92. John Milton, *Christian Doctrine*, ed. Maurice Kelley, in *Complete Prose Works*, vol. 6. Although several scholars have recently questioned Milton's authorship of this work, most students of Milton have not found their arguments persuasive. See the discussion of its authorship and survey of the contents of *Christian Doctrine* by Lewalski, *The Life of John Milton*, pp. 415–41.

93. John Milton, *A Treatise of Civil Power* (1659), ed. William B. Hunter, Jr.,in *Complete Prose Works*, vol. 7, rev. ed. In August of the same year Milton also published another tract related to toleration, *Considerations Touching the Likeliest Means to Remove Hirelings Out of the Church*, ed. William B. Hunter, Jr., printed in

ibid. In this work he argued that public taxation and compulsory payments for the support of ministers and the church were a violation of Christian liberty and the people's right.

94. See Lewalski, *The Life of John Milton*, chaps. 8–9, passim.

95. Williams might have met Milton during his first return visit to England in 1643–1644. During his second stay in 1652–1654. he gave the poet some instruction in the Dutch language, and it is quite likely that Milton had read his writings in support of religious toleration; see Lewalski, *The Life of John Milton*, p. 285.

96. *A Treatise of Civil Power*, pp. 242–48.

97. Ibid., pp. 247–55.

98. Ibid., pp. 259–64.

99. Ibid., p. 270.

100. Ibid., pp. 246, 254–55. Milton praised Parliament's ordinance of 1650 prohibiting blasphemy against God, and he spoke of idolatry as contrary to both the Old and the New Testaments.

101. Ibid., p. 254.

102. John Milton, *Of True Religion, Haeresie, Schism, Toleration, and What Best Means May Be Us'd against the Growth of Popery*, (1673), ed. Keith Stavely, in *Complete Prose Works*, vol. 8.

103. Excerpts from the Maryland Act of Toleration are printed in *Church and State in the Modern Age: A Documentary History*, ed. J. F. Maclear, 3 vols. (New York: Oxford University Press, 1995), pp. 45–47.

104. Gerald Aylmer, *The Levellers in the English Revolution* (Ithaca: Cornell University Press, 1975), p. 9.

105. On the Leveller movement and its program, see Aylmer, *The Levellers and the English Revolution*; Zagorin, *A History of Political Thought*, chaps. 2–3; H. N. Brailsford, *The Levellers and the English Revolution* (Stanford: Stanford University Press, 1961); Joseph Frank, *The Levellers* (Cambridge: Harvard University Press, 1955); Brian Manning, "The Levellers and Religion," in *Radical Religion in the English Revolution*, ed. J. F. McGregor and Barry Reay (Oxford: Oxford University Press, 1984); David Wootton, "Leveller Democracy and the Puritan Revolution," in *The Cambridge History of Political Thought 1450–1700*, ed. J. H. Burns (Cambridge: Cambridge University Press, 1991), chap. 12. Jordan discusses the tolerationist ideas of the Leveller leaders Walwyn and Overton in *The Development of Religious Toleration in England*, 4:180–90, 190–96.

106. John Lilburne, *A Copie of a Letter . . . to Mr. William Prinne Esq.* (London, 1645), printed in Haller, *Tracts on Liberty*, 3:182, 183–84, 187.

107. Richard Overton, *Mans Mortallitie* (London, 1643). The book, which appeared with only the author's initials on the title page, was printed in London on a secret press.

108. Overton used this pseudonym in tribute to the notorious Puritan anti-episcopal tracts of the 1580s by the pseudonymous Martin Marprelate, which were printed on an underground press.

109. Richard Overton, *The Araignement of Mr. Persecution* (London, 1645), printed in Haller, *Tracts on Liberty*, 3:221–22, 232–33, 241–42, 254. This work, although bearing an Amsterdam imprint, was secretly printed in London. It is

worth noting that one of its characters, Mr. Truth & Peace, recommends Roger Williams's *The Bloudy Tenent of Persecution* to the "necessary perusal" of England's House of Commons; ibid., p. 242.

110. Walwyn's life and thought are summarized in the introduction to *The Writings of William Walwyn*, ed. Jack R. McMichael and Barbara Taft (Athens: University of Georgia Press, 1989).

111. William Walwyn, *Walwyns Just Defence against the Aspersions Cast upon Him* (London, 1649), printed in ibid., pp. 398–400.

112. William Walwyn, *The Fountain of Slaunder Discovered* (London, 1649), printed in ibid., p. 372.

113. William Walwyn, *A New Petition of the Papists* (London, 1641), printed in ibid., pp. 57–60; for Walwyn's authorship, see the introductory note, pp. 55–56. This work was also printed under the title *The Humble Petition of the Brownists*, a circumstance that underlines its nondenominational character.

114. William Walwyn, *The Power of Love* (London, 1643), printed in ibid., pp. 80–81, 94–95; this work was published anonymously.

115. William Walwyn, *The Compassionate Samaritane*, 2d ed. (London, 1644), printed in ibid., pp. 102–3, 104–5, 107–14, 116. This work was published anonymously but is unmistakably Walwyn's.

116. William Walwyn, *A Helpe to the Right Understanding of a Discourse concerning Independency, Lately Published by William Prynne Esquire* (London, 1645), printed in ibid., pp. 136–37. This work was anonymous, but was later acknowledged by Walwyn; ibid., p. 131.

117. William Walwyn, *A Whisper in the Eare of Mr. Thomas Edwards, Minister* (London, 1645), printed in ibid., p. 178. This was the first of Walwyn's pamphlets to be published with his name.

118. William Walwyn, *Toleration Justified, and Persecution Condemn'd* (London, 1646), printed in ibid., pp. 156, 163–64, 166, 168. This work was published anonymously.

119. William Walwyn, *A Parable, or Consultation of Physitians upon Master Edwards* (London, 1646), printed in ibid., p. 258. This work was anonymous and was the last of five tracts by Walwyn against Edwards's intolerance.

120. This Leveller petition for a free press, sent to the House of Commons in January 1649, is printed in *Leveller Manifestoes of the Puritan Revolution*, ed. Don M. Wolfe (New York: Thomas Nelson & Sons, 1944), pp. 326–30; the quotation is on p. 328.

121. The statements are part of the Leveller declaration, *No Papist nor Presbyterian: But the Modest Desires and Proposals of Some Well-Affected and Free-Born People* (London, 1649), printed in ibid, pp. 307–10. The declaration also pointed out that Catholics were not idolaters according to the meaning of idolatry in the Old Testament.

122. For a discussion of the nature and significance of the Leveller *Agreement of the People*, see Zagorin, *A History of Political Thought*, chap. 3.

123. All three versions of *Agreement of the People* are printed in *Leveller Manifestoes of the Puritan Revolution*, pp. 226–28, 295–303, 400–410.

124. Ibid., pp. 405, 408.

125. On these Independent and Baptist writers, see Jordan, *The Development of Religious Toleration in England*, vol. 3, pt. 4, and McBeth, *English Baptist Literature*, chaps. 2–4.

126. On Winstanley's ideas, see Jordan, *The Development of Religious Toleration in England*, 4:196–202; Zagorin, *A History of Political Thought*, chap. 4; G. E. Aylmer, "The Religion of Gerrard Winstanley," in McGregor and Reay, *Radical Religion in the English Revolution*. For the Socinians, see H. J. McLachlan, *Socinianism in Seventeenth-Century England* (Oxford: Clarendon Press, 1951). On the Quakers, see William C. Braithwaite, *The Beginnings of Quakerism*, 2d ed., rev. by Henry J. Cadbury (Cambridge: Cambridge University Press, 1970); Barry Reay, *The Quakers and the English Revolution* (London: Temple Smith, 1985), and "Quakerism and Society," in McGregor and Reay, *Radical Religion in the English Revolution*.

127. On Vane, see Jordan's account, *The Development of Religious Toleration in England*, 4:52–61; Zagorin, *A History of Political Thought*, pp. 152–54; Margaret A. Judson, *The Political Thought of Sir Henry Vane* (Philadelphia: University of Pennsylvania Press, 1969); Violet A. Rowe, *Sir Henry Vane the Younger* (London: Athlone Press, 1970). Milton addressed a laudatory sonnet to Vane in 1652, which acclaimed him as a great statesman who knew "Both spiritual power and civil, what each means / What severs each thou has learnt, which few have done. / The bounds of either sword to thee we owe"; "To Sir Henry Vane the Younger."

128. On Taylor, see Tulloch, *Rational Theology and Christian Philosophy*, vol. 1, chap. 6, and Jordan, *The Development of Religious Toleration in England*, 4:378–409.

129. On Harrington, see Jordan, *The Development of Religious Toleration in England*, 4:281–91; Zagorin, *A History of Political Thought*, chap. 11; J.G.A. Pocock, *The Political Works of James Harrington* (Cambridge: Cambridge University Press, 1977), introduction.

130. Jordan discusses Prynne's Erastianism and opposition to toleration in *The Development of Religious Toleration in England*, 4:276–81; see also William M. Lamont, *Marginal Prynne 1600–1669* (London: Routledge, 1963).

131. Samuel Rutherford, *A Free Disputation against Pretended Liberty of Conscience* (London, 1649). This work was directed against the Independent John Goodwin and other proponents of toleration. On Rutherford, see Jordan, *The Development of Religious Toleration in England*, 3:292–97, and John Coffey, *Politics, Religion, and the British Revolution: The Mind of Samuel Rutherford* (Cambridge: Cambridge University Press, 1997).

132. Jordan deals with Hobbes as an Erastian in *The Development of Religious Toleration in England*, 3:291–320.

133. The texts of the legislation of 1648 and 1650 are printed in *Acts and Ordinances of the Interregnum*, ed. C. H. Firth and R. S. Rait, 3 vols. (London: HMSO, 1911), 1:1133–36, 2:409–12. William A. Shaw, *A History of the English Church . . . 1640–1660*, 2 vols. (London: Longmans, Green, 1900), 2:78n.2, contains a concise review of Parliament's actions against heresy during this period.

134. The act is printed in *Acts and Ordinances of the Interregnum*, 2:423–25.

135. The readmission of the Jews was debated during the Protectorate but not approved. The Quakers incurred great hostility because of their practice of

interrupting church services and sermons, refusal to take oaths, and unwillingness to remove their hats to magistrates and other authorities.

136. For an overview of the extent and limits of toleration and pluralism
under the English republic and Cromwellian Protectorate, see Jordan, *The Development of Religious Toleration in England*, 3:119–266; Blair Worden, "Toleration
and the Cromwellian Protectorate," in *Persecution and Toleration*, ed. W. J. Sheils
(Oxford: Blackwell, 1984); Coffey, *Persecution and Toleration in Protestant England*,
pp. 147–60.

Chapter 7
John Locke and Pierre Bayle

1. These developments are surveyed in the classic work of Paul Hazard, *The
European Mind 1680–1715* (1st French ed. 1935) (New York: Meridian Books,
1963). Their contribution in the long term to the growth of religious toleration
has been noted by many historians; see the essay by Richard Popkin, "Skepticism
about Religion and Millenarian Dogmatism: Two Sources of Toleration in the
Seventeenth Century," in *Beyond the Persecuting Society: Religious Toleration before the
Enlightenment*, ed. John C. Laursen and Cary J. Nederman (Philadelphia: University of Pennsylvania Press, 1998).

2. On the Anglican Church's return to power, see I. M. Green, *The Re-establish-
ment of the Church of England 1660–1663* (Oxford: Oxford University Press, 1978);
for the laws and persecution against Protestant dissenters and Catholics in the
period after the restoration of Charles II, see John Coffey, *Persecution and Toleration
in Protestant England 1558–1689* (Harlow: Longman, 2000), chap. 7; Michael R.
Watts, *The Dissenters* (Oxford: Clarendon Press, 1978), chap. 3; William C. Braithwaite, *The Second Period of Quakerism*, 2d ed. (Cambridge: Cambridge University
Press. 1961), chaps. 2–4; John Miller, *Popery and Politics in England 1660–1688*
(Cambridge: Cambridge University Press, 1973), chaps. 3, 8, and passim.

3. On the Declaration of Indulgence, see J. P. Kenyon, *The Stuart Constitution
1603–1688*, 2d ed. (Cambridge: Cambridge University Press, 1986), pp. 374–
78, 379–83, 389–91.

4. See above, chap. 2.

5. On the writings of Anglican apologists in defense of religious coercion, see
A. A. Seaton, *The Theory of Toleration under the Later Stuarts* (Cambridge: Cambridge University Press, 1911), and Mark Goldie, "The Theory of Religious Intolerance in Restoration England," in *From Persecution to Toleration*, ed. Ole Peter
Grell, Jonathan I. Israel, and Nicholas Tyacke (Oxford: Clarendon Press, 1991).

6. The three hundredth anniversary of the revocation of the Edict of Nantes in
1985 produced a considerable number of commemorative publications, among
which are the following: Elizabeth Labrousse, *Essai sur la révocation de l'Édit de
Nantes* (Paris: Payot, 1985); Janine Garrisson, *L'Édit de Nantes et sa révocation. Histoire d'une intolérance* (Paris: Éditions du Seuil, 1985); *La révocation de l'Édit de
Nantes et les Provinces-Unies 1685*, ed. J.A.H. Bots and G.H.M. Posthumus Meyjes
(Amsterdam: APA Holland University Press, 1985). See also Roland Mousnier,

The Institutions of France under the Absolute Monarchy, 2 vols. (Chicago: University of Chicago Press, 1979), vol. 1, chap. 8. On the coexistence of Protestants and Catholics, see Gregory Hanlon, *Confession and Community in Seventeenth-Century France: Catholic and Protestant Coexistence in Aquitaine* (Philadelphia: University of Pennsylvania Press, 1993).

7. The best modern life of Locke is Maurice Cranston's *John Locke: A Biography* (New York: Macmillan, 1957); John Marshall, *John Locke: Resistance, Religion and Responsibility* (Cambridge: Cambridge University Press, 1994), is an excellent intellectual biography that carefully traces the development of Locke's ideas in close connection with the events of his life. On the Reverend John Owen, see Geoffrey F. Nuttall, *Visible Saints* (Oxford: Blackwell, 1957), passim, and Peter Toon, *God's Statesman: The Life and Work of John Owen, Pastor, Educator, Theologian* (Exeter: Paternoster Press, 1971). In 1662 Owen was forced to leave the church with many other dissenting ministers and became a leading spokesman in behalf of toleration for dissenters. On Henry Stubbes's tolerationist work, *An Essay in Defence of the Good Old Cause* (London, 1659), see Perez Zagorin, *A History of Political Thought in the English Revolution*, new ed. (Bristol: Thoemmes Press, 1997), pp. 159–60; his conception of toleration is discussed in the biography by James Jacob, *Henry Stubbe, Radical Protestantism and the Early Enlightenment* (Cambridge: Cambridge University Press, 1983). The letter Locke wrote to Stubbe in 1659 about toleration is printed in *The Correspondence of John Locke*, ed. E. S. de Beer, 8 vols. (Oxford: Clarendon Press, 1976–1989), 1:109–12. He said in it that giving freedom of religion to Catholics would endanger England's national security, an opinion from which he never departed.

8. Locke's career as a revolutionary is well described, although with a number of exaggerated claims, by Richard Ashcraft, *Revolutionary Politics and Locke's Two Treatises of Government* (Princeton: Princeton University Press, 1986).

9. Both works are printed in John Locke, *Two Tracts on Government*, ed. Philip Abrams (Cambridge: Cambridge University Press, 1967), with a valuable introduction by the editor. A previous Italian edition called them writings on toleration: John Locke, *Scritti editi e inedite sulla tolleranza*, ed. C. A. Viano (Turin: Taylor, 1961). I cite the later edition by Abrams.

10. *Two Tracts*, pp. 120–21.

11. Edward Bagshawe, *The Great Question concerning Things Indifferent in Religious Worship, Briefly Stated* (London, 1661).

12. John Calvin, *Institutes of the Christian Religion*, ed. John T. McNeill, 2 vols. (Philadelphia: Westminster Press, 1960), vol. 2, bk. 3, chap. 19.7–8, pp. 838–40.

13. The nature and extent of things indifferent was one of the continuously contested issues between Puritans and Anglicans in the later sixteenth and seventeenth centuries; see the treatment of the subject by the great Anglican theologian and controversialist Richard Hooker, *Laws of Ecclesiastical Polity*, in *Works*, ed. John Keble, 2 vols. (New York, 1873), vol. 1, bk. 2, chap. 4.3–4, pp. 198–201; the first four books of Hooker's treatise were published in 1593. Bernard J. Verkamp, *The Indifferent Mean: Adiaphorism in the English Reformation to* 1554 (Athens: Ohio University Press, 1977), discusses the theological literature dealing with the question of indifferency. Abrams's introduction to *Two Tracts*, pp. 36–49,

examines some of the earlier seventeenth-century writings concerning indifferent things and the arguments of Bagshawe and Locke. See also the note on indifferent things in John Locke, *Epistola de Tolerantia. A Letter on Toleration*, ed. Raymond Klibansky, with English translation, introduction, and notes by J. W. Gough (Oxford: Clarendon Press, 1968), p. 157n.35.

14. *Two Tracts*, pp. 120–21, 125–26, 129, 131, 136, 138, 158, 159–60.

15. Ibid., pp. 127–28.

16. Thomas Hobbes, *Leviathan* (1651), ed. Edwin Curley (Indianapolis: Hackett, 1994), pp. 338, 354 = chap. 42.

17. See the passages on this point by Anglican writers and Owen, quoted in Seaton, *The Theory of Toleration under the Later Stuarts*, pp. 90, 117, 129; for Owen's views on toleration and its limits, see Marshall, *John Locke*, pp. 42–45.

18. Quoted in Ashcraft, *Revolutionary Politics and Locke's Two Treatises of Government*, p. 66n.

19. On Shaftesbury's life and career, see K.H.D. Haley, *The First Earl of Shaftesbury* (Oxford: Clarendon Press, 1968); chap. 11 contains an account of Locke's meeting with him and entry into his household.

20. In 1669, following a discussion with Charles II, Shaftesbury sent him a memorial of advice which spoke of the economic benefits that freedom of religion would bring England. It recommended that while Catholics and certain Protestant fanatics should be excluded from toleration, all other nonconformists to the Church of England should have freedom to assemble and worship as they pleased in public places of their own choice; this document is printed in W. D. Christie, *A Life of Anthony Ashley Cooper, First Earl of Shaftesbury*, 2 vols. (London, 1871), vol. 2, app. 1.

21. John Locke, *An Essay concerning Toleration*, printed in H. R. Fox Bourne, *The Life of John Locke*, 2 vols. (New York, 1876), 1:174–94, from which I cite it; it is also printed in Viano, *Scritti editie inediti sulla toleranza* and in *Political Writings of John Locke*, ed. David Wootton (New York: Mentor, 1993). I have not seen the edition by K. Inoue, *John Locke, An Essay concerning Toleration and Toleratio* (Nara, Japan: Nara Women's University, 1974), which is mentioned in Marshall's bibliography.

22. *An Essay concerning Toleration*, pp. 174–78.

23. Ibid., pp. 179–81.

24. Ibid., pp. 181–82.

25. Ibid., pp. 183–85.

26. Ibid., pp. 187–94.

27. On the four different versions of this essay, see J. W. Gough, *John Locke's Political Philosophy*, 2d ed. (Oxford: Clarendon Press, 1973), pp. 210, 214–15, which quotes the passage in the final version modifying the scope of indifferency to exclude everything related to religious worship. The texts of the work as printed in Fox Bourne, *The Life of John Locke*, and Viano, *Scritti editi e inediti*, reproduce an earlier version not containing this passage.

28. *The Fundamental Constitutions of Carolina*, printed in *Political Writings of John Locke*, pp. 228–30; see Wootton's comments in the introduction, pp. 41–42, on

Locke's authorship of this document and his probable reservations with regard to its establishment of the Anglican Church as the state religion.

29. Seaton, *The Theory of Toleration under the Later Stuarts*, pp. 154–72, discusses Parker's book and several of the answers to it; Cranston quotes passages from Parker and Locke's queries on them, pp. 131–33.

30. Seaton, *The Theory of Toleration under the Later Stuarts*, pp. 193–98, discusses Stillingfleet's sermon *The Mischief of Separation* (London, 1680), his book *The Unreasonableness of Separation* (London 1680), and some of the dissenters' replies; Marshall, *John Locke*, pp. 97–110, gives an account of Locke's *Critical Notes* replying to Stillingfleet's position. Although Locke undertook this critique in collaboration with his friend James Tyrrell, Marshall gives reasons to suggest that he was its sole author.

31. The books Locke collected are discussed and recorded in John Harrison and Peter Laslett, *The Library Catalogue of John Locke* (Oxford: Oxford University Press, 1965).

32. *An Essay concerning Human Understanding*, ed. Peter H. Nidditch (Oxford: Clarendon Press, 1975), bk. 3, chap. 9.22; bk. 4, chap. 16.4 = pp. 489–90, 659–60.

33. The 1689 Latin edition of the *Letter* bore only Locke's initials on the title page, and the English version was anonymous. Locke was always very cautious about revealing his authorship of his writings, and both his *Two Treatises of Government* and *Essay concerning Human Understanding* also appeared anonymously. His identity as the author of the *Letter* soon became known. On the circumstances and history of the publication of Locke's *Letter*, see Klibansky's preface to *Epistola de Tolerantia. A Letter on Toleration*. My references are to J. W. Gough's English translation in this edition, which is based on the original English version by Locke's friend William Popple in 1689. Popple's translation is reprinted in *John Locke: A Letter concerning Toleration in Focus*, ed. John Horton and Susan Mendus (London: Routledge, 1991), which includes the text and essays on the work by a number of scholars. There are many studies of the theory of toleration in Locke's *Letter*; see, among others, Gough's introduction to his translation; James Tully, "John Locke," in *The Cambridge History of Political Thought* 1450–1700, ed. J. H. Burns (Cambridge: Cambridge University Press, 1992); Wootton's introduction to *Political Writings of John Locke*, pp. 94–110; Marshall, *John Locke*, pp. 358–69 and passim.

34. *A Letter on Toleration*, pp. 59, 61, 63, 65, 113, 115.

35. Ibid., pp. 65, 67, 69, 71.

36. Ibid., pp. 71–91.

37. Ibid., pp. 91–99.

38. Ibid., pp. 101, 103, 105, 107, 109, 111.

39. Ibid., pp. 121, 123, 127, 139, 131, 133, 135.

40. Ibid., pp. 135, 137, 139, 141, 143, 145, 147.

41. Between 1690 and 1704, Proast wrote three short critical responses to Locke's arguments, which are reprinted in Jonas Proast, *Letters concerning Toleration* (New York: Garland, 1984). Locke replied to Proast in three further *Letters*, printed in *The Works of John Locke*, 10 vols. (London, 1823; reprint, Aalen: Scientia

Verlag, 1963), vol. 6. Their controversy is reviewed by Peter Nicholson, "John Locke's Later Letters on Toleration," in Horton and Mendus, *John Locke: A Letter concerning Toleration in Focus,* and by Richard Vernon, *The Career of Toleration: John Locke, Jonas Proast, and After* (Montreal: McGill-Queens University Press, 1997), which looks at the subject in the context of modern liberal political theory. Mark Goldie gives an account of Proast and the religious problems that formed the background of Locke's replies to him in "John Locke, Jonas Proast and Religious Toleration 1688–1692," in *The Church of England, c. 1689–c. 1833,* ed. John Walsh, Colin Haydon, and Stephen Taylor (Cambridge: Cambridge University Press, 1993).

42. John Locke, *A Second Letter concerning Toleration,* in *Works,* 4:68–71, 74–75.

43. John Locke, *A Third Letter for Toleration,* in ibid., pp. 143–45.

44. In an interesting essay, Jeremy Waldron has criticized Locke's defense of toleration on grounds similar to Proast's. Waldron holds that Locke conceived toleration solely as the absence of force in religion, and that he regarded persecution as irrational because belief is not under the control of the will. In his judgment, Locke's view was fatally flawed by its failure to prove in principle that force cannot influence belief; and he points to the fact that belief might be shaped, for example, by people's being forced to read or not read certain books or to engage in certain external practices. He also argues that Locke based his distinction between civil government and religion on the essential premise that the former uses force as a means, and that this distinction collapses if coercion by the magistrate can affect religion; see Jeremy Waldron, "Locke: Toleration and the Rationality of Punishment," in Horton and Mendus, *John Locke: A Letter concerning Toleration in Focus.* Waldron's critique seems to me to suffer, however, from a number of misconceptions. Thus for Locke toleration was not simply the absence of compulsion in religion but a positive condition of love, charity, and mutual goodwill among Christians. Moreover, he left no doubt that beside being contrary to reason, persecution is wrong because it is cruel, immoral, and unjust. He would have denied that a state of mind produced by the application of coercion could qualify as religious belief or faith. The basis of his distinction between civil government and religion was not that the former makes use of force, but the very different purposes or ends of each. That government uses force as a means is therefore not the premise of this distinction but a conclusion that follows from it.

45. The Toleration Act is printed in *The Eighteenth Century Constitution,* ed. E. N. Williams (Cambridge: Cambridge University Press, 1977). On its importance, see the comments by Watts, *The Dissenters,* pp. 258–62. The act required an oath that most dissenters had no difficulty in taking and from which Quakers were exempted.

46. Locke, *Correspondence,* 3:633 (letter to Limborch of 6 June 1689).

47. Elizabeth Labrousse, *Bayle,* 2 vols. (The Hague: Martinus Nijhoff, 1963–1965), has written the main personal and intellectual biography of Bayle; vol. 2, *Heterodoxie et rigorisme* contains a review of his philosophical, religious, and political thought and deals with his theory of toleration and liberty of conscience in chaps. 18–19. The same author's *Bayle* (Oxford: Oxford University Press, 1983),

presents an excellent short survey of his life, writings, and ideas. Hazard, *The European Mind*, discusses Bayle in chap. 5 and passim. Two of the most interesting studies of Bayle's thought that focus on his conception of toleration are Walter Rex, *Essays on Pierre Bayle and Religious Controversy* (The Hague: Martinus Nijhoff, 1965), and John Kilcullen, *Sincerity and Truth* (Oxford: Clarendon Press, 1988). See also Richard H. Popkin, *The History of Scepticism from Erasmus to Spinoza* (Berkeley and Los Angeles: University of California Press, 1979), passim, and "The High Road to Pyrrhonism," in *The High Road to Pyrrhonism*, ed. Richard A. Watson and James E. Force (San Diego: Austin Hill Press, 1980); Ruth Whelan, *The Anatomy of Superstition: A Study of the Historical Theory and Practice of Pierre Bayle* (Oxford: Voltaire Foundation, 1989); Thomas M. Lennon, *Reading Bayle* (Toronto: University of Toronto Press, 1999); *Bayle: Political Writings*, ed. Sally Jenkinson (Cambridge: Cambridge University Press, 2000), introduction. Guy Howard Dodge, *The Political Theory of the Huguenots of the Dispersion with Special Reference to the Thought and Influence of Pierre Jurieu* (New York: Columbia University Press, 1947), discusses Bayle's political ideas.

48. Bayle's works, except for his *Critical and Historical Dictionary*, are collected in his *Oeuvres diverses* (The Hague, 1727–1731); I have consulted the reprint, ed. Elizabeth Labrousse, 5 vols. (Hildesheim: Georg Olms, 1965–1970).

49. *Pensées diverses sur la comète* is printed in ibid., vol. 3. It appeared anonymously and pretends to be a letter written by a Catholic to a Catholic theologian of the Sorbonne.

50. For an argument to this effect, see the interesting essay by David Wootton, "Pierre Bayle, Libertine," in *Studies in Seventeenth-Century European Philosophy*, ed. M. A. Stewart (Oxford: Clarendon Press, 1997).

51. In his treatise on toleration, Bayle remarked on the great number of English writings on this subject, including "very excellent works." He attributed this fact to the multiplicity of sects in England that had been persecuted for such a long time by the established religion; *Pierre Bayle's Philosophical Commentary* (New York: Peter Lang, 1987), "Preliminary Discourse," p. 11.

52. See Klibansky's preface to Locke's *A Letter on Toleration*, pp. xxxii–xxxiii; Harrison and Laslett, *The Library Catalogue of John Locke*, p. 82.

53. These preceding statements on toleration occur in Letters 20.5 and 21.7 of his *Critique générale de l'histoire du Calvinisme de M. Maimbourg* (*General Critique of Monsieur Maimbourg's History of Calvinism*) (1682), a criticism of a work by a French Jesuit, and in letter 9 of its sequel, *Nouvelles lettres de l'auteur de la critique générale* (*New Letters by the Author of the General Critique*) (1684), both printed in *Oeuvres diverses*, vol. 2.

54. Bayle published most of his writings anonymously but could not conceal his authorship for long; see Elizabeth Labrousse's remarks in her introduction to *Oeuvres diverses*, 2:viii–ix. The *Philosophical Commentary* pretended to be the French translation of a work by an English author and to have been published in Canterbury. The French text is printed in *Oeuvres diverses*, vol. 2. I cite the English translation by Amie Godman Tannenbaum in *Pierre Bayle's Philosophical Commentary* with a few occasional changes.

55. On Saint Augustine's reliance on this text, see above, chap. 2.

56. *Philosophical Commentary*, pp. 9–10, 26.

57. In his *Discourse on Method* (1637) and *Meditations on First Philosophy* (1641), Descartes, as part of his effort to establish that "I think, therefore I exist," was a conception incapable of being doubted, argued that the clarity and distinctness with which the mind grasped an idea was a certain criterion of its truth.

58. *Philosophical Commentary*, pp. 27–33 = pt. 1, chap. 1.

59. Ibid., pp. 35–37, 39–43 = pt. 1, chaps. 2–3.

60. Ibid., pp. 45–49 = pt. 1, chap. 4.

61. Ibid., pp. 51–57, 71–72, 77–81, 83–86 = pt. 1, chaps. 5, 6, 9, 10.

62. Ibid., pp. 66–67 = pt. 1, chap. 6

63. Ibid., pp. 87–95 = pt. 2, chap. 1.

64. Ibid., pp. 97–105 = pt. 2, chap. 2.

65. Ibid., pp. 135–43 = pt. 2, chap. 6.

66. In his reference to half-tolerationists, Bayle probably had Jurieu in mind. The latter's *Le vraye système de l'eglise* (1686) advocated a limited toleration for sects whose doctrines were consistent with the foundations of the Christian religion, and was really an argument for the toleration of Protestants in France; see Lennon, *Reading Bayle*, p. 90, and Dodge, *The Political Theory of the Huguenots*, pp. 208–9.

67. *Philosophical Commentary*, pp. 145–50 = pt. 2, chap. 7.

68. Ibid., pp. 151–60 = pt. 2, chap. 8.

69. This is Kilcullen's phrase, *Sincerity and Truth*, pp. 8, 89–90, and passim.

70. *Philosophical Commentary*, pp. 151–60 = pt. 2, chap. 8.

71. Bayle based this example on the famous case of the sixteenth-century Frenchman Martin Guerre, whose wife lived for a time with a man who successfully impersonated her husband returned from the wars. When the real Martin Guerre reappeared, the impostor was executed; see Natalie Z. Davis, *The Return of Martin Guerre* (Cambridge: Harvard University Press, 1983).

72. *Philosophical Commentary*, pp. 161–72 = pt. 2, chap. 9.

73. Ibid., pp. 173–91 = pt. 2, chap. 10.

74. Ibid., pp. 193–94 = pt. 2, chap. 11. In this final chapter Bayle also stated his intention of writing a further treatise directly refuting Saint Augustine's justification for persecution, although he considered that he had "already enervated" most of Augustine's "logical fallacies and little moral maxims." He published this refutation in 1687 as the third part of his *Philosophical Commentary*, followed in 1688 by a *Suplement* that was a response to Pierre Jurieu's criticism of the *Philosophical Commentary*; both are printed in *Oeuvres diverses*, vol. 2.

75. Quoted in Dodge, *The Political Theory of the Huguenots*, p. 172n. Le Clerc, a major intellectual figure of his time, who left Switzerland on account of Calvinist bigotry and was a member of the Remonstrant church in Amsterdam, was likewise a champion of toleration; he is discussed in Jonathan I. Israel, *Radical Enlightenment: Philosophy and the Making of Modernity*, 1650–1750 (Oxford: Oxford University Press, 2001), passim, and Hazard, *The European Mind*, passim.

76. Among these authors were Noël Aubert de Versé, Henri Basnage de Beauval, Gédéon Huet, Isaac Papin, and Elie Saurin; see Dodge, *The Political Theory of the Huguenots*, pp. 165–66; a number of them are discussed in Frank Puaux, *Les*

précurseurs français de la tolerance au XVIIe siècle (1st ed. 1881) (Geneva: Slatkine Reprints, 1970).

77. *Suplement du commentaire philosophique*, in *Oeuvres diverses*, 2:539 = chap. 21. In the same work he commented that "nothing was more ridiculous in a dispute" than for adversaries to tell one another, "I am right and you are wrong," hitting the same tennis ball back and forth, "as if *petitio principii* were not the lowest and most infantile of all Sophisms"; ibid., p. 539 = chap. 20.

78. Printed in Fox Bourne, *The Life of John Locke*, 1:178, 306.

79. On the differences and quarrel between Bayle and Jurieu, see Labrousse, *Bayle* (1963), vol. 2, chaps. 14–19, passim, and *Bayle* (1983), pp. 34–39; Dodge, *The Political Theory of the Huguenots*, chaps. 3–7; Rex, *Essays on Pierre Bayle*, pp. 189–93, 216–43. Jurieu assailed Bayle's ideas in a number of works, including *Des droits des deux souveraines en matière de religion, la conscience, et le prince* (1687); *Courte revue des maximes de morale et des principes de religion de l'auteur des pensées diverses sur des comètes* (1691); and *Le philosophe de Rotterdam accusé, atteint, et convaincu* (1706). I quote the passages in the text from Dodge, *The Political Theory of the Huguenots*, pp. 199n, 203 and n.

80. See Rex, *Essays on Pierre Bayle*, pp. 187–88.

81. On this point see Jenkinson's comments in her introduction to *Bayle: Political Writings*, pp. xix–xx and passim.

82. Harry M. Bracken, "Toleration Theories: Bayle, Jurieu, Locke," in *Mind and Language* (Dordrecht: Foris Publications, 1983), p. 91.

83. This is the view of the French Locke scholar Raymond Polin, as expressed in his French edition of Locke, *Lettre sur la tolérance* (Paris: Presses Universitaires de France, 1965), and cited in Bernard Cottret, "La tolérance et la liberté de la conscience à l'épreuve. L'Europe du nord-ouest entre Révocation et Glorieuse Révolution (vers 1685–vers 1688)," in *La liberté de conscience (XVIe–XVIIe siècles)*, ed. Hans R. Guggisberg, Frank Lestringant, and Claude Margolin (Geneva: Droz, 1991), pp. 269–70.

84. Labrousse, *Bayle* (1983), p. 85. For several views of the differences and similarities between Bayle and Locke, see also S. O'Cathesaigh, "Bayle and Locke on Toleration," in *De l'humanisme aux lumières*, ed. M. Magdelaine, M.-C. Pitassi, R. Whelan, and A. McKenna (Oxford: Voltaire Foundation, 1995); Sally L. Jenkinson, "Two Concepts of Tolerance: Or Why Locke Is Not Bayle," *Journal of Political Philosophy* 4, no. 4 (1996): 302–21; Thomas M. Lennon, "Bayle, Locke, and the Metaphysics of Toleration," in Stewart, *Studies in Seventeenth-Century European Philosophy*.

Chapter 8
Conclusion: The Idea of Religious Toleration in the Enlightenment and After

1. Immanuel Kant, *What Is Enlightenment?*, printed in *Kant on History*, ed. Lewis White Beck (Indianapolis: Bobbs-Merrill, 1985), p. 3.

2. See Joachim Whaley, "A Tolerant Society? Religious Toleration in the Holy Roman Empire, 1648–1806," in *Toleration in Enlightenment Europe*, ed. Ole Peter

Grell and Roy Porter (Cambridge: Cambridge University Press, 2000), pp. 175, 185–86, and Karl Vocelka, "Enlightenment in the Habsburg Monarchy: History of a Belated and Short-Lived Phenomenon," in ibid., pp. 202–3.

3. Historians have looked upon the Enlightenment and its ideas from different points of view, and the literature on the subject is very large. Among good general accounts, all of which touch on the subject of toleration to some extent, are Ernst Cassirer, *The Philosophy of the Enlightenment* (Princeton: Princeton University Press, 1951); Paul Hazard, *European Thought in the Eighteenth Century* (London: Hollis and Carter, 1954); Alfred Cobban, *In Search of Humanity* (New York: Braziller, 1960); Peter Gay, *The Enlightenment: An Interpretation*, 2 vols. (New York: Knopf, 1966–1969); *The Enlightenment in National Context*, ed. Roy Porter and Mikulas Teich (Cambridge: Cambridge University Press, 1992); Jonathan I. Israel, *Radical Enlightenment: Philosophy and the Making of Modernity, 1650–1750* (Oxford: Oxford University Press, 2001). Grell and Porter, *Toleration in Enlightenment Europe*, contains a survey of Enlightenment thought on toleration in a number of countries in the eighteenth century; Robert Wokler's essay in this volume, "Multiculturalism and Ethnic Cleansing in the Enlightenment," is an excellent critique of the views of later-twentieth-century adversaries of the Enlightenment who speak of the failure of the Enlightenment project and accuse it of giving rise to new kinds of oppression in the form of social engineering and technological and bureaucratic domination.

4. On this point, see the essay by John Dunn, "The Claim to Freedom of Conscience: Freedom of Speech, Freedom of Thought, Freedom of Worship?" in *From Persecution to Toleration*, ed. Ole Peter Grell, Jonathan I. Israel, and Nicholas Tyacke (Oxford: Clarendon Press, 1991).

5. See Paul H. Meyer, "The Attitude of the Enlightenment towards the Jew," *Studies on Voltaire and the Eighteenth Century* 26 (1963): 1161–1205, and Arthur Hertzberg, *The French Enlightenment and the Jews* (New York: Columbia University Press, 1968), chap. 9.

6. Both Meyer and Hertzberg discuss Voltaire's attitude toward the Jews, as does Peter Gay, *Voltaire's Politics* (New York: Vintage Books, 1965), app. 3, "Voltaire's Anti-Semitism." Gay comments in *The Enlightenment*, 2:38n, that "the age of the Enlightenment was far from perfect," and that while some *philosophes* like Montesquieu and Lessing were philosemites, others, "with Voltaire in the lead, never overcame, or even tried to overcome, their prejudices against the Jews."

7. See the discussion of Toland's pamphlet and its historical context by Justin Champion, "Toleration and Citizenship in Enlightened England: John Toland and the Naturalization of the Jews, 1714–1753," in Grell and Porter, *Toleration in Enlightenment Europe*; the quotations are on p. 142.

8. Cassirer, *The Philosophy of the Enlightenment*, Hazard, *European Thought in the Eighteenth Century*, and Gay, *The Enlightenment*, vol. 2, all include discussions of Lessing's work and ideas; Meyer focuses on his view of the Jews.

9. See on Voltaire's life and ideas the biographies by A. Owen Aldridge, *Voltaire and the Century of Light* (Princeton: Princeton University Press, 1975), and Theodore Besterman, *Voltaire*, 3d rev. ed. (Oxford: Blackwell, 1976).

10. Voltaire, *Letters on England* (Harmondsworth: Penguin, 1980), letter 5; for the French text, see *Lettres philosophiques*, ed. Gustave Lanson, rev. André M. Rousseau (Paris: Didier, 1964). The first seven letters of this work deal with English religion, four of them on the Quakers, the other three on the Anglicans, Presbyterians, and Socinians.

11. Voltaire, *Philosophical Dictionary*, ed. Theodore Besterman (Harmondsworth: Penguin, 1983); the French text is printed in *Dictionnaire philosophique*, ed. Raymond Naves (Paris: Garnier, 1961).

12. Ibid., s.v. "Tolérance: Toleration."

13. See Raymond Klibansky's preface to John Locke, *A Letter on Toleration* (Oxford: Clarendon Press, 1968), p. xxix.

14. Voltaire, *Treatise on Tolerance*, ed. Simon Harvey (Cambridge: Cambridge University Press, 2000); the editor's introduction includes a brief account of the Calas case, on which see also David Bien, *The Calas Affair* (Princeton: Princeton University Press, 1959). The French text of Voltaire's work is printed in *Traité sur la tolérance*, ed. René Pomeau (Paris: Flammarion, 1989).

15. Ibid., chaps. 4–5.

16. Ibid., chap. 6.

17. In this connection, he mentioned in a note "Locke's excellent *Letter on Toleration*"; ibid., p. 49n.

18. Ibid., chap. 11.

19. Ibid., chap. 14.

20. Ibid., chap. 20.

21. Ibid., chap. 22.

22. Ibid., chap. 23.

23. See C. T. McIntire, "Changing Religious Establishments and Religious Liberty in France, pt. I: 1787–1879," in *Freedom and Religion in the Nineteenth Century*, ed. Richard Helmstadter (Stanford: Stanford University Press, 1997), pp. 251–52.

24. While there are numerous books on religious freedom, I am not aware of any work that traces the growth of the concept of toleration and the evolution of religious freedom in Europe and the world in the nineteenth and twentieth centuries. A helpful though incomplete survey is Helmstadter, *Freedom and Religion in the Nineteenth Century*, which includes discussions of the United States, several major European countries, and Jewish emancipation. I have also found helpful the collection of documents *Church and State in the Modern Age*, ed. J. F. Maclear (New York: Oxford University Press, 1995).

25. Extracts from the Maryland Toleration Act of 1649—which is mentioned above, chap. 6—the Rhode Island charter of 1663, and the Great Law of Pennsylvania of 1682 are printed in Maclear, *Church and State in the Modern Age*, pp. 45–48, 50–53. The Pennsylvania Great Law was an implementation of the tolerant ideas that the colony's Quaker founder, William Penn, expressed in his *The Great Case of Liberty of Conscience* (1670); a selection from the latter is printed in *Cornerstones of Religious Freedom in America*, ed. Joseph l. Blau, rev. ed. (New York: Harper Torchbooks, 1964), pp. 52–67.

26. Printed in Maclear, *Church and State in the Modern Age*, p. 54.

27. Printed in ibid., pp. 59–63.

28. See the essays by S. Gerald Sandler, "Lockean Ideas in Thomas Jefferson's *Bill for Establishing Religious Freedom*," *Journal of the History of Ideas* 21, no. 1 (1960): 110–16; Thomas E. Buckley, "The Political Theology of Thomas Jefferson," in *The Virginia Statute for Religious Freedom: Its Evolution and Consequences in American History*, ed. Merrill D. Peterson and Robert C. Vaughan (Cambridge: Cambridge University Press, 1988); Lance Banning, "James Madison, the Statute for Religious Freedom, and the Crisis of Republican Convictions," in ibid.

29. The Virginia Statute is reprinted in ibid., pp. xvii–xviii, and in Maclear, *Church and State in the Modern Age*, pp. 64–65.

30. See the illuminating essay by Nathan O. Hatch, "The Whirlwind of Religious Liberty in Early America," in Helmstadter, *Freedom and Religion in the Nineteenth Century*; the quotation is on p. 41. Hatch remarks (p. 30) that "colonial America surged with religious diversity well before any theory could fully explain or justify it."

31. See the discussion of Madison by John T. Noonan, Jr., *The Lustre of Our Country: The American Experience of Religious Freedom* (Berkeley and Los Angeles: University of California Press, 1998), chap. 3. The provision against religious tests and the First Amendment of the United States Constitution are printed in Maclear, *Church and State in the Modern Age*, pp. 65–66.

32. When it was adopted, the First Amendment of the Constitution applied only to the federal government, and not until many years later, in the case of *Cantwell v. Connecticut* in 1940, did the United States Supreme Court decide that it also applied to the individual states; see Maclear, *Church and State in the Modern Age*, pp. 395–98, and the discussion in Noonan, *The Lustre of Our Country*, pp. 34–35. Long before this, though, religious freedom existed in the states. The Congregationalist state churches in Connecticut and Massachusetts were disestablished in 1818 and 1833.

33. See the Declaration of the Rights of Man and Citizen, introduction and arts. 1–2, 10, in *A Documentary Survey of the French Revolution*, ed. John Hall Stewart (New York: Macmillan, 1951), pp. 113–14.

34. Ibid., pp. 231, 232.

35. See the account in McIntire, "Changing Religious Establishments," pp. 247–50.

36. See the discussion by Raymond Grew, "Liberty and the Catholic Church," in Helmstadter, *Freedom and Religion in the Nineteenth Century*, p. 201–10, and Roland Hill, *Lord Acton* (New Haven: Yale University Press, 2000).

37. See J. P. Ellens, "Which Freedom in Early Victorian Britain?" in Helmstadter, *Freedom and Religion in the Nineteenth Century*, pp. 90–91.

38. John Stuart Mill, *On Liberty* (Boston, 1868), p. 20.

39. On Jewish emancipation, see David C. Itzkowitz, "The Jews of Europe and the Limits of Religious Freedom," in Helmstadter, *Freedom and Religion in the Nineteenth Century*, and David Vital, *A People Apart: The Jews of Europe* 1789–1939 (Oxford: Oxford University Press, 1999), introduction and pt. 1.

40. I take these facts from the excellent work by Mary Ann Glendon, *A World Made New: Eleanor Roosevelt and the Universal Declaration of Human Rights* (New

York: Random House, 2001), which gives a very interesting account of the origins and making of the Universal Declaration. Malik's speech is summarized on pp. 164–65; the countries that abstained included the USSR, other states in the Soviet bloc, South Africa, and Saudi Arabia; ibid., pp. 169–70.

41. The Universal Declaration of Human Rights is printed in ibid., pp. 310–14.

42. See the comments by the editors in *Human Rights: Documents That Paved the Way*, ed. B. de Villiers, D. J. van Vuuren, and M. Wiechers (Pretoria: HSRC Publishers, 1992), p. 1. Glendon, *A World Made New*, chaps. 10–12, contains an analysis of the Universal Declaration of Human Rights and discusses its post-1948 history and its position today.

43. See Noonan, *The Lustre of Our Country*, chap. 13, which gives an interesting account of the Second Vatican Council's Declaration on Religious Freedom.

44. Quoted in ibid., p. 339; Noonan notes that the theological draftsman of the pope's encyclical was familiar with Thomas Jefferson's Virginia Statute for Religious Freedom.

45. Noonan discusses John Courtney Murray's ideas on religious freedom and his role in the Second Vatican Council; the quotation is in ibid., p. 343.

46. The Declaration on Religious Freedom is printed with an introduction by John Courtney Murray in *The Documents of Vatican II* (New York: Guild Press, 1966), pp. 675–96.

47. Ibid., p. 673.

48. John Rawls, *Political Liberalism* (New York: Columbia University Press, 1996), p. xxvi.

49. "Was du ererbt von deinen Vätern hast, / Erwirb es, um es zu besessen"; *Faust*, pt. 1.

INDEX

❧